ethics
at the cinema

ethics
at the cinema

EDITED BY
WARD E. JONES
AND
SAMANTHA VICE

OXFORD
UNIVERSITY PRESS
2011

OXFORD

UNIVERSITY PRESS

Oxford University Press, Inc., publishes works that further
Oxford University's objective of excellence
in research, scholarship, and education.

Oxford   New York
Auckland   Cape Town   Dar es Salaam   Hong Kong   Karachi
Kuala Lumpur   Madrid   Melbourne   Mexico City   Nairobi
New Delhi   Shanghai   Taipei   Toronto

With offices in
Argentina   Austria   Brazil   Chile   Czech Republic   France   Greece
Guatemala   Hungary   Italy   Japan   Poland   Portugal   Singapore
South Korea   Switzerland   Thailand   Turkey   Ukraine   Vietnam

Copyright © 2011 by Oxford University Press, Inc.
Published by Oxford University Press, Inc.
198 Madison Avenue, New York, New York 10016
www.oup.com
Oxford is a registered trademark of Oxford University Press

Ethics at the cinema / edited by Ward E. Jones and Samantha Vice.
  p.   cm.
  ISBN 978-0-19-532040-4 (pbk. : alk. paper)—ISBN 978-0-19-532039-8 (hardcover : alk. paper)
1. Motion pictures—Moral and ethical aspects. I. Jones, Ward E. II. Vice, Samantha, 1973–
  PN1995.5.E84   2011
175—dc22   2010007429

---

1 3 5 7 9 8 6 4 2

Printed in the United States of America
on acid-free paper

For Alan, with whom we wish we could have shared this book.
W.E.J. and S.V.

CONTENTS

ETHICS AND PERSONAL RELATIONSHIPS

ethics
at the cinema

PHILOSOPHY AND THE ETHICAL SIGNIFICANCE OF SPECTATORSHIP

AN INTRODUCTION TO *ETHICS AT THE CINEMA*

WARD E. JONES

THE CONTRIBUTORS TO *Ethics at the Cinema* were invited to engage with ethical issues raised within, or within the process of viewing, a single film. All of the contributors have previously written in ethics and/or the philosophy of film, but they come from a wide range of traditions and backgrounds within both.

We asked contributors to concentrate on only one film in their essays. We have two reasons for this. First, as I hope to make clear in this introduction, we see merit in forcing both authors and readers to engage with a single narrative in detail; discovering the ethical import of narratives requires digging into the fine points of those narratives. Second, one of the constraints inherent to writing and reading about narratives is that the reader needs to be familiar with the narrative being discussed. Limiting the essays in *Ethics at the Cinema* to discussions of single films ensures that even if the reader is not already familiar with the narrative being discussed, she can without too much time commitment view the film with which an author is concerned.

The contributors to *Ethics at the Cinema* were given the freedom to write on a topic and film of their choice. The result is a group of films—including one television series—that vary not only in terms of when and where they were made, but also in terms of their artistic quality.[1] The earliest film discussed is Jean Renoir's *La Grande Illusion*, from 1937, one of two classic French films in the collection; the most recent is Paul Haggis'' *Crash*, a film released in 2005 and one of several films in the collection coming from Hollywood. Not surprisingly, *Ethics at the Cinema* includes papers on some masterpieces. In particular, *The Third Man*—on which three of our authors have chosen to write—has some claim to being the greatest motion picture yet made, and *The Sopranos* has had a number of writers call it the greatest television show yet aired. Less expected is at least one film at the other end of the spectrum: the best reason I can find to see *Fools Rush In* is that it will allow one to fully appreciate Paul C. Taylor's fine contribution to this collection. Taylor's paper raises the interesting question of whether a rich philosophical engagement with a mediocre narrative might justify higher aesthetic appraisal of the narrative. More important, it illustrates that the richness of a philosophical engagement with a film is not dependent upon the artistic worth of the film itself. Indeed, Taylor is explicit that it is precisely the populist nature of *Fools Rush In* that concerns him; his aim is to "excavate and illuminate the meanings that constitute the shared culture that mass entertainments presuppose and that help constitute us as individuals."[2]

We have divided *Ethics at the Cinema* into two parts: "Part 1: Critique, Character, and the Power of Film," and "Part 2: Philosophical Readings." The papers in Part 1 wear their philosophical and ethical credentials on their sleeves; these papers engage explicitly with meta-issues surrounding film, film narratives, and film viewing. The papers comprising Part 2 are engaged less with issues *about* film than with the details of their chosen film: its characters, its plot, and its particular uses of images. Authors of these latter papers are more involved in what would be traditionally understood as *interpreting* their films. I do not want to exaggerate this difference; authors of papers in Part 1 do make interpretative commitments, and papers in Part 2 often address meta-cinematic issues. Nor do I wish to exaggerate the similarities among papers within each part; the authors of papers in Part 2, especially, take very different approaches to their films. Nonetheless, the emphases of the papers in this collection naturally place them in these two fairly distinct categories.

The papers in Part 2, however, raise two questions: What is the significance of a reading of a film to the philosophical study of ethics, and why should we not think that in reading a film philosophers are doing something that other academics—like film critics and theorists—do less naïvely? The answers to these questions are not, in my opinion, obvious. The papers of Part 2 require more explanation and, perhaps, justification than the obviously philosophical enterprise of the papers in Part 1. The main aim of this introduction is to defend the significance of the philosophical reading. I sketch a general framework for theorizing the kind of interaction that films and other narratives invite us to have with them. As will be seen, spelling out this framework requires that I touch on large issues in aesthetics and ethics, relevant to all of the papers in this collection. After laying out the basics of this framework in the next section, I use it to situate the papers that comprise Part 1 of this collection. In order to understand how engagement with the finer details of filmed narratives can have both philosophical interest and ethical importance, however, I will need to defend more of its features; this will be done in the second section below.

I. NARRATIVES, SPECTATORS AND THEIR ATTITUDES

Perhaps the simplest answer to the question of why films and other narratives have philosophical significance is offered by Stephen Mulhall, in the introduction to his discussion of the *Alien* quartet of films.

> I do not look on these films as handy or popular illustrations of views and ar-
> guments properly developed by philosophers; I see them rather as themselves
> reflecting on and evaluating such views and arguments, as thinking seriously
> and systematically about them in just the ways that philosophers do. Such
> films are not philosophy's raw material, nor a source for its ornamentation;
> they are philosophical exercises, philosophy in action—film as philosophizing.[3]

If, as Mulhall suggests, some films are themselves "philosophizing", then this would both explain and justify philosophers' engagement with them. Since films are doing philosophy, then at least some of them are philosophically significant. There- fore, philosophers are *prima facie* justified in bringing films into the realm of philo- sophical discourse, and philosophers have *prima facie* reason to be interested in *other* philosophers' engagement with such narratives. While provocative, Mulhall's suggestion that (some) films are doing philosophy needs a great deal of filling out. In particular, he needs to provide us with a conception of philosophy under which a narrative can instantiate it; such a conception would need to tell us which prop- erty narratives—which are, at bottom, simply depictions of characters in a series of events—possess such that they could count as "philosophy in action."[4]

I will take a different approach. I think it unlikely that the philosophical signifi- cance of film lies in the fact that films "philosophize", that is, that philosophy and film are *in the same business*. As we will see in a moment, there is, indeed, an impor- tant similarity between the two—both manifest attitudes toward their subject matter, and both invite their audience to do the same. Nonetheless, we should not conclude that the philosophical significance of film has anything to do with its *sharing* that feature with philosophy, that is, with the fact that films have features that can make them appear "philosophical". Film, like (say) science, is a fit subject for philosophy not because it shares something with philosophy, but because of its potentially complex, pervasive, and deep role in our lives; in the case of film, it is largely because of the importance of narrative-spectatorship in our ethical lives.

As a spectator of a film (or any other narrative), I am fully aware that it was made for an audience; it was produced to be viewed. The narrative before me is a *creation*, it is *someone else's presentation* of a series of events. In this regard, the spectatorship of a film differs centrally from my direct perception of the world; I am aware that my view of a film's world is controlled by another person's (or persons') choices. As such, the film constitutes, we might say, a certain "take" on the world within the film. A film presents its audience with a point of view of its characters and events, and it invites us to adopt that point of view as we follow the film and its sequence of events to the film's conclusion. This thought provides the core of the position that I wish to develop here. A spectator's confrontation with a narrative is ethically significant because the narrative (1) manifests an evaluative *attitude* toward its own characters, events, and context, and (2) encourages the spectator, through the latter's enjoyment of and satisfaction with the narrative, to adopt a similar attitude. Conceiving of our interactions with film narratives in this way, I will suggest, allows us to readily grasp the significance of philosophical engagements with them, and the significance of the contributions to *Ethics at the Cinema*.

An attitude is best understood in terms of the dispositions of some person who possesses that attitude. A person with a certain attitude toward something S (a particular or kind of object, property, or event) will be, among other things, *attentive to certain features* of S, *inclined to describe or understand* S in certain ways, disposed to feel certain *emotions* toward S, disposed to certain *beliefs* about S, disposed to *praise* or *blame* S in certain conditions, and disposed to *act* in certain ways toward S.[5] Forgiveness, resentment, compassion, wariness, suspicion, trust, and admiration are among the many examples of attitudes that we take toward others, and that in turn manifest themselves on occasion in emotions, beliefs, and actions. Racism, sexism, and xenophobia are also plausibly understood as attitudes toward a certain kind of person; to have a racist attitude toward someone is to have tendencies to be attentive to certain things she does, to have certain beliefs about her, and to have certain emotions toward her.

As the examples above suggest, attitudes have an *evaluative* component; one's attitude toward something can be said to embody, in part, one's evaluation of it. Resenting someone involves adopting a negative, disapproving posture toward her for what she has done; admiring someone involves a disposition to praise her character or actions; taking a racist or sexist attitude toward someone involves a tendency to devalue her character or actions. The central component in the evaluative feature of attitudes is the tendency of the attitude holder to feel certain emotions toward the object of his attitude. Recent work on the emotions has made it clear that in feeling an emotion, one reveals one's evaluation of the emotion's object; my emotion toward something reveals my evaluation of that thing. That this is so is strongly suggested by examples. The surprising extent of someone's grief over the loss of a pet reveals how valuable the pet was to him. Someone's shame or indignation reveals his evaluation of his own or someone else's integrity or entitlements. The philosopher Robert Gordon has divided a long list of emotions into the "positive" (e.g., "is proud", "is grateful") and the "negative" (e.g., "is embarrassed", "regrets").[6] The appropriateness—in principle, at least—of Gordon's division is a manifestation of the fact that many emotions either themselves express a positive or negative evaluation of something (e.g. "loves", "is disgusted") or are a kind of response to the positive or negative status of something of value (e.g., "is delighted", "is disappointed"). In expressing an emotion toward some state of affairs, these examples suggest, we express an evaluation of that state of affairs. Accordingly, in attributing to someone a disposition to feel certain emotions toward something, we are able to say something about his attitude toward that thing.

In general, then, attributing attitudes to someone allows us to identify and explain patterns in the mental states and actions that she possesses and takes toward another person or thing. Attributing to someone an attitude toward S allows us to explain, for example, his selective attention to certain features of S, his tendencies to pass judgment on S in certain ways, or his tendency to act in certain ways rather than others with regard to S. In attributing an attitude to an agent, we move to a higher level of description than we would were we to speak only of his emotions, beliefs, or patterns of attention or judgment; attitudes are higher in that they are "bundles" of, and thus allow us to organize, these lower-level phenomena. As such, the ethical importance of attitudes should be clear. To adopt an attitude toward another person is to take on characteristics in relation to her—for example, the kinds of emotions and actions that one will undertake toward her—that may have deep moral significance.

It is important to bear in mind three features of attitudes, as we turn to examine how they are manifested in narratives. First, while some attitudes may have common names and familiar features, this is not going to be true of most of them. A huge range of patterns in our attitudes toward others is possible, and it may be that most of them are too rare to be named or too subtle and complex to be spoken about in everyday discourse. This is not to say that attitudes cannot be described. On the contrary, while the content of many attitudes will not be *easily* describable, it will always be possible to describe some of the lower-level states and actions that the attitude includes. Second, as with any other mental state, we can identify, describe, or create an attitude that does not belong to any actual person. Although an attitude is necessarily something that *could* be attributed to a person, an attitude can be described, discussed, debated, or even named without ever actually belonging or being attributed to someone. Third, attitudes can be held not only toward real persons, but toward fictional, nonexistent characters; one can admire or be suspicious of a fictional character just as one can a real person. All three of these features are likely to characterize the attitudes manifested in fictional narratives. Indeed, they are all three pivotal to the suggestion that I am developing —the ethical importance of philosophical readings of narratives derives from the fact that they are involved in elucidating the often complex attitudes that narratives invite us to take toward their characters, their context, and their actions.

If the attitudes manifested in a narrative are not necessarily attributable to any single person, then how are such attitudes manifested in narratives? In many cases, this is a complex and often subtle affair. It is uncommon in films to find direct statements that reveal an evaluative attitude toward the personalities or actions of their protagonists, or of things that happen to them. Even on the rare occasions in which there are such direct statements, it is often clear that the narrator making such statements is *himself* a character in the narrative; in such cases, while the narrator is directly expressing an attitude toward the other characters and events he is relating, the narrative itself will express in other ways an attitude toward the *narrator* and *his* attitudes. Because narratives can distance themselves from their narrators, a narrator's attitude need not, and in many cases will not, be identical with that of the narrative. As a consequence, in film, as in much written literature, a narrator's direct statement can be—ironically—the *least* direct way for a narrative to express its attitude toward its characters.

More commonly, and more effectively, it is in the choices of the narrative creator (e.g., filmmaker, author) regarding focus and description that a narrative's attitude is revealed. In his book *Engaging Characters*, Murray Smith usefully classifies two elements here, *recognition* and *alignment*, both of which encourage the spectator to take a certain attitude toward a character in a film.[7] "Recognition", he writes, "describes the spectator's construction of character: the perception of a set of textual elements, in film typically cohering around the image of a body, as an individuated and continuous human agent."[8] Creating a narrative involves choosing certain (kinds of) characters, choices that in themselves manifest an attitude toward those characters; indeed, at a minimum it reveals that certain (kinds of) characters are deserving of narrative attention. In addition, narratives invite spectators to become *aligned* with certain characters, as "spectators are placed in relation to characters in terms of access to their actions, to what they know and feel."[9] Any telling of a series of events must involve a choice as to which information to give its spectators about its characters, their properties, their actions, and their contexts; such choice will manifest an attitude toward the characters, as it reveals which characters deserve how much and what kind of attention from the spectators. Some characters get more attention than others; all characters have certain features described and others ignored. The consequence is that a narrative necessarily manifests evaluations of its characters in the various ways that it invites spectators to adopt various allegiances with—that is, attitudes toward—the narrative's characters.

In what is perhaps the most significant element in the process by which narratives manifest attitudes, a narrative leads its spectators to respond with certain emotions—and the desires and evaluations that go along with them—toward its characters and events.[10] In encouraging a spectator to feel a certain emotion toward a character or event, the narrative reveals *its own* attitude toward that person or event. So, for example, in so far as a narrative displays a character in such a way that the spectator is encouraged to pity or fear him, it encourages the spectator to form an evaluation of the character as, in part, the kind of thing *to be pitied* or *to be feared*. This invitation to emotion both reveals the narrative's attitude toward the characters and calls upon spectators to share that attitude, along with the evaluative desires and thoughts that are a part of it. In the paradigmatic case, then, the spectator "sees" a series of events in film, emotionally responds to those events, and, as a consequence, forms an attitude toward the characters involved.

The thought that we should see narratives as inviting and endorsing emotional and broader attitudes toward their characters and events is familiar from literary theory. Indeed, the expression of attitudes in a narrative seems to be one of the main concerns of interpretation and criticism, and many theories of interpretation can be understood as claiming that attention should be paid to certain aspects of the creation, the nature, or the context of the narrative's attitude toward its characters and events. What we might call "author-centered" theories of interpretation (which, e.g., psychoanalyze authors, or seek out an author's intentions) advocate an interpretative focus on the psychological features—however that is to be understood—of the creator or the presented narrative attitude. "Reader-response" theories of interpretation advocate an interpretative focus on the narrative's spectator, what the narrative asks of her, and how she responds to the narrative attitude. Here is the reader-response theorist Wayne C. Booth, describing the scene from *King Lear* in which Cornwall gouges out Gloucester's eyes: "We have in this scene . . . . a revolting act that in its very portrayal *insists on our revulsion* . . . ."[11] What we might think of as "agenda-driven" theories of interpretation (e.g., Marxist, feminist, post-colonial) advocate an interpretative focus on context, history, and bias factors in the creation and nature of a narrative attitude. We also see literary-minded philosophers working with a conception of narratives as inviting spectators to share an attitude; writing generally of irony in the novels of Jane Austen and Henry James, the philosopher Cora Diamond writes, "The reader of them is invited to share a way of viewing human nature and its failings, in which amusement, sympathy, critical intelligence, and delicacy of moral discrimination all play a role. . . . "[12] In all of these interpretative traditions, there is a core focus upon the attitude the narrative expresses toward its characters, and/or the attitude that the spectator is invited or encouraged to adopt.

If, as I have suggested, films manifest and invite us to take attitudes toward their characters and the events in which they occur, it naturally follows that they can invite improper attitudes, or invite attitudes in improper ways. The first two papers in Part 1 of *Ethics at the Cinema* address this issue. Andrew Gleeson follows a number of writers in exploring the thought that there is something fundamentally powerful and direct about the "moving image".[13] Gleeson argues that the power of film means that it can readily be used in the service of mendacity rather than truth. The immediacy and power of the moving image raises problems of manipulation, stereotyping, and downright lies. In the second paper in the collection, Stephen Williams continues with the theme of cinematic lying, focusing on the propagandist film *The Life and Death of Colonel Blimp*. Williams, however, is concerned not just with the film's attempt to manipulate its audience, but also with the tension between its manipulative nature and its status as a great film. This connects with recent philosophical discussion regarding the relationship between the aesthetic and moral qualities of an artwork.[14] Williams thinks that there is an intimate relationship between a film's ethical status and its aesthetic status, and he endorses the view that ethical flaws in a film detract from its aesthetic status. He argues, however, that *Colonel Blimp* overcomes these flaws (or at least has the potential to do so), and it has the potential to gain or retain greatness in spite of its propagandist aims.

The third and fourth papers in Part 1 address a different issue arising from the attitudes that films and other narratives encourage us to adopt. The power of a narrative to influence a spectator's attitude derives, at least in part, from the spectator's satisfaction, pleasure, and approval of the narrative as a whole, including a satisfaction, pleasure, and approval of the kind of emotional responses that the narrative asks of her. What we might call a "standard" film narrative invites us to take certain straightforward attitudes toward its characters—partly, as we have seen, in the form of emotions we feel toward them and desires we develop on their behalf—and then the narrative plays out in accordance with those created emotions and desires. The result is—if things go as planned—the spectator's overall pleasure and approval of her experience. She is satisfied both by how the narrative events play themselves out and in the way it encourages her to feel about those events. As Noël Carroll writes, "Most movies elicit a gamut of garden-variety emotions over the duration of the narrative. . . . The pleasure that attends the conclusion of the film is a function of the desires that subtend these different emotions being finally satisfied."[15] If we are shown, for example, a character committing a horrifyingly immoral act, we may form an attitude toward that character that involves, in part, the desire for this action to be avenged as the narrative unfolds. A standard narrative will unquestioningly fulfill this desire—without, say, leading us to wonder whether we *should* have formed this desire at all—and we will feel the potency of such a desire being satisfied. As the standard narrative proceeds, events favor the characters we like and admire, and disfavor those we dislike and condemn; as a result we feel a certain pleasure at this fulfillment.

Not all narratives follow a simple procedure of inducing attitudes and straightforwardly satisfying the desires those attitudes bring with them. Some narratives lead us to feel more complex emotions and unclear desires toward their characters, and others invite us to take attitudes toward characters and then invite us to question or examine those attitudes. The issue of a film's inviting challenging and ambivalent attitudes is the main concern of the papers by Murray Smith and myself. *The Sopranos*, an episode of which Smith discusses in his paper, is remarkable for the sympathy that we feel for its protagonist, but this sympathy is by no means unequivocal, and most of us have no clear desires regarding what we wish to happen to Tony Soprano. Smith focuses on the first feature, seeking to explain the appeal of the violent, lying, womanizing Soprano. In my contribution, I address a related issue, aiming to account for our laughter with the deceitful, conniving Walter Burns and the lengths to which he goes in *His Girl Friday* in order to be reunited with his ex-wife. As with the first two papers in the collection, these papers are primarily concerned with a meta-issue in the philosophy of film: Why and how do we enjoy—an enjoyment that is manifested in laughter with, concern for, and bias toward—those characters (like Tony Soprano and Walter Burns) who morally transgress? Although Smith and I ask very similar questions in our papers, our answers are very different; side by side, these two papers reveal how complex the issues in this area are.

These and related themes are also briefly raised throughout Part 2 of this collection. As previously mentioned, however, meta-cinematic and meta-narrative themes lie more in the background of the papers in Part 2. These papers are "philosophical readings", largely dedicated to interpreting and elucidating the narrative and characterization of individual films. I need to delve further into the framework I have so far introduced—that of seeing narratives as inviting us to take attitudes toward their characters—in order to reveal the ethical significance of the philosophical reading.

II. THE PHILOSOPHICAL READING

The kind of philosophical work found in Part 2 of *Ethics at the Cinema* belongs to a tradition with more pedigree outside English-language philosophy than within it. At some point in their careers, Nietzsche, Kierkegaard, Heidegger, and Derrida each directly engaged with specific narratives. Works in this genre of philosophy are not necessarily written in service of the artwork itself; the philosophical reading should not be seen, primarily, as a kind of literary criticism. On the contrary, these writers were doing, or took themselves to be doing, *philosophical* work. Nor are their works appropriating an artwork as a mere thought experiment, trotted out in the service of a philosophical argument; on the contrary, it is *in* the engagement with the artwork that these writers see themselves as doing philosophy. This kind of work was not prominent in the English-language tradition in philosophy until the work of Stanley Cavell in the 1960s. Cavell wrote essays on the work of Samuel Beckett and Shakespeare, as well as essays on film, publishing them alongside essays on J.L. Austin, Wittgenstein, and meaning and knowledge. In the 1980s, Martha Nussbaum began to do the same, engaging at length with Greek tragedies and the novels of Charles Dickens, Henry James, and others. There is a growing body of philosophical work in this vein, on film in particular, in books by Peter A. French, Joseph Kupfer, Andrew Light, Stephen Mulhall, Thomas Wartenberg, and others, and to which the papers in Part 2 of this collection contribute.

The philosophers of literature Peter Lamarque and Stein Haugom Olsen express a reason to be skeptical about the value of such work:

> Literature offers its own alternative realm of application. It offers an imaginative rather than a discursive interpretation of the concepts. And this possibility of applying thematic concepts in literary application makes no direct contribution to philosophical. . . . insight, nor is it tied to any such aim. It

constitutes its own form of insight, its own kind of interpretation of thematic concepts.[16]

To some extent, the division that Lamarque and Olsen describe between the literary and real world is undeniable. In narrative fictions, we are requested to accept things that we know are not true and, even, that we know are not possible. We are asked to stretch our use of the concept *pig* or *spider* or *playing card*, for example, to apply to a thing with the property of *being able to talk*, and this is an application that we would not be willing to accept outside of a fictional world. So, Lamarque and Olsen are no doubt right that, to some degree, "literature offers its own alternative realm of application."

This is not true for all concepts, however. As I suggested in the previous section, narrative films invite us to adopt the attitudes that they manifest toward their characters. In accepting these invitations, we apply certain evaluative concepts to these characters—we come to see one character as someone *to be pitied* because his life has not gone well, another as one *to be praised* because he has done something good, or another as one *to be resented* or *punished* because he has done something blameworthy. These attitudes involve an application not of some stipulated or stretched concepts, but of *our* evaluative concepts. When a film invites its spectators to take an attitude toward its characters, it is addressing them as moral beings; we are being asked not to use concepts invented or stretched by the filmmaker, but to use the evaluative concepts that we use every day. We are being asked to use our ethical concepts as we would use them toward our fellow human beings.

At this point, however, it will now be objected that a film spectator's attitude is toward *fictional beings* and *events*.[17] Why should we think that it is important to discuss stipulated fictional characters, their events, and their contexts, much less the attitudes that the narratives and we as spectators adopt toward these fictional worlds? With limited exceptions, it may be claimed, philosophers are—and should only be—concerned with the *real* world and our attitudes toward what exists in the real world. The attitudes manifested by a fictional narrative, however, are toward its own characters, and those characters and their actions do not exist in the real world, the world in which we exist, the world of what matters. As a consequence, our adopting evaluative attitudes toward fictional beings is not of ethical significance, and *a fortiori* philosophers' discussions of films and the attitudes that they invite us to take are not of ethical significance, either.

I see two ways to respond to this worry. One would be to point to the ways that adopting attitudes toward fictional characters would *affect* the attitudes we adopt toward real creatures. Those who tend to adopt certain kinds of attitudes in the cinema, it might be claimed, will tend to adopt similar kinds of attitudes in the real world. In virtue of this effect, philosophical examinations of the attitudes invited by films can be ethically worthwhile. I do not doubt that there is some such effect, but its nature is intricate and complex, and it is one that can only be determined by observation and testing.[18] Fortunately, an alternative response to skepticism regarding the ethical significance of a spectator's attitudes toward fictional characters is available, and it is this response that I will defend here. This response involves a straightforward denial of the objection expressed in the previous paragraph: the attitudes we adopt as spectators of fictional characters and events are of ethical significance. As spectators, it can *matter* to us whether or not we adopt attitudes that films invite us to take, and so philosophical discussions of the particular attitudes that films invite us to take can matter as well.

The fact that the attitudes that we as spectators adopt towards fictional narratives are important to us is manifested most strikingly in the occasions that we resist or refuse to accept, on moral grounds, the attitudes that a narrative invites us to take. From time to time, a spectator may find it difficult or impossible to join a narrative in taking a certain attitude towards its events. This is one of the cluster of phenomena discussed under the rubric of "imaginative resistance".[19] David Hume was perhaps the first to describe this phenomenon:

> Where vicious manners are described [e.g., in a poem] without being marked with the proper characters of blame and disapprobation, this must be allowed to disfigure the poem, and to be a real deformity. . . . A very violent effort is requisite to change our judgment of manners, and excite sentiments of approbation or blame, love or hatred, different from those to which the mind from long custom has been familiarized.[20]

Imagine a film or novel inviting you to celebrate or enjoy a horribly immoral action. As a spectator, you are not likely to have any difficulty in simply imagining the immoral action; difficulty arises, if it does, when you are invited to take a certain attitude toward that action—to celebrate or enjoy it. In such a situation, as Hume puts it, "vicious manners" are being "described without being marked" with disapproval; you are being presented with vicious manners without being asked to appropriately disapprove of them. The same difficulty arises when we are invited to like a character whom we find repulsive, or praise a character who has acted in an evil way; these attitudes may be difficult or impossible to adopt, precisely because such invitations are inappropriate given what we take to be the conditions for devotion or blame.

There is a difference, then, between *imagining that* a fictional character does something and *taking an attitude* toward the character for what she has done. The latter will be resisted by spectators even when the former is not. This distinction is nicely captured by Richard Moran in a recent discussion on imaginative resistance:

> If the story tells us that Duncan was *not* in fact murdered on Macbeth's orders, then *that* is what we accept and imagine as fictionally true . . . However, suppose the facts of the murder remain as they are in fact presented in the play, but it is *prescribed* in this alternative fiction that this was unfortunate

only for having interfered with Macbeth's sleep that night . . . The [latter]
seem to be imaginative tasks of an entirely different order. . . .[21]

A spectator's opposition arises not when she is asked to imagine something that is
not true, but when she is asked to take what she sees as an inappropriate attitude
toward it. Moran writes that "[w]hatever the ultimate explanation of such conflict,
it seems to argue against thinking of the fictional world of the work as a separate
domain, existing purely by stipulation."[22] A more accurate way of putting Moran's
point would be this: while it may be that a fictional world exists by stipulation, our
responses to it do not. While we can be invited to take certain evaluative attitudes
toward characters, our accepting such invitations is not a matter of simple stipulation; our evaluative responses to fictional characters are not a matter of pure pretense. It follows that there is *something at stake* for the spectator of fictional
narratives, in the attitudes that she is being asked to take.

One expression of there being something at stake here is that my refusing to
adopt the attitudes invited by a narrative may result in my condemnation of the
narrator, or even the narrative itself. If I find an invitation to be inappropriate,
that may—as Hume puts it—"disfigure" the narrative in my eyes. In a recent
discussion, Kendall Walton imagines a story that includes the following sentence: "In killing her baby, Giselda did the right thing; after all, it was a girl." We
agree to imagine that Giselda killed her baby, but we *do not* agree to imagine that
what she did was right, and as Walton adds, "A reader's likely response . . . is to
be appalled by the moral depravity of the *narrator*."[23] This simple example nicely
illustrates our inability to stipulate our evaluative responses to events in a narrative. Rather than accepting that Giselda did the right thing—which involves
adopting a positive attitude toward Giselda—our response is to imagine that
someone else—for example, the narrator—has this attitude. If there is no narrator,
as is true in most films, then we may find ourselves—as Hume points out—
condemning the work itself (or its creators) for inviting an offensive attitude.
Rather than accept the invitation to take an approving attitude toward a fictional
character like Giselda, we refuse the invitation and condemn the narrator or the
work itself.

So, what is it that is at stake in the attitudes spectators adopt toward fictional
characters? One candidate is suggested by Moran:

> Imagination with respect to the cruel, the embarrassing, or the arousing
> involves something. . . . like a point of view, a total perspective on the situa-
> tion, rather than just the truth of a specifiable proposition. . . . It is some-
> thing that I may not be able to do if my heart is not in it.[24]

One way of understanding Moran's reference to "my heart" is to my *character*, to
my emotional and evaluative dispositions with respect to others. When a spectator is
invited to take pleasure in or laugh at a character's being physically attacked, for

example, and she resists doing so, her resistance may be a matter of her refusing to be the kind of person who relishes or laughs at physical abuse, whether fictional or not. The question of whether "my heart is in it" does not arise with respect to the factual stipulations that a fictional narrative invites me to have; I can easily imagine a playing card that talks or a spider that saves a pig. With respect to the emotional and attitudinal response that the narrative asks of me, however, my character is at stake. It can matter deeply to me that I am the kind of person who does not relish physical abuse, whether imagined or not, and when I am asked to do so, I may find myself refusing.

The thought that it is a spectator's character that is at stake in the attitudes we take to fictional characters fits well with the fact that there is a good deal of variance in the attitudes that we, as spectators, are willing to adopt. Some spectators are happy to be invited to laugh at, or approve of, characters that other spectators would not. This is why, for example, some people enjoy dark comedy while others do not. On the view that it is my character that dictates what attitudes I can adopt as a spectator, this variance is not surprising; as we all know, our moral characters vary. Nonetheless, almost all of us have our limits. Even the most lenient of us will not be able to enjoy or laugh at just *anything* in a fictional narrative, be happy with just *anyone's* success or downfall. And this fits well with the fact that, for all of us, our moral characters matter to us.

The suggestion that it is the value of a spectator's character that leads her to refuse certain narrative invitations is only a suggestion. Precisely *what* is at stake deserves, in my opinion, more exploration in the philosophical literature. What does seem clear, however, is that we risk or expose something as spectators of fictional narratives, and that in coming to understand what we risk or expose as spectators—such that we can at certain points resist the invitation that the narrative extends to us—we will better understand why our daily engagement with narratives is important, and why it should be of interest for philosophers in particular to join in on the discussion regarding the attitudes invited by particular films. More pertinent to my purposes here, the existence of imaginative resistance shows us why philosophers should be interested in exploring the attitudes that particular narratives manifest and invite, even though those attitudes are toward fictional beings: as spectators, we are asked not just to join in a stipulated imagining of an alternative world, but to expose ourselves evaluatively to that world, and our evaluative exposure to fictional worlds—and not only the real world—matters to us. Once this is recognized, then one can readily see that the spectatorship of narratives belongs in the broad area of moral psychology. And with this recognition, one has a framework with which to understand why the contributions to Part 2 of *Ethics at the Cinema* are philosophically and ethically relevant.

I can summarize the position I have been outlining here by comparing the spectators of narratives to the receiver of another's *moral endorsement*. Imagine someone describing a politician to you in order to get you to see her as honest, or someone describing your new boyfriend in order to get you to see him as conniving, or a lawyer describing a defendant in order to get a jury to see him as unlikely to have committed the crime of which he is accused. Film makers do not (usually) set out to deliberately change or entrench our attitudes. Nonetheless, in all of these situations, we are presented with a depiction constructed in such a way that we are encouraged to take a certain evaluative attitude to what is being described. Both the moral endorsement and the narrative are, in short, created appeals to our evaluative attitudes toward their objects. As such, the narrative (like the moral endorsement) has a range of features that deserve attention: the nature of its descriptions, the information that we are given and which is withheld from us, the points of view offered to us, the way descriptions of narrative and events unfold, the characters upon which we are invited to focus our attention, and many other features of the techniques that are being used to elicit our emotions and encourage us to adopt certain attitudes. It seems clear that certain experts will have something to tell us about these features of narratives. This includes philosophers.

Many of the writers in Part 2 of *Ethics at the Cinema* have something to say about the general relationships among philosophy, ethics, film, and spectatorship, and some of them may disagree with the framework that I have defended here. Some of them, for example, find the notion of *illustration* useful. Peter Goldie suggests that the world of his film has an illustrative relationship to the world; Samantha Vice and Thomas Wartenberg both suggest that their films illustrate philosophical or theoretical claims about the world. I do not wish to discourage the exploration of the morally salient relationship between the film world and (claims about) the real world. On the contrary, there is much to say about the similarities and differences between our attitudes toward the real and the fictional, as well as about the similarities and differences among ways in which our characters are formed, entrenched, and challenged by our engagements with the real and the fictional. I am convinced, however, that any relationship between the two is neither the only nor the most basic one at stake in the spectatorship of film. On the contrary, the phenomenon of the spectator's imaginative resistance, described above, suggests that there is something morally important entirely within the relationship between spectator and narrative.

My suggestion, then, is that the framework defended here best explains the philosophical and ethical importance of what these writers are doing when they "read" their films, that is, when they delve into the details of plot, dialogue, characterization, imagery, technique, and thematic development. Let me illustrate this by looking at one familiar feature of narratives and how philosophers discuss them. Films often have spectators follow the moral development of a character; as they do so, spectators are invited to have a range of complex, challenging, and perhaps ambivalent attitudes toward him. In doing so, the film can, if a spectator is so inclined, lead her to reflect upon these attitudes and the changing features of the characters that led to them, and to come to certain intellectual conclusions. One contribution in Part 2, for example, Thomas Wartenberg's discussion of *The*

Third Man, intricately charts the moral development of Holly Martins and attempts to make explicit the kinds of intellectual conclusions spectators may be led to draw. A spectator's early attitude of disapproval toward Martins' loyalty toward Harry Lime may lead her to conclude that (and see how) Martins' initial moral position is flawed, and her later attitude of approval may lead her to conclude that (and see how) Martins' moral position has improved; all the while, her attitude of sympathy toward the likeable Martins may lead her to appreciate his journey as genuine and sincere. Wartenberg does not himself make explicit reference to the spectator's engagement with the features of *The Third Man* that he discusses, but when we do so, a fundamental ethical dimension of the film and of his discussion comes into clear view.

Several of the writers in Part 2 ask whether philosophical readings can be generalized to tell us something about our interactions in the real world. This is an appropriate (and interesting) question, but the importance of the philosophical reading—just like the importance of the narratives they discuss—does not rely on its being answered. In these narratives, we observe, come to know, and are invited to have, emotional attitudes toward persons. What we gain from discussions of those narratives is not just a matter of whether they can give us lessons that we will transfer to real-life situations, or even descriptions of what we might encounter or how we might behave in real-life situations. On the contrary, their discussions tell us about our complex and ethically significant encounters *with these films*, and how it is that aspects of our characters were enlivened or ignored, accommodated or challenged in those encounters.

In sum, the intellectual insights that a philosophical reading offers up to us are wholly dependent upon the fact that films, like all narratives, invite us to take certain evaluative attitudes toward the goings-on in its world. Most fundamentally, it would not make sense to speak about a narrative offering intellectual moral insight unless it invited evaluative attitudes. Stated roughly, a narrative is simply a depiction of a series of events, of a character or characters doing things and having things happen to them. That description, in itself, does not include the conceptual resources for understanding how a narrative can carry or convey moral insights about those characters, actions, or events. It is only when we add to our description of a narrative—as I did in the previous section—the possibility of a spectator, and with it the possibility of that spectator's being encouraged to *evaluate* those characters, actions, or events, do we see how a narrative might contain moral insights to be excavated by a philosopher. It is in the potential *presentation* of a series of events that we get the possibility of evaluation of that series of events, and with that, of the possibility of there being a moral conclusion to be explicitly drawn.

A second way in which the intellectual insights of a philosophical reading are dependent upon the attitudes that films invite us to take is that this very feature of films is ethically significant. My claim in this section has been that philosophical readings can be seen as making explicit the many ways in which we, as spectators,

morally expose ourselves to films and other narratives. All films invite us to inter-
act with them, and those invitations and interactions can be reflected upon. Stanley Cavell once wrote, "If philosophy can be thought of as the world of a particular
culture brought to consciousness of itself, then one mode of criticism (call it philosophical criticism) can be thought of as the world of a particular work brought to
consciousness of itself."[25] The interest of the papers in Part 2, I think, lies here. A
philosophical reading is an instance of a philosopher bringing the world of a film
"to consciousness of itself"; philosophical readings can be seen as describing, examining, and in some cases evaluating the kind of moral interactions that spectators (can) have with these films, and in doing so, they make explicit the kinds of
insights to which these films can lead their spectators.

The kinds of topics in Part 2 of *Ethics at the Cinema* will be, to readers familiar
with the history of film, unsurprising. Ever since their inception, film and television have been sensitive to the prevailing social and cultural mood, either demo-
cratically reflecting it or exploring it more self-consciously or critically. It was
therefore to be expected that many of the papers in this collection would concentrate on topics relating to our social identities—race and class division, national
and cultural identity. The first five papers in Part 2 address one or more of these
issues. In addition, films have long been concerned with more universal, interpersonal themes of love, friendship, parenting and sexuality; the final six papers in the
collection all address issues in these areas. Our division of the papers in Part 2 into
these two thematic groups, however, does not do justice to the complexities of
these papers. All of the authors here are philosophers, and so in bringing aspects
of their respective films to "consciousness of themselves," they are concerned, not
surprisingly, with particularly philosophical aspects of the themes in their respective films. Tom Martin writes on the meaning of life, Samantha Vice on ethical
ideals, Lawrence Blum on stereotyping and prejudice, Torbjörn Tännsjö on ethical
dilemmas, Thomas Wartenberg on moral intelligence and perspective, Julia Driver
on justice and mercy, Deborah Knight on irony; other philosophical issues arise
throughout.

Most of the authors of papers in Part 2 bring a tradition of philosophical work
to bear on the world of their film. In the beginning of his paper on *The Believer*,
Tom Martin looks at philosophical theories of racism, and he finds them lacking
in their ability to account for Danny Balint's anti-Semitism; Martin thinks that the
real source of Danny's hatred lies in another area of crisis about which philosophers have had a great deal to say—namely, the specter of life's meaninglessness
and absurdity. Other papers are similarly explicit. Paul C. Taylor, for example, uses
American Pragmatism in his reading of the intercultural romantic comedy *Fools
Rush In*. Samantha Vice brings philosophical work on moral ideals to bear on *Meet
John Doe*. Lawrence Blum uses his own extensive work on prejudice and stereotyping to explore the ways in which *Crash* affects its viewers. The thought driving
Torbjörn Tännsjö's discussion of *Sophie's Choice* is that recent philosophical work
on moral dilemmas will help us understand the kind of dilemma that Sophie

Zawistowska faces when she arrives at the concentration camp. The re-emergence within philosophy of forms of virtue ethics is well represented in *Ethics at the Cinema*. Joseph Kupfer brings a virtue framework to his reading of *Dangerous Liaisons*, interpreting it as a portrayal of the goodness of sexual integrity and virtue. Aristotle's account of friendship and moral intelligence provides the background to papers by Julia Driver and Thomas Wartenberg, two of the three authors who independently chose to write on *The Third Man*. The third paper in this trio, by Deborah Knight, approaches *The Third Man* as a philosopher, but without any kind of philosophical theory in hand; Knight portrays the film as an ironic study in "moral weakness". In a similar manner, Peter Goldie attempts to derive some quite fundamental insights about human bonding from *La Grande Illusion*. Karen Hanson brings *Jules et Jim* to bear on philosophy, concluding that the film provides "welcome corrections" to the Aristotelian picture of male/female relationships and reveals Plato's view of communities to be "boringly unattractive".

There is a growing awareness, from a number of areas within philosophy, of the role of narratives in our lives, in such disparate areas as theories of action and emotion, practical reasoning, personal identity, and ethics. Related to this is a growing sense that a serious engagement with sophisticated narratives can enrich not only ethical debate within philosophy, but also our ethical lives. This commitment has guided the majority of the contributors to *Ethics at the Cinema*. If *narratives in general* can contribute to ethical debate, then filmed narratives should be studied equally with written narratives. Film is a serious and popular conveyance of ethically laden narratives, and the narratives of many important films have been written especially for the screen and are not widely available in any other format. Indeed, only three of the filmed narratives discussed in this collection (*Dangerous Liaisons*, *Sophie's Choice* and *Jules et Jim*) are widely available in written form.[26] Were we to ignore film, we would ignore a rich source of serious and influential narratives. Those involved in the debates surrounding the role and nature of narratives in ethical discourse, persuasion, and commitment simply cannot close their eyes to the cinema.

My suggestion has been that the most crucial feature of spectatorship of filmed and other narratives is that the spectator is being made privy to a particular attitude toward a constructed world, an attitude that she is encouraged to embrace in her emotional and other responses to the events in the narrative. Furthermore, whether or not the spectator takes this attitude is not just a matter of her joining in the stipulation of the imaginary world, but rather flows from, and is a reflection upon, her character. Various features of our engagement with not only complex and challenging film narratives, but also those that are more straightforward and pedestrian, deserve philosophical attention. At bottom, I think, are questions about the nature of the attitude a narrative is inviting the spectator to take, and the details of how the film presents its world and encourages the spectator to see and respond to it in a particular way. This feature of the spectatorship of narratives (fictional and otherwise) brings it into the realm of the concerns of mainstream moral philosophy, and it is to this realm, I think, that all the papers in *Ethics at the Cinema* make sophisticated and enjoyable contributions.[27]

NOTES

1. In what follows, I refer to "film" to avoid clumsy repetition, but have in mind both film and television narratives.

2. "Melting Whites and Liberated Latinas: Identity, Fate, and Character in *Fools Rush In*," this volume, page 142.

3. *On Film*, 2.

4. For a concise summary of some of the issues here, see Murray Smith's review article, "Film and Philosophy," in Donald and Renov (ed.), *The Sage Handbook of Film Studies*, Chapter 10.

5. My thoughts on attitudes have been influenced by Lucy Allais' excellent work on the attitude of forgiveness. See, e.g., her "Wiping the Slate Clean: The Heart of Forgiveness," Section III, and "Dissolving Reactive Attitudes: Forgiving and Understanding." In recent work, Bas van Fraassen has described a similar state, which he calls a "stance" and which he defines as "a cluster of attitudes, including propositional attitudes as well as others, and especially certain intentions, commitments, and values." ("Précis of *The Empirical Stance*," 128. See also *The Empirical Stance*, Lecture 2.)

6. Gordon, *The Structure of Emotions*, 28.

7. Smith, *Engaging Characters*, Chapter 3. I have also been influenced by the work of Berys Gaut in this area; see, e.g., his "The Ethical Criticism of Art."

8. Smith, *Engaging Characters*, 82.

9. Ibid., 83.

10. I am ignoring the debate over whether the spectator's emotions are make-believe or real.

11. "Of the Standard of Moral Taste," 257, emphasis added.

12. Diamond, "Anything but Argument?," 300.

13. See, e.g., Noël Carroll's "The Power of Movies."

14. See, e.g., the papers collected in Jerrold Levinson (ed.) *Aesthetics and Ethics*.

15. Carroll, "Film, Emotion, and Genre," 23.

16. Lamarque and Olsen, *Truth, Fiction, and Literature*, 409.

17. This, of course, is not always true; there are nonfictional films. Nonetheless, it is often true, and it is true of all of the films discussed in this collection.

18. For a discussion of some of the empirical work and the issues surrounding it, see Hakemulder, *The Moral Laboratory*.

19. For a useful taxonomy of the various phenomena in this area, see Weatherson, "Morality, Fiction, and Possibility."

20. Hume, "Of the Standard of Taste," in *Selected Essays*, 152.

21. Moran, "The Expression of Feeling in Imagination," 95.

22. Ibid., 99.

23. Walton, "Morals in Fiction and Fictional Morality," 37–38.

24. Moran, "The Expression of Feeling in Imagination," 105.

25. *Must We Mean What We Say?*, 313.

26. The script for *Dangerous Liaisons* is adapted from the novel *Les Liaisons Dangereuses*, by Choderlos de Laclos; *Sophie's Choice* is based on the novel of the same name by William Styron; *Jules et Jim* is based on the novel of the same name by Henri-Pierre Roche. Graham Greene's screenplay for *The Third Man* is also widely available in written form, although it was written to be filmed.

27. Thanks to Elisa Galgut, Lindsay Kelland, Hafiz Sadeddin, Murray Smith, Ken Walton, Tom Wartenberg, and, especially, to Samantha Vice.

PART ONE

CRITIQUE, CHARACTER, AND THE POWER OF FILM

THE SECRETS AND LIES OF FILM

ANDREW GLEESON

I T IS TEMPTING TO BELIEVE that film is the most powerful of media, and that with that power comes a pre-eminent capacity either for conveying truth or for falsification. This paper is very largely an attempt to identify the senses in which this is true (or false), making use of Mike Leigh's 1996 film *Secrets and Lies*.[1]

I begin by concentrating on the ways in which film may falsify. In the first section, I give an account of the way in which film may well be pre-eminent among media in falsifying in a straightforward, factual sense (lying). In the second section, I identify a deeper, value-related sense of truthfulness, and thus of falsification, which permeates our lives and to which serious art is necessarily responsive. I argue that, once again, film quite likely has a pre-eminent capacity to be exploited for falsification in this sense, an exploitation very much on display in modern culture. This kind of falsification does not just deliberately misinform us: it can make us contemptuous of the very idea of truth. In the third section, I turn matters around from a focus on falsification to a focus on truthfulness in the sense I have identified. Using a scene from *Secrets and Lies* I show how film can enlarge our sense of the nature of human sexuality, friendship and life itself – but only by keeping in check its own characteristic power to stimulate the senses. I also argue that, in contrast to its power to falsify, film's power to convey truth is unlikely to be greater than that of other media. In the final section, I apply the conception of truthfulness I have developed to *Secrets and Lies* as a whole, and I find the film wanting in its ending. This demonstrates the exacting demands of truthfulness to which art in general—and especially film, with its outstanding power to affect viewers—must be responsive.

I.

The power in question is the power to control what we think, what we feel, and how we act—not just in relation to film itself, but in the world at large. Thus, advertisers use film—especially television—to try to get us to want and buy products; public relations firms use it to promote the popularity of pop stars and politicians; propagandists use it to persuade us to believe in and die for their ideologies.

The key to this power is film's capacity to control our two most important senses—seeing and hearing—to control appearances. If we pay only minimal attention, it will get us to see and hear just about anything at all. How does that power to control appearances translate into a power over belief, feeling, and action? The simplest answer is by straightforward deception. A doctored newspaper photograph making a celebrity look better or worse than he or she does is an example.[2] Faked documentary footage presented as real is another. If, as some people believe, the moon landings were faked, that would be a perfect example on a grand scale.

That sort of plain deception exploits one kind of realism that is often supposed to be distinctive of photography and, especially, film. We might call this realism physical *lifelikeness*. More than in painting or sculpture, the way things *look* and *sound* in a film strongly resembles (or can strongly resemble) the way they look and sound in real life (if the film purports to be a true story) or (if the film is a fiction) the way they would look and sound if some reasonable precisification of the story were real—it is *as if* we were seeing the real thing, as if we were "really there". Thus, on our television news, we see Barack Obama looking and sounding very much as he looked and sounded to people present at his press conference earlier in the day. There are films (*Gandhi*) in which we see Gandhi looking and sounding very much as he actually did when he did various things, or (on reasonable supposition) would have looked and sounded had he done them. And still other films (*King Kong*) in which we see King Kong looking and sounding as he would have looked and sounded were some reasonable precisification of the *King Kong* story true.

This resemblance—between what we see in watching the film and what we would have seen in real life or if the story were true—is possible because either (1) the person, events, etc., the film is about have themselves been filmed (as in the Obama press conference case), or (2) the filmmaker has photographed actors, sets, props, etc., which bear a strong resemblance to the actual (or hypothetically actual) events. (Often there is a mix of the two, as when films are shot at well-known locations that have a place in the story.) Of course, it is not being denied that what one sees in looking at or watching other media besides modern, hyperrealistic, colored, talking films resembles things as they appear in real life. Painting, sculpture, animated film, silent film, black-and-white film, photography—all can have this resemblance, but overall they have it to a lesser extent than full-blown (colored, etc.) film.

Some philosophers may take exception to my saying that, for example, when we watch *King Kong* we see King Kong.[3] It should abate my offense in their eyes to point out that I am using "see" in its *intentional* sense—the sense in which I can see things and hear things regardless of whether they are "there". Thus, mishearing a word or seeing a cow when it was really a horse are examples of intentional perceiving. Notice that so, too, is *hearing* a word correctly, and seeing the horse veridically—because *all* seeing is intentional—to see at all is to see *as* something (even if it be a mere blur or "buzzing, blooming confusion"). In contrast, not all seeing is *extensional*—only that which is veridical. In this sense, I see the horse rather than a cow, I see colored images flickering on a screen (or perhaps, at a greater, prosthetic distance, actors and sets, and so on), but anything lacking the relevant causal connection (though exactly what that is is a matter of debate) is not seen (not Barack Obama if he is not relevantly connected, and certainly not King Kong). Now in the case of film (and other depictive, visual media), when I say that we see King Kong or Barack Obama (or whatever), I mean that this is what we intentionally see when we attend to the film (or documentary, or television news report) qua content—what we see *when we see what it depicts* (rather than as the physical thing doing the depicting), filtering out the hum of the projector or the glare of the TV, any reflections in the screen, the curtain or wall on which the film is projected, etc. Unless I indicate otherwise, whenever I speak of seeing and hearing in relation to film and other depictive media, it is the intentional sense of seeing what is depicted that I shall have in mind.

Notice that such seeing of what is depicted does not depend on a life-likeness to what one extensionally sees. Even a very faint resemblance can (perhaps with context) ensure the perception. One can see Barack Obama in black and white, with a big nose and short legs in a caricature—and so on; one can see things (or at least identify them) without seeing them *as they literally are* in every, or even most, respects (just as one can depict them without depicting them as they literally are). Similarly (as I have already noted) any visual depiction will control intentional seeing of what is depicted to some extent. And of course, nonrealistic depictions can be used to lie too. Falsification is not unique to hyperrealistic media.

But are hyperrealistic media like film more *effective* at it? Certainly the popular *reach* of film is greater than that of most other media—in that sense, it is probably responsible for more falsehood in the world. But—assuming equal exposure—is a photograph or a film more convincing (and thus a better liar) than the same falsehood stated in, say, a newspaper column? That is a hard question to answer—there are so many factors (subject matter, the credibility of the author or filmmaker, the audience) that need to be kept constant. Still, I am inclined to think (though I cannot demonstrate it) that film is a more effective liar than other media because its hyperrealistic lifelikeness stimulates us in ways resembling the stimulus of personal presence, and thus lowers our guard. There is a greater—or better, perhaps a more readily created—sense of excitement and personal involvement, triggered by the intense visual and auditory bombardment.[4] This might be especially so when personal (or otherwise strongly felt) connections are involved—think of the importance to us of representations of loved ones, in which the most realistic, meaning the photographic, are strongly preferred. Humans have always made physical images of the dead, of gods and so on. (And when this is prohibited, as it is in some cultures, its potency is testified to by the strength of the prohibition.) Think of the sense of intimacy, or at least identification, transcending time, that we can feel in looking even at old, dog-eared, black-and-white family photographs. Hence, the lengths to which we go to ensure the desired appearances, especially of important moments in our lives, are preserved:

PHOTOGRAPHER [Maurice] *is arranging the bride's train on the floor. She is posed on a sofa, holding her bouquet.*

PHOTOGRAPHER: Let's make the most of this beautiful train . . . that's it—okay . . .

(He smiles at her, a friendly smile. He has a beard. He goes over to another sofa, and picks up a camera. A severe middle-aged man in a morning suit, presumably the bride's father, paces up and down in the doorway, occasionally looking at his watch. The PHOTOGRAPHER looks through his viewfinder.)

Yeah . . . that's really great, yeah—yeah. Okay, now, as I said before, you're under no obligation to, but you can if you want to give me a . . . tiny little twinkle—yeah, that is—(*He snaps.*) lovely! Get a bit closer . . .

(He does so. The bride looks nervous.)

Don't you worry—you'll be alright! (*He chuckles. He looks up from his camera, and adjusts a lock of her hair delicately.*)

There's just a little bit . . . . that's it! And you've got an eyelash on your nose—we don't want that, now we. . . . (*He removes it.*) Supposed to be on your eye, not on your snitch.

(He laughs and the bride smiles.)

That's it—you've got a lovely smile when you smile, 'aven't you? Right, okay; and keep that lovely gorgeous smile! (*He snaps.*) That's the easy bit.

(He laughs. Sarah smiles, but her smile quickly fades.)[5]

Thus can photography—and of course film—magnify, disperse and preserve a lie. The example is from *Secrets and Lies*, a film centrally about appearances, true and false. I shall be returning to it in Section III. First, however, I want to investigate whether film—again, in virtue of that "sensory bombardment" that controls seeing and hearing—has a pre-eminent potential to be used, not simply to deceive, but *to subvert the very place of truth in our lives*. To rob us of not just facts, but truth itself. To make us not just ignorant, but contemptuous of truth.

II.

I think it does. To show this, it is necessary to turn attention away from straightforward factual truth and to consider truth concerning matters of value.

Of course, there is a long philosophical tradition—the most familiar strand taking its inspiration from Hume—that is deeply skeptical of truth and falsity in relation to value. That is much too big a topic to take on here. I shall simply assume the legitimacy of the following notion of "true" and "false", one that I take to mark a distinction of value (certainly, it is not a straightforward distinction of fact). Many of our emotions are what one might call "morally calibrated". That is, the identification and understanding of them requires distinguishing genuine from bogus forms. For example, love must be distinguished from infatuation and possessiveness, grief from self-pity, righteous indignation from personal pique, self-respect from vanity, courage from bravado, and so on. Raimond Gaita calls this distinguishing among "the real and the counterfeit forms of the inner life."[6] We often use the very words themselves, or their close cognates. We speak of a true love or genuine friendship, or we talk of a "false note" in a person's emotional tone, or of self-deception. The distinctions are of the greatest importance. Our moral lives are partly defined by the demand to achieve a lucid self-scrutiny in regard to them. When a person systematically avoids this demand in some part of their lives, and produces rationalizations for it, we may speak of them as "living a lie." The effort to achieve this lucidity is the effort to live a truthful life in a sense much broader than simply trying to tell the truth in a plain, factual sense.

Most story telling (fiction and nonfiction) explores this domain of human truthfulness and the various ways in which we may succeed or fail in rising to its demands. This is not to say that a concern with such truthfulness is a principal and explicit aim of the story. An author (or film director) may merely set out to tell a good yarn. As long as it is dealing with human beings, or anthropomorphized creatures, however, the characters in a story can be assessed from this point of view. That means that the story, too, can be assessed for its truthfulness—for how seriously, perceptively, subtly it portrays the characters and the significance of their responses to the situations they confront, and whether it manages to convey a sense that they have responded well or poorly. (This need not mean the story is overtly "moralistic"; far from it.)

A novel, play, or film that does this well provides the audience with material for reflection of a broadly ethical sort. The better the work, the deeper the possibilities for reflection it creates. Conversely, the poorer the work, the less rich those possibilities. Works that deliberately disregard the moral distinctions I have been speaking of, or which actively confuse them, have the potential to be corrupting— that is, to encourage us in some profoundly mistaken view of the distinctions, or in a frivolous indifference to or contempt for them. When a work does this, it is usually because its exclusive preoccupation with some other end has driven out all such considerations—a preoccupation with ideology, or with impressing a certain constituency, or with making money. In the last case—in modern, commercial publishing and broadcasting—the twisting, at the limit even the annihilation, of value distinctions characteristically results from the creator's overriding goal of stimulating not the audience's capacity for civilized reflection, but, rather, a bald and undiscriminating tsunami of excitement. A thoughtful work creates space for reflection, on the responses of the characters in the story and, sometimes, on one's own response to the story. Thoughtless works of the type I have in mind deny material for reflection by creating characters and stories whose only purpose is to solicit a "sugar rush" of feeling. Since that feeling is ethically unconditioned, what one gets is primarily the bodily constituents of emotion—the physical arousal of pulse, adrenalin, etc. A superficial, sensory excitation is purchased at the expense of deeper, ethical exploration.

Here is an example from G. K. Chesterton. It concerns value in the artistic use of pure color, but its description of the exploitation of the senses, at the expense of the capacity to discriminate reflectively, applies equally well to the presentation of human beings.

> . . . we live in a world which gives us a vast exhibition of that vividness which is symbolised by colour, but which is wholly without that concerted unity of rule or tradition which is symbolised by harmony in colour. The illuminated advertisements of a big city like London. . . . exhibit exactly that contradiction between colour and design. The design, even in the sense of the purpose, is patchy and personal and not only vulgar but essentially venal. The colour is often the best and most beautiful experience given to the senses of man, if only man were in a position to make the best of it. The psychological effect produced by random commercial illumination is something which is to the real possibilities of colour what a drunken slumber is to the divine gift of wine. Or rather, it should be compared to that habit, which springs up so easily in Prohibitionist or semi-Prohibitionist countries, of trying to get the best out of the divine gift of wine by preceding it with excessive quantities of whisky, following it by equally excessive quantities of beer, or possibly beginning the whole banquet with liqueurs and ending it with cocktails. In short, Prohibitionists get drunk because they have never been taught to drink; and commercial advertising wastes its artistic materials, even when it possesses them, because it has never been taught to colour or even to enjoy colours. Colours are being killed; and they are being killed by being worked to death. The nerve is being killed; and it is being killed by being overstimulated and therefore stunted and stunned.[7]

Chesterton was writing in the 1930s. Already, however, he could see that mass advertising debased sound and color to produce an addictive excitation in auditors and spectators. Film and video have taken this to a new level in the three quarters of a century since. Vast amounts of popular advertising and entertainment (most of it film, video or print photography) rely on the relentless stimulation of the senses—beating them to death, in Chesterton's image—a stimulation that *fixates* attention, preventing the development of appreciation and reflection by locking us into a frenzy of excitement. In sound, it prefers volume to harmony or even tunefulness; in sight and color, it elevates garishness and glitter over beauty and taste; in general, a formless hubbub and commotion dominates over coherence, proportion and meaningfulness—all with the effect of substituting titillation and intoxication over reflection or even serene enjoyment. Intensity and repetition of a single glaring beat or image are its simplest elements. Notoriously—in some of its more extreme manifestations—the aim is to attack the mind and produce a kind of permanent numbness and distraction from reality (and when the image or noise cannot do this, direct chemical attack on the brain can).[8]

Of course, one needs to distinguish the content of the film—what materials for reflection it does or does not provide, what attitudes and values it encourages—from its actual effects on viewers, both to what extent they get caught up in the "sugar rush", and then to what extent a heavy diet of such films (and similar entertainments) affects their values and behavior. The first is a moral-cum-artistic judgment. The second is an empirical question. I cannot hope, in an essay like this, to convince skeptics that the empirical effects are large enough to be a matter of concern. The most I can do is to describe the general phenomenon (which is all around us) and appeal to the reader's own familiarity with it in the hope that he or she will see the plausibility of such effects coming to pass, at least on developing minds. In what follows, the more skeptical reader may take my empirical claims as claims about what the effects on viewers *would* be *if* they, so to speak, succumbed to the moral content of the films (and other entertainments) I have in mind and the attitudes and values they, in effect, endorse and encourage.

Consider pornography. The exploitation of image and sound in film is readily joined to the visceral bodily cravings and reactions of sex, considered simply as genital arousal. In relation to sex, film's realism-as-"lifelikeness" comes into its own again, conferring a power to control our seeing and hearing at a level of attention dominated by genital excitation, or the physiological prologues thereto. The *sine qua non* of pornography is its dissociation of sex from meaning or significance of any sort—that is, its divorce from the distinctively human dimension of our lives, the dimension in which we may assess the truthfulness of our emotions and actions, including our sexual lives—in the way described earlier. It does, as we say, treat people, especially women, as "objects", as machines for gratification.[9]

Contrasting written pornography with D. H. Lawrence's writing about sex, Richard Hoggart writes of how the latter expresses:

. . . . a weight of respect—reverence, Lawrence would have said—for another; a sense of pity for another's grief and weakness; a recognition that our lives exist in time—have a past and a future—rather than a shuttered focussing on to the thrill of the moment.[10]

It is the "shuttered focussing on to the thrill of the moment"—with its necessary annihilation of all issues about truthfulness—that is pornographic film's distinguishing characteristic. Even when a human context is provided in a work as a whole, any lapse into salaciousness, into savoring sexual stimulation for its own sake, is apt to bring the shutters down, and it remains an artistic failing, even when it does not constitute a work's main appeal. (None of this is to say that nakedness, passion, comic bawdiness, or the depiction—as opposed to the actuality—of salaciousness, are objectionable. Needless to say, there are cases in which distinguishing them from pornography will be a very subtle matter indeed.)

The depiction of violence can also take on a "pornographic" quality. For example, in some modern film genres (e.g., the "action" movie), the audience is excited by cruelty and invited to admire—with video games, even to participate in—its cleverness. Again, the violence appeals because of the way it arouses bodily excitement (affording something of the sensation of danger, without the real risk) at the expense of thoughtfulness and of imagination, which, in such films, exists as little more than variation on the same plot lines, more or less flashily effected.

I have concentrated on pornographic sex and violence because they are particularly clear cases of the more general phenomenon I am trying to identify—the capture and manipulation of an audience through the provision of bodily and emotional excitation at the expense of thoughtfulness and imagination, including, crucially, the inclination (and eventually perhaps even the capacity) to examine the truthfulness of human lives and especially one's own life   that is, as I explained at the start of this section, to distinguish true from false emotions, reactions, and qualities of character. Here are three more examples[11]:

- Celebrity gossip, which plays on our unadmirable proclivities for envy, prurience, voyeurism, and *schadenfreude*.

- Racial and nationalist propaganda, which plays on our even more unadmirable proclivities for racism and xenophobia.

- Much (not all) advertising, which plays on greed or desire for social prestige—or anything it can—to sell anything it can.

Of course, none of these is unique to film. But film's pre-eminent capacity to control seeing and hearing seems plausibly to give it a pre-eminent capacity to stimulate bodily and emotional responses. Otherwise, it is hard to explain its widespread use for these purposes (think of television's triumph, music aside, over print and radio).

In a Platonic idiom of thought, these phenomena constitute a flight from reality into fantasy, a flight deeper into the shadows of the cave. The shadows inevitably disappoint. They exhaust the senses and the emotions rather than refresh them, leaving a potentially addictive craving for a satisfaction they promise but can never provide—hence, a perpetual escalation in the levels of explicitness, in the vain hope of satisfaction. The result may be a widespread loss of the very moral and artistic vocabulary and meanings that are necessary to ask those questions about our lives—and their representations in the arts—that seek to distinguish the true from the false semblances, the sun from the shadows.

This is precisely the fear Plato held for the popularisation of the arts. As a contemporary Platonist, R. F. Holland, explains it:

Enquiries [in science and art] trivialize themselves in subservience to exploitation and the arts are commuted into instruments of gratification. The
more they gratify the more they falsify and they proliferate with cancerous
fecundity while in this state.[12]

The falsification Holland speaks of deliberately seeks to abolish ethical and artistic
distinctions in a fog of thoughtless excitation. In short, it wilfully attacks understanding, insight, and hence *truth*, in the sense I began this section by explaining.

Now we can see what I meant in the last section when I said that film has a
pre-eminent capacity not just to attack *truths*, but to promote a contempt for *truth*
itself. I meant that, in the way I have been trying to explain, it can undermine our
willingness and capacity to examine our lives for their truthfulness—that is, for the
genuineness of their love, grief, friendship, courage, loyalty, etc.

Does all this have a connection to prosaic, factual truth? To the virtue of factual
honesty? Simply, if we are not moved to examine our lives for the quality of their
love, grief, etc., then we are not likely to examine the quality of our speech—and
a central criterion of that quality is honesty. The orators and sophists whom Plato
presents Socrates struggling against prostituted language as merely a means to an
end—the end of controlling an audience. Their modern counterparts—advertisers, propagandists and ideologues, ministerial "spin-doctors", public relations
experts—treat it the same way as sex and violence are treated. When a politician
panders to popular prejudice to win votes; when a newspaper columnist polemi-
cizes in order to satisfy a readership craving to hear a certain opinion; when public
relations shysters set out to burnish a flagging image; when an artist puts his talents at the service of an ideology; when a performer recycles the same uninspired
songs just to keep his name in the public eye, they all falsify their talents (the arts
they employ) by aiming them at something other than truth—at money, popularity, or worldly advancement, but not truth. When language, in particular, is seen
in such an exclusively instrumental light, its relation to truth becomes at best accidental. Where language is for sale, honesty disappears.

III.

If I am right in arguing that film has a pre-eminent capacity to falsify in the sense
described, this presents filmmakers with an unprecedented temptation that they
need to identify and resist. When film succeeds in such resistance, it does so by
restraining its characteristic power (over seeing and hearing) rather than by exercising it. It must, so to speak, exercise a certain anti-filmic discipline. This is not
necessarily to deny that certain distinctively cinematic techniques—the close-up,
for example—can be employed to enhance a film's capacity to convey and explore
human life. It is to say that such powerful imagery must not be used simply for the
addictive power it can so readily exert. To avoid that danger, such techniques need
careful integration with plot, characterization, acting and so on.[13] Thus, rather

than narrow our focus to the momentary sensation, a film must enlarge that focus, so as to bring into view the human context of events. It must give the sense of human beings with "a past and a future"—it must tell, or imply, a story or stories (that is, people with a history) and it must take the time, and by the detail of its observation of people and their lives, convey a sense of (and create an interest in) the characters as people, so that the viewer comes to care about their history and their fate the way we care about friends or family. To do this, it must, as I say, resist the temptation merely to excite us with the power of its images. Attention, must, so to speak, be transferred from the image to what it is an image of—to the story and characters.

Sometimes this can be accomplished in part by pausing, by taking a break from the main plot development, and allowing the viewer to spy on, or relax with, the characters in those many episodic moments that have no place on our resumes but that make up so much of life. Then, even two young women gigglingly discussing a casual sexual encounter need not be a prurient event, but a finely observed—that is, a *true*—portrait of female friendship,as demonstrated here, from Leigh's *Secrets and Lies*:

> *That evening, another bright summer's one,* HORTENSE *and her friend* DIONNE *are sitting at* HORTENSE'S *kitchen table. They have had supper, and are sipping white wine. They are looking reflective.*
>
> DIONNE: I saw 'er, [HORTENSE'S LATE MOTHER] you know?
>
> HORTENSE: Did yer?
>
> DIONNE: Yeah, eight o'clock in the morning, she's down Harlesden, buyin her yam and banana; she says like, "You got a boyfriend yet, Dionne?" (*She laughs.*)
>
> HORTENSE: Nearly everyone 'oo went to the funeral reckoned they'd seen 'er, and she'd given them some kind of sign. (*Ancient West Indian lady's voice:*) "Me see your mudder two days before she dead an she hol on to me an' look in me eye as if she did know."
>
> (*They both laugh. Then* HORTENSE *becomes reflective again.*)
>
> I mean if she knew, I wish she'd told us.
>
> DIONNE: You're getting better, though.
>
> HORTENSE: It's a nice day.
>
> DIONNE: (*Looking out of window*) Yeah.
>
> (*Pause.*)
>
> HORTENSE: I dunno. My 'ead can't contain it all—it's too soon. There's nothing rational about grief. Maybe you're crying for yourself.

DIONNE: Have you been out much?

HORTENSE: No, I can't. Some days . . . I'm completely vulnerable—I can feel everything; other days, I'm numb.

DIONNE: You wanna come out with me?

HORTENSE: No! I've got stuff to sort out.

DIONNE: What?

HORTENSE: Life.

DIONNE: Look, if there's anything I can do . . . .

HORTENSE: No—thanks. I'll be all right.

DIONNE: Have you heard from Bernard?

HORTENSE: No. Yes! He sent a sympathy card.

DIONNE: Did he?

HORTENSE: Which I thought was a very nice thing to do.

DIONNE: Mm.

(HORTENSE *makes a funny, grotesque face, a sort of pouting kiss, presumably some private reference to Bernard.* DIONNE *imitates this, and they both burst into naughty, conspiratorial laughter.*)

I did something really bad.

HORTENSE: Oh, no, I don't think I can deal with no confessions.

DIONNE: Cleanse my soul!

HORTENSE: Mm—mm!

DIONNE: I did the do!

HORTENSE: Do it!

DIONNE: Did the deed!

HORTENSE: Did it!

DIONNE: With a complete stranger.

HORTENSE: No—who?

DIONNE: Dunno. (*She giggles.*)

HORTENSE: Well, what did 'e look like?

DIONNE: Dunno. 'E was in advertising.

HORTENSE: (*West Indian accent*) Oh, Lard!

(*They laugh.* HORTENSE buries *her head in her arm. Normal voice:*)

Did you use a condom?

DIONNE: Yes.

HORTENSE: Did you use two?

DIONNE: Yes.

HORTENSE: One on top of the other?

DIONNE: One after the other.

HORTENSE: Oh, God!

DIONNE: (*Laughing*) D'you despair of me?

HORTENSE: (*Looking at her*) No.

DIONNE: Yes, you do.

HORTENSE: I don't. Did you 'ave a good time?

DIONNE: Yeah.

HORTENSE: That's all that matters, then, innit?

DIONNE: Yeah.

(*She smiles, and sips some wine.* HORTENSE *laughs quietly.*)[14]

Hortense has recently lost her adoptive West Indian mother and begun the search for her birth mother. Even without knowing this, the scene succeeds in implying for the viewer some such past and future, a life extending far beyond this languid moment of reflection, and bearing all the unrationalizable human importance that something like *having parents* has for us; it makes that truth apparent to us. Then the placement of sex, even in this casual connection, in relation to friendship, then death and grief—wondered at, in this cool moment, for their sheer power over us—rescues the reference from any merely titillating effect, and the whole scene succeeds in conveying Hoggart's "weight of respect"—a nonsolemn, unportentous seriousness—for human life. It does not matter greatly that in the scene itself the characters are not engaged in searching self-examination. In making evident the importance that parents, and friendship, and so on have for us, it implicitly raises questions about what demands of truthfulness these place on us: What is it to be a genuine friend, a loving parent or child? Moreover, in its depiction of the characters (say, of Hortense's grief) the film can be assessed for its alertness to the distinctions implicit in these questions. Once again, this is a matter of distinguishing the real from the counterfeit in our lives.

The above vignette is one of several marvellous "stand alone" episodes that break into *Secrets and Lies'* plot development. At first, this might seem like a Brechtian alienation device, designed to remind us that this is, after all, a film, but in fact, the effect is to deepen the film's realism, its truth, as a picture of what human life is like.

IV.

So far I have tried to develop an account of film's characteristic power (in distinction from other media) and then to relate that power to a capacity to undermine, or to uphold, both plain, factual truthfulness and the profounder truthfulness that human lives, and their depiction in the arts, are appraised in the light of. In this final section, I want to give a fuller example of such appraisal, using *Secrets and Lies*, a film that itself takes the search for truth, and for truthfulness—especially in families—as a central theme. The example brings out how great are the demands of artistic truthfulness; how art, because it depicts our lives, is answerable to questions like those our lives are answerable to. Has the film, in its depiction of character X or Y, appreciated the distinctions between genuine and spurious love, courage, or friendship? Does the film itself succumb to sentimentality, jadedness, kitsch, or sensationalism?

Hortense is seeking the truth about her parentage. On one level, she is seeking truth in the plain, factual sense. If that were the end of it, she might be satisfied when the authorities (in the person of a finely drawn instance of the "caring" but harried and bureaucratized professional) inform her that her mother is a white woman. Of course, however, Hortense is seeking more than simply information—she wants to know who her mother is in a sense that requires (if it is possible) a personal encounter with her, an encounter that (whatever its outcome: which may be that they never meet again) raises all the opportunities for human accountability (on both sides) that exist between mother and daughter. What sort of mother are you (am I)? What sort of daughter can I (you) be to me? Why did you (I) give me (you) away? Can I (we) rise to the demands, and the joys, of this newly uncovered relationship? These questions are all, implicitly, demands to scrutinise our lives in the spirit of truthfulness I have described. (This is not to say, of course, that the questions are necessarily ever overtly stated.)

The first hurdle is overcoming the shock and fear of actually meeting, of finding the courage to meet. The mother—a lonely, uneducated, working-class woman, Cynthia—reacts with horror to the first approach, which is by phone. She hangs up, refusing all contact. Hortense persists and eventually talks Cynthia into a meeting. In one of those scenes that, while profoundly serious, is also marked by that rich vein of slightly dark comedy that erupts into the film from time to time, they begin to explore the issues of mother and daughter that bind them together— Hortense, the educated, middle-class black professional, and her white mother from the other side of the tracks:

An empty café. CYNTHIA *and* HORTENSE *sit side by side at a table. Each has a cup and saucer.* HORTENSE *is getting out the documents.*

CYNTHIA: I 'ope you find yer mum, sweet'eart. You keep lookin.' Go on. (*Offers* HORTENSE *a cigarette.*)

HORTENSE: No thanks. I don't smoke.

CYNTHIA: (*Lighting up*) Nor should yer. My daughter smokes like a chimney.

HORTENSE: You got a daughter?

CYNTHIA: Yeah. I ain't never been in 'ere before. They shouldn't go raisin' yer 'opes like that—it ain't fair!

(HORTENSE *puts a document on the table.*)

HORTSENSE: Is this your signature?

(CYNTHIA *looks at it. Then she picks it up.*)

CYNTHIA: This is stupid—I don't understand it. I mean, I can't be your mother, can I?

HORTENSE: Why not?

CYNTHIA: Well, look at me.

HORTENSE: What?

CYNTHIA: Listen, I don't mean nothin' by it, darlin,' but I ain't never been with a black man in my life. No disrespect, nor nothing. I'd a' remembered, wouldn't I?

(HORTENSE *looks at* CYNTHIA. CYNTHIA *thinks about things. Long pause. Suddenly, something comes back to her.*)

Oh, bloody 'ell . . . . ! (*She looks at* HORTENSE.) Oh, Jesus Christ Almighty! (She bursts into uncontrollable tears, and turns away from HORTENSE.) I'm sorry, sweet'eart . . . (*Sobbing.*) I'm so ashamed.

HORTENSE: You shouldn't be ashamed. (*She puts away the documents.*)

CYNTHIA: I can't look at you. (*She turns to* HORTENSE.) I didn't know, sweet'eart, honest, I didn't know.

HORTENSE: What didn't you know?

CYNTHIA: I didn't know you was black. See, I th—I thought they got the dates all wrong; all this time I thought you was born six—six weeks premature, but you wasn't . . . you wasn't . . .

(*Pause.*)[15]

It is too easy to dismiss Cynthia's shame here as an unnecessary burden of guilt that more enlightened attitudes would sweep away That she should at least face the possibility of needing to feel shame is an indispensable dimension of what makes the relationship of mother and daughter something momentous. That momentousness cannot exist without the disposition to scrutinize our lives (as mothers or daughters) in the way Cynthia is doing here. Without that momentousness, there would be no need on either side to meet at all; there would not be motherhood or daughterhood in anything but a biological sense. None of this is to pass any judgment on what Cynthia *did* (quite apart from the fact she was only 15 and very largely had the decision made for her), much less to deny the propriety of Hortense's reassurance (forgiveness?).

The need to know the truth of her human origins that Hortense responds to is not of any instrumental sort. It is not as if, for example, she pursued it for any happiness, or relief of unhappiness, it might bring, for her happiness depends upon it only in so far as it has a significance for her in its own right—if she did not care about her parentage *per se*, why would it affect her happiness? Anyway, there is no guarantee that the discovery of the truth—in any matter— will be pleasant, happy, or liberating. That fact is behind the irony in the manufactured smiles and jolliness that Maurice—Cynthia's photographer brother—is professionally engaged in producing (and of which we saw an instance in the first section): they are attempts to convince ourselves, in the medium of photography, of a (once-upon-a-time) "true happiness" that in reality eludes most of us.

It certainly eludes Cynthia's family. Maurice and Cynthia were once close, he the protective elder brother, after their parents died. He, however, became distant after marrying the socially ambitious Monica, who encouraged his professional talent, which, together with some hard-earned money left by his father, enabled them to rise in the world—specifically, to a nice house in a good suburb. Polished Monica looks down on the uncouth Cynthia, while Cynthia resents Monica for taking Maurice from her. Cynthia and Monica quarrel over the money. Cynthia— unable to resist interfering and offering motherly advice—quarrels, too, with her other, younger (also illegitimate) daughter, the unhappy Roxanne.[16] Roxanne knows nothing of Hortense. Maurice and Monica know Cynthia adopted out an older daughter, but they do not know her identity. They hide a secret of their own. When Cynthia decides to introduce Hortense to her family—having grown closer to her in a number of meetings—she does so under the disguise that Hortense is a friend from work.

The occasion is Roxanne's twenty-first birthday party, celebrated as a barbecue at Maurice and Monica's—the first time Cynthia or Roxanne has been there. Cynthia is unable to contain the emotions that the arrival of Hortense in her life has stimulated, and she blurts out the truth in the middle of the party (while Hortense is in the bathroom). As I said, the effect of truth is never guaranteed to be positive, and in this case the initial result is explosive.

CYNTHIA: She [Hortense] takes after her mother.

MAURICE: Does she?

MONICA: D'you know her as well?

MAURICE: Work in the factory, does she?

CYNTHIA: You're looking at 'er.

ROXANNE: Eh?

CYNTHIA: She's my daughter.

(MAURICE *and* MONICA *look startled.*)

ROXANNE: What's the matter with yer?

CYNTHIA: Maurice . . . it's me daughter.

ROXANNE: Don't be *stupid*! She's 'ad too much to drink.

. . . .

MONICA: She can't be the one that . . . .

(MAURICE *looks at her.*)

ROXANNE: What?

(MONICA *looks away.*)

CYNTHIA: Hortense, sweet'eart . . . . she's yer sister. (*She breaks into tears.*)

ROXANNE: What?

. . . . [*Hortense returns to the table. Cynthia offers her cake. Otherwise there is dead silence.*]

HORTENSE: Thanks. What's the matter?

CYNTHIA: I'm all right, darlin.'

(HORTENSE *looks round the table.*) I told'em.

(*Pause.* HORTENSE *is nonplussed.*)

Tell 'em 'oo you are sweet'eart.

(*Pause.*)

HORTENSE: It wasn't supposed to happen like this.

CYNTHIA: Yeah, well it 'as, ain' it? So you tell 'em—go on.

MAURICE: Is it true?

HORTENSE: Yes, it is.

MAURICE: (*To* CYNTHIA) You never told her, then?

CYNTHIA: (*To* ROXANNE) I'm sorry, darlin' . . . .

ROXANNE: Will someone tell me what the fuck's goin' on?

CYNTHIA: SHE'S YOUR SISTER![17]

From this point, the party dissolves into mayhem. Everyone is distressed, especially Roxanne, who storms out in a fury. The host of family "secrets and lies" bubbles to the surface, including the chronic quarreling between Cynthia and Roxanne and the seething enmity between Cynthia and Monica. Cynthia accuses Monica of being more interested in money than in having the children Maurice so wants. And that's the tipping point for Maurice:

> MAURICE: Why can't you [Monica] tell'er [Cynthia]? (*Pause.*) She can't have kids. Simple as that. She's physically incapable of having children. We've had every test known to medical science. She's been pushed around, prodded, poked, had operations—we've had fifteen years of it, and she can't have a baby. (*To* MONICA) I love you to bits . . . . but it's almost destroyed our relationship . . . . you know it has.

At this point, the film could swing either way. It could leave a family in ruins. Instead, it swerves toward the revelation of truth as catharsis. Maurice—who, as I have said, is professionally engaged in using photography to gloss and conceal truth—now goes on:

> There. I've said it. So where's the bolt o' lightning? (*Pause.*) Secrets and lies! We're all in pain. Why can't we share our pain? I've spent my entire life trying to make people 'appy, and the three people I love most in the world 'ate each other's guts, I'm in the middle AND I CAN'T TAKE IT ANY-MORE!!!
>
> (*Long pause. Everybody is shaken.* MONICA *weeps, fraught. Then* MAURICE *goes over to* HORTENSE.)
>
> I'm sorry Hortense. But you are a very brave person.
>
> HORTENSE: A very stupid person.
>
> MAURICE: No you're not. You wanted to find the truth, and you were prepared to suffer the consequences. And I admire you for that. I mean it.
>
> (*He sits beside her at the table.* ROXANNE *looks at them.* PAUL [Roxanne's boyfriend] *looks at* ROXANNE. CYNTHIA *looks at* MONICA. MONICA *weeps.* CYNTHIA *gets up and goes over to* MONICA. *She takes her in her arms.* MONICA *sobs.* MAURICE *watches them.*)[18]

The film ends in a general reconciliation and healing. If there is a significant failing in this wonderful film, this is it. Of course, sometimes such events in families do result in "happy endings". But just as often (more often?) they do not—and a more ambiguous ending would have been truer to this fact. The most fundamental demand on art (very generally expressed) is not to falsify human life—to, say, gloss over its pain with saccharine deceit (or, equally to make things out to be worse than they are). The tone of the ending as it stands encourages the sentimental—and so, falsifying— thought that truth is to be pursued primarily because it will yield good consequences, a thought that misrepresents the nature of Hortense's quest and betrays Maurice's praise of it. Thus, the film itself fails in the necessary self-scrutiny that is required to remain truthful in the sense I have tried to elucidate. That a film as attentive to the detail of human life as this one should itself succumb, however subtly, to a falsifying emotional manipulation, only goes to show how hard the filmmaker must work to resist—or even to recognize— secrets and lies.[19]

NOTES

1. A CiBy2000/Thin Man production in association with Channel Four Films. The screenplay, from which my extracts are taken, is published as Mike Leigh, *Secrets and Lies*. Page references for the extracts are to this work.

2. Though my concentration is on film, I will occasionally refer to still photography in this way, because of its potency in controling seeing.

3. For example, Kendall Walton, who believes (in relation to fictional films) that we *imagine* ourselves seeing the events of the fiction. See Walton's "On Pictures and Photographs: Objections Answered," 60–75.

4. It may also be that people's trust in film—whatever its extent—is partly based on the notion of the *mechanicalness* of photography, which some writers regard as characteristic of it, as opposed to writing and painting. There is an interesting discussion of this in Irving Singer, *Reality Transformed: Film as Meaning and Technique*. Of course, people realize that deception is possible in photography, but they also realize it is harder to achieve.

5. Leigh, *Secrets and Lies*, 1–2.

6. *A Common Humanity*, 240.

7. G. K. Chesterton "Killing the Nerve," 108–109.

8. I am exaggerating, of course, but in order to capture one salient tendency in popular, commercial culture. There are many good things too and sometimes a sugar-rush is innocent fun. But it is the continual, ubiquitous *excess* of the sort of material I describe that gives much pop culture an ugly and troubling aspect.

9. For reflections on pornography along these lines see David Holbrook, *Sex and Dehumanisation in Art, Thought and Life in Our Time*. See also the discussion of the obscene in Roger Scruton, *Sexual Desire: A Philosophical Investigation*.

10. Richard Hoggart, "Introduction" to D. H. Lawrence *Lady Chatterley's Lover*, viii.

11. The cases I cite are also fairly clear. A more subtle example would be the general tendency to sentimentality in most popular culture. We are only too willing to

avoid the *hard* questions about the truthfulness of our lives. I should add that in criticizing sentimentality I am not criticizing the presence of sentiment (feeling, emotion) in film and in thought about film (sentimentality is excessive or affected feeling, often flattering to the feeler, who imagines himself a person of particular sensitivity). More generally, the distinction on which I am relying in my overall argument is one between mindless frenzy and reflective attention. It would be a mistake to identify one with "emotion" and the other with "reason", or, indeed, within reflective attention, to try and tease apart reason from emotion. For some further reflection on the place of emotion in film and film criticism see Carl Plantinga, "Spectator Emotion and Film Criticism."

12. R. F. Holland, *Against Empiricism*, 108.

13. An exception is the primarily visual cinematic genre of films like *Koyannisquatsi* and Derek Jarman's *Blue*, in which it is beauty that must bear the weight of pleasing the senses without deranging them.

14. Leigh, *Secrets and Lies*, 29–31.

15. Ibid., 52–53.

16. Quarreling—not least over money—is a sad truth of families that the film does not shrink from (and does not use to denigrate the idea of family, either). In one of the few glimpses we get of Hortense's adoptive family, she is sitting in the bedroom going through her late mother's papers. She listens, "concerned and detached," to the voices of her brothers and sister-in-law, who are arguing downstairs over what to do with the family home.

17. Leigh, *Secrets and Lies*, 93–94.

18. Ibid., 100.

19. I am grateful for helpful comments from Ward Jones and Samantha Vice.

2

PROPAGANDA AND ARTISTIC MERIT

THE CASE OF *COLONEL BLIMP*

STEPHEN G. WILLIAMS

I. INTRODUCTION

ONE OF THE MOST REMARKABLE British films to emerge from the Second World War was Michael Powell and Emeric Pressburger's *The Life and Death of Colonel Blimp*.[1] With the explicit aim of representing as illusory a certain picture of British military life, it takes on, as it moves through the first half of the twentieth century, great themes of war, nationhood and home, of loss and nostalgia, of freedom and tolerance, and of love and friendship across national boundaries. It lays considerable claim, if any film does, to be a masterpiece. Yet, there is a tension. Great film it may be—but it is also propaganda, deliberately created by Powell and Pressburger to help further the British war effort. How can this be? How can a film be a great work of art when it has been devised as a vehicle of propaganda? Partly through an exploration of *Colonel Blimp*, this is the question that I wish to address in the present essay.[2]

Some philosophers will reject the idea that there is a tension in the first place, taking propaganda in itself to be value neutral. For them, whether a work of art is propaganda will be irrelevant to its artistic merit. In the first four sections of this essay, I indicate why I think this view is wrong by arguing that the fact that a work of art is created as propaganda provides a *pro tanto* reason for supposing it to be flawed or diminished aesthetically. I shall begin, in Section II, by making some detailed remarks about what I take propaganda to be, comparing it with the related phenomena of lying and advertising. Using considerations similar to those advanced by Sissela Bok in her peerless discussion of lying,[3] I shall then argue, in Section III, that we should take something's being propaganda to be a *pro tanto* reason for supposing it to be *ethically* flawed. In itself, this will not show that being propaganda is a *pro tanto* reason for taking a work of art to be *aesthetically* flawed as well, but I shall then, in Section IV, exploit a now familiar argument of Berys Gaut's to establish the connection.[4] I am not convinced that the argument Gaut advances applies with quite the generality he envisages, but works of art that are purpose-built propaganda provide some of its more compelling instances.

That such works are *pro tanto* flawed aesthetically does not, of course, entail that they are aesthetically flawed in any absolute sense, aesthetically flawed *tout court*. For although a work's being purpose-built propaganda may provide a *pro tanto* reason for taking it to be flawed aesthetically, such a reason may be overridden, silenced, or otherwise made irrelevant. What is interesting, however, is how this may come about, and it is at this point, in Section V, that I shall turn in detail to *Colonel Blimp*. Through this film, I shall explore how its principal propagandist themes can be seen not merely to be silenced or overridden, but to be overtaken, as the film shifts from a wartime to a post-war context—as its audiences or their concerns alter, and its broadly historical-cum-journalistic register changes to one that is more future oriented and considerably more normative.

In itself, this will not entail that the film is a great work of art. Indeed, insofar as the context may change again, any verdict will necessarily be provisional. For instance, one of the film's most powerful themes is its espousal of tolerance and the welcoming of strangers. As we shall see in Section VI, however, this may seem in retrospect nothing more than a sick joke if (as seems to be the case in our own time) the British culture in which the film is embedded becomes increasingly authoritarian and illiberal. In such circumstances, to claim that the reasons for taking it to be aesthetically flawed have been overridden, silenced, or overtaken may appear distinctly empty. In the end, whether *Colonel Blimp* turns out to be a great film, or at least to be properly recognizable as such, may—via the more familiar idea of moral luck—simply be a matter of aesthetic luck.

II. WHAT IS PROPAGANDA?

According to Harold Lasswell's influential entry on propaganda in the first edition of the *Encyclopaedia of the Social Sciences*, although propaganda "may be employed for subversive, fraudulent, libellous and lascivious purposes," "as a mere tool [it] is no more moral or immoral than a . . . pump handle."[5] And in an attempt to warrant this conclusion, Lasswell deploys the following characterization of propaganda: "Propaganda in the broadest sense is the technique of influencing human action by the manipulation of representations. These representations may take spoken, written, pictorial or musical form."[6]

Now whether this characterization does indeed warrant his conclusion depends upon whether the term "manipulation" is used pejoratively or nonpejoratively. (If it is used nonpejoratively, it does; otherwise, not.) Either way, it cannot be correct. If it is used nonpejoratively, then merely talking to someone or writing them a letter would count as propaganda, since both would involve "the technique of influencing human action by the manipulation of representations." But even if the term "manipulation" is used pejoratively—and henceforth, I shall take it to be used in this way—it would allow any lie to count as propaganda. If I ask a policeman where the post office is, and he maliciously sends me off in the opposite direction, then although he will certainly have influenced my behavior by "manipulating representations" in the pejorative sense, he will hardly have been engaged in the dissemination of propaganda.

It is clear, I think, that what Lasswell's characterization omits to mention is the kinds of reasons someone has for "manipulating representations" when he or she engages in propaganda; we can gain some clue what these are from Peter Lamarque's confident assertion, when speaking about propaganda, that "[a]ny work of art whose princip[al] purpose is to promote some ideology or morality is potentially flawed as art."[7] Here Lamarque is concerned to argue that propaganda is not *aesthetically* neutral, and I will return to this presently. What is important for the moment, however, is his idea that propaganda is something of which the principal purpose is "to promote some ideology or morality."

Now on its own, this cannot be quite right either. On the one hand, something can be propaganda even if promoting "some ideology or morality" is not its *principal* purpose. (It might be just one important purpose among many.) On the other hand, if I tell some schoolchildren that it's a good idea to call an ambulance if they see someone being knocked down by a car, my principal purpose in so doing may well be to promote a certain kind of morality. But in any ordinary way of thinking this would not count as propaganda; it is merely the kind of information that any conscientious, practical educator should be imparting. So something is still missing. The first objection, of course, is trivial to answer. We need only require that for something to count as propaganda, *one* active reason for engaging in it must be "to promote some ideology or morality." The second, however, is more difficult. The answer, I think, lies in the fact that in pointing out circumstances in which they should call an ambulance, I am not in any way trying to deceive the children or manipulate their beliefs.[8] But this needs to be articulated in more detail.[9]

It will help here if we compare propaganda with the related phenomenon of lying, beginning with St Augustine's famous observation that "every liar says the opposite of what he thinks in his heart, with purpose to deceive."[10] Although this captures the essence of lying very well, it will not hurt to unpack it a little. The notion of *thinking in one's heart that such-and-such* is reasonably straightforward, since for Augustine it consists in believing that such-and-such. So liars, according to him, say the opposite of what they believe: they say things they believe to be false.[11]

However, Augustine's requirement that liars say something "with purpose to deceive" is more difficult. On the face of it, it seems very attractive. It certainly explains why rehearsing a lie on one's own beforehand is not yet telling a lie. Nevertheless, it also leaves the content of the intended deception unclear. Here, I think, there are two possibilities. In the typical case, liars intend to get their audiences to believe what they are saying (or to reinforce that belief). Sometimes, however, they intend merely to get their audience to believe that they believe it (or to reinforce the belief that they believe it). This allows for cases like the following, in which a Zoroastrian (say) wants to convince an audience he knows to be Muslim that he believes in God, without admitting that he is a Zoroastrian. To this end, he might say that Christ is God. In so doing, it seems to me, he would be lying, even though he does not intend to convert his audience to Christianity, and the natural explanation of this would be that he is trying to persuade them falsely that he is a Christian.[12]

Using resources made available to us by Paul Grice,[13] we might express these ideas in more detail as follows. Here A is a speaker and B is A's intended audience.

In making the claim that p to B, A *lies* if and only if

1. A believes that the claim that p is false, and

2. A intends either (a) to induce or sustain in B the belief that p in part by getting B to recognize that A is trying so to do, or (b) to induce or sustain in B the belief that A believes that p in part by getting B to recognize that A is trying so to do.

Notice that the requirement in (2)(a) and (b) that A should intend B to recognize what A is trying to do is to exclude brainwashing, hypnosis, and the like by A. In suggesting something to someone under hypnosis or the influence of drugs, or brainwashing them into thinking it, one is hardly lying, even if one believes it to be false.[14]

How then does lying differ from propaganda? Several things are apparent. First, the reasons liars have for wanting to get others to believe things do not belong to a common category. It is not even necessary, for example, that liars should lie for bad reasons: some lie to spare a relative pain, others to help a friend through a difficult period, and so on. By contrast, if Lamarque is right, propaganda is always created to promote an ideology or morality.[15] Second, I do not think it would be enough for propagandists that their audience should believe that *the propagandists* believe the claims in question. What they intend is that the audience should believe the propagandists themselves. Third, propaganda does not require its authors to disbelieve what they are saying. Indeed, there is little doubt that some of the best propagandists genuinely believe their own propaganda. But if *this* is so, in what way is it deceptive or manipulative?

When propaganda *does* consist of lies, of course, it certainly is deceptive and manipulative, but there are other ways it may be so, too. Consider for a moment a sincere, honest, and critically reflective communicator. Such a person will not lie, but, equally, he will not try to manipulate his audience's emotions without their realizing it in order to make what he is saying seem more attractive to them; nor will he try to make out that he has evidence he does not have, hide persuasive counterevidence he does have, or deceive them about the strength of the evidence. However, these are precisely the kinds of things that the truth-telling propagandist—and often the lying propagandist as well—will do. Let us call anyone who does none of these things in a particular piece of communicative discourse *epistemically virtuous* (relative to that piece of discourse). And let us take those who do nothing to indicate that they are not being epistemically virtuous in such a piece of discourse to be *representing* themselves as being epistemically virtuous.[16] Then what marks out propagandists is that in promoting their propaganda, they will try to represent themselves as being epistemically virtuous when they know they are not, intending thereby that their audiences will take them to be such and hence believe their propaganda. They will lie to their audiences, or try to manipulate their emotions, or try to deceive them in some significant way about the available evidence, all the while trying not to let on that this is what they are doing. This is how I take propaganda to be deceptive or manipulative.[17]

These considerations suggest the following elucidation, again formulated in the Gricean manner. Here, A is the putative propagandist and B is A's intended audience.

In making the claim that p to B, A *propagandizes* if and only if

1. In making the claim, A tries to represent himself to B as being epistemically virtuous—thereby intending B to take A to be such—knowing that he is not;

2. In part by trying to get B to take A to be epistemically virtuous in making the claim, A intends to induce or sustain in B the belief that p; and

3. A's principal reason, or one of them, for intending to induce or sustain in B the belief that p is that A would thereby be furthering some ideological interest.

We may then say that a work of art is a piece of propaganda if someone—typically the author of the work[18]—propagandizes through it.[19]

It must be conceded immediately, of course, that propagandists often will not be anything like as self-conscious as the definition seems to imply. Indeed, some propagandists may not only be persuaded of the truth of a piece of propaganda, they may even be convinced that they are conveying it in what is, in fact, an epistemically virtuous manner. Whether through foolishness or self-deception, however, such propagandists will typically be acting as conduits for others, and it will be the latter who are the primary propagandists. Henceforth, I shall ignore this complication.[20]

Much more important, however, is the fact that the proposal does not embrace advertising.[21] This is something that social scientists almost always take propaganda to include[22]—and their doing so is not without merit. In addition to the considerable convergence in the methods of advertising and of propaganda (as conceived above), the very same vehicles can be used for both. For example, the advertisements of certain oil companies not only try to get the companies' customers to buy their petrol, they encourage them to take at face value the claim that the companies care about the environment. On the reasonable assumption that the principal activities of such commercial organizations are invariably subordinate to the pursuit of profit, however, such claims are liable to be misleading at best, and so the advertisements will be commercial propaganda, too.

Still, I think it is worth keeping the two notions apart. First, although advertisements are often deceptive and manipulative, they do not have to be. One may advertise a second-hand bicycle in a local newspaper with no manipulative or deceptive intentions at all (and without being the conduit of such). By contrast, however, if I am right, propaganda is an essentially deceptive or manipulative phenomenon.

Second, it is typically the primary aim of advertisers to get their target audience to *do something*—for example, if the advertising is commercial, to buy a product or refrain from buying someone else's. It does not much matter whether the advertiser succeeds in getting the buyer to believe anything special about the product. Thus, someone who bought Heineken beer because of the advertisements would have been successfully engaged, irrespective of whether he or she believed it refreshed the parts that other beers cannot reach. By contrast, propagandists—again, if I am right—will not ordinarily have a specific course of action in mind when they engage in propaganda. To be sure, they will often desire action, but they will desire the kind of action that fits in more generally with the kind of belief or beliefs the propaganda is intended to promote. For propagandists, it is getting people to believe things that is crucial. It follows that to the extent that both are manipulative, propaganda is in essence *intellectually* manipulative—its purpose is to manipulate people's beliefs in specific ways—while *advertising* is at root *practically* manipulative—it is designed to manipulate their behavior in specific ways.[23]

Finally, advertisers, at least in paradigm cases of advertising, intend their target audiences to recognize that what they are seeing or hearing is advertising.[24] This means it is often difficult to get people to believe the claims of advertising, and it helps explain why what counts in advertising is not what they end up believing, but what they end up doing. (No doubt the Heineken people would have been delighted if drinkers really did believe that Heineken refreshed the parts that other beers could not reach; however, knowledge that their customers were not quite that foolish rightly did not put them off launching their campaign.) This is in marked contrast to propaganda. Not only do propagandists not intend that members of the target audience know that they are on the receiving end of propaganda, propagandists would doubtless be delighted if their audiences did not know. Of course, as audiences become more sophisticated, they begin to realize when they are being fed propaganda, and it then becomes correspondingly more difficult for propagandists to get people to believe what they want them to believe. Indeed, this is one reason why propagandists use ever more sophisticated techniques. All this shows, however, is that propagandizing successfully is increasingly difficult in our media-savvy times. It should not militate against our characterization of the practice.

III. IS PROPAGANDA IN ITSELF ETHICALLY NEUTRAL?

Despite being grounded in an inadequate conception of propaganda, Lasswell's claim that propaganda is an ethically neutral tool that can be used for either moral or immoral purposes expresses an undoubtedly appealing view. In its simplest form, propaganda will be censurable if it is put to use in the service of an unpleasant ideology and commendable if it is put to use in the service of a worthwhile ideology; in itself, propaganda will have no more ethical value than a pump handle.[25]

How might we resist Lasswell's claim? Some insight into this question can be gained by comparing propaganda, again, with lying. For although certain consequentialist philosophers have claimed with Bentham that even lying is ethically neutral, considerations drawn from the way we naturally think about lying, as Bok has highlighted,[26] can make this seem thoroughly alien; and even though there are important differences between lying and propaganda—the latter is certainly not a species of the former—the features they have in common are nevertheless sufficient to show that if lying is not ethically neutral, neither is propaganda. Or so I shall try to argue.

So why should lying not be ethically neutral? To answer this question, it is important to note an obvious asymmetry in our attitudes to lying and to truth telling: we think that lying requires a justification or excuse, whereas we do not think the same holds of truth telling. Why is this? Bok suggests two kinds of reasons, one that depends on the deceiver and one that depends on the deceived. For deceivers, lying is a morally risky business, since it always has the potential to strike at the deceivers' own integrity: they know, or should know, that they risk becoming tainted by the lie, and typically their self-worth will be bound up with not being so tainted. At the very least, therefore, they will have to provide a justification to themselves. More important, however, are those who are deceived. For when they are lied to, their freedom to choose is automatically compromised, since (as Leibniz long ago recognized) freedom not only requires an ability to do other than one actually does, it also requires a proper understanding of the choices available;[27] and lying impairs that proper understanding. It follows that the deceived are automatically being subjected to coercion and manipulation, however trivially and ineffectively. Hence, those shown to be liars are under an obligation to provide an excuse or justification, since coercion and manipulation are themselves wrong. Lying, therefore, is *pro tanto* wrong—though obviously for a particular lie, a good justification or excuse may well be available, and so it will not be wrong absolutely. (One of the most important features of Bok's book is her demonstration of how difficult it is in practice to provide convincing justifications or excuses for lying.)[28]

Armed with the conclusion that lying is *pro tanto* wrong, how, then, can we argue that propaganda is, too? Similar considerations, I think, apply. For although propaganda does not always involve lying, it does involve a form of deception: through the propaganda, propagandists deliberately misrepresent themselves as being epistemically virtuous (which includes not lying) when they are not. So propaganda shares with lying the same need for justification. In particular, the propagandists must justify it to themselves given the serious risk they run of loss of integrity: if they are found to be mere propagandists, they risk becoming seriously tainted again. Moreover, in falsely representing themselves as epistemically virtuous, the propagandists are being coercive and manipulative: since their audiences' understanding of the choices available is once again impaired, their freedom to choose is correspondingly compromised. This, too, needs justification.[29]

As with lying, all this shows at best is that propaganda is *pro tanto* wrong. For specific propaganda in *particular* circumstances, it may well be possible to justify it or justify ignoring it—I will touch upon what is involved in doing so in the final two sections. Next, however, I want to consider whether in being *pro tanto* wrong a propagandist work of art is *pro tanto* flawed aesthetically too.

IV. IS PROPAGANDA IN ITSELF AESTHETICALLY NEUTRAL?

Suppose, then, that we accept that propaganda is *pro tanto* wrong, because in promoting it, its authors deliberately misrepresent themselves as being epistemically virtuous. Does it follow that when the propaganda is a work of art, it is *pro tanto* aesthetically flawed as well? With one small qualification, the answer, I think, is "yes". Why should this be?

A first suggestion might be to appeal to one of the traditional marks of the ethical, the idea that it is action-guiding. For insofar as we take the aesthetically valuable to be worth attending to, it is possible to think of aesthetic value as action-guiding, too. It would be too quick, however, to conclude that aesthetic value is a species of ethical value, since the values that guide us even in what is worth looking at may come from different sources. The beauty of an abstract painting may make it worth seeing even if it is devoid of moral content, and the graphic reminders provided by photographs of military brutality may make it salutary to look at them, even if to speak of their aesthetic value would be impertinent or tasteless.

A more promising line of thought emerges from Lamarque's development of the remark quoted earlier that "[a]ny work of art whose princip[al] purpose is to promote some ideology or morality is potentially flawed as art." Citing Dickens's *Hard Times*, he continues, "Precisely because it presses its message home so relentlessly about social justice it exaggerates and distorts some of the central characters."[30] Now it would be hard to deny that works of art designed to promote an ideology are apt to exaggerate and distort, particularly when the work takes a narrative form. In careful hands, however, it need not—or the fact that it does need not matter. Subtle propagandists will present their propaganda in a way that either does not require realism or connives with more realistic elements in the audience's world view. Given this, it remains open for someone to insist that although propaganda can be realized in forms that are either flawed or commendable aesthetically, in itself it is aesthetically neutral. It follows that we are not yet in a position to conclude that a propagandist work of art is *pro tanto* flawed aesthetically.

Lamarque's attempt to warrant the claim that propaganda is aesthetically flawed in effect appeals to instrumental connections between ethical and aesthetic value,[31] but such connections are too flimsy for our purposes, too contingent. What we need is a conceptual connection. It is at this point that I want to turn to Berys Gaut's familiar argument that purports to establish precisely such a connection. Here it is in its most abstract form. Suppose that a work of art "manifests an attitude," that is, it prescribes certain responses—rural nostalgia, say, or support for a certain war. Suppose further that some of these responses are ethically unmerited—perhaps the nostalgia is racist or the war unjust. Then, according to Gaut,

> we have reason not to respond in the way prescribed. Our reason not to respond in the way prescribed is a failure in the work. What responses the work prescribes [are] of aesthetic relevance. So the fact that we have reason not to respond in the way prescribed is an *aesthetic* failure of the work, that is to say, is an aesthetic defect, . . . [and] a work's manifestation of ethically bad attitudes is an aesthetic defect in it.[32]

Such a defect, of course, need only be one aesthetic feature among many possessed by the work, and these other features may override, silence, or otherwise render irrelevant the defect. It follows that the most the argument shows in itself is that a work of art that manifests ethically bad attitudes is *pro tanto* diminished or flawed aesthetically; it does not establish that the work is aesthetically diminished or flawed *tout court*.

Does the argument apply to works of art that are propaganda? It is clear, I think, that it does. For given the elucidation of propaganda above, any such work will prescribe certain types of response: it will prescribe not only that particular views should be adopted (or held onto), but that its audience should take them to be promoted in good faith. However, it is precisely this last prescription that is not merited: the propagandized beliefs are not being promoted in an epistemically virtuous way, but rather, for example, through emotional or epistemic manipulation.[33] Hence, a propagandist work of art is aesthetically defective; it is *pro tanto* aesthetically flawed.

Should we accept the argument? Powerful and appealing though it is, I am not persuaded that it has quite the generality that Gaut intends. What I do think, however, is that it applies to works of art devised or conceived principally as propaganda.

The crucial premise in Gaut's argument is the claim that responses prescribed by a work of art are always of aesthetic relevance. It is this claim—call it "AR"— that I wish to call into question. For this purpose, it is important to distinguish between attitudes manifested by the work irrespective of how it is used and attitudes it manifests simply by virtue of how it is used. We might call the former attitudes *intrinsic* to the work, and the latter, being tacked on to it or there by special fiat, *extrinsic* to the work.[34] When AR is restricted to responses the prescription of which is manifested by attitudes intrinsic to the work, it is, I think, highly plausible, but when it includes responses the prescription of which is manifested by attitudes extrinsic to the work, it is not. For example, suppose that an artist working in fraught political circumstances has painted two portraits of a nobleman, one in which he is smiling and one in which he is frowning. He is then told to send the smiling portrait to his companions elsewhere if the political circumstances have improved, and to send the frowning portrait to them if they have not. Clearly, if the artist sends the smiling portrait, it will manifest (to those with eyes to see) a certain attitude; it will prescribe a certain response, perhaps of joy or quiet satisfaction. But if the artist has unfortunately misread the political situation, such a response would equally clearly not be merited. Would this count as an *aesthetic* criticism of the work? It is hard to see why it should—and the obvious reason for this is that the response prescribed by the work is introduced only by special fiat, the attitude manifested by the work is wholly extrinsic to it.

Occasionally, no doubt, it will be difficult to decide whether attitudes manifested by a work of art are intrinsic or extrinsic to the work. Indeed, in some cases, there may be no fact of the matter. But what is important is that there are cases that can be decided. How does propaganda fare in this respect? Well, it is certainly possible that a work of art should manifest propagandist attitudes, and prescribe propagandist responses, only by special fiat. This may happen when a work of art that was not originally devised with propagandist purposes in mind is, by administrative decree (say), used for such purposes—for example, when a regime decides to adopt a particular work as an expression of national identity.[35] If the propaganda is built into the work of art from its inception, however, the salient attitudes will not be extrinsic to it. It follows that if we restrict AR to such works, we achieve our desired connection. *Purpose-built* propaganda is *pro tanto* aesthetically flawed.

V. COLONEL BLIMP

Again, of course, it does not follow that it is aesthetically flawed *tout court*. To understand concretely how this can be, I want now to turn to *Colonel Blimp*, one of several major propaganda films—conceived and executed as such—that Powell and Pressburger produced and directed during or just after the Second World War (WWII).[36] I begin by indicating in what way the film is indeed propaganda. By exploring its relation to different kinds of audiences, I then suggest reasons why the fact that it was made initially as propaganda—and hence is *pro tanto* aesthetically flawed—provides no grounds *now* for taking it to be aesthetically flawed *tout court*. Indeed, in the light of its other estimable qualities, it is hard to resist the conclusion that it should be numbered amongst Powell and Pressburger's finest films, that it warrants what Mary Devereaux refers to as "the highest aesthetic praise."[37] As we shall see in Section VI, however, that it does warrant such praise—or can at least be recognised as doing so—may yet be undermined by circumstance.

In what way then is the film propaganda? To answer this properly, if what I have said about the concept of propaganda is right, we must not only identify the ideological interests that Powell and Pressburger are promoting through the film, we must also indicate how, in promoting those interests, they deliberately misrepresent themselves as being epistemically virtuous. Let us begin with the areas of ideological interest. I think we may discern at least three.

The first relates to the conduct of the war, and is best understood against the background of the film. Its central character, Major-General Clive Wynne-Candy, VC, was himself based on a cartoon character—the Colonel Blimp of the title—invented by the *London Evening Standard* cartoonist David Low, whose intention, at least in part, was to lampoon what he took to be the outdated military practices of certain elements in the British army. By treating Candy similarly as an aging military man of the old school, the film was able to continue in pretty much the same vein. Indeed, its principal aim at the time was not only to indicate the inadequacies of the old ways of soldiering to the wartime circumstances in which Britain found itself, but also—and this is where Powell and Pressburger went beyond Low—to imply that such ways had, by 1943, been supplanted by methods commensurate with those circumstances.

Such ideas are foreshadowed during the middle period of the film, when we witness Candy's encounters in the First World War with members of the U.S. military and, more controversially, with a South African officer, all of whom are shown to possess a greater sense than Candy does of the realities of war and the compromises that apparently must be made in it.[38] These ideas emerge again in a speech made by Candy's great friend and rival, Theo Kretschmar-Schuldorff,[39] to a

"WE ARE PRESENT AT THE END OF COLONEL BLIMP"— *SAYS CRIPPS*
(Copyright in all Countries

Figure 2.2

WWII British "enemy aliens" tribunal, in which Theo highlights the very different nature of the enemy Britain now faces. But they are present most explicitly in the success of a young, recently commissioned officer—Lieutenant "Spud" Wilson—in forestalling a WWII military exercise in which he is effectively pitted against Candy. Here Spud's success—and the fact that Candy is finally pensioned off—illustrates directly not merely the inadequacy of the military practices that Candy represents, but also that such practices are now absent from those who are conducting the war—or from what Powell and Pressburger refer to, in the film's original dedication, as the "New Army of Britain."[40]

The second ideological theme that Powell and Pressburger wish to promote relates to the idea of unity. In particular, they are concerned to emphasize that their wartime audiences, the armed forces, and those in power really are fighting together in the same way against a common enemy—that there is genuine unity of thought, purpose, and action in the New Army of Britain. The idea is present most poignantly perhaps in Candy's belated acceptance of the merits of Spud's case, after the latter has pre-empted the military exercise. It also exists in the film's explicit attitude to women, particularly as manifested by the different incarnations of the actress Deborah Kerr, who plays all three of the main female protagonists. Naturally, each demonstrates in her different way a mixture of courage, independence, and integrity. This simply anticipates or reflects the ethos of the New Army. But in two of them—Barbara (Candy's wife) and Angela (his ATS driver[41])—we see British women contributing directly toward the respective war efforts of WWI and WWII: Barbara as a nurse and, more important, Angela as a member of the armed forces. Even if, as some thought at the time, it should turn out that women were in the army only for the duration of the war, they were there and pulling in the same direction as the men.

Such ideological interests—the methods employed by the armed forces and the unified spirit in which the war is to be fought—represent a major wartime cinematic concern of Powell and Pressburger's: namely, how to fight the war. It is important to remember, however, that even in *Colonel Blimp*—and this is the third area of ideological interest that I want to highlight—they are no less concerned with the question of what the war is for, and although they naturally place their main emphasis on victory over the unspeakable ideology of Nazism, they are also looking to develop various strands of what I shall call the *National Myth*—commonly understood and undoubtedly powerful—the image of an essentially rural Britain, free, tolerant, and welcoming of strangers. Although not all the strands of the myth have equal prominence in *Colonel Blimp*,[42] the myth itself is nevertheless an important theme in the film. It is promoted powerfully again through Theo's impassioned speech to the tribunal, in which he celebrates all the strands of the myth, and also through various familiar iconic figures: Barbara (Candy's solid and reliable wife), Barbara's father (a salt-of-the-earth Yorkshireman), and, of course, Candy himself, whose decency, fair-mindedness, and tolerance of others are, at least outside the military sphere, by no means wholly rejected. Not only is the war being fought to defeat a monstrous ideology, the audiences are being told, it is also being fought to restore or reaffirm these elements of their national identity and culture.

These, then, are the principal ideological themes that Powell and Pressburger are promoting in the film. As I noted above, however, if they are to count as propagandist themes, we must also establish that in promoting them they deliberately misrepresent themselves as being epistemically virtuous. It is logically possible, after all, that their ideological interests should have been epistemically innocent, that they were genuinely promoting them in the manner of honest and critically reflective communicators.

The evidence, however, is against this, at least when they have their wartime audiences in mind.[43] No doubt the idea that Britain was facing an enemy whose defeat required different methods from those represented by Candy was by 1943 transparently correct, but the thought that Britain was properly prepared and that there was unity in the land was not. By presenting such characters as Spud, Angela, Candy, and Theo as attractive, if flawed or complicated, representatives of these ideas, Powell and Pressburger were trying to manipulate their wartime audiences into accepting the ideas even though, as troublesome filmmakers peripheral to the establishment, they could scarcely have been in a position to justify them properly.[44] Equally, through Theo, Candy, and the other iconic figures mentioned above, they were trying to induce their wartime audiences to connive with the National Myth. Much of the myth, however, Powell and Pressburger recognize as half-truth at best. Even within *Colonel Blimp*, they allow their audiences to feel a certain tension in it. The reason Candy goes to Berlin early in the film is to help rebut charges of British atrocities in South Africa, but (quite rightly) the charges are never refuted, and the implied cruelty of the South African officer during WWI is simply left hanging.[45] In addition, Powell and Pressburger were scarcely unaware that a sizeable proportion of the population of Britain in 1943 lived and worked in the industrialized cities.

The themes I have highlighted, I therefore claim, ensure that the film is purpose-built propaganda. Via the fact that it is therefore *pro tanto* flawed ethically (Section III), it follows that it is also *pro tanto* aesthetically flawed (Section IV). How, then, does it avoid being aesthetically flawed *tout court*? What could silence, override, or otherwise make irrelevant the aesthetically diminishing or corrupting effect of its being propaganda?

As a first thought, it would be natural to try to find features of the film that justify the propaganda, features that excuse it.[46] Certainly, the prescription that its audience should take what is in fact propaganda to be promoted in good faith will then cease on balance to be unmerited. It is plausible that there are such features. Thus it helps that *Colonel Blimp* does not promote an evil cause; indeed, it promotes the very obliteration of such a cause. But in itself this would not be enough. For instance, the propaganda would hardly be excused if the film promoted a viciously racist attitude toward Germans. Not only is *Colonel Blimp* not a viciously racist film, however, one of its extraordinary merits, given that it was made during the war, is that in part it manages to celebrate German culture and the artists who created it.[47]

Even if the propaganda in *Colonel Blimp* can be fully justified in this way, however, it is not, I think, the most important way in which the film avoids being flawed *tout court*. For—or so I wish to argue—Powell and Pressburger so conceive of their film that the original propagandist concerns get overtaken by other considerations. Not wishing to rest content with producing something that would turn merely into a dated propaganda film,[48] they aimed to draw on what counted as propaganda in 1943—justified or not—to create something that would later on not principally be propaganda at all.

To understand how they do this, it is important to remember that the efficacy of propaganda is almost always liable to be ephemeral. A work of art that was once propaganda may lose its power to manipulate or deceive when experienced by audiences who are more sophisticated or less conniving than, or do not share the same concerns as, its original target audience. Hence, its authors may be able to adhere to different aims and pursue different effects as the audience changes. And this is certainly how Powell and Pressburger conceived of *Colonel Blimp*. Replying to objections to the film made by the Ministry of Information, they remark in a memorandum to the Ministry's Films Division (June 16, 1942) that "if Blimpery[49] were not a danger, in prosecuting and winning the war with Germany, we would not be interested in it at the present time."[50] So even if the internal evidence of the film were insufficient, their words suggest that they took themselves to be concerned with orthodox morale-boosting of audiences principally preoccupied with fighting the war.[51] In the same memorandum, however,[52] they also remark that "it is . . . . possible to make films for future audiences and for future occasions," adding that the purpose of *Colonel Blimp* "is to tell people what happened after the last war was won, and our reason is that the winning of this war will be in sight [by the time the film is released]."[53] So they also thought of themselves as preparing for audiences concerned with the likely aftermath of war, and it was partly by concentrating on such audiences that they aimed to create something that in the end would not principally be propaganda.

How successful were they? First of all, despite what would undoubtedly be a residual resentment, fueled to some extent by returning members of the armed forces, about how ill prepared British forces actually were, propaganda about Britain's military preparedness and unity of purpose would naturally fade into the background after the war. To be sure, it would still be possible for audiences to empathize with such propaganda (in much the same way as we can now), but for the most part, they would, quite properly, leave it in the cinema. Such propaganda, therefore, would—and indeed did—simply become irrelevant in the fullness of time. More problematic, however, were the various elements of the National Myth. For one reason for fighting the war, according to the propaganda that originally informed the film, was to restore and reaffirm those elements, and this idea would surely not disappear with the end of the war.

It is here that we can see Powell and Pressburger taking two very different attitudes to the myth, one for during the war and one principally for afterwards. During the war—and doubtless with the wishful connivance of their audiences—they encourage those audiences to conceive of the myth as largely factual, that is, to think of Britain as an essentially tolerant nation that welcomes strangers and refugees, that lights a beacon of freedom, that in its natural naivety espouses fair play, that celebrates home and countryside, and so on, even if some of these ideas have to be partially shelved for the duration of the war. For post-war audiences, however, or for those who during the war were concerned principally with its likely aftermath—groups to whom much of the myth would appear absurd[54]—Powell and Pressburger move from the broadly historical-cum-journalistic register of the original propaganda toward a more normative vision of how a post-war Britain *ought* to be and to act. For them, the myth is then not a description of how Britain was, but an expression in part of how Britain should be and what it should do.

To see this, consider again the June 16 memorandum. As it intimates, Powell and Pressburger were explicitly concerned to emphasize in the film what happened to Germany after WWI. The resentment of Theo and other German officers at the treatment of Germany after that war (exhibited during and after the scenes in the British prisoner-of-war camp) and Theo's subsequent speech to the tribunal serve to indicate to audiences the dangers of a disempowered and impoverished Germany. Here they are exhorting the audiences not to make similar mistakes at the end of WWII. By taking aspects of the National Myth, not as historical fact but as a pointer perhaps to how things should have been and certainly as a guide to how things could and should be in post-war Britain, they are also indicating how, in practice, to avoid making those mistakes again. In celebrating freedom and fair play, tolerance, and the welcoming of strangers, particularly in Theo's speech but also through Candy's behavior toward Theo throughout the film, they are urging their future-oriented audiences to learn from the experience of the interwar period, not merely by avoiding the political and financial humiliation of the defeated powers, but by actively embracing Europe in all its cultural variety.

The rural elements of the myth, it is true, are more complicated, and I am not sure that even Powell and Pressburger themselves had a clear idea of what their role should be in British life. What does seem evident, however, is that in celebrating them primarily in *A Canterbury Tale*, but even in *Colonel Blimp*—they were not recommending a return to some fantasy-laden rural idyll, nor even that the continuing rush to the city, to industrialization, should be halted.[55] But by alluding to the attractions of countryside, both in Theo's speech and through Barbara's family seat in Yorkshire, they were, I think, recommending at least that rural concerns should not be neglected as Britain tries to embrace change in the post-war era.

This shift in focus across audiences indicates how propaganda in the film may not only fade, but also mutate into material that is not propaganda; accordingly, I contend, it provides a strong additional case for saying that the film's having been created initially as propaganda does not in the end show it to be flawed aesthetically *tout court*. If this is right, we can see how, in principle, *Colonel Blimp* could be a great film, despite its having been conceived originally as a vehicle of propaganda. This, of course, does not show that it really is a great work. Although I myself am inclined to think that it is, I wish to conclude this essay on a note of caution.

VI. A CAUTIONARY NOTE

I wrote at the beginning that whether *Colonel Blimp* does turn out to be a great film, or at least to be recognizable as such, may—via the more familiar idea of moral luck—be simply a matter of aesthetic luck.[56] Because works of art are subject to ethical evaluation, they can, in principle, become exposed to the vagaries of moral luck. Hence if Gaut-like arguments are right—if, that is, the aesthetic value of a work can be affected by moral considerations—we can sometimes expect the aesthetic evaluation of works of art to be exposed to luck too. This is especially likely with propagandist works of art, since propaganda, if I am right, promotes ideology. For although the ideology that a particular piece of propaganda promotes may seem to be acceptable at the time the propaganda is produced, changing circumstances may reveal it not to be. Hence, what seemed merely *pro tanto* flawed for being deceptive or manipulative may be revealed as flawed absolutely for promoting as acceptable what is not. And given that it is a matter of luck whether the new circumstance comes to obtain, the disclosure of this new moral insight may well be a matter of luck, too. To be sure, it still does not follow that a work in which some moral flaw comes to light in this kind of way will also be aesthetically flawed *tout court*, since the moral flaw is only one aspect of a larger aesthetic whole. But we can now see how to allow for the possibility.

Of course, this is not how it is with *Colonel Blimp*. For no circumstance could reveal the defeat of Nazism during WWII to be wrong. Nor, I think, could any circumstance show that in peacetime the promotion of freedom, tolerance, and the welcoming of strangers is unacceptable, at least in a flourishing and stable democracy. Nevertheless, the eventual circumstances in which the film comes to promote these things may result in its prescriptions seeming profoundly hypocritical. It is precisely because *Colonel Blimp* locates itself within British culture—identifies with it and promotes in part an ultimately normative conception of it—that Powell and Pressburger cannot wash their hands of its future development; they risk throwing in their lot with something that may in the end prove unworthy of our respect and loyalty. Strictly, one could not accuse *them* of hypocrisy, but the film itself might take on an aspect of hypocrisy, in that the national values it celebrates might prove to be rejected in practice, even if affirmed in name, by the very society it identifies with. In such circumstances—which may well be partly the product of electoral luck—it would be hard to acknowledge that the film warranted the highest aesthetic praise. Even if the qualities of a great work were still present in it—and they might not be[57]—the course of history might be such that later audiences could no longer see in it a convincing representation of the ideals its authors tried honestly to convey. This, I fear, is precisely what is risked in today's Britain as it becomes increasingly authoritarian and illiberal, and its governments treat immigrants and refugees to the country with ever more contempt. The practical rejection, or the endorsement in name only, of values celebrated by *Colonel Blimp* may not be permanent. If it does continue, however, we risk losing what may be a great film—at least in the sense that no one properly informed of the culture in which it is embedded could recognize it as such. To risk losing such a film in this fortuitous way pales in comparison with the continuing abuse and vilification of strangers. But it is not a trivial epiphenomenon.

NOTES

I gave a version of this paper as a talk to the Oxford Interdisciplinary Film Seminar in 1999. Thanks to Judith Buchanan, who organized the series of talks, Sabina Lovibond, Lutz Becker, Markus Schrenk, Gary Jenkins, and the editors for immensely helpful comments on subsequent drafts. I have tried to take account of as many as possible; but a response that did them full justice would have greatly lengthened the paper.

1. Or *Colonel Blimp*, for short.

2. The film was made in 1942 and first shown in 1943. The screenplay (with variations and additional documentation) can be found in Powell and Pressburger, *The Life and Death of Colonel Blimp*. A history of the tribulations they had to endure in the making of the film, particularly at the hands of the British government and civil service, can be found in Christie, *Introduction to Powell and Pressburger*; Aldgate, "What a Difference a War Makes"; and directly from the documentation to be found in Powell and Pressburger, 25–53.

3. Bok, *Lying*.

4. See Gaut, "The Ethical Criticism of Art."

5. Lasswell, "Propaganda", 21.

6. Ibid. 13.

7. Lamarque, "Reflections on Current Trends in Aesthetics," 6.

8. Remember that I am here using the term "manipulation" pejoratively.

9. Compare Smith, "Propaganda", 579, who suggests that it is the deliberate manipulation of other people's thoughts or actions "by means of symbols" that distinguishes propaganda from "merely casual communication . . . the 'free' exchange of ideas [and] education." It is worth noting that the notion of propaganda has not always contained the elements of manipulation and deception. Many of the original Roman Catholic "propagandists" of the seventeenth century who took on the task of recovering those countries lost to the Church in the sixteenth century will doubtless have been disseminating Church doctrine properly and in good faith. (See Smith, "Propaganda", and esp. Robert Jackall's introduction to Jackall (ed.), *Propaganda*, for helpful historical background information.) Lenin, moreover, famously took propaganda to be what amounts to properly sourced and evidenced scientific belief; see Lenin, *What*

is to be Done?, Ch.3, esp. 132–133, and Smith, "Propaganda". To a modern ear—or so is one of the contentions of this essay—the term "propaganda" does not have the respectable overtones of either Lenin or the cardinals. It is closer to what the former called *agitation*.

10. This comes from *The Enchiridion*, and is quoted in Bok, *op. cit.*, 32. Bok's own definition (13) echoes this: "I shall define as a lie any intentionally deceptive message which is stated."

11. Lies, therefore, need not actually be false.

12. Whether Bok's definition (10) covers the second alternative depends upon whether a message that states that p also states (indirectly) that the speaker believes that p.

13. See, e.g., Grice, "Meaning".

14. Some might say that Augustine's intention to deceive is not required. Can people not lie by asserting in the presence of an audience something they believe to be false, not caring one jot whether there is any audience uptake? Consider a guilty young delinquent who insists in court that he is not guilty, despite not caring what the outcome is. It is perhaps tempting to think of him as just "playing at lying" here or "lying in a loose sense." I suspect, however, that he would only be doing so if it is commonly acknowledged between him and the court that he is guilty. If not—that is, if he does not know, e.g., whether the court believes him to be guilty or not—then his insistence that he is not guilty would surely count as a lie. To accommodate such cases, we would have to abandon the simple intention to deceive as a necessary condition, and say something along the following lines: in making the claim that p to B, A lies if and only if (1) A believes the claim that p is false, and (2′) for all A knows, B is in a position to take A as having the intentions in clauses (2)(a) and (b) in the text. We may think, therefore, of the suggestion in the text as applying to the basic case.

15. Henceforth, I shall use the term "ideology" to cover both, taking an ideology to be a broadly integrated set of, e.g., national, political, economic, social, ethical, or religious ideas, concepts, and beliefs possessed by an individual or shared by a group of individuals. This is close to the original, nonpejorative sense of the term. It probably does not, however, correspond to informal contemporary use, which has a Marxist background and is undoubtedly pejorative. (In this respect, the notion of ideology has evolved informally in a similar way to that of propaganda.) If I were to essay a provisional and tentative elucidation of informal present-day use, it would be to say the following: an ideology is a broadly integrated set of, e.g., national, political, economic, social, ethical, or religious ideas, concepts, and beliefs possessed by an individual, or shared by a group of individuals, the beliefs in which do not track the truth (in Robert Nozick's sense: see Nozick, *Philosophical Explanations*, 178.). An ideological belief, then, is roughly one that its believers would still believe in circumstances close to the actual circumstances in which it was not true. An ideological belief can therefore be true; it's just that its adherents are apt to take it as being unfalsifiable—at least with respect to circumstances close to the actual ones. I have here chosen the more anodyne suggestion, since (as we shall see presently) it is perfectly possible for propagandists to propagandize in the service of beliefs and ideas that they know to be well-founded.

16. The default assumption concerning participants in a piece of communicative discourse will therefore be that they are representing themselves as being epistemically virtuous.

17. It is worth emphasising that although the manipulation of an audience's emotions may often be very helpful in practice to the propagandist, it is not essential. A propagandist may manipulate people's beliefs by using distorted newsreel footage, for example, without the interpolation of their emotions. Indeed, even if their emotions become engaged, it need not follow that they believe the things in question *because* their emotions have been engaged.

18. Though not necessarily—see Section IV.

19. Or at least propagandizes *substantially*. One may feel that a major work that makes in passing a few fairly trivial propagandist claims hardly counts as propaganda. Some may wonder—indeed, one of the editors did so wonder—how a filmmaker can represent himself as being epistemically virtuous through a fictional film. This follows directly, however, from the fact that an author of a work of fiction can say things about the world through the work. If he does so sincerely—or at least gives no indication that he is lying or relevantly manipulating either the evidence or his audience's emotions—then he will be representing himself as being epistemically virtuous. If he does give some indication—perhaps the work is propaganda and the propaganda is blatantly inept—then he will not so represent himself.

20. As we shall see, Powell and Pressburger were not at all unclear about the propagandist implications of what they were doing, and so, in their case, the complication is irrelevant.

21. Whether commercial, political, or charitable.

22. Along with public relations (which I shall not discuss here, but which I think also should be excluded). See, e.g., Lasswell, "Propaganda", Smith, "Propaganda", Jackall, "The Magic Lantern," and Hirota, "Making Products Heroes."

23. I do not mean to imply here that propagandists never have specific courses of action in mind. Thus, propaganda posters of Lord Kitchener proclaiming "Your Country Needs You" were specifically aimed at getting people to volunteer for the armed forces during the First World War (WWI). But they tried to do this partly by suggesting to them, however falsely or misleadingly, that they had a duty to volunteer; it was this that turned the posters into propaganda. Notice that this shows that the content of propaganda, what propagandists try to get their audiences to believe, can be normative.

24. In the light of subliminal advertising and certain kinds of product placement, I have stopped short of treating such transparency as a necessary condition of genuine advertising. There are grounds, however, for excluding such phenomena, or at least for treating them as advertising in a loose sense. For instance, the former is arguably too close to, e.g., post-hypnotic suggestion to count as genuine advertising. We need not decide the issue here.

25. In a more complicated form, it would also allow for the fact that even propaganda that promotes a laudable ideology may for other reasons be distasteful, contemptible, or otherwise unacceptable.

26. See Bok, *Lying*, esp. Ch.2. My brief observations below on the question whether lying is ethically neutral draw heavily on her rich discussion; I cannot do it full justice here.

27. See Leibniz, *Theodicy*, Section 288.

28. Note that such considerations would hardly convince rigid consequentialists. The fact that lying, unlike truth-telling, appears to require justification is for them just an

echo of the fact that lying generally has unacceptable consequences. It may indeed be coercive and manipulative, and it may invariably risk undermining the integrity of the liar; but it is not these features in themselves that make lying require justification for them, but the fact that coercive or manipulative acts, or acts that result in loss of integrity, tend to be harmful, unpleasant, or distressing. However, given that this line of thought does considerable damage to our ordinary ways of thinking about coercion, manipulation, and integrity, it should, I think, be resisted. At any rate, we should not set aside such ways of thinking in favor of something quite so alien without powerful reasons.

29. Notice that because advertising does not necessarily involve deception, it is not, at least for that reason, *pro tanto* wrong. This is another reason not to lump it together with propaganda.

30. Lamarque, "Reflections on Current Trends in Aesthetics," 6.

31. Thus, in Lamarque's example, Dickens's failure to be epistemically virtuous in *Hard Times* results in serious character distortion.

32. Gaut, "The Ethical Criticism of Art," 195–196. As he notes, the argument applies *mutatis mutandis* to ethically commendable attitudes.

33. In the case of propaganda, therefore, it is a *second* order prescription that is by definition unmerited.

34. There is an analogous distinction in the realm of artefacts that separates genuine Fs from things that are merely used as Fs. Something is a genuine chair in part because it falls under the functional description "thing for sitting on" irrespective of whether it is used with that function, whereas a wooden box used as a chair is not a genuine chair, since it only has that function *insofar as* it is used with that function.

35. It might be thought that a simpler way of ruling out this type of example would be to appeal to the fact that the propagandists are not the original authors of the work. Such considerations, however, would not allow for cases in which the original authors come to support the propaganda and collude with the issuers of the decree. (They could even be the people who issue it.)

36. Including *49th Parallel* (1941), *One of Our Aircraft is Missing*, (1942), *A Canterbury Tale* (1944), and *A Matter of Life and Death* (1946).

37. Devereaux, "Beauty and Evil," 250.

38. What makes the incidents with the South African officer especially controversial is the fact the audience is led to believe, though not encouraged to accept with equanimity, that he is willing to use considerable cruelty to elicit information from captured German soldiers.

39. Whom Candy befriends early on in the film—when he visits Berlin near the end of the Boer War, in 1902, and after they have dueled. Theo at this point is a young German officer.

40. It is worth relating the original dedication in full: "THIS FILM IS DEDICATED to the New Army of Britain, to the new spirit of warfare, to the new toughness in battle, and to the men and women who know what they are fighting for and are fighting this war to win it."

41. "ATS" referred to the Auxiliary Territorial Service, the women's branch of the army in WWII. By April 1941 it had full military status.

42. The idea that Britain is essentially a rural nation is in fact only briefly touched upon in *Colonel Blimp*, but it is explored in depth in *A Canterbury Tale*.

43. That is, audiences who were not yet principally concerned with the likely after-math of war. For evidence additional to that which immediately follows, see the text surrounding notes 49–51, below, along with the notes themselves.

44. They could scarcely have known, for example, whether Britain's forces were properly armed; nor would they have been able to find out whether, say, morale in each of Britain's blitzed industrial cities was at breaking point. Their sources of infor-mation—whether they were newspapers, the BBC, or simply hearsay—would not have put them in a position to decide such matters.

45. Compare Moor, *Powell and Pressburger: A Cinema of Magic Spaces*, 71–72, 76.

46. In accordance with Bok's third type of "excuse"; see Bok, *op. cit.*, 74–77.

47. Notably in Theo's speech to the tribunal and in a concert of German music both performed by and attended by German prisoners-of-war in the second period. Powell and Pressburger were not alone in daring to celebrate German culture in WWII British propaganda films; compare, e.g., Dame Myra Hess's performance of Beethoven in Humphrey Jennings's *A Diary for Timothy* (completed in 1945, though not released until 1946), together with Michael Redgrave's voiceover: "I do like the music that lady was playing. Some of us think it is the greatest music in the world. Yet it's German music. And we're fighting the Germans. There's some-thing you'll have to think over later on." (The commentary was specially written by E. M. Forster.)

48. Like, e.g., Brian Desmond Hurst's *Dangerous Moonlight* (1941) or William Wyler's *Mrs. Miniver* (1942), an American production set in wartime Britain.

49. The perceived idea that Britain's military top brass was populated by outdated thinkers like Candy.

50. Powell and Pressburger, *The Life and Death of Colonel Blimp*, 37.

51. As Judith Buchanan has pointed out to me, one should not automatically take their words here at face value, since in the memorandum they were trying to get Min-istry approval for the film. However, Low's famous cartoon of Blimp's funeral early in 1942 (see Figure 2.2, page 54 above), which was drawn in response to a speech by a government minister proclaiming that Blimp was dead, and in which Blimp's half-open coffin is attended by identical Blimps and Blimp himself is showing distinct signs of life, suggests that Blimpery was still publicly perceived as a threat.

52. Ibid., 36.

53. Ibid., 37.

54. Should anyone be tempted by it even now, I recommend Robert Winder's account of Britain's extraordinarily ambivalent attitude to foreigners in Winder, *Bloody Foreigners*.

55. Compare, e.g., the infamous "glue man" plot in *A Canterbury Tale*. For an excel-lent discussion of the pastoral themes in Powell and Pressburger's work, see Moor, *Powell and Pressburger*, Ch.3. Moor himself is inclined to think that they genuinely do endorse a return to a rural idyll. Speaking of *A Canterbury Tale*, he remarks that "It is ideologically dedicated to the encouragement of a shared sense of national identity, based upon values which predate the urban, industrialised structure of modern society. It craves a cosy re-imagination of half-timbered Englishness." (100) He then takes their treatment of those features—like the "glue man" plot—that "[sit] oddly with the film's predominantly effusive representation of [this kind of] Englishness" (109) as

exposing an "ideological contradiction" (110). It is much simpler, however, to take their treatment of such features merely as demonstrating their awareness of the limitations of the rural mythology.

56. By the term "moral luck", philosophers usually mean the idea that the moral worth of people or their acts can, even with the best will in the world, depend upon factors outside their control (compare., e.g., Nagel, "Moral Luck"). Similarly, "aesthetic luck" may be taken to connote the idea that the aesthetic worth of a work of art can depend on factors outside its authors' control, no matter how skilfully and sensitively the work is executed. It is possible, however, to give these terms an epistemological gloss. Thus, we may take "aesthetic luck" to mean the idea that being able to *recognize* the aesthetic value of a work of art can depend upon factors outside its authors' control, again no matter how skillfully and sensitively the work is executed.

Evidently, the claim that something is an instance of moral or aesthetic luck is less controversial if given the epistemological gloss. For without it, the claim allows for the possibility, e.g., that a work of art may *lose* certain moral or aesthetic properties merely because of a change in external circumstances; it allows apparently intrinsic properties of the work to come and go simply as a result of extrinsic change. By contrast, the epistemological version requires only that audiences of a work of art are no longer able to appreciate the work as having such properties. I do not, however, wish to rule out the more controversial version of the claim. Accordingly, I propose to take "aesthetic luck" here as meaning that *the aesthetic worth of a work of art, or our ability to recognize it as having such worth*, may be contingent upon circumstances beyond its authors' control, no matter how skillfully and sensitively it is executed; and similarly with "moral luck".

57. So that the qualities we were once able to see in the film did not merely disappear from view, but ceased to apply to it altogether; see Note. 56.

3

JUST WHAT IS IT THAT MAKES TONY SOPRANO SUCH AN APPEALING, ATTRACTIVE MURDERER?

MURRAY SMITH

SOPRANO: Why me, huh? Doesn't every parent make mistakes?

DR MELFI: Why not you?

SOPRANO: Cos I'm a good guy. Basically. I love my family.

'The Second Coming,' *The Sopranos*, Season 6, Episode 19.

TONY SOPRANO (JAMES GANDOLFINI), GODFATHER of a powerful New Jersey Mafia family and the central character of *The Sopranos*, is recovering from a gunshot wound in his stomach—inflicted by his deranged and estranged uncle, Junior (Dominic Chianese)—that has almost killed him. It is his first week back at work, and he is burdened by anxiety over his frailty and threatened authority, undermined (at least in his own mind) by his physical weakness and by his absence for many weeks. Gathered with his team of "captains" and "soldiers", Soprano accuses his driver Perry Annunziata (Louis Gross)—a well-meaning, eager-to-please but none-too-bright bodybuilder, new to the gang—of slamming the refrigerator door, without thought for The Boss. The slight, however, is clearly fabricated by Soprano as a means of provoking a fight with the driver. When Perry responds to a blow from Soprano by striking back, Soprano weighs in viciously, knocking the driver down and beating him into bloody submission. The rest of the gang looks on in troubled, but awed, silence. Mission accomplished, Soprano retires to the lavatory, vomiting from the strain of his exertions.[1]

Like so many moments in *The Sopranos*, this is a troubling scene, and not merely for its display of moderately graphic violence. More profoundly disturbing are the social and psychological dynamics it explores. Soprano is an admired leader among his men, and as the "general" of this clan, he is no longer often called upon to exercise his physical fighting skills—such tasks as require them can usually be delegated to those of lower rank. As Soprano himself realizes, however, the authority of the alpha male is, in this social world, underpinned by his willingness and ability to assert himself, violently and definitively, when necessary. This authority is absolute and brooks no serious dissension or doubt; thus, while the members of the gang recognize that the driver has done nothing wrong—not until he strikes Soprano in self-defense, an action that they probably do regard as not only foolish, but wrong—they believe that there is nothing they can or should do when Soprano launches his assault.

What's more, this is business as usual; indeed as an instance of violent intimidation in the show, this is chicken feed. It is worth reminding ourselves of the extent
of Soprano's immorality. He is thoroughly immersed in a world in which the
extortion of money and favors is the norm; as a godfather, he is, of course, one
of the leaders of this world. The mechanism of extortion is most often physical
violence or the threat of such violence, though other methods, such as blackmail,
are on the books. While this violence is normally directed outward toward his
enemies, Soprano is fully capable of imposing it on friends, members of his own
gang, and associates when the need arises. The assault on his driver is a minor
example; one of the major, and truly shocking, examples occurs late in Season
6, when Soprano murders his nephew Christopher (Michael Imperioli). Whether
Soprano metes out the physical violence himself, as he does on this occasion, or
delegates the task, he is fully responsible for these acts of terrorization (an over-
used word these days—but surely apt in this context). Soprano also regards it as his
right to maintain a "goomah" (mistress), and more generally to sleep with prostitutes and other women as and when it suits him. As a system of social manage-
ment, the Mafia is also shown to be corrupt, injust and irresponsible in numerous
ways: a string of episodes in Season 6, for example, shows Soprano's building company illegally dumping asbestos without regard for its effect on the environment
or human population.

Now, the remarkable thing is this: though most committed viewers of the show
will be repelled by Soprano's dishonesty and violence and the gang's quiescence,
they'll continue to find Soprano a fascinating, and even appealing, character. As an
Amazon UK commentary puts it, "[t]he genius of his [James Gandolfini's] performance, and of the programme-makers, is that, despite Tony being a whoring,
unscrupulous, sexist boor, a crime boss and a murderer, we somehow end up
feeling and rooting for him."[2] The show explicitly thematizes this issue, through a
variety of strategies. Occasional individual episodes focus on the theme of sympathy and admiration for Soprano. 'A Hit is a Hit' (Season 1, Episode 10), for example, articulates a three-layer parallel between the Soprano family; a black
criminal turned gangsta-rapper, Massive Genius (Bokeem Woodbine), who tries to
extort money from Soprano's associate Hesh Rabkin (Jerry Adler); and the Sopranos' neighbors, fellow Italian-Americans Bruce and Jeannie Cusamano (Robert
LuPone and Saundra Santiago), who oscillate between fascination, pride, and
unease in response to the fact that they live next door to a notorious Mafia godfather. In addition, *The Sopranos* features two characters whose sympathy with and
loyalty to Soprano becomes an ongoing dramatic focus. Most centrally, there is
Soprano's wife, Carmela (Edie Falco), who periodically agonizes about her husband's activities and her complicity with him (more on Carmela below). More
peripherally—but still significantly—there is FBI agent Dwight Harris (Matt Ser-
vitto), who, while investigating Soprano through all six seasons, always treats him
with remarkable civility, even in the face of Soprano's muted hostility toward him.
In Season 6, Episode 21, Harris is shown assisting Soprano in relation to internal

Mafia strife, literally and explicitly rooting for Soprano in his war with rival gang leader Phil Leotardo (Frank Vincent); "We're gonna win this thing!" exclaims Harris, upon hearing that Leotardo has been dispatched. If this sort of "sympathy with the devil" is something of a staple within the gangster genre, in *The Sopranos* it becomes a rich and central dramatic conceit. The representative scene that I have begun by recounting, then, helps us to pose two distinct but related questions (or, more properly, two sets of questions): first, what is the appeal of Tony Soprano? Or, more precisely: how is it that we can find a character who routinely acts in the ways exemplified by this scene attractive? These first questions, then, treat *The Sopranos* as an instance of the *problem of personality*: how can we care about, or sympathize with, someone who would repel us in reality?[3]

The second major question posed by *The Sopranos* is: what are the moral (and aesthetic) implications of the fact that we find Soprano an appealing character? The air of philosophical debate in recent years has been thick with ethical questions and worries of this sort, many of them citing Hume's claim that:

> where vicious manners are described, without being marked with the proper characters of blame and disapprobation; this must be allowed to disfigure the poem, and to be a real deformity. I cannot, nor is it proper I should, enter into such sentiments . . . We are not interested in the fortunes and sentiments of such rough heroes: We are displeased to find the limits of vice and virtue so much confounded: And whatever indulgence we may give to the writer on account of his prejudices, we cannot prevail on ourself to enter into his sentiments, or bear an affection to characters, which we plainly discover to be blameable.[4]

If ever there were a "rough hero" who confounds "the limits of vice and virtue," Soprano is that figure. Are fictions that do not merely depict, but also involve us imaginatively in immoral actions, necessarily morally harmful, as Hume implies? Is Tony Soprano mad, bad, and dangerous to know? Should fans of the show be hastening to the nearest confessional, seeking moral guidance to overcome their corrupt attachment to the show? Or are the moral implications of the show more complex and less obviously bleak? This problem, then, is not the recently much discussed "problem of imaginative resistance," so much as it is the problem (if such it is) posed by those of us—fiction makers and fiction appreciators alike—who exhibit relatively limited imaginative resistance.[5]

As the contemporary example *par excellence* of the gangster drama, *The Sopranos* is a very apt case to explore the grounds for ethical worries over the nature and effects of fictions that focus on immoral characters and actions. For along with the horror film, and certain related genres of popular song like the "murder ballad", the gangster film is one of the paradigms of the morally "dangerous" cultural object.[6] From its inception, the world of moviemaking has drawn hostile moral fire and censorious attention, but, as we have seen, essentially the same sort of moral worry has been around since at least Hume, and it has been developed in detail in contemporary aesthetic debate under the guise of the "ethicist" theory of artistic value.[7]

One way of heading off these moral worries is to urge that, while thrilling and compelling, a drama like *The Sopranos* is but "harmless entertainment". Entertaining it certainly is; and harmless it may be, but if it is so, that is not because it sidesteps the moral domain. Susan Sontag claimed that Jack Smith's underground classic *Flaming Creatures* (1963) exists outside "moral space", and Pedro Almodóvar has signaled his intention to make narratives that exist outside of the moral domain ("I like big melodramas," Almodóvar has stated, "but I can't actually make a big melodrama because my point of view is amoral.")[8] Whatever we make of these examples, it is surely true that a cartoon like *Tom and Jerry* (1940–1958) engages us in an amoral fashion; and if it does engage us morally, then it does not do so on the same direct terms as dramatic narrative. In a similar vein, one reviewer has written of the *Harry Potter* films (2001–2011):

> Some have asked whether we should fear, or cheer, for a world whose kids have derived some elements of their childhood morality from Harry Potter's Manichaean world. I think the question is overblown. For one thing, the movies have ensured—as movies often do—that the stories have acquired the shape of pure fun, detached from the darkness and light that can reside within private readings of text.[9]

There are some questionable assumptions here (bearing on the putative differences between films and novels), but what strikes me as exactly right is the idea that not all narratives engage with morality in the same way. There is plenty of moral language, and notionally moral action, in the world of Harry Potter, and it is probably an exaggeration to say that the story assumes the shape of "pure fun", as perhaps it does in *Tom and Jerry* or *SpongeBob SquarePants* (1999-present). *Harry Potter*, however, does not engage us morally in the way that *Crime and Punishment* does. In moving from *Krazy Kat* to *Middlemarch*, we encounter many different grades of "moral concentration" and moral seriousness in works of fiction.

In order to clarify the idea that a work of fiction might invoke morality without that entailing full-blown moral engagement and deliberation, let me draw a parallel. In the sport of rugby union, the New Zealand national side—the All Blacks—begins each game with a ritual war dance known as the "haka". The dance is directed at the opposing team and is a fittingly bellicose affair, involving various aggressive postures, gestures, and facial and vocal expressions. Occasionally opposing teams will respond to the challenge by, for example, squaring up to the All Blacks as they perform the haka. So the dance invokes the idea of war, and in this way sets the game to be played within the frame of a serious, angry, and unresolved conflict between rival groups. Then the whistle is blown and the game begins—and we know that that is all it is: a game, no matter how much might be at stake in these terms (sporting reputations, national pride, and the like). So while ideas of warfare are evoked, in part to arouse powerful emotions and strong commitment on the part of players and spectators alike, only the pathological will take the idea literally. So it is, I argue, with morality in the case of many types of fiction: evoking the moral framework helps to engage and arouse us, but we understand that, depending on the type of fiction, we should not necessarily construe the action in fully moral terms. The degree to which we do apply our normal moral preconceptions is something that we work out by engaging with individual works.

Given that our focus here is on a television drama, we might think this through in terms of other recent, high-profile television series. On one extreme, we have shows like *The Sopranos* and its HBO sibling *The Wire* (2002–2008). While both begin from generic bases (the gangster and police procedural genres, respectively), and create interest in part through the familiar iconography and narrative patterns of these genres, they are also designed as dramas that engage us on a direct moral level, focusing on the moral dilemmas, psychology, and compromises that characterize the situations and characters they depict. Some distance away from these shows is *Prison Break* (2005–2009), a show that generates most of its drama from the ingenuity with which its central characters escape from apparently impossible circumstances. As with Harry Potter, there is some moral engagement; indeed, superficially, there is a great deal of moral deliberation and action going on. T-Bag (Robert Knepper) is a truly vile character, but for the most part, he plays the role of "the man we love to hate," a pantomimic villain. We take the action of the show, in moral terms, with more than a pinch of salt. Occasionally *Prison Break* attempts to modify its tone, bestowing a more serious moral light on the story, but such passages stand out rather awkwardly because the prevailing moral mode is more instrumental and playful than sincere. *Lost* (2004–2010) occupies terrain somewhere between *The Sopranos* and *Prison Break*, appealing to us through its often outlandish and unpredictable narrative turns, and the unfolding implication that we cannot be sure that we properly understand the fundamental narrative context. Nevertheless, the action on the island, and the narration of the various characters' backstories, often engages us on the level of serious moral action, in a way that seems more convincing than *Prison Break*'s moral "digressions". I do not offer these brief comparative remarks as exhaustive or exacting analyses of the shows, but merely to suggest the ways in which even narratives from the same period and cultural context may differ in their uptake and rendering of moral matters. The variety of examples is enough, I hope, to point up the absurdity of treating all narrative representations of human action as seeking the same form of engagement with morality.

So there may well be, in certain cases, something to the idea that a fiction may be "harmless entertainment" even as it appears to engage with serious moral matters. That will not wash for *The Sopranos*, however. A dramatic narrative like *The Sopranos* engages us to a very considerable degree by depicting characters whose lives are recognizably informed by moral deliberation, even as the social world occupied by these characters remains distant from ours. Thus, to go along with the view that *The Sopranos* is nothing more than harmless entertainment would be to neuter the show, protecting it from moral censure at the cost of denying, or failing to fully acknowledge, the extent to which the power of the show derives from its engagement with moral questions.[10]

One particular episode of the show that I want to focus on in this essay, "Second Opinion" (Season 3, Episode 7), explicitly brings these questions to the surface, through the figure of Carmela. Undergoing a crisis of conscience, Carmela is referred to Dr Sig Krakower (Sully Boyar), a psychotherapist. When afflicted by moral doubts about her lifestyle in the past, she has turned to Father Phil (Paul Schulze), a Catholic priest who offers her solace and advises her to try to stay with her husband and attempt to reform him. Carmela expects something along the same lines from Krakower—marriage counseling with tea and sympathy. This, in slightly abridged form, is what she gets:

CARMELA: . . . well then, you know. How difficult it can be. He's a good man. A good father.

KRAKOWER: You were telling me he's a depressed criminal—prone to anger, serially unfaithful. Is that your definition of a good man?
[. . .]

CARMELA: So what, so what? He betrays me every week with those whores.

KRAKOWER: Probably the least of his misdeeds. [*Carmela goes to leave, but Krakower stops her with a look*]

CARMELA: You're wrong about the accomplice part, though.

KRAKOWER: Are you sure?

CARMELA: All I do is make sure that he's got clean clothes in his closet, and dinner on his table.

KRAKOWER: So "enabler" would be a more accurate job description for you than "accomplice". My apologies.
[. . .]

CARMELA: My priest said I should try to work with him, help him to be a better man.

KRAKOWER: [dryly] How's that going?
[. . .]

KRAKOWER: One thing you can never say: that you haven't been told.

CARMELA: I see. You're right, I see.

Krakower confronts Carmela with the moral reality of her husband and her relationship with him, and so assaults her moral self-deception (or what Meadow

(Jamie-Lynn Sigler), the Sopranos' daughter, terms her mother's "bullshit accommodational pretense"). In its own way, Krakower's unflinching assertion of the truth may be as much of a challenge to the viewer as it is to Carmela, in the sense that Carmela might be seen as the closest analog, within the fictional world, of the viewer: one who finds herself emotionally attached to someone who, at the same time, she knows is guilty of the most abhorrent crimes. "I see. You're right, I see." Does Carmela really see? If so, can she help herself from looking away from the truth, and staying with Soprano? Are we appreciators of the show guilty of the same sort of prevarication—if on a smaller scale—when we stay with the show?

Of course, there are important asymmetries between our position and Carmela's, both ontological and epistemic. Carmela is part of the fictional world of *The Sopranos*, so Soprano is real for her, but fictional for us. But we see the whole array of Soprano's actions, especially his "professional" activities. Carmela, by contrast, while fully aware in a general sense of the nature of her husband's lifestyle, deliberately shields herself—and is shielded, by Soprano—the details of his activities, so that a shared pretense of domestic normality is maintained in the Soprano residence much of the time. The ontological divide separating us from Soprano may, as we will see, have important consequences for the extent to which we can maintain a sympathetic disposition toward him, even in the face of his extensive immorality.

My focus from this point on will be on the first of our pair of questions, concerning the appeal of Soprano and the problem of personality. I hope to have established, in my comments above, that there *is* a second question—concerning the moral status of *The Sopranos* and our appreciation of it—and will say a little more about it in the conclusion. The second question, however, really requires an independent essay, and so I postpone further substantial discussion of it. I approach the first question initially by examining *The Sopranos* in considerable detail. Only through the "thick description" and detailed consideration of a fictional world and its presentation will we be in a position to ask and answer moral questions about it. Broad-brush characterizations of fictions are likely to lead to equally crude moral answers in which fictions are merely placed in a kind of periodic table of moral rectitude, a gesture about as precise and illuminating as the "thumbs up-thumbs down" mode of film reviewing.

A PORTRAIT OF THE GANGSTER AS A REGULAR GUY

The character of Tony Soprano is not, of course, the whole of *The Sopranos*, but he looms large in the show in every sense, so our examination of the world of the show will begin with Soprano and revolve around him, even as we look at various other characters and the behavior and values of the Mafia community as a whole. The first thing to note about Soprano, and a feature that distinguishes him from most earlier iconic gangster figures, is that he is in many ways *a regular guy*. The show has been widely understood as a hybrid of the gangster drama and the domestic soap opera, a blend intimately related to Soprano's "ordinariness" as a character. Often all Soprano wants is a few minutes' peace to read his newspaper, but the chlorine unit on the swimming pool keeps rattling, and they just will not leave him alone in his office. He maintains relationships with friends, neighbors, and acquaintances outside of the Mafia, including his old school friend Artie (John Ventimiglia), who runs the restaurant patronized by Soprano and his team (though Soprano's Mafia commitments routinely intrude upon his relationship with Artie). Scenes in the show are split, roughly equally, between those focusing on Soprano's suburban family life and those tracking his Mafia activities; the show pivots around the conflict, uneasy balance, and impact of each of these domains on the other. Soprano conceives of himself as the put-upon family man, constantly bombarded by the demands of not one, but two, families—his immediate family, and the "extended family" of his Mafia confederates (a few of whom are actual relatives). One source of ongoing, low-level friction between Soprano and Carmela is his neglect of day-to-day family routines. He is often late for dinner—"That's what microwaves are for," he provocatively quips in the episode "Second Opinion".

One of earliest and most remarkable commentaries on the gangster film, Robert Warshow's "The Gangster as Tragic Hero" (1948), treats the gangster as a tragic figure in part because he is "doomed" to fail.[11] Setting *The Sopranos* within the framework of tragedy is instructive in terms of understanding how it is that we may sympathize with Soprano. In his commentary on tragedy in the *Hamburg Dramaturgy*, G.E. Lessing argues that it is essential that the protagonist of a tragedy is "'one of ourselves'—that is, recognizable as a human being, a mix of virtue and vice, rather than 'an incarnate devil.'" Lessing's remarks are prompted by the character of Richard III in Christian Felix Weiss's play *Richard III* (completed in 1765), whom Lessing called "the most loathsome monster that ever trod the stage." In Lessing's view, this ensured that the play could not succeed as a tragedy. According to Lessing, the emotions of pity and fear, prompted by tragedy, are interrelated in a particular fashion: our pity for the tragic protagonist hinges on seeing him as precisely *not* monstrous, enabling us in turn to fear such a fate for ourselves. Now, my point in mentioning Lessing's analysis of tragedy is not to suggest that *The Sopranos* takes the precise form of classical tragedy, but to stress that Soprano is rather more like the protagonist of a tragedy—"neither a wholly virtuous nor a wholly vicious man" —than he is like Weiss' monstrous Richard III.[12] Soprano is sufficiently ordinary that we may, in Lessing's terms, recognize him as "one of ourselves."

A crucial part of our sense that Soprano is "one of ourselves," in Lessing's sense, arises from the fact that, however we might assess Soprano in moral terms, he certainly has a moral code, and the idea of family is central to that moral code. In a moment of quiet intimacy with his daughter in "Second Opinion", he tells her that "everything that I do . . . it's all for you and your brother." Early in Season 6, he articulates similar sentiments, advising his son A.J. (Robert Iler) that friends will always eventually let you down, and for this reason it is family that counts. In

Season 5, Soprano risks the stability of the entire regional Mafia regime by protecting his cousin Tony Blundetto (Steve Buscemi) on the grounds that he is "family". (Blundetto has killed, with neither Mafia "justification" nor Tony's authorization, a member of a neighboring New York Mafia family, with whom Soprano's Mafia family maintains generally good relations.) In "Second Opinion", Soprano has to manage and contain a smaller-scale conflict within his own team, between long-time captain Paulie "Walnuts" Gualtieri (Tony Sirico) and Soprano's nephew Christopher, before it gets out of hand. He is also driven to violence in dealing with the creeping demands of Angie Bonpensiero (Toni Kalem), whom Soprano supports financially, vandalizing her car as a warning to her.[13] Thus, while the show hinges on the contrasts and conflicts between the domains of the domestic and the criminal, the idea of family cuts across them and structures both; within that structure, Soprano sees himself as a hard-pressed patriarch doing the best he can with a demanding and difficult job. Soprano conceives of this job not only in practical and financial terms, but in *moral* terms—he believes he has responsibilities and obligations to his families, and he often wrestles with the question "what should I do?" To the extent that the show gives Soprano's self-perception some salience and legitimacy—which it does—Soprano can be understood as a "regular guy", subject to pressures and responsibilities that any ordinary Joe can appreciate, including moral ones. In everyday parlance, we can, in these respects, "identify" with Soprano, no matter how distant his world and his personality may be from our own in other respects.

One particularly important source of Soprano's "regularity" is his relationship with conventionally powerful professionals, such as Dr Kennedy (Sam McMurray) in "Second Opinion". Kennedy is Junior's surgeon, operating on his cancer in this episode. The prognosis immediately following the operation is good, and Soprano attempts to show his gratitude—by thanking Kennedy warmly and personally, and hinting that he would happily reciprocate in the way only a Mafioso can: "If there's anything I can do, let me know." Kennedy is wholly unimpressed by Soprano's reputation and brushes him aside with the same polite and condescending contempt that he uses with all his patients (overt disdain and impatience being reserved for any medical colleague who disagrees with him). As the episode progresses, and it emerges that Junior's cancer has not been cured by the surgery, Kennedy distances himself from the case and refuses to return calls from Junior and Soprano. Soprano is finally driven to confronting, intimidating, and humiliating Kennedy as he plays golf, with the assistance of Soprano's Italian right-hand man, Furio (Federico Castelluccio). In one way this is all very much out of the ordinary—few of us pursue our frustrations with doctors and other professionals we depend upon in this way (though we might have fantasies of doing so). Nevertheless, the fact that Soprano finds himself at the mercy of an arrogant surgeon like Kennedy is something that any person without exceptional wealth or status can relate to, and herein lies Soprano's ordinariness. It is also worth stressing that, once again, our allegiance with Soprano on this score has a strong moral dimension. Kennedy fails in his duty of care for Junior (and by extension, for Soprano); and Soprano acts out of a sense of duty toward his uncle—an uncle who he believes may once have tried to kill him. Soprano's *means* doubtless strike us as immoral, but his motivations here are, in fact, morally laudable.[14]

Soprano is also, famously, in therapy, with fellow Italian-American Dr Jennifer Melfi (Lorraine Bracco). If we shift the class locus of our notion of "ordinariness" upward a little, this feature of Soprano's life also bestows an air of typicality on it, since psychotherapy is almost as commonplace among middle-class Americans as jogging or working out in a gym. Soprano does not enter the space of Melfi's office as a typical middle-class American, however, and he never feels fully at ease there. His uneasy relationship with her has a number of sources. Like Kennedy, Melfi is a professional, and Soprano is eager to be treated as her equal but convinced that she looks down upon him. He also lusts after her and continually flirts with her, in his own brusque fashion; her refusal to be drawn into a sexual relationship with him is an affront to him in just the same way as Kennedy's initial refusal to accept a gift from him—Soprano is not used to being told "no", and that is why he is often ill at ease outside of his own social and cultural space. The very idea of having a psychological problem in need of treatment is a source of shame to him; it is a "feminizing" trait that, if it ever became known within the Mafia community, would put him in danger.

The most important ramification of Soprano's psychotherapy from our point of view, however, is that it highlights his vulnerability and sense of guilt. Although capable of terrible viciousness, Soprano is not without remorse. In Season 2, Soprano encounters a former school friend, Davey Scatino (Robert Patrick). Scatino, a compulsive gambler, persuades Soprano to allow him to join Soprano's elite circle of high-roller card players. When Scatino gets into debt with his mob friend, Soprano assumes control of Scatino's sports store, Ramsey Outdoor, driving Scatino into bankruptcy as he strips the business of its assets, credit, and good standing. Pressed by Scatino to explain how he can so ruthlessly exploit his friend's misfortune, Soprano smilingly alludes to the fable of the spider and the fly: it's just in his nature, he claims, to prey on weaker entities. Soprano, however, rarely lives up to the Nietzschean "ideal" of remorseless strength that he extols here.[15] His guilt often surfaces in unexpected ways, manifesting itself—in classic pop Freudian fashion—in dreams and in relation to objects onto which his anxieties have been displaced. A toy singing fish in "Second Opinion" reawakens guilt over Pussy's murder (a dead fish being a traditional symbol of death within the Mafia world). When Soprano encounters two of his men joking over the toy, he spins into a rage, assaulting (and permanently injuring) the hapless barman Georgie (Frank Santorelli) who has brought the toy into the Bada-Bing (the strip club that functions as one of the fronts for Soprano's operations). As with the attack on his driver, recounted at the opening of this essay, Soprano's behavior here is shocking and repellent. In both cases, however, it is closely enmeshed with his vulnerabilities, and this goes some way toward exculpating him—dramatically, if not strictly morally. (Warshow: "In the end it is the gangster's weakness as much as his power and freedom that appeals to us; the world is not ours, but it is not his either . . . ")[16] That is, Soprano's guilt reveals him to be a moral being even as it drives him to further deplorable acts. He is without question *morally sentient*. Soprano's limited but active conscience, his passionate and divided character, contrasts strongly with the icy coolness of Michael Corleone (Al Pacino), his dramatic equivalent in the first two *Godfather* films (Francis Ford Coppola, 1972 and 1974, respectively), whose ethos is succinctly captured by his wife, Kay (Diane Keaton): "reason—backed up by murder."

The moral core at the heart of Soprano's being is vital in triggering *our* moral "instinct" in a sympathetic fashion. As Noël Carroll has suggested, our propensity to detect and ally ourselves with the most moral—and thus the most trustworthy—agents in a given community or situation likely has deep evolutionary roots. Soprano is at the very heart of *The Sopranos*, to the extent that one might even see the show, to a considerable degree, as a drama of Soprano's conscience. He is at least as moral as all other major characters in the world of the show (and considerably more moral than many of them): "In a world of moral midgets, insofar as [Soprano] is the closest approximation of probity we find, we ally our selves with him."[17]

THE ALLURE OF THE TRANSGRESSIVE

. . . . There seems to be a limit to how much morality we can stand.[18]

But, you might say, Soprano is not exactly a moral paragon, nor is he so regular as to be *merely* ordinary. And you would be right to say this. This fact is implicit in many of the remarks above, and dramatized in an extended fashion over Episodes 2 and 3 of Season 6, in which Soprano—critically ill from the gunshot wounds inflicted by Junior—hallucinates a whole parallel life as a *truly* ordinary, respectable businessman, "Kevin Finnerty". In the fictional reality of *The Sopranos*, however, Soprano is a man held in awe within and beyond the Mafia community. (The dialectic between Soprano's ordinariness and extraordinariness is intensified further as Finnerty, within the hallucination, imagines being mistaken for notorious gangster Tony Soprano!) Soprano's exceptional standing is played up in at least two further ways.

First, as we have seen, Soprano's gang members conceive of themselves in quasi-military terms. Soprano himself is fascinated by military documentaries, and in "Second Opinion" he avidly watches a film about General George Patton, seeing himself as a military leader of comparable stature in charge of his own army. However crooked and unlikely the comparison may seem to us upon reflection, Soprano seems to think of himself at least partly in terms of those "sublime" character traits that Hume associated with military heroism: "[c]ourage, intrepidity, ambition, love of glory, magnanimity . . .,"[19] Hume notes how the appreciation for such sublimity of character "paint[s] out the evils, which this supposed virtue has produced in human society; the subversion of empires, the devastation of provinces, the sack of cities."[20] If what Hume says is true of genuine military heroes, it holds still more firmly for a "sublime" figure like Soprano, a character who lacks any legitimate underlying moral rationale that might mitigate against the destructive consequences Hume limns. Nevertheless, Hume's point is to insist on the seductive psychological power of the sublime character, which impresses us in spite of our better judgment.[21] Soprano may thus benefit from, and appeal to us through, such sublimity.

In addition to Soprano's metaphorical status as a military leader, there lies the fact that Soprano is a crime boss. Thus far, I've treated Soprano's status as a gangster in wholly negative terms with regard to his appeal to us: racketeering implicates Soprano in all manner of immoral activities, and so cannot be a source of his appeal. But things are not so straightforward. Behind Soprano as an individual gangster stands the full force of the mythology of the charismatic cinematic gangster, from Cagney and Robinson to Pacino and de Niro. The opening credit sequence of *The Sopranos* reasserts this mythology while reinventing it. The sequence tracks Soprano as he drives from New York City out to New Jersey, traversing various industrial and blue collar districts which gradually give way to the leafier suburbs where Soprano lives. Accompanied by the Alabama 3's "Woke Up this Morning," a propulsive hip-hop song complete with Howlin' Wolf samples and a swelling gospel choir, the entire sequence is shot and cut like a music video, in sync with the dynamics of the song: a succession of rapidly-cut shots—of tollbooths, traffic, Soprano puffing a fat cigar, factories, shops and houses—rolls along, turning a routine car trip along overcrowded highways into an edgy, vibrant ride. The lyrics of the song sketch Soprano's anti-heroic status: "Woke up this mornin', got yourself a gun, Mama always said you'd be the Chosen One." So even as the credit sequence reaches its conclusion, with Soprano driving up to his suburban house—an image stressing, along with the very title of the show, the importance of the domestic sphere in *The Sopranos*—it has evoked the traditional, countercultural glamour of the gangster. In these terms, the icon of the gangster embodies status, dynamism, insouciance—in a word, *power*; including the power to do as he pleases, to contravene social conventions and moral norms. Picking up on this aspect of the gangster hero, Michael Wood aptly characterizes the figure as "an embodiment of rogue power, a Robin Hood without the sentimental interest in the poor"; Warshow described the gangster as an emblem of "the unlimited possibility of aggression."[22]

Think back, in this connection, to Soprano's intimidation of Dr Kennedy at the golf club. If we isolate the miniature drama that unfolds between Soprano and Kennedy during "Second Opinion", there's no doubt that Soprano comes across as the more sympathetic character, largely on moral grounds (as I argued earlier). When Soprano and Furio threaten Kennedy on the golf course, pushing him back into the edge of a river and knocking his cap off, we are not led to condemn this action. Instead the show, on this occasion, allows us to enjoy the humbling of Kennedy by Soprano. An important part of the pleasure we take in the scene, I submit, consists in imagining acting transgressively but with impunity, as Soprano does. The moral underpinning, so to speak, of Soprano's immoral act is certainly important, and we'll return to this point. The key point to recognize here, however, is that the appeal of Soprano is paradoxical, conjoining the attraction of regularity (and morally grounded sympathy as part of that) with the allure of the transgressive (including moral transgressiveness). The combined force of these appeals is visually emblematized by the climax of the credit sequence, the title *"The Sopranos"* emblazoned across the screen as Soprano arrives at his suburban home, the "r" rendered by the image of a pistol standing on its tip (see still, page 66). Note also that the example of Soprano's dealings with Kennedy provides a good instance of the importance of fine-grained analysis, if we are to understand and assess the moral dynamics of a narrative fiction. If asked whether a scene involving a gangster intimidating a doctor would likely evoke morally based sympathy for the gangster, with no more detail or context provided, we would probably answer in the negative. Only by following the interaction of Soprano and Kennedy closely do we see how morally driven sympathy can flow into sympathy for an understandable but morally dubious action; how (moral) duty comes to support (immoral) inclination. The details matter.

Susan Wolf's essay on "moral saints" sheds some indirect, reflected light on the case of Soprano and the blend of moral, immoral, and amoral factors that inform our responses to him.[23] Part of Wolf's concern is to explore the tensions, both practical and logical, between properly moral ideals and various amoral "personal ideals". The moral saint, in her view, while by definition extraordinarily morally good, fails as a model of (maximally desirable?) human life because of the degree to which it shuts out all sorts of other achievement and quality that we do, as a matter of fact, value. Wolf focuses on cases of basically good and decent individuals who are accomplished in other ways: high-achieving athletes, virtuoso musicians, witty raconteurs. Is it rational for us, or for these individuals themselves, Wolf asks, to desire that they trade in some of their personal accomplishment for greater moral virtuosity? Whatever the case for such individuals, Soprano does not fit into this category. Even if we grant that his ascension to the leadership of his Mafia family counts as a personal achievement—certainly, he sees it that way, as do his peers—it is pretty clearly reasonable that he trade in this achievement for a morally better life, since the achievement in this case is so thoroughly entangled with immoral, rather than amoral, actions and goals. It simply is not imaginable, moreover, within the framework of the show, that Soprano will voluntarily renounce his immoral lifestyle.

So it might seem that the kind of case Wolf is concerned with has no relevance for Soprano. The show, however, creates much of its drama from the question of *just how bad* Soprano is, or is capable of being. His most brutal actions can shock and disappoint us; his better actions surprise us. By any ordinary standard,

Soprano is sunk in moral depravity, and yet we recognize his recognition, diminished as it may be, of moral considerations. He is recognizably a moral being, albeit an all too *human* moral being. It is this pull between Soprano's moral impulses on the one hand and his self-interested, immoral and amoral acts on the other hand, that connects Soprano with Wolf's musicians and raconteurs. Soprano embodies the tension between the moral and amoral motivations and ideals identified by Wolf, albeit reflected in a dark and distorted mirror.

What sort of an answer to the "problem of personality"—that is, the problem of liking and caring about characters who we would dislike, or be indifferent to, in reality—does this analysis of Soprano furnish? Two points come to the fore. Soprano's "regularity", and the moral foundations of many of his acts, allows us to care about him precisely because, in these ways, he is "one of ourselves," notwithstanding the fact that he is a racketeer. So, in this respect, we share more with him than meets the eye, and to that extent we have reason to come to care for him. On the other hand, there are those transgressive aspects of his character that may make him appealing, and an object of care, for a very different sort of reason: his ability to flout moral and other constraints with impunity. This source of appeal is likely to be much more salient and powerful in the context of fictional engagement, where the imagined pleasures and benefits of such behavior do not have to be set against any real costs (i.e., worries about the potential harm that such agents of "rogue power" might inflict on oneself and those one cares about). This is where the ontological divide separating Soprano from appreciators of *The Sopranos* makes a difference: contemplating the actions of Soprano in the imagination simply is not the same, in all respects, as encountering the actions of a real equivalent to Soprano. It might be objected that this is no answer at all to the problem of personality, insofar as it proposes a paradox—we care about Soprano because he is moral and because he is immoral—as a solution to the problem. The paradox in this case, however, is not a product of faulty thinking about an aspect of behavior, but, rather, a description of our behavior. If it is behavior itself that is paradoxical, then "resolving" the paradox in the traditional sense, by redescribing some aspect of it such that the paradox is eliminated, may be simply misleading. The real "solution", in such cases, may be to stare hard in the face of the complexity, and even inconsistency, of certain aspects of human behavior.

OBJECTIONS AND REFINEMENTS

What we have now is a portrait of Soprano, suggesting the various sources of his appeal and the ways in which the situations in which he finds himself, and the actions he undertakes in these situations, may resonate with us in spite of the evident gap between Soprano's lifestyle and those of most viewers of the show. This gives us an answer to the first, descriptive, question derived from Hume, a question that I cast in two variants: what is the appeal of Tony Soprano? and how is it that we can find a character who routinely acts in morally troubling ways attractive? There may, however, be other ways of accounting for our interest in *The Sopranos* and Soprano that dissolve this question rather than providing an answer to it, as I have assumed is necessary. A consideration of these alternative approaches to the nature of our interest in the show will, in addition, have the virtue of allowing me to refine the idea of "psychological appeal", specifying more precisely the stance we come to adopt toward Soprano.

The first alternative to the idea that, in some important way, we like or even admire Soprano is the proposal that it is the show itself, *The Sopranos*, rather than the character, that elicits our admiration and appreciation. It is relatively easy to see why the show might be admired. It works within an established tradition of American drama, evoking a semi-mythical world and set of character types that have engaged audiences for more than a century. It alludes to numerous earlier works in this tradition, while developing the norms of the tradition in an original manner. The show exploits the expansive canvas afforded by the format of the television series to present a richly detailed world, with notable shifts of tone and dramatic focus from one season to the next. As an HBO production—indeed, its flagship show—*The Sopranos* has benefited from high production values and freedom from many of the constraints attached to U.S. network television, as well as unusually long periods of gestation and development between seasons (a privilege won by David Chase on the basis of the early and continuing success of the show). For all these reasons—and, of course, much more could be said to flesh out each of them—one might think that it is enough to say that we find the *show* appealing and admirable.

The problem with this position is that it is, at best, incomplete, and at worst, question-begging. It is incomplete in the following sense. It is obviously true—indeed a tautology—that admirers of the show admire the show. This fact, however, leaves open the question of our stance toward the show's protagonist: the fact that we admire the show does not preclude the possibility that we might also admire its protagonist. Indeed, it is normally the case that our liking of a film goes along with our basic approval of its central character. A commonly articulated reason, in movie reviews and everyday talk about films, for disliking a film is the lack of appeal and likeability of the central protagonist: "The movie left me cold because the hero just turned me off." I do not say that there are no films with unappealing protagonists that are nevertheless admired; but if a film is admired, it is highly probable that we will find a basically likeable character at its core. Indeed, it is quite plausible that, in a great many cases, a viewer's admiration of a drama is heavily *contingent upon* their admiration of the protagonist. So two possibilities emerge here, with regard to the idea that viewers of *The Sopranos* might admire the show rather than its protagonist. The first is that radical divergence between our stance toward a drama and its protagonist is atypical, and so the burden of proof lies with the advocate of this view to show that we dislike Soprano even as we admire the show. The second is that it is quite plausible that our admiration of the show is actually driven, in part, by the appeal of Soprano, in which case, far from dissolving our problem, pointing to our admiration of the show begs the question (and, indeed, heightens the importance of the question). Our interest in Soprano cannot be explained by our admiration for *The Sopranos* if our admiration for the show is partly driven by our interest in and admiration for Soprano.

This brings us, however, to the second alternative to my assumption that we find Soprano likeable and appealing in many respects. Perhaps, it might be urged, we are *fascinated* or *intrigued* by Soprano; we are interested in him and curious about him, but "bear no affection" toward him. As with the first alternative, a certain amount of ground can be conceded here. Soprano *is* fascinating (at least, for committed viewers of the show); fascinating because he is powerful, charismatic, corrupt, complex. As with the first alternative, however, a question is left dangling: is Soprano *merely* fascinating, a mere object of curiosity to us, or does he engage us sympathetically—that is, in moral terms—as well? I submit that the latter is much the more plausible of these options. As I have argued elsewhere, the attitude of fascination, in isolation, implies a combination of focused attention with a kind of moral detachment.[24] "Fascination" in this sense more aptly describes our attitude toward nonhuman subject matter than human drama.[25] Watching *The Blue Planet* (2001), I find myself intrigued and fascinated by the wonders and cruelties of the natural world—the prolonged, almost ritualized, physical abuse of baby seals by killer whales, for example—but my moral sensibility is not substantially engaged. It is true that we find some species "cuter" than others, and some are more readily anthropomorphized than others. It is hard, however, to imagine Roger Ebert complaining that he did not like *The Blue Planet* because those killer whales left him cold. There is a difference in kind between the attitude of fascination we adopt in relation to nature documentaries and the morally engaged stance we adopt in relation to human drama, even if each attitude may play a subordinate or complementary role in the domain in which it does not constitute our primary attitude.

The advocate of "fascination" might retort that there is a class of human subject that might be said to evoke our interest without any hint of sympathy— figures of unalloyed evil, of whom Hitler would be the modern prototype. Clearly, Hitler is a figure of fascination, if only due to the lamentable impact of the man on our world, and much of the interest we take in biographies of Hitler and histories of the Nazi period arises from curiosity concerning the manner of Hitler's rise to power and the way in which, under his dictatorship, a nation committed itself to such a profoundly noxious ideology. Watching *Downfall* (2004), we might say that we find the film compelling and that we are intrigued by Hitler and his relationships with the narrowing circle of intimates and functionaries confined to the bunker with him; but we find Hitler himself neither appealing nor admirable. Is not our relationship with Soprano cut from similar cloth?

The comparison is certainly instructive. Our relationship with a figure like Hitler very obviously engages us morally, and in this sense the detached amorality of fascination—as I have defined it—is clearly inadequate as a description of our stance toward him. In *Downfall*, Hitler is presented as deceptively kindly in certain relationships and contexts, before he unravels over the course of the film, assuming the role of ranting megalomaniac that one anticipates. The first third of the film puts Hitler in a relatively sympathetic light, partly as a means of explaining how the young secretary—the film's true protagonist—is drawn into accepting the world she finds upon working for Hitler. Such is the strength of our foreknowledge of Hitler, however, and our negative judgment of all that he represents, that even these early scenes hardly touch the antipathy in which we hold Hitler, an antipathy consolidated by the unfolding of the film.

It should be said that the film does not simply demonize Hitler as an individual. Instead, by situating him within a circle of collaborators, ranging from naïve and perhaps self-deceiving agents like the secretary to dedicated adherents of Nazi ideology, the social dimension of—and collective responsibility for—the events we witness is emphasized. Indeed, one of the most appalling scenes in the film involves not Hitler, but Goebbels and his wife. Unable to face capture, the two of them systematically murder their six children—by doping them and then administering a lethal poison while they sleep—before committing suicide. The film emphatically personalizes the moral disaster zone it depicts while never representing immorality as a simple matter of individual moral failure. The moral actions of individuals are set within an immediate and larger social context.

So, *Downfall* engages us morally, eliciting strong antipathy toward Hitler and the other Nazi leaders, while inviting a more complex stance toward dramatically central but politically peripheral characters like the secretary. If there is a kinship between *Downfall* and *The Sopranos* in terms of the sort of attitude each elicits toward its central characters, that kinship is not between Soprano and Hitler, but between Soprano and the secretary, in spite of the disanalogies between them in terms of status within their social worlds. The key point, however, is that the attitude in play with regard to all three characters is a morally evaluative one, rather than a morally detached fascination. As such, our judgments of Hitler, of the secretary, and of Soprano can be more or less favorable or negative, approving or (to use Hume's term) disapprobatory.

In his discussion of Weiss's *Richard III*, Lessing explores two ways in which we might respond to figures of great monstrosity and evil. The first of these is curiosity, equivalent to the amoral fascination that I have discussed. The second might be termed "sublime terror"—a feeling of awe in the face of something or someone profoundly evil. Does such terror have any purchase on the case of Soprano? It might constitute an element of our response to him; certainly there are moments when we are amazed and appalled at his viciousness. As with fascination, however, this is problematic as a solution to the extent that it discounts the fact that we *do* feel sympathy for Soprano. The sympathy that we feel for Soprano, moreover, is the full-bloodied variety that Lessing terms "compassion" or "pity", based on our judgment that Soprano is "one of ourselves"—not the weaker sympathetic response that Lessing labels "philanthropy", which can be triggered by the contemplation of any suffering human being, irrespective of his or her moral character.[26]

As I noted earlier, *The Sopranos* is, if not exactly a modern tragedy, then certainly closer to tragic form than it is to the forms that give rise primarily to fascination, curiosity, and sublime terror, precisely in virtue of our morally informed, sympathetic stance toward Soprano.

This sort of moral evaluation lies at the heart of what I term *allegiance*. Allegiance refers to the business of assessing a character's attitudes, traits, and actions, a process that results in a more *or* less sympathetic or antipathetic attitude on our part toward a character. Allegiance in this sense is to be differentiated from *alignment*, which bears on the way a film organizes our access to a character—the degree to which it makes characters central to the action and gives us access to their states of mind. The sympathy (or lack of it) that allegiance gives rise to is also to be distinguished from empathy, in the sense that while the latter refers to a process whereby we "feel with" a character, sympathy involves feeling *for* (or *against*) a character without necessarily mimicking their states, or feeling them "from the inside".[27] The degree to which we find a character sympathetic or antipathetic is probably not *wholly* a matter of moral evaluation; we might be inclined to find a character sympathetic—likeable, attractive—because he or she is droll, or charming, or lively, or clever.[28] Yet I maintain that moral evaluation lies at the core of allegiance. It is hard to think of cases in which a film elicits strong sympathy toward a character largely on the basis of amoral attributes; characters who appeal through wit or charm, for example, command our sympathetic allegiance because these amoral traits co-exist in the character with at least some morally positive traits (as in the case of Soprano). Similarly, it is hard to think of cases in which powerful antipathy is generated by amoral traits; dullness or inarticulacy are not hanging crimes. Consequently, they warrant indifference or irritation rather than outrage or hostility. Moral assessment of characters, I aver, constitutes a kind of center-of-gravity that amoral factors may inflect, but not displace.

How, then, do we stand toward Soprano in terms of allegiance? To what degree and in what ways does *The Sopranos* elicit sympathy or antipathy toward Soprano, or some admixture of the two? To what degree do amoral factors play a role in determining our degree of allegiance with him? As the previous section sought to demonstrate, while our attitude toward Soprano is an ambivalent one, in many respects he is presented sympathetically. The sources of our sympathy for him are various: we sympathize with his anxieties, his vulnerability, with his everyday frustrations. Lopsided and inadequate as it is, Soprano has a strong sense of moral duty, and that sense of responsibility (toward his immediate and extended families), along with his human weaknesses, establishes a core, morally grounded, sympathetic disposition toward him. Conjoined with this, however, is the allure of the transgressive—that very different source of appeal founded on Soprano's ability and willingness to flout social norms, including some moral ones. Recognizing this last source of our sympathy with Soprano compels us to specify more precisely what sort of ambivalence we may feel toward Soprano—to explore *how* our ambivalence toward him plays itself out. Soprano's transgressiveness will, I suggest, at different moments trigger revulsion, pleasure, or some sort of hesitation between or mixture of the two.

Consider the scene with which we began, in which Soprano assaults his driver, without any justification—not even in the terms of Mafia morality. As I've suggested, this is surely one of those instances in which any positive allegiance we have with Soprano is put under pressure. Yet there is a dimension of the action here that is intimately connected with the sympathy that we do have for Soprano. Recall that after the assault, Soprano collapses in the bathroom, vomiting blood. Cleaning himself up, he smiles at himself in the mirror with what seems like demonic self-satisfaction. Then, however, he is thrown into a further bout of vomiting. In short, Soprano's aggression is bound up with his vulnerability, and that, as we have seen, is an important factor in the underlying allegiance the show forges between Soprano and the spectator. Episodes of this sort, which conjoin elements that draw our sympathy with other elements that are apt to repel us, best demonstrate that our allegiance with Soprano is, in the most exact sense of the word, ambivalent.

It is also worth considering in more detail, in this context, Soprano's murder of his nephew Christopher. Soprano's relationship with Christopher is established from the very first episode of the series as a crucial one. Even as he raises his own children at arm's length from the world of the Mafia, he treats Christopher as a son apprenticing in the family trade. A troublesome and sometimes wayward son, to be sure, but in one whom Soprano invests great affection, trust, and hope. By Season 3, Christopher is a made man. In the penultimate episode of the entire series, Soprano and Christopher are involved in a serious car accident. Christopher is at the wheel, high on drugs, as they drive along a remote country road at night. Drifting and weaving, he is forced to swerve abruptly to avoid an oncoming vehicle. The car flips and rolls numerous times; Christopher is badly injured. He tells Soprano to call a cab rather than an ambulance. Soprano starts to make the call, but he hesitates. Instead of following through on the call, he asphyxiates an already ailing Christopher by holding his nose.

This is a dreadful action. Far from helping a man who has been, at times, as close as anyone to him, who occupies a privileged position as a member of both Soprano's literal family and his symbolic family, and who is in a state of extreme vulnerability, Soprano exploits the occasion to kill Christopher with impunity (since he knows that his death will appear to have been caused by the accident). What are Soprano's motivations? Personal resentments are part of the picture: Christopher has recently had an affair with a woman whom Soprano tried but failed to seduce. Christopher himself has been anxious about this, knowing that it violates a norm of the sexual morality of the tribe, potentially diminishing Soprano's status as the dominant male of the group. Soprano's motivations go well beyond this, however. In Soprano's eyes, Christopher has become a liability. The accident provides evidence that Christopher still has not kicked his longstanding drug habit. In the aftermath of the accident, as Soprano contemplates what to do, he glances twice at the child seat in the rear of the car. Exactly what Soprano is thinking is not clear, but the shots play up the fact that Christopher has recently become a father (and, in a later conversation, Soprano draws attention to Christopher's irresponsibility as a father). When not in the throes of drug-induced intoxication, Christopher is often in a state of angry alienation from Soprano, resentful of what he sees as a lack of recognition by Soprano for his gang-related efforts. Soprano sees evidence of this resentment in Christopher's recently completed film, *Cleaver*, a gangster-horror flick in which a godfather figure rules his gang with violent authority.

So how are we likely to respond to Soprano's action? On the one hand, we are appalled. Of all the murders we have seen Soprano undertake or authorize, this may be the blackest, precisely because of the deep personal bond between the two men. Yet, we recognize that Soprano is not acting merely out of self-interest. He believes that Christopher has become a danger to the entire gang and to all those it supports. We have been here before, with the murders of Pussy Bonpensiero, Christopher's girlfriend Adriana, and Soprano's cousin Tony Blundetto. In the immediately preceding episode, we have seen Soprano come close to murdering Paulie for similar reasons (Paulie is prone to reckless mouthing-off about his Mafia exploits and connections). My point is not that Soprano's "moral" motivation redeems the action, making it somehow attractive. I believe, though, that it does attenuate our judgment of the action because we recognize that Soprano acts out of what he conceives of as a moral motivation; we do not judge the murder as one borne of pure malice. Our allegiance with Soprano might thus best be characterized as *partial* allegiance: we ally ourselves with some of his actions and attitudes and not others; indeed, some of his actions and attitudes draw our antipathy rather than sympathy. Our sympathy for Soprano is "not unconditional".[29] Moreover, to compound matters, a single action may draw out distinct and contrasting responses from us.[30]

There is at least one other possibility, however. It might be argued that our stance toward Soprano constitutes a kind of *perverse allegiance*, in which we find him sympathetic *because* of his wrongdoing, in contrast to the ambivalent, partial allegiance I have just described, in which different actions, and different facets of particular actions, elicit approbatory and disapprobatory responses from us (sometimes simultaneously).[31] For obvious reasons, the idea of perverse allegiance with a figure like Soprano is attractive to theorists who are inclined to stress the transgressive allure of the gangster figure. For such a theorist, the gangster figure allows us to play out in the imagination socially and morally proscribed actions. As I acknowledge above, this is certainly an important part of Soprano's appeal. The idea that *The Sopranos* does *no more than* feed transgressive fantasies is unconvincing, however. Rather, the structure of the show is one that continually plays off the transgressive appeal of Soprano against both his immorality and his ordinariness. That is, his transgressive behavior is sometimes alluring and sometimes repellent, and he is by turns extraordinary—larger than life—and remarkably ordinary.

Put in structuralist terms, much of the complexity of Soprano as a character arises from the complex variation and intersection of the two axes, "moral—immoral" and "ordinary—extraordinary". Whatever charisma Soprano possesses is offset, qualified, and diminished by his cruelty, egoism, and dishonesty, as well as his over-weight frame, heavy breathing, and frequent ill temper. The sublime "greatness" of Hume's generals and the potency of the classic gangster figure are still evident in Soprano, but they are distressed and debased. The problem, then, with the idea of perverse allegiance is that it does scant justice to the complexity of our re-sponses to Soprano and *The Sopranos*.

We have canvassed a variety of responses to the first, descriptive question (or cluster of questions) I posed at the outset: what is the nature of our interest in So-prano? Do we really sympathize with him, in whole or in part, and for what reasons? If we do sympathize with him, how is it that we can care for such a "rough hero"? I have argued that our relationship to Soprano is characterized by partial allegiance. The alternative responses to these questions that we have considered include the idea that we sympathize with Soprano mostly or wholly on the basis of his trans-gressive, immoral actions and attitudes; that *The Sopranos* is a harmless slice of ge-neric entertainment that does not truly engage us on a moral level; and that our interest in Soprano as a character takes the form of amoral fascination rather than morally-informed sympathy. We can add here one more perspective. One might hold that the show principally elicits an *antipathy* toward Soprano; that it functions as an unambiguous moral fable detailing the corrosive effects of the Mafia lifestyle (much as the antipathy that *Downfall* generates toward Hitler and other committed Nazis plays a crucial role in the film's critical depiction of Nazism). What we see is emphatically *not* the good life, and this must be obvious to any sensitive viewer. This position, then, forms the mirror image of the argument concerning perverse alle-giance. To hold that we are perversely allied with Soprano is to hold that we sympa-thize with him *because of*, and not *in spite of*, his immorality; according to this final position, this same immorality ensures wholesale antipathy rather than sympathy.

This last position, however, is no more persuasive than any of the other alter-natives to partial allegiance that we have examined. None of them captures the complex, multilayered, perhaps even downright messy nature of our moral and emotional responses to Soprano and *The Sopranos*. Rather, the show fosters toward its protagonist that partial, ambivalent, and fluctuating sympathy that I have tried to describe and analyze here. What of the second, overtly moral question that we put on the table at the beginning: what are the moral implications of the fact we do sympathize with Soprano in the manner I describe? Or, as Noël Carroll puts it, "Is it morally permissible for the creators of *The Sopranos* to produce a fiction that elicits our alliance with a creature like Tony? Is it not simply immoral to do this?" Carroll argues that because "our pro-attitude toward Tony is highly circum-scribed," the moral anxiety is not really a "serious" one; indeed the show is "mor-ally salutary".[32] While I agree with Carroll that the import of the show is ultimately a morally as well as an aesthetically positive one, unlike Carroll I think that the sheer complexity of our stance toward Soprano makes the moral question a live one. Fuller consideration of that question, however, will have to wait for another day.[33]

NOTES

1. The incident takes place at the conclusion of Season 6, Episode 5, "Mr. and Mrs. John Sacrimoni Request . . ."

2. David Stubbs, on the Season 2 DVD, http://www.amazon.co.uk.

3. The phrase "problem of personality" comes from Gregory Currie, "The Paradox of Caring." Currie describes the "problem of personality" in the following terms: "We frequently like and take the part of people in fiction whom we would not like or take the part of in real life . . . Why the disparity?" (65) The problem of personality is a particularly pressing problem for those of us committed to a mimetic account of character—that is, to the principle that characters are fictional analogues of real persons, and that characters are thus both created and understood on the basis of the same psychological skills and assumptions that we depend on in our interaction with real persons. Since this mimetic principle clearly includes the moral dimension, the question arises as to why our moral judgments and dispositions do not appear to carry over in their entirety to fictional characters—in other words, we find ourselves facing the problem of personality. A nonmimetic approach to character might, from this point of view, seem like a solution worth pursuing; but I do not think it is a live option, for reasons set out in my *Engaging Characters*, especially in Chapter 1.

4. Hume, "Of the Standard of Taste," 282.

5. The current debate was initiated by Kendall Walton, "Morals in Fiction and Fictional Morality"; Walton cites the passage in Hume's essay. Subsequent essays on "imaginative resistance" include Michael Tanner's initial response, "Morals in Fiction and Fictional Morality—A Response"; and Tamar Szabo Gendler, "The Puzzle of Imaginative Resistance."

6. Pornography might appear to be an odd omission here. While widespread, pornography takes the form of a parallel cultural practice, in practice widely tolerated and regulated even as it is legally proscribed. By contrast, horror and gangster fictions and murder ballads all occupy highly visible places in mainstream culture—the middle shelves of culture, so to speak, as opposed to the top shelf and the space under the counter, where pornography resides.

7. For an overview, see Berys Gaut, "Art and Ethics."

8. Susan Sontag, "Jack Smith's *Flaming Creatures*," 234; Pedro Almodóvar, quoted in George Wilson, "Rapport, Rupture, and Rape: Reflections on *Talk to Her*" in Anne Wescott Eaton (ed.), *Talk to Her*, 68, note 12; see also Wilson's commentary on the quote, 65. In an earlier essay on related matters, I invoked Sontag's claim about *Flaming Creatures* in order to question the idea that that film, and other works in the "decadent" tradition, really does seek to exist outside "moral space". There, I argued that a certain class of such works adopts an apparently amoral stance as an indirect form of moral intervention. "Apparently amoral, [such works] are in reality assaults on moralism, on the intolerance of Puritanical moral doctrines and precepts," Murray Smith,

"Gangsters, Cannibals, Aesthetes; or, Apparently Perverse Allegiances," 231. I am not seeking now to revise this argument, but rather to argue in addition that narrative works may engage with moral questions in a variety of ways, and that there may indeed be a class of works that, in effect, sidestep morality—albeit a very different class from the one that Sontag had in mind.

9. Tunku Varadarajan, "Generation Hex", 3.

10. I am thus half in agreement with Gaut, who expresses a similar skepticism about the idea that art is "a kind of pleasant and harmless pastime" (Gaut, "Art and Ethics," 341). In my view, Gaut is right about what I am simply calling "dramatic narrative"—narrative in the morally serious mode—but he fails to acknowledge or accommodate the fact that there are a variety of such modes.

11. "The gangster's whole life is an effort to assert himself as an individual, to draw himself out of the crowd, and he always dies *because* he is an individual; the final bullet thrusts him back, makes him, after all, a failure." Warshow, "The Gangster as Tragic Hero," 103.

12. Lessing, *Hamburg Dramaturgy*, 176, 194, 175.

13. Angie is the widow of Pussy Bonpensiero, a former colleague of Soprano's secretly "whacked" by Soprano at the climax of Season 1 for acting as an FBI informant. The "official" Mafia line is that Pussy was put into hiding by the FBI when it became known by his Mafia brothers that he was "ratting" on them.

14. Note that the action concerning Soprano and Kennedy takes place much earlier (Season 3) than the shooting of Soprano by Junior (Season 6). In the very first season of the show, Junior plots to have Soprano assassinated in the wake of the death of Jackie Aprile (Michael Rispoli), whose demise leaves Soprano and Junior vying for leadership of the northern New Jersey Mafia.

15. In *The Genealogy of Morals*, Nietzsche invents a similar dramatic exchange, between lambs and birds of prey, in order to argue against the idea of free moral agency—and thus against morality as traditionally conceived: "There is nothing very odd about a lamb's disliking birds of prey, but this is no reason for holding it against large birds of prey that they carry off lambs." Nietzsche, *The Birth of Tragedy* and *The Genealogy of Morals*, 178.

16. Warshow, "The Gangster as Tragic Hero," 107.

17. Noël Carroll, "Sympathy for the Devil," 132. See also the discussion of similar cases in Smith, "Gangsters, Cannibals, Aesthetes; or, Apparently Perverse Allegiances," 223.

18. Susan Wolf, "Moral Saints", 423.

19. David Hume, "Of greatness of mind," 316.

20. Ibid., 317.

21. The effect of the sublime character upon us works, according to Hume, through the mechanism of "sympathy", i.e., our tendency to "take on" in some measure the mental states of those with whom we engage. In contemporary terms, what Hume describes is much closer to the notion of *empathy*, especially as it is conceived by simulation theorists. For discussion of empathy in relation to narrative artworks, see Currie, "The Paradox of Caring;' Smith, *Engaging Characters*; and Smith, 'Imagining from the Inside." For a broader discussion, see Alvin Goldman, *Simulating Minds*.

22. Michael Wood, "At the Movies: *The Departed* directed by Martin Scorsese," 20; Warshow, "The Gangster as Tragic Hero," 102. Similarly, in "Movie Chronicle: The Westerner," Warshow remarks that the gangster movie is at root "anti-social, resting on fantasies of irresponsible freedom" (122).

23. Wolf, "Moral Saints".

24. Smith, "Gangsters, Cannibals, Aesthetes," 233–236.

25. Michael Tanner suggests that we may adopt something like this attitude to works either historically or culturally very remote: " . . . the more distant the culture represented, the less likely we are to read about it in any other than an anthropological spirit. Given the general view of life, and the circumstances in which it is endured, of, say, the *Saga of the Volsungs*, our reactions to the behavior of the characters in it are certainly not those that we would experience to approximately similar behavior on the part of people who inhabit 'the real world'" (Tanner, "Morals in Fiction and Fictional Morality—A Response," 368). In the present context, the point is that *The Sopranos* does not fall into this category, in which extreme remoteness has the effect of attenuating or even extinguishing a morally informed engagement with the work.

26. See Lessing, *Hamburg Dramaturgy*, 184-6.

27. See Smith, *Engaging Characters*, for discussion and elaboration of each of these concepts.

28. On this point, see Ward Jones, "Transgressive Comedy and Partiality," this volume, Chapter 4.

29. Carroll, "Sympathy for the Devil," 134. In a similar spirit, Jones notes that caring about someone, and wanting things to go well for them, is "consistent with recognizing the limitations of her capabilities." Jones, "Transgressive Comedy and Partiality," this volume, Chapter 4, 77.

30. I introduce the notion of "partial allegiance" in "Imagining from the Inside."

31. I propose and discuss the concept of "perverse" allegiance in "Gangsters, Cannibals, Aesthetes," 221ff.

32. Carroll, "Sympathy for the Devil," 134.

33. My thanks to audiences at the University of Kent, the symposium on "characters in fictional worlds" in Bielefeld, 2007, and the editors of the current volume, for helpful feedback. Special thanks to Katja Mellmann for pointing me in the direction of Lessing's *Hamburg Dramaturgy*.

4

TRANSGRESSIVE COMEDY AND PARTIALITY

MAKING SENSE OF OUR AMUSEMENT AT *HIS GIRL FRIDAY*

WARD E. JONES

ONE OF THE MORE COMMON experiences of the film viewer is that of finding something on the screen funny or humorous. This occurs not only within the genre of comedy—even a viewer who assiduously avoids comedies will find herself amused at certain places in the films she watches. One would find it next to impossible to avoid all films that include scenes intended to bring about some form of amusement.

Some of this amusement will be in response to what I will call *transgressive actions*—that is, the kind of events that would, in many other, easily imaginable instances, appropriately bring about very different kinds of responses. In humor at the transgressive, we find ourselves laughing at acts of violence, abuse, or cruelty—at the kinds of occurrences that (as we well realize in calm reflection) are more likely to generate—and that are, perhaps, more deserving of—anger or indignation at the perpetrators, sympathy or sadness for the victims. This phenomenon is *prima facie* perplexing, since our default response to wrongdoing does not (nor should it) include amusement. The present paper explores one kind of transgressive comedy—that which invites viewers to laugh with a perpetrator of wrongdoing. While there has been considerable discussion of when, if ever, amusement *itself* is immoral, there has been little discussion dedicated to understanding how and why there is apparently acceptable laughter *at the prima facie immoral*.[1]

I will not be attempting to explain all examples of humor at the transgressive. Indeed, much of the present paper will be concerned with laying out some of the complex terrain at the junction of humor and ethics, much of it terrain that I do not even begin to attempt to understand. My positive claim, developed in Sections 4–6, will be that our favoritism toward certain persons or characters plays a role in some examples of humor at wrongdoing; in particular, I will suggest that it plays a central role in our amusement at the events in the 1940 Howard Hawks film *His Girl Friday*.

I. WHAT WE FIND AMUSING: THE INCONGRUOUS

At the heart of humor and comedy is a familiar state of mind that I will throughout this paper refer to as "amusement", a state of mind characteristically (but not always) manifested in the external behavior of laughing, giggling, and smiling. Amusement is an intentional state, both dependent upon and intertwined with an agent's beliefs or imaginings; it is always a response to and about something—one always finds *something* amusing. What is this "something?' In writings on humor, the only real contenders for the intentional object of amusement all more or less fall within the broad family of the *unexpected*, the *inappropriate*, or most generally, the *incongruous*.

The claim that the incongruous is what we find funny can be traced back to Aristotle, but the position was not given a significant airing until Francis Hutcheson's brief *Reflections on Laughter* in 1750.[2] A recent defender of the incongruity thesis, John Morreall, writes:

> The basic idea behind the incongruity theory is very general and quite simple. We live in an orderly world, where we have come to expect certain patterns among things, their properties, events, etc. We laugh when we experience something that doesn't fit into these patterns.[3]

I will refer to this claim as the "Incongruity Thesis":

> *Incongruity Thesis*: the intentional content of S's amusement is to be found in S's believing or imagining that an incongruous state of affairs obtains.

The claim that incongruity is the object of all humor has its critics, and there is a great deal of work that still needs to be done in making more precise both the notion of incongruity involved in humor and the kinds of incongruity that give rise to humor (as opposed to those that do not).[4] There is, however, no shortage of support for the thought that humor is a response to, at, and about incongruities or something closely related to them.

The Incongruity Thesis predicts that any instance of humor involves a violation of expectations or norms. This prediction seems remarkably well borne out: some kind of incongruity characterizes the vast majority of what we find amusing. From childish laughter at physical differences and deformities, to laughter at embarrassments, to sophisticated puns and wordplay, the object of amusement involves something like a juxtaposition that one does not anticipate or a norm that is violated. In embarrassing situations, amusement usually arises in the face of an incongruity between, on the one hand, the embarrassed person's expectations of herself, and, on the other hand, what happens to her. In riddles and jokes, we get an incongruity between the question and the answer, or the joke and its punch line. This is strikingly revealed in what are sometimes called "meta-jokes:" "What are the last three hairs on a dog's tail called? Dog hairs."[5] A meta-joke relies on the incongruity between the norms governing answers to riddle questions (namely, that they be unexpected or incongruous) and the answer we get in a meta-joke riddle (namely, one that is straight). Meta-jokes violate the expectations of jokes themselves, which explains why they are most popular among young children who have recently learned the expectations and norms involved in joking.

If humor involves a violation of expectations or norms, then understanding what is humorous in an instance of comedy will require identifying the expectations or norms that it violates. Such situations can be extremely complex, especially in film. An early scene in *His Girl Friday* involves Walter Burns marching out to meet Hildy Johnson's new fiancé, Bruce Baldwin. Walter marches straight to an elderly man sitting in the lobby and enthusiastically introduces himself. A spectator viewing this scene in isolation from the rest of the film would take this is to be a case of mistaken identity, something that can be funny when and because it results in inappropriate behavior from the person making the mistake and elicits confusion or surprise from the person who is taken for someone else. Those of us who have watched *His Girl Friday* from the beginning, however, quickly catch on that this is not a case of mistaken identity. Rather, Walter is *pretending* to be committing a case of mistaken identity, a fact that makes the situation, and its humor, far more complex than it would otherwise have been were it a simple case of mistaken identity. Why is pretending to mistake someone's identity funny? Part of what is going on is that Walter is violating the norms of introduction; he is not following the norms that govern our behavior when we meet a friend of a friend. More than this, however, we can see that Walter is putting on a private show; he is intentionally acting *for Hildy*, a pretense that is both hidden from Bruce and at Bruce's expense. In short, where Bruce (humorlessly) sees a straightforward case of mistaken identity, in reality we see a *practical joke* being played on Bruce. Thus, another incongruity lies in the disparity between Bruce's view and ours; it is Bruce who is mistaken about what is going on, not Walter. While brief, this rich scene is riddled with incongruities.

Revealing the incongruities in comedic situations is not the only way in which we can defend the Incongruity Thesis. Supporters of the claim have used it to explain a number of features of humor, such as why humor is unique to human beings, why what is found funny varies from person to person and culture to culture, and how comedy can be seen as a catalyst of social or attitudinal change.[6] The Incongruity Thesis is also revealed in the dialectical phenomena that surround amusement. Like all mental states, amusement is susceptible to challenge and disagreement.[7] When someone finds a performance funny that I do not, I might explain to her that I found the performance "obvious", "predictable", "old", or "monotonous". Each of these responses fits nicely with the thought that what we find funny is the unexpected or incongruous.

The claim that incongruities are the intentional object of amusement—that incongruities are *what* we find amusing—has a good deal going for it. There are, however, many questions that it leaves unanswered. As we clearly do not find *all* incongruities amusing—some incongruities frighten us, some of them make us curious[8]—we still need to know which incongruities are amusing. Relatedly, the claim that it is incongruities that we find amusing does not tell us what role amusement is playing in our behavioral economy: what is this mental response to an incongruity doing *for us*? We need to know what is accomplished when we find something funny, what function it serves. We need to know, in short, why we find incongruities amusing. What follows touches on this broad question, by way of focusing on a small but puzzling subset of the incongruities that we find amusing.

II. HUMOR AT THE TRANSGRESSIVE

One subset of incongruous events comprises transgressive events, events that appear to cross ethical boundaries; one kind of incongruous event will be, in other words, the *ostensibly wrong* or the *ostensibly bad*. Accordingly, if what we find amusing is the incongruous, then we might expect that a subset of what we find amusing is the transgressive. That is, we might expect there to be a great deal of humor that is at or about the transgressive, in which we see or are invited to see as amusing something that would more typically—and in most situations more appropriately—invite an emotion like indignation, anger, pity, or sympathy.

This expectation is clearly borne out. A great deal of successful humor concerns transgressive actions. There are jokes about the transgressive, like the following:

The Secret Service has an opening in its ranks, needing to recruit someone to join those who guard the President of the United States. They post a notice in bulletins for government workers, and soon they receive three applications: one from an FBI man; one from an agent from the Bureau of Alcohol, Tobacco, and Firearms; and a third from a Chicago city policeman. Each is given a qualifying exam, beginning with the FBI man.

The FBI man is given a revolver and told to go into the adjacent room and shoot whomever he finds there. When he has been gone only a few seconds, the FBI man returns, saying, "You must be out of your minds! That's my wife. I'm not shooting her."

"Fine", say the examiners. "You must be a good family man, but you are not cut out for the Secret Service."

Next, the ATF agent is sent in with the revolver, with the same instructions, to shoot whomever he finds in the next room. He, too, returns in minutes, exclaiming, "That's the mother of my children, you lunatics!"

"Good for you," say the examiners. "Enjoy your family and your career in the bureau; we can't use you in the Secret Service."

Finally, the Chicago policeman is given the same test. When he has been in the adjacent room for a few seconds, shots are heard, then sounds of struggle and muffled groaning. Afterwards, the cop reappears, looking somewhat mussed, and says, "Some moron put blanks in the gun; I had to strangle her."[9]

This is (in my experience) a fairly successful joke, but it is also clearly about a transgressive event. The punch line—that which triggers our amusement—involves a man having just strangled his wife in order to get a job.

Moving from jokes to performance comedy, we might first think of clowns and their antics. One of the standard fares of clowns is abuse: they push each other over, hit each other with large hammers, and even shoot each other out of cannons. Clown behavior found its way into early television with the very successful and long-running American ensemble *The Three Stooges*, whose humor largely depended upon the various ways in which the members of the ensemble physically abused each other. Humorous but abusive actions can, of course, be far more sophisticated and interesting than those we find at the circus and in *The Three Stooges*, as is revealed (among other places) in the institution of practical jokes. Setting out to perform a practical joke on someone involves thinking up a more or less clever way of doing something that will cause her inconvenience, fear, shock, or embarrassment. Practical jokes are a kind of performance in which one abuses an acquaintance in some way.

From early in cinematic history, films have taken humor about the transgressive to extremes. As early as 1925, we get cannibalism: Charlie Chaplin's *The Gold Rush* involves a scene in which a starving man, hallucinating that the Little Tramp is a chicken, tries to kill and eat him. More recently, the 1981 comedy *Eating Raoul* centers around a couple luring, robbing, and murdering men, one of whom they eat at the end of the film, and the 1989 comedy *Parents* involves a young boy discovering that his otherwise straight-laced suburban parents are cannibals. In the 1940s, we get mass murder: *Arsenic and Old Lace* (1944) is about a man discovering that his elderly aunts have poisoned twelve men, and Ealing Studios' *Kind Hearts and Coronets* (1949) is about a man who kills six people in order to ascend to a minor dukedom. What about mutilation and torture? No problem, try the black knight scene in *Monty Python and the Holy Grail* (1975), or the musical sequence set during the Inquisition in Mel Brooks' *History of the World Part 1* (1981). As one looks through the history of film, one comes to suspect that few kinds of transgressions have been left untouched as sources of humor.

Compared to these films, *His Girl Friday* looks somewhat tame on the scale of transgressive seriousness. Nonetheless, there must be no doubt that it does include transgressive actions. Walter arranges to have Bruce put in jail three times in the film, and he has Bruce's mother kidnapped. All of these Walter does merely in order to get Hildy back. Even if Bruce or his mother are never *physically* hurt, they have clearly been wronged; their respective freedoms have been taken away, and in each case, they deserve nothing of the sort. In framing Bruce and kidnapping his mother, Walter has wronged them in ways that can in no way be said to be justified by either his aims in doing it or the consequences that result from it. While *His Girl Friday* should perhaps not be categorized as a "dark" or "black" comedy, it should be uncontroversial that it prominently includes humor about transgressions.

It is important to see that humor *about* transgressive actions is not the only kind of what we might call "transgressive humor". Some instances of humor are not *about* transgressions at all. Take the following joke: One good thing about

Alzheimer's disease is that if you get it you can hide your own Easter eggs.[10] This joke, playing as it does on the symptoms of a tragic and fatal disease, is not about any transgressive action or wrongdoing. Rather, it seems as if the joke *itself* is transgressive. To invite an audience to find amusement in a disease that brings about the kind of suffering that Alzheimer's disease does, is to transgress; widespread and fatal diseases are not the sort of thing that one usually laughs about. This kind of comedy—in which we are invited to laugh at the wretched or the unfortunate—has very old roots, going back (at least) to the Elizabethan genre of tragicomedy. It is heavily present in early comedic films, in the bumbling, underachieving, and pitiable characters created by Charlie Chaplin and Buster Keaton.[11] *His Girl Friday* has elements of tragicomedy as well; the plot revolves around the press coverage of a gentle, quirky, amiable man who has been convicted of murder, and who is waiting to be hanged the following day. Nonetheless, while these aspects of the film have a transgressive aspect to them, they do not involve an invitation to laugh at transgressions *themselves*. It is the latter category—humor *at* wrongdoings—with which I am concerned here.

While it is clear that there is humor involving the transgressive, it is important to recognize that the transgressive events here are not *incidental* to our amusement. In all of these cases, the very *transgressiveness* of the events involved is something that we are laughing at. The joke about the Chicago cop would either not be funny, or it would be a very different joke, were it to not involve the transgression of its punch line. This is equally true of practical jokes; what, if anything, is funny about a practical joke is precisely that it involves the abuse of the joke's butt. It is also true of the films that involve humor about the transgressive. What is so funny about the premise of *Parents* is precisely the incongruous spectacle of a suburban, prim couple with a penchant for human flesh. Part of what is funny about *His Girl Friday* is that Walter chooses the means he does—that of framing Bruce and kidnapping his mother—in attempting to gain his ends. The wrong of these events is not incidental to the humor at hand; on the contrary, the wrong is essential to their being funny at all. We would not be laughing if Walter had spent the film pleading with Hildy to come back, just as the joke about Alzheimer's disease would not be funny if it were about amnesia. This fact must be accommodated by any attempt at explaining amusement at the transgressive. A satisfactory account of humor at transgressions must accommodate the fact that a viewer who finds *His Girl Friday* humorous does not think that putting an innocent person in jail in order to get your ex-wife back is morally acceptable. The incongruity, and humor, depends upon the transgressiveness of the actions involved, and any acceptable explanation of humor at transgressions must respect that fact.

It should be clear by now that amusement at transgressions is not an unusual phenomenon; on the contrary, one would suspect that humor at transgressive actions will be found wherever comedy and amusement exist. Nor, I think, should it lead us to disparage ourselves, modern society, or the film industry. While I will not argue this point here, I see no reason to believe that *His Girl Friday*, and all other comedic films involving transgressions, are themselves wrong or offensive. This is not to say that there are no offensive films or jokes involving the transgressive. The thought that they are offensive *simply* in virtue of their involving transgressions, however, seems implausible. The philosophical interest in humor at the transgressive derives not from its being wrong, but, on the contrary, from its being both possible *and* permissible. How is it that a great deal of successful and unobjectionable comedy invites us to laugh at *what we know to be* wrongdoings?

There are two questions here: (1) What is going on when we find wrongdoings humorous? (2) Why is our doing so not itself wrong? My concern in this paper is with the first question, and I will leave the second question for future work.

III. FACT, FICTION, AND POINT OF VIEW

Many of the examples in the previous section concerned our laughter at *fictional* transgressions, and, accordingly, one might be tempted into concluding that the phenomenon of humor about the transgressive is heavily dependent upon the fact that the events about which we are laughing are not real. Humor at the transgressive, goes this thought, occurs when and because the transgressive actions did not actually happen. While I do not want to deny that knowing that a transgression has or has not really occurred can have *some effect* upon one's amusement, this can at best be only part of the story in any one case. A wrongdoing's being fictional is neither necessary nor sufficient for our finding it humorous.

That a portrayed wrongdoing is fictional is clearly not sufficient for its being humorous, as some fictions about transgressions are not funny, even when they are attempting to be. On the contrary, in some cases humor at transgressions seems to become stronger when we know that the depicted events *are* true. Both "hidden camera" comedy and the interview-comedy of Sasha Baron Cohen, for example, rely on verity for their amusement. Both of these comedic techniques are related to practical jokes, and in this regard it is revealing that in many cases one will find a *realized* practical joke funnier than an imagined one. The imagined practical joke often will not be as funny as one that has actually been executed, for at least part of what is so funny about a practical joke is its having been carried out. This is likely to be true even if one did not observe the prank first hand, but was merely told about it: "Did that really happen?," we might ask, laughing even harder when we are assured that it did.

This is, of course, not true of most fictional portrayals. Films that include transgressive events do not, in contrast to practical jokes, generally get funnier if the transgressions being portrayed are true. In many cases, however, it is not clear that knowing whether or not a wrongdoing really occurred will affect the extent to which we find a narrative funny. If, for example, *His Girl Friday* began with a title card that told us that the events that happened in the film were true, would that detract from our amusement at the film? I find it implausible to think that it would. Such a title card does appear at the beginning of Joel and Ethan Coen's comic thriller *Fargo*. This title card is false—the film does not depict true events—but it is not clear that it matters either way to the amusement that the transgressions in the film generate.[12]

The effect of our knowing that the transgressive events in a narrative really did occur should not be understated. If we approached, say, *Kind Hearts and Coronets* believing that it was made about a real serial killer, then we might not find the film as funny as we do. In fact, we might find it inappropriate and offensive that the filmmakers were inviting us to laugh at a lighthearted presentation of real serial murder. It is not obvious, however, that it could not be carried off, that a portrayal of a series of murders that really occurred could be very funny indeed. Although they do not involve transgressive actions, we might compare the so-called Darwin Awards, which describe real people who have hurt themselves, and even lost their own lives in some spectacular fashion due to their own mistakes. The Darwin Awards invite us to laugh at these unfortunate individuals by placing them in the context of natural selection; in accidentally killing themselves, they are "chlorinating the gene pool."[13]

What this final consideration suggests is, I think, something quite deep about humor: finding something amusing is most centrally dependent upon the portrayal of the event, upon the way the narrative is laid out or contextualized. Whether or not it did or did not occur, our amusement at an event is dependent upon the *point of view* that we have or are given of the event. This should not be surprising, given the content of humor. Something will appear incongruous to me only from a certain point of view; had the same thing been approached from another direction or within another framework, it might not have been funny. On the contrary, it may have appeared mundane, routine, sad, pitiful, unpleasant, or odious.

The point of view that leads to amusement, however, must be more than one that makes some event incongruous. The point of view from which we find a transgressive action amusing is one from which (in contrast to other points of view of the same transgression) we are somehow led to respond with not pity or anger, but with mirth. What are the components of this point of view? We have already looked at two of them: First, the transgressive comedic point of view is not one in which the wrongness is neutralized, for the very wrongness of transgressive actions—as a kind of incongruity—seems to contribute to our finding them amusing. Whatever are the elements of a portrayal of, or a point of view on, transgressive actions that invite amusement, they are not elements that *hide* their transgressiveness. Second, the transgressive comedic point of view may or may not include our being informed that the events related are fictional. In some cases, fictitiousness may contribute our to amusement in others (e.g., practical jokes) verity may do so.

What are the other components of the point of view from which we find the transgressive humorous? In the remainder of this paper, I want to explore the suggestion that in some cases our amusement at transgressive actions will be dependent upon our attitudes toward the persons or events involved in the situation before us. That some such attitudes will be relevant is easy to see; if someone close to me was murdered by her spouse, or if I have just had a run-in with the police, then I may not find the joke about the Chicago policeman who kills his wife at a job interview humorous. Similarly, if I am the person on whom a practical joke is played, or if I am very close to that person, I may not find the joke amusing. This is true even though I may recognize the incongruity in both jokes. Interpersonal attitudes are not always relevant in our amusement at transgressive actions; many of those who *do* find the Chicago policeman joke funny will have no strong feelings toward or against any of its character types. I want, however, to argue that such attitudes, in the guise of *partiality* toward the perpetrator of transgressive actions and/or our *partiality* away from its victim, play a role in some narratives involving transgressions. In particular, I will suggest that it plays an important role in our amusement at *His Girl Friday*.

IV. HUMOR AND PARTIALITY

Everyday and experimental observations together reveal that some generalization like the following is true:

> A person's being amused at something is significantly correlated with the person's partiality toward or away from certain features of the humorous situation.

In finding something amusing, I tend to be "disposed toward" the maker or performer of the joke and/or "disposed against" the butt of the joke, and the degree of one's amusement increases or decreases with the degree of these dispositions. This I will call the *Principle of Partiality in Humor*. I do not want to overstate the strength of this principle. There are exceptions, where humor and partiality cut across each other, and the social dynamics of humor are complicated well beyond what the Principle maintains.[14] The Principle says only that amusement and partiality—and their magnitudes—*generally* correspond with each other.

One prominent arena in which we can see the partiality/amusement relationship at work is that of *social grouping*. There has been a good deal of discussion, in the empirical literature on comedy, of the dynamics of humor interactions in grouping. In his review of the sociology literature on humor, for example, Gary Alan Fine writes: "Often if the members of one group laugh at the actions of another group, it serves to integrate the first group, through what Dupréel (1928) calls 'the laughter of inclusion.'"[15] And in his review of the psychology literature on humor, Antony J. Chapman writes that

> for members of one group, a joke may increase morale and consolidate them as a group while at the same time sustaining or intensifying aggression

towards outsiders. Those outsiders may be encouraged by the same joke to reciprocate hostilities. Such effects have been reviewed extensively . . . .[16]

What these studies and observations reveal is that amusement allows groups to gain and maintain their existence. Amusement, it appears, promotes cohesiveness. If amusement plays a role in grouping, however, we have reason to believe that it generates attitudes of partiality toward and against other persons. As the internal dynamics of a group are intimately related to the individual psychological attitudes of the individuals who make up that group, it would appear that humor generates personal attitudes that encourage grouping. That is, humor tends to generate the attitudes associated with partiality toward and against other persons, attitudes that contribute to the behavioral patterns of inclusion and exclusion that constitute interpersonal groups.[17]

The Principle of Partiality in Humor seems to be made true by the influence that *being amused by* and *being partial toward* have on each other, an influence that works in both directions. In one direction, being amused seems to affect one's partiality toward things in a humorous situation; in the other direction, one's partiality toward something in a humorous situation affects how funny one finds it. The effects of both relationships are observable in everyday interactions and revealed in social psychological studies.

On the one hand, my being amused either by or on your behalf can influence how I feel toward you. When I laugh at your joke, this tends to lead me to have a positive attitude toward you; when a joke successfully makes fun of Jones, this can lead me to a disparaging attitude toward Jones. While it is clear that this is a complex influence with exceptions, the existence of such a tendency is illustrated by one common use of *ridicule*. Ridiculing, or mocking, is often undertaken with the intention of bringing about the state of amusement in others for the purpose of garnering their favor or agreement. Think of schoolchildren making fun of others in order to be popular or in order to make someone else unpopular. Here, humor is being *used* in order to bring about social preferences and grouping, a use that is possible only because amusement encourages a partiality toward some people or things, and/or away from other people or things. Political cartoons and caricatures, in which a leader is ridiculed in order to get the viewer to side against her, work in the same way. This same effect of amusement can, of course, be put to less pernicious and more mundane uses: a teacher may crack jokes in order to get his students to like him, or a woman may joke in order to get her date to like her.[18] All of these cases reveal the propensity of a person who finds something funny to develop biased or partial attitudes for or against a person involved.

The reverse influence—in which my partiality affects whether, and the extent to which, I find you or something you say funny—is slightly more difficult to show. It is suggested by certain familiar patterns of amusement: happy couples eagerly laugh at each other's jokes, and groups of friends more readily laugh with each other than with strangers. Such patterns can also be explained in other ways, how-ever. Perhaps the existence of couples and groups of friends is to be partly explained by their having similar senses of humor. Or, perhaps this result stems from acquaintances *understanding* each other better—the better I understand you, the better I am going to understand your wit. While this may be the right explanation for many cases, controlled empirical studies reveal that feelings of partiality out-side of love and friendship can affect one's amusement. In one study, for example, subjects examined cartoons in which either a professor is hurling a pie in a gradu-ating student's face, or a graduating student is hurling a pie in a professor's face. Faculty members reported finding the first funnier than the second, while stu-dents found the second funnier than the first. In another experiment, the experi-menter herself was rude to certain subjects and polite to others. Subjects were then all shown the same video (subjects believed that this was a live link-up) in which the experimenter accidentally spills hot tea on herself. Subjects who were treated rudely by the experimenter found the accident funnier than those who were treated politely. These and other studies are described by a leading proponent of the Principle of Partiality in Humor, the psychologist Dolf Zillmann, who sum-marizes the findings thus: "The more intense the negative disposition toward the disparaged agent or entity, the greater the magnitude of mirth. The more intense the positive disposition toward the disparaging agent or entity, the greater the magnitude of mirth."[19]

V. HUMOR AND PARTIALITY IN *HIS GIRL FRIDAY*

So, according to the Principle of Partiality in Humor, (1) my finding something funny inclines me to side with and/or against other persons, and (2) my biased attitudes toward persons affect the extent to which I find something funny. In this section and the next, I want to bring the partiality/humor relationship described in the previous section to bear on *His Girl Friday*. I will suggest that this relation-ship is doing a great deal of work in our engagement with the film. Humor leads us to side with the devious, conniving Walter (as opposed to Bruce), and this resulting partiality allows us to laugh at what Walter does to Bruce and his mother.

There is some disagreement, among philosophers who write about fiction, as to whether we feel *proper* emotions toward fictional characters or in the face of fictional events. The pressure away from thinking of our feelings toward fictional characters as real emotions derives from the fact that we clearly do not *believe* that what we are encountering in a fiction is real, and that, consequently, our feelings do not have the consequences in action that they would otherwise have. In watch-ing a horror film, our heart rates may increase, our eyes may get wider, and we may even scream, but we have no temptation to flee or to kill the monster before us. As a response to this kind of consideration, Kendall L. Walton speaks of the horror film viewer as being in "quasi-fear".[20] Quasi-fear is similar to fear, but when I feel the former, I do not believe that something dangerous is before me. Rather, quasi-fear is the result of imagining or making believe that I am in a dangerous situation. Those who oppose Walton on this point claim that real fear need not be based on belief in the way that Walton supposes.[21]

Whether our affective responses to films are proper or *bona fide* emotions, it is clear that what we feel often amounts to something like what Murray Smith describes as "allegiance" with some characters and against others: as we watch films, and follow their characters, we feel differently toward them. Put very crudely, we like some and dislike others; we approve of some and disapprove of others. In this way, our feelings involve an *appraisal* or an *evaluation* of the characters we follow. This is allegiance, "the moral evaluation of characters by the spectator." Smith writes:

> Evaluation, in this sense, has both cognitive and affective dimensions; for example, being angry or outraged at an action involves categorizing it as undesirable or harmful to someone or something, and being affected— affectively aroused—by this categorization. On the basis of such evaluations, spectators construct moral structures, in which characters are organized and ranked in a system of preference.[22]

Whether the anger that Smith describes is, in the cinema, *bona fide* anger or quasi-anger, it is clear that this feeling would bias the spectator against the character who arouses such feeling. She sees the character as a villain, as a scoundrel, as insensitive, as self-centered, as greedy . . . . a list that can go on and on. In some manner or other, the spectator is said to have *negative* feelings toward such a character. The spectator can, of course, have more *positive* attitudes toward the characters she follows on screen. She may like or be touched by a character, she may feel pity or sympathy if the character has suffered, or she may see the character as courageous or full of life.

It may be possible for the spectator to feel both positive and negative attitudes at the same time; this may happen, for example, if we are encouraged to feel pity or fondness toward a wrongdoer.[23] It may also be possible for a spectator not to develop *any* feelings toward the characters, either positive or negative; this may be because the film has no real narrative or because the narrative is so puzzling or fragmented that the viewer is not able to make enough sense of the characters' actions to feel anything toward them.[24] Nonetheless, when a film includes enough of a plot that it can be said to have character development, the viewer will begin to feel toward, and in the process make evaluations of, the film's characters. It takes very little cinematic characterization for a viewer to begin to feel partiality toward or against a character on screen.

Humor may have a distinct and deciding role in the development of a spectator's allegiance. Indeed, another way of stating the Principle of Partiality in Humor is that humor can both augment and be augmented by what Smith calls allegiance. On the one hand, our partiality toward one person is often the result of our amusement *with* him, while our partiality away from another person is often the result of our amusement *at* her. On the other hand, our partiality toward one person leads us to be more likely to laugh with him, and our partiality away from another person leads us to be more likely to laugh at her. All of these tendencies are instantiated in our engagement with *His Girl Friday*.

Our laughter *with* Walter, and *at* Bruce, does a good deal of work, early in the film, in developing our allegiance with Walter rather than with Bruce. The fact that viewers do side so readily and quickly with Walter should, upon reflection, come as some surprise. We know that Hildy is both suspicious and wary of Walter, we know that he did not treat her as she wanted to be treated, and we also know that Walter is devious, bossy, and self-centered. Bruce, on the other hand, is an upright, solid, and virtuous man who has a great deal of affection, respect, and admiration for Hildy; he clearly seeks her happiness on her own terms. Given these two characters, it is certainly not a foregone conclusion that we will side so early in the film with Walter rather than with Bruce, and we can imagine many other similar scenarios in which our allegiance would go in the opposite direction. Nonetheless, the attentive viewer of *His Girl Friday* is likely to develop a fondness for Walter, and this is in no small part due to his making her laugh. Laughter, it must be admitted, is not the only mechanism by which *His Girl Friday* has us side with Walter. We get far more time with Walter in the first part of the film, Walter is played by the eminently captivating and likeable Cary Grant, and we see a rapport and passion between Walter and Hildy that does not exist between Bruce and Hildy. All of these features of watching the film collude in our allegiance with Walter. Nonetheless, our amusement with Walter, at Bruce's expense, is surely one of these features. As we saw in Section 1 above, Walter's first meeting with Bruce is characterized by Walter's mocking him, in a ridiculing act that is utterly hidden from Bruce. This continues through the restaurant scene, as Walter continues to mock-compliment Bruce's staid clothing, personality, job, and attitudes. Once again, all of this is lost on Bruce, as he takes Walter's continual faux compliments to be genuine. *His Girl Friday* is carefully constructed—its humor included—in order to lead us to allegiance with Walter.

Subsequently in the film, and more centrally to my concerns in this paper, the humor/partiality relationship begins to work in the opposite direction. The Principle of Partiality in Humor predicts that once our allegiance to Walter is established, we are primed to continue laughing with Walter and at Bruce, supporting the former over the latter. Our allegiance with Walter in his competition with Bruce, the Principle predicts, sets us up to be disposed to laugh at Bruce (and his mother), should the latter be appropriately incongruous. As Walter begins his scheming to get Hildy back, this prediction is borne out. We continue laughing with Walter throughout the film, *even though* many of his actions have a tinge of cruelty. It is this latter feature of the film that now needs to be explained. While the Principle of Partiality in Humor explains our tending to side with Walter in our amusement, it does not, by itself, explain why we find amusing

Walter's *ostensibly cruel* treatment of Bruce and his mother—his having the former repeatedly put in jail and the latter kidnapped. In order to do so, I need to add, to what has been said so far, a proposal about the effect of partiality (and, by consequence, of amusement) upon our ethical responses to wrongdoing. This is the aim of the next section.

VI. PARTIALITY AND ETHICAL RESPONSE

The Principle of Partiality in Humor holds that amusement encourages partial attitudes toward other persons. Our partiality toward others, however, is in *prima facie* conflict with our attitudes toward their ethical shortcomings. The conflict here is a psychological one, and it arises between the attitudes involved in being partial toward—or caring about—someone and the attitudes involved in *recognizing* that the person cared for has committed a wrong. My being partial to you can lead me to be, in some ways, *more lenient* toward you with respect to what you do.

Lying behind this conflict is our tendency to endorse the goodness of those we care about—to care about someone involves seeing that they are, essentially, good, and seeing their goodness. To care about someone is, in part, to be willing to *endorse* or *vouch for* the goodness of this person. This is not to say that I will vouch for her in all, or even most, situations. Endorsing the goodness of a person is not inconsistent with seeing her as lazy, slow, untrustworthy, or unmotivated; I may not feel comfortable, say, providing a letter of reference for her latest job application or acting as her guarantor when she borrows from the local bookie. Caring for someone is consistent with recognizing the limitations of her capabilities.[25] When I care for someone, however, I vouch for her in the sense that I will have a tendency to claim that she is (at bottom) a good person, that she lives a good sort of life, that she makes (at bottom) the right sort of life decisions, and that she has (by and large) a decent character. This is not to say that we cannot disagree with those we care about, or that we cannot wish they would change bits of their lives. To care for someone, however, is to be disposed toward seeing his decisions as having a basis in his sense of what is good and right. It is to be open and sympathetic to the cared-for person's way of evaluating the world.

A consequence of this aspect of being partial toward someone is that her wrongdoing can have a distressing psychological affect on me. This is one of the dangers, one of the risks, of caring. Imagine a man who hears about an act of vandalism in another town, by and against people he knows nothing of. It would surprise us were he to feel strong emotions toward this event; indeed, a very strong reaction would lead us to question his mental health. If we now imagine that this man discovers that the vandal is his son, however, then we would not be surprised to see the father becoming deeply upset and disappointed. Caring for someone can readily escalate one's reaction to his wrongdoing.

If those who care for others are in danger of experiencing strong negative emotions, then we would expect there to be "mechanisms" by means of which those who care can avoid such strong emotions. Such mechanisms do, indeed, exist. One familiar way to avoid the pain of believing that someone one cares about has done wrong involves *deceiving* oneself into believing otherwise. The stock philosophical example, often trotted out in discussions of wishful thinking, is that of the mother who cannot believe that her son has committed the crimes of which he is accused. The plausibility of the example trades upon the general thought that there is a tension between a mother's love of her son and the belief that he has committed some heinous crime. Another familiar way of avoiding the tension between caring for someone and believing that she has done wrong is *explaining away* or *excusing* the badness of the person one cares about. There are an extraordinary number of ways in which this can be done, and we are very adept at doing so: the cared-for did not know what she was doing, she did not intend to cause harm, she was under the influence of alcohol or drugs, or she was led to do so by her friends. At their limit, such moves appeal to very distant conditions that, in spite of our not being able to clearly spell out their force, seem to us to distance the person cared for from responsibility for the action, and thus, from wrongdoing itself: she has some or other genetic make-up, she was neglected or beaten as a child, or she had no role models to give her a moral education.[26]

A third way in which someone who cares can avoid the pain of knowing the cared-for has done wrong is one, I suggest, that plays a role in our amusement at Walter's transgressions in *His Girl Friday*. One can simply *play down* the badness of what the person one is partial toward has done. In taking this response to the cared-for's wrongdoing, one does not change one's mind, in general, about what is or is not bad (although that may, in some cases, be true). Rather, one brushes it off as *not all that bad*. A tendency like this may explain how close-knit families can be deeply involved in crime; my love for you, involved as you are in immoral and criminal activities, leads me to a weaker condemnation of your activities.[27] More familiarly, perhaps, this tendency will be behind the "boys-will-be-boys" attitude that our imagined father might take to his vandalizing son. In this way, the father minimizes or (a revealing phrase in the context of this paper) *makes light of* his son's behavior. By thinking that his son's action is not really all that bad—by dismissing it with a boys-will-be-boys response—the father can avoid the more extreme reaction that he may otherwise have felt in fully recognizing the harm that his son has caused, the wrong that he has perpetrated, or the kind of person he has become.

It is important to see what the father is not doing:

1. He has not changed his commitment to a *generalization* like "One should not wantonly destroy another person's property."[28] He is not rethinking the wrong of vandalism, or adding a *ceteris paribus* clause to his belief in its general wrong; he will not now say things like, "Vandalism is wrong *except*

when my son performs it." It would be wrong to see the father's playing down his son's vandalism in terms of a change in the father's beliefs. Rather, what we have before us is a father's *emotional response* to an action he believes to be wrong having been affected by his love for his son. The father is not *aroused* by the wrongdoing before him; such an arousal would, if it were to occur, be painful, and the father is avoiding it by minimizing the wrong his of son's actions.

2. At the same time, the father should not be seen as *ignoring* the fact that his son has transgressed. The attitude "boys will be boys" only makes sense in the context of a recognition that "boys transgress". The former statement entails, and is a particular response to, the latter. Were the father wholly ignoring the iniquitous nature of what his son is doing, he would not need to make light of it. He would not need to portray it as a boyhood prank.

3. It would also be wrong to see the father as doing this consciously or voluntarily. He would no doubt bristle were we to suggest to him that he is playing down his son's crime in order to keep from facing the fact that his son is something of a hooligan. Rather, the boys-will-be-boys response is a hidden, and more or less temporary, suppression of painful moral emotions.

In sum, then, the father's caring for his son entails that he would feel shame, disappointment, or distress were he to focus on the harm his son has caused to someone else. In order to avoid this shame and disappointment, the father recognizes, but does not emotionally focus on, the harm that his son has caused; on the contrary, he sloughs off the action as a harmless boyhood prank.

There are some striking similarities between the father's treating his son's vandalism as a prank, on the one hand, and our laughter at Walter's abuse of Bruce and his mother, on the other. Both cases are significantly characterized by an agent's partiality toward a wrongdoer—that is, the father's toward his son, the spectator's toward Walter. In both cases, someone (involuntarily, unconsciously) makes light of something that she knows is, and is aware of as being, a wrongdoing. My suggestion is that the spectator's *partiality*—like that of the father— explains the *making light of*. The model is not a perfect fit. One difference is that the spectator knows that she is, and the father knows that he is not, responding to a fiction. This may make it easier for the spectator to avoid the distress that endangers her.

What, precisely, is this danger in the case of the film spectator? I have claimed that the source of the father's making light of his son's wrongdoing is his need to avoid the pain that would result from fully acknowledging that someone he cares for has done wrong. We, as viewers of *His Girl Friday*, cannot be in the same danger, for—as just mentioned—we know that our allegiance is with a fictional character. Nonetheless, there is a certain sense in which we do need to avoid recognizing, fully and emotionally, what Walter does. Imagine what we would feel were Walter to do something that we could not laugh at, something that we could not play down: imagine he pulls out a knife and stabs Bruce, or he begins viciously beating and kicking Bruce's mother. We would be shocked by such a display. Such a shock would reveal our expectations of Walter; we take him to be, essentially, a better man than this, and we would feel disturbed by such a display. We are partial toward Walter, and we would feel violated by him, distressed not just by such actions but by the fact that *he* has carried them out. Once we become partial toward Walter, there are things that we expect from him, things at stake in our relationship with him.

That which is most at stake here is the success of the narrative of *His Girl Friday*. It depends upon the spectator's continuing and unfettered partiality toward Walter. The plot, and our humor-driven interest in it,could not recover from the shock of our becoming disappointed or distressed by what Walter does. Some works of fiction, like *The Sopranos* or Vladimir Nabokov's novel *Lolita*, in which characters we are fond of do horrible things, thrive on filling the viewer with an anxiety regarding characters of whom he is fond. As a narrative driven mainly by humor, however, *His Girl Friday* requires that the spectator avoid this tension. Its success as a comedy necessitates that the spectator not feel the kind of tension that characterizes *Lolita* or *The Sopranos*, that the spectator not be slowed down or pulled away from her immersion in the narrative by such conflict. In order to be swept away by the rapid comedy of *His Girl Friday*, the spectator needs to avoid any knocks to her attitudes toward its characters. Her partiality toward Walter must not be shaken; the film would be ruined, or it would at least not be the same film, were that to occur.

It comes as a surprise to many viewers of *His Girl Friday* to realize, on reflection, that Walter has done such cruel things to Bruce in the film. This is revealing, and it well fits the account given here. The film works very well in "hiding" Walter's transgressions in our partiality toward him, so well that most of us are not "aware" that Walter is treating Bruce so badly. The words in scare quotes in the previous sentence must be understood in a particular way, for we must not deny that we know that Walter has put Bruce in jail—after all, this is one of the things we are laughing at—nor must we deny that we know that this is wrong—after all, the transgressiveness of his act is one of the things that makes it humorous. The awareness that we lack, I suggest, is a kind of emotional awareness, an *affective* acknowledgement of and response to the wrongdoings that occur in the film.[29] The film achieves this by developing, and then utilizing, our partiality toward Walter, a partiality that leads us to emotionally play down his wrongdoings.

It is important that Walter's first encounters with Bruce are harmless, that he does not abuse Bruce in any way. Nevertheless, Walter's clever *teasing* of Bruce, in the office lobby and over lunch, in a way that only Hildy and the viewer are privy to, contributes to our feeling a certain partiality toward Walter over Bruce.

This allegiance with Walter, I suggest, sets up our response to Walter's abusive treatment of Bruce later in the film; it leads us to make light of Walter's treatment of Bruce. This "making light of," in the film, takes the form of humor, but, as my example of the father of a vandal shows, it need not. We are amused that Walter *put Bruce in jail* in order to get his ex-wife back; such an extreme tactic is, to say the least, incongruous. Most important, for my explanation of humor at transgressions, our amusement at Walter's actions is itself a way of *not being disturbed by* Walter's treatment of Bruce.

In arguing that our partiality toward Walter contributes toward our humor at his transgressions, I am committed to the claim that if a viewer were not led to be partial toward Walter, the film would not be, for her, as funny as it is for others. This seems plausible. If one were not taken by Walter, if one were put off by his conniving and deviousness, then it seems that one would not find what he does to Bruce and his mother as funny as one otherwise would have. In short, if you are not partial to Walter, then I suspect the film—as a comedy—does not work for you as well as it does for those of us who are partial toward him. If, say, you find yourself partial to the kind, gentle, and respectful Bruce instead of the self-centered, arrogant, grandstanding Walter, then I predict that you are likely to find what Walter does to Bruce leading you to indignation or pity. If you are not partial toward Walter, then the humor driving *His Girl Friday* simply will not work for you.

VII. CONCLUSION

In closing, I would like to consider two responses to the position I have defended. Both point to some of the directions in which fruitful work in this area could be taken.

The picture that I have drawn of our response to transgressions in *His Girl Friday* will be applicable to other comedies involving transgressions, films like *Monsieur Verdoux* (1947), *The Ladykillers* (1955), *Eating Raoul* (1982), *The King of Comedy* (1983), *Heathers* (1989), and *Pulp Fiction* (1994). In all of these films, we are invited to feel sympathy for, and to laugh with, characters who commit transgressions. In addition, however, there is a large body of comedies involving transgressive actions in which our sympathies lie with the *victim*, and not the perpetrator; Charlie Chaplin and Buster Keaton both tended to work this way, and the more recent films *The Jerk* (1979) and *The Big Lebowski* (1998) are nice examples of films in which our sympathies lie with the victims of wrongdoing. *Prima facie*, it looks as if this is going to be a problem for my account. If, as I have argued, our partiality toward a wrongdoer can lead us to laugh at transgressions he commits, then how does our partiality toward a *victim* lead us to laugh at transgressions *done to* her?[30]

I am not convinced that this is a problem. Even if partiality toward a character does contribute toward our amusement at his victimization, this is not necessarily in conflict with the account that I have defended in this paper. As is well known, something can cause X to happen in one context, while in another it may prevent X from happening; to take a very simple case: a gust of wind may, on a calm day, cause a glass sitting on a table to fall and break; on a windy day, however, that same gust of wind may prevent that same glass from falling and breaking, because it counterbalances wind from other directions. Similarly, in different narratives, our partiality may play very different roles in our laughter at transgressions. That partiality plays a role in our amusement at *His Girl Friday* that is very different from its role in our amusement at, for example, *The Big Lebowski*, is suggested by the fact that in the first film the challenging question is, "Why do we not get angry with Walter?" while in the second film, the challenging question is, "Why do we not *pity* Lebowski?" I have argued that partiality toward Walter plays a role in allowing our laughter in the first, but it is *prima facie* plausible that our partiality toward Lebowski plays no role at all in allowing our amusement in the second. It seems more likely that our laughter at what happens to Lebowski is *in spite of* our partiality toward him. Rather than allowing for our amusement at his victimhood, it seems that our partiality for Lebowski must be overridden by some other factor in order for us to laugh at what happens to him. This "other factor" may be that we do not see Lebowski as *only* a victim; like the Little Tramp and Wile E. Coyote, we believe in Jeff Lebowski's resiliency, that he is not really being harmed by what is happening to him. There is a good deal of work to do in understanding what conditions—other than partiality—are present or absent in these and other cases of transgressive humor, but it is by no means obvious that the outcome of this work will count against my claims in this paper.

I admit that my account might be seen to suffer if someone were to find a story that unifies both kinds of amusement: that with perpetrators and that with victims. Jessica Gildea has attempted to unify both with the interesting suggestion that we tend to share the viewpoint of the character to which we are partial.[31] This seems to work well in some cases, as when Lebowski jokes while his head is being dipped in the toilet. It does not, however, work in all cases of laughter at the victimization of those we are partial to: the Little Tramp and Lebowski really do appear *scared* when the former is being chased by his hallucinating and hungry fellow prospector and the Nihilists drop a marmot in the latter's bathtub. Yet we laugh.

A second objection is to the starting point of my argument. I began with the thought that our base or default response to wrongdoing is pity, anger, or condemnation, and, accordingly, I have approached the problem of humor at transgressions by attempting to understand how such responses are *averted*. That is, I have approached humor at transgressions as something that happens when other, particular conditions push the default emotions aside. These conditions, I have claimed, include partiality toward the transgressor. Partiality introduces mechanisms for avoiding the pain of recognizing that the one to whom one is partial has wronged; these mechanisms open the door for other responses to the wrongdoing, including that of amusement at the incongruity that the transgression is. An alternative, more direct approach toward transgressive humor would deny that the default response to wrongdoing is pity, anger, or condemnation. On the contrary, humor at transgressions reveals that transgressive actions *just are* something that we take pleasure in or enjoy. In an interesting debate between Noël Carroll and Cynthia Freeland on the pleasure derived from horror, Carroll takes a position analogous to that which I have defended in this paper, while Freeland takes a more direct approach.[32] Carroll argues that fear and disgust at monsters and their deeds are "the price to pay" for the pleasure of having our curiosity satisfied by the horror film's "narrative of disclosure"; on his account, the pleasure we gain from horror is not a direct response to that which horrifies us. Freeland disagrees, suggesting that we take pleasure in the "spectacle" of violence itself. Freeland's account of the pleasure of horror depends upon a certain picture of human nature, one in which we are shown to enjoy or become thrilled at violence and suffering. A similar approach to humor at transgressions would be one in which we, quite "naturally", become amused in the face of wrongdoings. The issues here seem to me to be deep, and I have said nothing in this paper to rule out the alternative picture. While I am sympathetic to Freeland's account of our immediate and direct fascination at horror and disgust, I am less sympathetic to the analogous position regarding our humor at transgressions. Someone's shock, pity, or anger at a wrongdoing does not seem to me to be in need of an explanation in the same way that someone's amusement at a wrongdoing does. This, however, I must leave as an issue for future exploration.[33]

NOTES

Thanks to Tom Martin, Murray Smith, Pedro Tabensky, Samantha Vice, Dean Ween, an audience at Smith College, and the students who participated in my seminars on philosophy and film at Rhodes University and Bennington College.

1. Although see Gruner, *The Game of Humor*, and the comments on comedy in Smith, "Gangsters, Cannibals, Aesthetes." Carroll, "Horror and Humor," an investigation into why humor and fear so readily coincide is related in spirit to this paper.

2. Hutcheson, *Reflections Upon Laughter*. See also Schopenhauer's comments, found in *The World as Will and Representation*, at I:13.

3. Morreall, *Taking Laughter Seriously*, 15–16.

4. For a criticism of the centrality of incongruity to humor, see Scruton, "Laughter", Section 5. For useful attempts to clarify the kinds of incongruity involved in humor, see Morreall, "Enjoying Incongruity", and Feinberg, "The Absurd and the Comic."

5. Also see Ted Cohen's discussion of "shaggy dog" stories in his *Jokes*.

6. For the first two points, see Hutcheson, *Reflections Upon Laughter*, Section II. For the third point, see Morreall, *Taking Laughter Seriously*, Chapter 10.

7. See Brandom, *Making it Explicit*, Chapter 3.

8. Morreall, "Enjoying Incongruity".

9. I have taken this joke verbatim from Cohen, *Jokes*, 84–85.

10. Another joke taken verbatim from Cohen, *Jokes*, 43.

11. More recent films that could be categorized as tragicomedies: Robert Altman's *M*A*S*H* (1970), which takes place in a surgical field hospital during the Korean War, Hal Ashby's *Harold and Maude* (1971), which is about a death-obsessed teenager who falls in love with a 79-year-old woman, and Bruce Robinson's *How to Get Ahead in Advertising* (1989), which is about a man who discovers another head growing out of his neck and taking over his life.

12. Although, as Elizabeth Spelman pointed out to me, it would clearly make a difference as to whether we were watching the events themselves (as opposed to a re-enactment of them). While she is right about *Fargo*, I doubt that this is true of *His Girl Friday*.

13. The Darwin Awards are recorded and awarded online by Wendy Northcutt at http://www.darwinawards.com.

14. For an extensive discussion of the social sources and consequences of humor, see Mulkay, *On Humour*.

15. Fine, "Sociological Approaches to the Study of Humor," 173.

16. Chapman, "Humor and Laughter in Social Interaction," 149–150.

17. Neuropsychologist Robert R. Provine, *Laughter: A Scientific Investigation*, suggests that laughter, rather than humor, is the more basic grouping phenomenon. Such a position is not incompatible with the claims I depend upon here.

18. For a discussion of literature on what he calls "humour in a sexual marketplace," see Mulkay, *On Humour*, 84–90.

19. Zillmann, "Disparagement Humor", 91–92. See also Martineau, "A Model of the Social Functions of Humor."

20. Walton, "Fearing Fictions", Section II.

21. See, e.g., Lamarque, "How Can We Fear and Pity Fictions?"

22. Smith, *Engaging Characters*, 84.

23. Viewers of, say, *A Bout de Souffle* (or, *Breathless*) (1959), *Dead Man Walking* (1995), or the U.S. television series *The Sopranos* may find themselves feeling this way. See Murray Smith's contribution to this volume.

24. See, e.g., *Last Year at Marienbad* (1961).

25. Although it is perhaps worth noting here that social psychology experiments show that lovers vouch for their beloveds in many ways. Hall and Taylor, in "When Love is Blind," for example, find that people who observe their spouses in group tasks tend to explain the success of the group task on the spouse and the failure of the group task on other members of the group.

26. See, e.g., the essays collected in Tabensky, *Judging and Understanding*, and Part II of Wasserman and Wachbroit, *Genetics and Criminal Behavior*.

27. This is a phenomenon widely explored in U.S. film (e.g., *The Godfather* films) and television (e.g., *The Sopranos*).

28. Murray Smith suggests (in correspondence) that spectators of fiction often suspend their moral commitments. I am suspicious of this, largely because of the so-called phenomenon of imaginative resistance; see Hume "Of the Standard of Taste," Moran "The Expression of Feeling in Imagination," and Gendler "The Puzzle of Imaginative Resistance." This is a large issue that I cannot pursue, however.

29. This feature may separate *His Girl Friday* from what are commonly referred to as "black" or "dark" comedies, in which the wrongdoings are made more evident to the spectator.

30. I thank John Garfield and Jessica Gildea for pressing me on this point.

31. Unpublished class essay, Bennington College, 2007.

32. Carroll, *The Philosophy of Horror*, Chapter 4, and Freeland, "Realist Horror".

33. In his "Gangsters, Cannibals, Aesthetes," Murray Smith takes some steps toward developing the Freeland-type position.

PART TWO

PHILOSOPHICAL READINGS

ETHICS AND SOCIAL BEING

5

REASON, ABSURDITY, AND ANTI-SEMITISM IN *THE BELIEVER*

TOM MARTIN

ENRY BEAN'S FILM *THE BELIEVER* bears the following epigraph from Catallus:

> *I hate and I love*
> *Who can tell me why?*

The task of the current essay is to address Catallus's question as it might apply to the film's main character, Danny Balint (Ryan Gosling). Danny is an anti-Semite who is at the same time a (secretly) self-identifying Jew. If this were not curious enough, he also presents through the film a diverse array of considerations that supposedly motivate his anti-Semitism, many of which dazzlingly contradict each other. With this in mind, the viewer may be tempted to give up early the task of making sense of Danny's hatred of the Jews, perhaps casting it as a pathology unlikely to yield anything to rational interpretation., He comes across as an intelligent and articulate young man, however—not clearly mad and certainly no mere thug. Catallus's question is, in this context, *prima facie* a good one. Why is Danny an anti-Semite? And what of love? How and why does Danny love the Jews, and what role does this love play in his relationship to Judaism?

My aim is to piece together a coherent account of Danny's anti-Semitism. This task is rendered difficult given the complexity of just *what* "anti-Semitism" amounts to in Danny's case (let alone the questions of "Why?"). While several of the film's minor characters exhibit what we might think of as "straightforward" Jew hatred (of varying degrees and for varying reasons), the "anti" of Danny's anti-Semitism takes a variety of forms emerging from his complex and changing relationship to the people he is at once against and a member of. These forms range from disgust and homicidal hatred to a pathos and despair born of love (hence the appropriateness of Catallus's question). Furthermore, through the course of the film a development takes place in Danny's relationship to the Jews. In the early stages of the film, Danny's anti-Semitism appears as hatred and disgust for the Jews combined with a bemused curiosity born of detached familiarity. By the end of the film, following an engaged reacquaintance with Judaism, Danny's anti-Semitism has transformed into something perhaps more appropriately thought of as disappointment and despair, emerging from a still negative assessment of Judaism combined with a love that eliminates the possibility of detached judgment.

I will begin working toward answering the question, "Why is Danny an anti-Semite?" by considering what Danny has to say about it. When Danny attempts to explain to others his anti-Semitism, why he is against the Jews, he does so in two broad ways. The first is to attempt to provide rational justifications for his hatred—there are, he claims, features of the Jews that warrant his antagonism. The kinds of justifications that Danny attempts to give here are considered by Kwame Anthony Appiah in his account of racism, and, in Section I, I will explore the possibility that Appiah's account will assist us in answering Catallus's question. The second type of explanation Danny employs is to claim that the hatred of Jews that he and other anti-Semites harbor is not the result of something that can be rationally discovered. If anything, this hatred is a primary fact about anti-Semites. In Section II, I consider this tack in conjunction with Jean-Paul Sartre's account of anti-Semitism, an account that gives passion a central explanatory role. Neither of Danny's expressed accounts, however, emerges as adequate to understanding Danny's hatred of the Jews. In Section III, I turn to what I take to be a more fundamental and inclusive account of Danny's anti-Semitism, one that focuses not just on the accounts he gives, but rather on constructing an account from a number of diverse, even contradictory, claims that he makes. There, I argue that the thread running through Danny's key beliefs about the Jews and Judaism is the link between them and various forms of meaninglessness. It is the meaninglessness that Danny takes to be entailed by Judaism that evokes his ire. Yet Danny recognizes that he has been constituted by Judaism, such that he cannot divorce himself entirely from love and respect for his people. For this reason, I claim that Danny's relationship to the Jews bears the characteristics of absurdity, as defined by Thomas Nagel.

I. APPIAH, REASON, JUSTIFICATION, AND RACISM

Danny Balint has a strong aversion to Jews, an aversion that he is not only prepared to act upon, but one that also provides a pivotal purpose in his life. In many places in *The Believer*, Danny attempts to justify to others his anti-Semitism by sharing with them beliefs he holds about the Jews, morality, religion, and politics. How are we to understand the nature of the reasons that he gives and the role that they play in his anti-Semitism? Do these beliefs, presented by Danny as reasons, provide *the* reasons for his anti-Semitism?

Kwame Anthony Appiah has explored the nature of racism in terms of how it could best be justified by a racist and, or so I will claim, some of his results are useful in framing what is and what is not going on when Danny seeks to provide rational justification for his anti-Semitism. Appiah claims that there are two basic ways in which a racist could seek to justify her racism. In the first, *extrinsic racism*, the racist attempts to justify discrimination against members of another race by pointing to undesirable, morally relevant character traits that she holds are reliably linked to that race and the presence of which warrant the discrimination.[1] In the second, *intrinsic racism*, the racist attempts to justify her discrimination against members of another race, not because of the presence in them of any race linked character traits, but simply by virtue of their being of another race. Just as it might be held that one owes *more* (in terms of kindness, solidarity, sharing of goods, etc.) to members of one's own family, for no other reason than that they are members of one's family, the intrinsic racist might hold that she owes more to members of her own race.[2] In order for her to be an intrinsic racist, however, she must hold further that she owes *less* to members of other races (by virtue of their being members of other races) than would normally be morally required of her and/or she is morally required to act against them in morally significant ways. Should the extrinsic and intrinsic racists' beliefs about race-linked character traits, on the one hand, and race-based duties, on the other, be true,[3] then we could say that they have reason to be racists. Even if untrue, if they are genuinely held,[4] they could provide (at least part of) an answer to the question "Why is she a racist?" Answer: "Because she believes . . .". . . .

Can Appiah's account of extrinsic and intrinsic racism direct us to the reason for Danny's anti-Semitism? In order for that to be possible, to begin with, we would need to accept that an account of *racism* would be germane in considering Danny's *anti-Semitism*. While anti-Semitism can be racist, through relying on a racialized notion of "Jew", it need not be. If Danny were a *racist* anti-Semite, then the relevance of Appiah's account would be clear. He does display racism at times. He identifies with a paradigmatically racist anti-Semitic organization (the Nazis), describes his own group as a "racialist movement" that believes in a hierarchy of races, is happy to direct some of his violence toward blacks, and so on. There are, however, two telling and considered claims that he makes that count against casting his *anti-Semitism* as racist. The first, in his interview with the *New York Times* reporter Guy Danielson (A. D. Miles), is that the Israelis are not Jews because they now have land (while "the real Jew is a wanderer") such that they no longer require Judaism. The second, in his meeting with a businessman and potential donor to the fascist cause, Roger Brand (Jordan Lage), is the claim that he (Brand) has become a Jew through his adherence to capitalism. From these claims it seems that, for Danny, Jews can become non-Jews, and non-Jews can become Jews. A core feature of any notion of race, however, is that it is something a person is born with and that they will carry with them throughout their lives. "Race" precisely is not the kind of thing that can be either shed or adopted. If this is so, then Danny does not hold a racialized view of the Jews, which entails that his anti-Semitism cannot be racist. Whether or not Danny's anti-Semitism can be shown to be racist, I would maintain that Appiah's account of racism can still be useful. We can certainly make sense of an extrinsic anti-Semitism that attempts to justify itself through reference to morally relevant character traits reliably linked to Jews. The link between the characteristics and being a Jew could be by virtue of racial essence, or it could be for some other reason. As long as the link is sufficiently reliable for an anti-Semite to be satisfied that by having identified someone as a Jew he has at the same time identified someone with that character trait, then extrinsic anti-Semitism can stand. Similarly, we can make sense of an intrinsic anti-Semitism that attempts to justify anti-Semitic actions through reference to group-based duties and anti-duties. The groups could be drawn along racial lines, or they may be drawn along some other lines. As long as, in the mind of the anti-Semite, the groups identified are such as to bear the weight of morally relevant differential treatment, then intrinsic anti-Semitism can stand.

Having established that Appiah's extrinsic/intrinsic account of racism could be applied to Danny's case, let us begin by asking if Danny's anti-Semitism can be explained in intrinsic terms. Intrinsic anti-Semitism or racism may well be applicable to other characters in the film. In our first meeting with fascist leader Curtis Zampf (Billy Zane), we hear him defending fascism on the basis of previously culturally (and, by implication, racially) homogeneous neighborhoods having been infiltrated by destabilizing foreign elements. There is a strong "us and them" message to his speech. His audience is all white. His story is of creeping disadvantage to whites specifically, not to the plight of present-day communities in general. His audience is, presumably, supposed to at least sympathize, if not identify, with these white people, and it is difficult to see on what basis they might do so other than by virtue of shared race. Should this then motivate morally relevant differential treatment of nonwhites, we are clearly in the camp of intrinsic racism. The "race family feeling" might also be present among Danny's fellow gang members. In Danny's case, however, intrinsic racism/anti-Semitism does not seem to predominate, at least in the claims he makes to others to justify his anti-Semitism.[5] Rather, in dialogue with others, it seems to be the case that Danny believes that there are bad characteristics associated with Jews, and that it is the presence of these that motivate anti-Semitism.[6] As such, under Appiah's scheme, extrinsic racism/anti-Semitism seems to predominate in Danny's case.

At several points Danny provides extensive lists of Jewish characteristics that, he claims, warrant Jews being acted against. For example, in his interview with Guy Danielson, Danny claims that Jews bear a number of character traits with respect to sexuality and economic and cultural life, including a fascination with oral sex, impotence, hedonism, being "essentially female", undermining traditional life, and deracinating society. These features Danny takes to be worthy of condemnation. Furthermore, there is the implication that if you identify a Jew, then you have identified someone with these features. We have, then, in this excerpt from the film, a *prima facie* case of extrinsic anti-Semitism.

Does this extrinsic anti-Semitism provide an answer to the question, "Why is Danny an anti-Semite?" It would seem that it does not, at least not entirely. Danny at times plays the reason- or justification-giving game and, when he does, he does so in a primarily extrinsic fashion. He might even believe much of what he says in these moments, and these beliefs may provide impetus for his antagonism toward the Jews. It is clear, however, that these beliefs do not fully explain why he is an anti-Semite, and in the film Danny explicitly claims as much. During one of his public speaking engagements he says:

Why do we hate them?. . . . Do we hate them because they push their way
in where they don't belong? Or do we hate them because they are clannish
and keep to themselves? Because they are tight with money, or because they
flash it around? Because they are Bolsheviks, or because they are capitalists?
Because they have the highest IQs, or because they have the most active sex
lives? Do you want to know the real reason why we hate them? Because we
hate them. Because they exist. Because it's an axiom of civilization: just as a
man longs for woman, loves his children, and fears death, he hates Jews.
There's no *reason*. And if there were, some smart-assed kike would try and
come up with an argument, try and prove us wrong, which would only
make us hate him even more. And really we have all the reasons we need in
three simple letters: J-E-W.[7]

Through the conjunction of (supposedly) flagrantly contradictory claims,[8] all of
which he may well have heard put forward by different apologists, Danny parodies
attempts to provide rational justification for anti-Semitism. In fact, he even cites
here the Jew's propensity to engage in argument (to demand reason, perhaps) as
one of the very features of them that attract his disdain.

In summary, Danny at times attempts to provide rational justifications for his
anti-Semitism, and, when he does, these justifications tend to be cast in extrinsic
terms by pointing to undesirable traits that he takes to be characteristically
linked to Jews. While he might even believe some of what he says in these
moments, however, his willingness at other times to depart from the justifi-
catory reason-giving process entirely casts suspicion on the status of these
"reasons" as ultimate foundations for his anti-Semitism. It is possible, of course,
that Danny is simply wrong about his motivations, that in fact his anti-Semitism
is fully explicable in terms of his beliefs about the nature of the Jews, and that
his resort in the above-quoted passage to a notion of a primitive disdain for the
Jews is the result of justification fatigue (or some such other unprincipled condition) rather than a genuine turning away from reason giving *per se*. I am inclined,
however, to trust Danny on this score and accept that, at least at times, his anti-
Semitism has a basis in something other than extrinsic anti-Semitic beliefs. In the
passage quoted above, Danny suggests that anti-Semitic hatred plays a central,
perhaps even foundational, role in explaining anti-Semitism. In the next section
I turn to an analysis of anti-Semitism which provides a focus on passion over
reason.

II. SARTRE, PASSION, AND ANTI-SEMITISM

In *Anti-Semite and Jew*, Jean-Paul Sartre constructs a portrait of what he takes to
be the paradigmatic French anti-Semite of the 1940s. Sartre's account of anti-
Semitism is a potentially useful one in investigating Danny's case though, in the
end, I argue that Sartre's anti-Semite and Danny are importantly different.

For Sartre, anti-Semitism is most immediately not about reasons at all—it is more a matter of passion (particularly the passions of hatred and disgust).

> Indeed, it [anti-Semitism] is something quite other than an idea. It is first of all a *passion*. No doubt it can be set forth in the form of a theoretical proposition. The "moderate" anti-Semite is a courteous man who will tell you quietly: "Personally, I do not detest the Jews. I simply find it preferable, for various reasons, that they should play a lesser part in the activity of the nation." But a moment later, if you have gained his confidence, he will add with more abandon: "You see, there must be *something* about the Jews; they upset me physically."[9]

Here Sartre claims that anti-Semitism is "first of all a passion." While this is not quite accurate, even by his own account, as there are motivations for the passion that support it (as we shall see in Section III), it is certainly the case in Sartre's account that anti-Semitic passion comes prior to evidence that is cited in support of anti-Semitism. Impassioned, physical disgust at the Jew is something that Danny (like Sartre's anti-Semite) experiences and reports on.

> People hate Jews, don't you agree? . . . Deep down, beneath all the tolerance that they learn on television, nothing has changed. The very word makes their skin crawl. It's not even hate. It's the way you feel when a rat runs across the floor; you want to step on it. You just want to crush it; you don't even know why. It's a physical reaction and everyone feels it. Jew.

Here, Danny seems to acknowledge in himself and others the truth of Sartre's diagnosis that passion plays a primary role in motivating anti-Semitism.

What, according to Sartre, is the link between this passion and the reasons given by anti-Semites to justify their opposition to Jews?

> Everyone understands that emotions of hate or anger are involved. But ordinarily hate and anger have a *provocation*: I hate someone who has made me suffer, someone who contemns or insults me. [But] anti-Semitic passion could not have such a character. It precedes the facts that are supposed to call it forth; it seeks them out to nourish itself upon them; it must even interpret them in a special way so that they may become truly offensive.[10]

It is the presence of anti-Semitic hatred that explains the anti-Semite's purportedly justifying experiences. This hatred generates an "idea of the Jew," and it is through this lens that dealings with, or things about, the Jew are read. So we still might have reasons being presented for anti-Semitism but, with Sartre, we should be under no illusion that these supposed reasons actually result in anti-Semitism. These reasons (perhaps similar to those of an extrinsic anti-Semite) are given to justify the hate, but the evidence they intend is in fact not the source of the hate. The actual motivations for anti-Semitism have nothing to do with the reasons the anti-Semite puts forward to justify his anti-Semitism.

What, then, are the motivations for anti-Semitic hatred? Sartre thinks that hating Jews might appear to confer certain benefits on the Jew hater, and that in nonreflectively pursuing these benefits anti-Semitic hatred is strategically (though, again, nonreflectively) adopted. These benefits include a strong and stable sense of self ("impenetrability");[11] a justified outlet for violence ("It is *fun* to be an anti-Semite");[12] a privileged position to the mediocre ("In representing the Jew as a robber, they put themselves in the enviable position of people who could be robbed. Since the Jew wishes to take France from them, it follows that France must belong to them. Thus they have chosen anti-Semitism as a means of establishing their status as possessors");[13] equality ("anti-Semitism brought the duke closer to his coachman");[14] and a purpose in life (combating Jews) that is beyond question ("If all he has to do is to remove Evil, that means that the Good is already *given*").[15] These are things that Sartre can imagine the anti-Semite might want, and Sartre sees anti-Semitism as a misguided route toward attaining them.[16] These purported benefits are held out to explain, at least in part, why the anti-Semite hates Jews. Why can they do so only in part? Because while we might accept that these considerations motivate anti-Semitism, the question "Why *anti-Semitism* in particular?" still persists.

Sartre's anti-Semite seeks to profit from hatred, and his hatred requires an object. The Jew is that object but, given another context, it might just as well be someone else. "The Jew only serves him as a pretext; elsewhere his counterpart will make use of the Negro or the man of yellow skin."[17] The anti-Semite's choice of the Jew to play the role of object of hatred is not quite arbitrary. There is a history and current climate of anti-Semitism that presents the Jew as a likely, available target. Beyond these factors, however, there is no investment that the anti-Semite has in targeting the Jew in particular, and it is this feature of Sartre's anti-Semite that makes him deviate importantly from Danny. Danny may well want the benefits that Sartre mentions the anti-Semite aiming for the Jew clearly means much more to Danny, however, than he does to Sartre's anti-Semite. Danny's hatred and despair is more closely linked to Jews than Sartre's account would suggest. Danny really does seem to have a problem with Jews. In the next section, I offer an account of Danny's particular "problem" in terms of his concerns about absurdity, which rely on his intimate acquaintance with the Jews.

III. DANNY BALINT, ABSURDITY, AND ANTI-SEMITISM

As human beings, we desire lives that have both value and meaning. We want our lives to include purpose through the pursuit of valuable projects that give meaning to existence. That our lives might not possess such meaning may be seen, by some of us, at least, to be a most lamentable possibility. Some put their hopes in religion to provide guidance on how to lead a valuable and meaningful life. God loves us and He lays out guidelines on how to structure our lives so that they are valuable and purposeful. It may be the case, however, that we should expect something further from God than just providing our lives with meaning. In addition, perhaps, we should expect that God will also make it such that we see or understand our lives as meaningful. As Thomas Nagel writes:

> If God is supposed to give our lives a meaning that we can't understand, it's not much of a consolation. God as ultimate justification, like God as ulti-mate explanation, may be an incomprehensible answer to a question that we can't get rid of. On the other hand, maybe that's the whole point, and I am just failing to understand religious ideas. Perhaps the belief in God is the belief that the universe is intelligible, but not to us.[18]

As can be seen, Nagel ends this passage by considering that the hopes for finding meaning to our lives through God might not include comprehending that meaning. No doubt some believers would accept, or even relish, this state of ignorance and the necessity for blind obedience. If God, however, has possessed us with the fac-ulty of reason, in addition to a disposition to be anguished at the thought of our lives being meaningless, we might hope not only that our lives in fact do have meaning, but that we would *understand* how and why they do so. This would assist greatly in providing the "consolation" we seek from a loving God with respect to assuring us that our lives are meaningful.[19]

The God that Danny Balint discovers as a child in yeshiva class, however, is not a God that assists him in appreciating the meaningfulness of his life. On the contrary, the guidance he finds provided by God makes no sense to him at all. For example, this is the God who, in Genesis 22 commands Abraham, His most faithful servant, to take his beloved son, Isaac, to the land of Moriah and sacrifice him there as a burnt offering. Abraham is prepared to carry out this deed, but, just as he is about to do so, God sends an angel to stop him and provides a ram to substi-tute Isaac in the sacrifice. While Danny's classmates view the Akedah (the story of Abraham and Isaac), which in various guises stands as the film's most persistent *leitmotiv*, as a lesson in faith, he encounters there a God who is an uncaring bully. Danny claims that the true message of the tale is: "It's not about Abraham's faith, it's about God's power. God says, 'You know how powerful I am? I can make you do anything I want, no matter how stupid, even kill your own son, because I'm everything and you're nothing.'" For Danny, the Akedah depicts God as unbridled and unprincipled power, as "everything", and the Jew as powerless, as "nothing". God is a conceited bully, a megalomaniac, and the Jews (God's most beloved people) merely pawns in a stupid game. The "stupidity" of God's commands extends beyond His demand that Abraham sacrifice his son. In fact, for Danny,

Judaism is just riddled with such demands, and the unreasonable, "not making sense" element of Judaism is a recurrent theme in the film. The rules for observing the Sabbath and the kosher dietary laws are, for Danny, hopelessly complex and pointless, and, above all, they make no sense. Consider the scene in which Danny attempts to get the café waiter, Steve (Christopher Kadish), to admit that kosher rules are "stupid":

STEVE: Religion's not about making sense.

DANNY: It's about the incomprehensible Steve, not about the idiotic.

STEVE: Fuck you.

DANNY: Fuck you. That explains it. Now we understand.

While this is said somewhat tongue in cheek,[20] there is a serious side to this utterance. For Danny, "Fuck you" does describe (at least one aspect of) the Jews' relationship with God (encapsulated in kosher dietary rules), and it does explain the meaningless tasks he gets them to perform. That the Jews are required to follow an intricate set of rules that fly in the face of reason is an affront to their dignity. That God would require them to live lives that reason could not accept as valuable or meaningful is a sign of utter contempt on His part.[21]

Additionally, in Danny's eyes, the Jews willingly perform these tasks—they are prepared to sacrifice their very selves to this bully (and to other bullies, such as, ironically in Danny's case, the Nazis). Their impotence and refusal to fight back appalls Danny. In an ill-fated sensitivity training session, Danny becomes furious upon hearing an old Jewish man's account of how he had been forced to watch his young son killed by a soldier during the war, a story that, for Danny, seems to have strong parallels with the Akedah. Danny says it would have been better if the man had jumped the soldier and been killed, because now he is worse than dead, he is "a piece of shit," and he claims that "we have nothing to learn from these people" as he storms out in disgust. A second example comes from the film's opening, a violent scene in which Danny assaults a young Jewish man he has seen on the train. Here, Danny seems to play out the relationship between God and man, again cast in terms of the Akedah. Having knocked the man to the ground, Danny then says: "Get up!. . . . What do you think this is? Do you think it's a fucking test? Do you think God's going to provide a fucking ram instead of you? No! Do me a favor. Won't you fucking hit me, OK? . . . Hit me, please, hit me!" To the extent that Danny believes that the Jews have, in a cowardly fashion, submitted to the unreasonable whims of others, combined with his own identification with being a Jew, there is a snowballing of loathing and self-loathing that takes place. Here, we have some insight into why Danny is an anti-Semite. That the Jews did not fight back against oppressions (both divine and worldly) disgusts him. In addition, though, it is the senselessness or "stupidity" that Danny takes to be associated with what Judaism requires of its people which is both a target for and, I would suggest, a motivation for, much of Danny's antagonism toward the Jews.

This is only half of the story, however. For while the God that Danny hates is at times presented in terms of a power-crazed bully, as everything, at other times God is presented as being nothing at all. The theme of God's absence emerges in a conversation Danny has with his girlfriend, Carla (Summer Phoenix), in his bedroom.

> CARLA: [reading from the Torah] "Make no graven image of the Lord . . . . because He is not like anything." Not only can you not see him or hear him, but you can't even think about him? What's the difference between that and him not existing at all?
>
> DANNY: There is no difference.

Here, God is depicted not as providing us with "stupid" reasons to be and meanings to life, but as providing us with no values or meaning at all. And to the extent that the Jews accept this picture of God, Danny tells us that "what the Jews want is nothingness, nothingness without end." What would the "something" be, which is Danny's preferred alternative to this nothingness? I suggest that it is a life of stable meaning, a life that makes sense. This is precisely, however, what, according to Danny, the modern world, "that Jewish disease," denies us.

Danny bemoans the inventions of "three great Jewish minds:" class warfare (which draws into question traditional society), relativity (which also draws our commonsense understanding of the universe into question), and unconscious urges (we do not even know ourselves any more). What is fascinating about these complaints, however, is that they are complaints about questioning, about *not* simply submitting to the way things are, about *not* just taking "stupid" orders. In considering Abraham, the old man at the encounter group, and the young man from the train, it was submission to unreason and refusal to stand up for oneself in the face of it that was the occasion for Danny's disgust. Now it is *refusal* to submit that bothers him. At one point Danny claims that, "Before the Jews, we lived in a world of order and reason." I would suggest, however, that the world Danny claims we have lost is a world in which we had an order that we obeyed and *took for granted that it was reasonable*. What these Jews—Marx, Einstein, and Freud—have done is to draw into question such a world. In this instance, these Jews are precisely on the side of reason, not against it. It is Danny who is now demanding that we do not dig too deep, demanding that we do not question the order of things. The fear is that if we pursue reason too vigorously—the Jewish drive for "abstraction" to which Danny refers—we will be left with nothing, "nothingness without end."

Danny, it appears, holds two opposing views of God (everything and nothing) and, relatedly, two opposing views of the Jews (submissive to a set of seemingly stupid commands and refusing to lie down and just accept the way things are).

This all seems just hopelessly confused and contradictory. If we are to make sense of Danny, we need to find what these seemingly completely opposed views have in common. The common thread running through them is that, for Danny, they all entail meaninglessness.

If we have God #1 (a capricious maker of stupid rules) then we are faced with meaninglessness, as the core guiding principles and practices of our lives turn out to be pointless and arbitrary. If we have God #2 (nothing—or next to nothing—at all) then we are left alone in a world without guiding principles and practices at all, and so face lives devoid of meaning. If we respond to our situation as Jew #1 does (submitting to God's caprice) then we are accepting that our lives are meaningless. If we respond as Jew #2 does, we may well discover through rigorous questioning that our lives have no stable value and meaning. Whichever way we go, it seems, we are faced with meaninglessness, and this is what Danny rails against.

For someone in Danny's position, the association between the Jews and this crisis of meaninglessness is multilayered. First, the Jews, according to the tradition in which Danny was raised, are the chosen people of God. If anyone should expect divine protection from meaninglessness, it should be the Jews. That they have not received this protection is outrageous, and that they accept this state of affairs is more outrageous still. Second, as the chosen people, perhaps the Jews stand as representatives or figureheads of the relationship between God and humanity and could thereby (following a rather twisted logic) stand as fitting scapegoats for the anger and despair at the shortcomings or failures of that relationship in terms of the meaningfulness to life that it affords. Third, with respect to the threat of mean-inglessness resulting from rigorous questioning which disrupts accepted practices and worldviews, the Jews (i.e., Jews #2), to Danny's mind, are the key players (through their fascination with "abstraction"). Finally, of course, there is Danny's own identification with the Jews, which exacerbates his concerns with and for them, both in terms of scrutinizing them and holding them to account (the Jews' failures reflect on him),[22] and in terms of caring about their status.

It is particularly through considering this last point—Danny's own identification with Judaism—that the theme of his concerns can be understood as not simply meaninglessness, but absurdity. In speaking of absurdity here, I do so following Thomas Nagel's account, captured well in the following passage:

> We see ourselves from outside, and all the contingency and specificity of our aims and pursuits become clear. Yet when we take this view and recognize what we do as arbitrary, it does not disengage us from life, and there lies our absurdity: not in the fact that such an external view can be taken of us, but in the fact that we ourselves can take it, without ceasing to be the persons whose ultimate concerns are so coolly regarded.[23]

According to Nagel, absurdity arises when we view our lives (and the projects and values embodied therein) as meaningless, and yet at the same time recognize that we are nonetheless committed to them. Now, *anyone* who comes to the judgment that human life (in general) is ultimately meaningless, recognizes herself as the bearer of such a human life, and, regardless of this, also finds herself committed to her projects, will encounter absurdity as described by Nagel. In Danny's case, however, there is something more pointed and exigent about the absurdity he faces. Certainly, his belief about the Jews' relationship to God and the meaninglessness that some of their number have revealed has bearing on the meaning of human life in general. If he recognizes himself as a human who must, nonetheless, pursue a human life, however, then he is faced with absurdity. It is not as examples of "humans in general" that he is interested in the Jews, however. It is as *his people* that he is concerned with them. Their meaningless projects and habits have a hold on him and concern him despite his judgment that they are meaningless. This care and despair with respect for the Jews *and himself as a Jew* is something that develops and increases as Danny re-establishes his intimacy with Judaism through the course of the film, by doing such things as rescuing and repairing a vandalized Torah, helping his (gentile) girlfriend to read and understand it, reacquainting himself with childhood friends, and so forth. Yes, for Danny, Judaism is associated with meaninglessness, but it is also associated with him, and he with it. It is not something he can just give up. In terms of Catallus's question: Danny hates the Jews because of the meaninglessness associated with them, and he loves the Jews through knowing them and counting himself as one of them. It is through this combination of distance and intimacy that "absurdity" is writ large in Danny's life.

I claim that we should view Danny's anti-Semitism in terms of a revolt against absurdity.[24] If, for Danny, however, the current situation is beyond the pale, completely unacceptable, how will the suppression or destruction of the Jews be of any help? Danny gives two quite divergent models of the destruction of the Jews. One (introduced only toward the end of the film) is to love them so that they will assimilate.[25] By assimilating him, bringing him into the fold, the Jew will no longer be able to maintain a critical distance from society and will cease his relentless and disruptive questioning, and we can live in a somewhat self-deceived peace, resting comfortably in our beliefs and values. This would be to deprive the Jew of conditions necessary to him being Jew #2. Hence, it would be to destroy Jew #2, and it would provide some insurance for us all against being faced with meaninglessness.

The other, and in the film the more often cited model, is to destroy the Jew completely. While this solution would, naturally, encompass Jew #2, I think it is imagined by Danny with Jew #1 primarily in mind. Jew #1 disgusts Danny through her acceptance of God's order, and much of his claims and actions against the Jews are cast in terms of fury, contempt, and hatred. As such, there is a vengeance theme to Danny's demand for their destruction. There is at the same time, however, a loving, redemptive theme. Danny has a preferred version of the Akedah, in which Isaac is killed on Mount Moriah, and then reborn "in the world to come." What is this world to come? Danny does not say, though presumably it is different from this one; perhaps it is one in which there is value and meaning to be found and appreciated, perhaps one in which *we* are different such that we can rest content without value and meaning at all. At any rate, in Danny's estimation, it would be better *for Isaac* to die/be killed in this world, with all its absurdity, and move on to the next world. By implication, it would be better *for the Jews* similarly to depart this world. While they deserve to die, for having allowed themselves to be so shamed and humiliated by God, it would also be better for them to die. By the end of the film, however, Danny's reattachment and love for the Jews has risen to such an extent that he finds himself unable to follow through with an earlier plan to blow up a synagogue full of worshippers. Instead, he sets the bomb to destroy only the pulpit that he knows he will be standing in, and prior to the moment of detonation he has all the worshippers evacuated. Danny chooses to die alone, taking the place of his people as their Passover lamb.

My claim, then, is that Danny's anti-Semitism is best understood as being motivated by concerns regarding absurdity—by hate and love. Prior to reaching this conclusion, I considered the works of Appiah and Sartre to see how they might be used to understand Danny's anti-Semitism. While I ultimately found them unable to fully capture what lay behind Danny's relationship to the Jews, I take it that both provide worthwhile interpretive tools regarding the nature of attempted justifications for anti-Semitism, in the case of Appiah, and the role of passion in anti-Semitism, in the case of Sartre. Both of these philosophical works on racism and anti-Semitism have proved to be illuminating when considering *The Believer*. Furthermore, I think that the interpretation of *The Believer* that I have offered can remain compatible with, and possibly even, in its own way contribute to, both.

Interpreting Danny's anti-Semitism as being based in his revolt against meaninglessness and absurdity provides an explanation for the phenomena that were examined earlier when considering the works of Appiah and Sartre. Both Appiah and Sartre hold that there must be something underlying the phenomena they analyze. In the case of Appiah's account of racism, that racist beliefs (extrinsic or intrinsic) in turn require explanation is a point made clear. The persistence of such beliefs despite the presence of (what should be) ample counterevidence (a persistence that Appiah refers to as "cognitive incapacity") points to the possibility of non-epistemic motivations for such beliefs. Appiah claims that "ideology" can motivate us to not "give up beliefs that play a part in justifying the special advantages we gain (or hope to gain) from our positions in the social order."[26] I would suggest, further to Appiah's claims, that not merely the persistence of racist beliefs, but their very generation requires recourse to non-epistemic motivations. In Danny's case, I have suggested, anti-Semitism is promoted by a concern with absurdity. Danny believes that there is the threat of absurdity in connection with the Jews, and he has a number of anti-Semitic beliefs which revolve around or concern this threat. It is important, however, to understand these beliefs not simply as *concerning* this threat, but stemming from the possibility of it. Firm beliefs in the absurdity generating properties of the Jews stand, ironically, as a bulwark against absurdity itself. As such, absurdity plays two roles here. First, the Jews are to be fought against because they stand for absurdity. Second, the fight against the Jews itself is an exercise in stemming absurdity—by providing (however misguidedly) purposeful, meaningful activity. Concern with absurdity—at least over and above, if not instead of, the concerns for economic, political and social station that Appiah gestures toward—plays the role of key non-epistemic motivation for Danny's anti-Semitic beliefs. Absurdity may then stand as another item that, depending on the case at hand, Appiah might add to his list non-epistemic motives for racist beliefs.

It is also the case, with respect to Sartre's account of anti-Semitism and its parallels to Danny's case, that absurdity could play an explanatory role. I mentioned in Section II that Sartre envisages a number of perceived "benefits" that might accompany anti-Semitism. For Sartre these benefits, in turn, require explanation, and this explanation is to be found in the role they play in stifling anxieties in connection with the human condition.

> [The anti-Semite] is a man who is afraid. Not of the Jews, to be sure, but of himself, of his own consciousness, of his liberty, of his instincts, of his responsibilities, of solitariness, of change, of society, and of the world—of everything except the Jews. . . . The existence of the Jew merely permits the anti-Semite to stifle his anxieties at their inception by persuading himself that his place in the world has been marked out in advance, that it awaits him, and that tradition gives him the right to occupy it. Anti-Semitism, in short, is fear of the human condition.[27]

For Sartre, the human condition is characterized by, among other things, a radical freedom that imparts immense responsibility at the same time as it brings deep uncertainty. I suggest that one way of casting this uncertainty is in terms of the threat of meaninglessness and absurdity. Sartre's anti-Semite seeks "his place in the world" and, presumably, this "place", with its prescribed values and projects, carries with it the promise of meaningfulness. This "place", then, would be a refuge from absurdity. If we view matters in this light, the parallels between Sartre's anti-Semite and Danny become very strong indeed. There still remains a clear difference between Sartre's anti-Semite and Danny. For the former, the Jew is simply a place holder as he against whom the anti-Semite's place in the world can be secured. For Danny, the Jew is not just some replaceable enemy, but an intimate who is peculiarly apt as an object of both hate and love.

Apart from being compatible with, and possibly illuminating with respect to, two important philosophical works on racism/anti-Semitism, we might ask if there is any other value *The Believer* might have in assisting us to understand anti-Semitism, or racism more generally. Perhaps the story told in the film is simply such an unusual one, and Danny Balint such an idiosyncratic character,[28] that it would be in vain for us to hope to draw any general lessons from it. Then again, we might ask if any work of fiction can contribute to understanding real social phenomena. Contrary to these suggestions, I would submit that the unusualness of Danny's story may make *The Believer* potentially very useful indeed and that its status as "fiction" does not diminish this usefulness. Lester Hunt claims that a contribution that films can make to philosophy is through their provision of illustrations of ideas.

> As such, they play a role that is quite different from convincing us that some proposition is true or not. Rather, they help us to decide what a given idea is, or should be. They help us to distinguish, among other things, between what is truly part of a concept and what is merely associated with it by habitual associations. This function is in particular one of the benefits of the sort of film that has genuine value as a work of art, inasmuch as such films have a marked tendency to avoid clichés.[29]

According to Hunt, then, some films, and I suggest *The Believer* should be included among them, have the power to stretch our conceptual imagination by confronting us with what is both familiar and unfamiliar. Unlike being faced with more run-of-the-mill racist characters (such as those in *American History X* and *Crash*),[30] the audience of *The Believer* (even without Catallus's prompting at the film's opening) feels compelled to dig deeply into conceptual resources to understand the main character, as I have tried to do here. The possibility that racism or anti-Semitism might in some cases at least (perhaps even more generally) be related to existential crises such as the threat of absurdity, and not simply (or even primarily) to the more commonly cited causes (political, social, cultural, and class indoctrination) is worth considering seriously. Danny's case simply does not allow for pat understandings in such familiar terms. At the very least, the film makes the viewer consider this possibility (and perhaps other possibilities offered by the film which I have overlooked) seriously, even if later, on reflection, she decides that it cannot assist her in understanding the more general phenomena of anti-Semitism and racism.[31]

NOTES

Work on this paper began during a period of academic leave funded by the National Research Foundation of South Africa, the Ernest Oppenheimer Trust, Rhodes University, and Flinders University, and I wish to thank those institutions for their support. I am also grateful to Samantha Vice, Ward Jones, and the "Philosophy and Film" class at Rhodes University for some excellent feedback on previous drafts.

1. Appiah, "Racisms", 5.
2. Ibid., 5–6.
3. Appiah denies that these beliefs are true. For a start, the realist concept of race that he claims both kinds of racism rely on is an empty one. There simply is nothing in

human biology that corresponds with it. Even if there were races, as these categories are conventionally drawn, Appiah thinks both kinds of racist justification fail. The extrinsic racist's doctrine fails on the basis that there are no morally relevant character traits reliably linked to conventionally identified race groups. The intrinsic racist's doctrine fails because (1) races are not like families, and (2) even if they were, the sorts of morally relevant differences in treatment that racists seek to justify are not justifiable along family lines anyway. (Ibid., 6ff.)

4. Appiah holds little hope for either of these doctrines providing the *actual* basis of racism in practice, gesturing instead to ideological pressures that motivate the holding of such beliefs in the face of counterevidence.

5. One apparent reason for discounting the possibility that Danny is an intrinsic anti-Semite might be that he is a part of the group that he despises, in which case, how can the "family feeling" be at play? This, however, is not convincing. While Appiah seems to have in mind that intrinsic racism involves pro-attitudes to fellow "family" members, I can see no reason why it should be limited in this way. For example, an individual consumed by *self*-loathing or *self*-criticism might well extend this loathing or criticism (and morally relevant differences in treatment that follow on from them) to others with whom she identifies racially or culturally, for no other reason than that they are so identified with. I will return to a similar point to this later in the paper. It may also be noted that several commentators, including the film's writer/director, claim that *The Believer* deals explicitly with the theme of Jewish self-hatred. For examples, see any of the essays contained in Henry Bean, *The Believer: Confronting Jewish Self-Hatred*.

6. It should be noted that extrinsic and intrinsic racism are not mutually exclusive. Someone could hold *both* that racial others are inferior by virtue of their possession of race-linked traits that render them so *and* that she owes special allegiance to her own race irrespective of the presence of inferiorizing, race-linked traits in the other. In such a case, racism is overdetermined. In Danny's case, however, when he presents reasons for his anti-Semitism, these reasons tend not to be cast in intrinsic terms.

7. All dialogue quoted in this essay has been transcribed directly from the film.

8. "Highest IQs" and "most active sex lives" are not obviously contradictory (one might hope), though in the speech under consideration, Danny appears to take them as so.

9. Sartre, *Anti-Semite and Jew*, 10.

10. Ibid., 17.

11. Ibid., 18.

12. Ibid., 46–47.

13. Ibid., 25.

14. Ibid., 29.

15. Ibid., 44.

16. Misguided in two key ways. First, anti-Semitism is clearly morally misguided. Second, and putting to one side its moral status, these benefits are not attainable via anti-Semitism anyway. In the case of building equality across the classes and raising mediocrity up to a noble quality, it is, perhaps, a contingent fact that anti-Semitism simply will not achieve these states. With respect to "impenetrability" and finding a stable and unquestionably worthwhile purpose in life, it is a necessary fact within

Sartrean existentialism that, given the kinds of creatures we are, these goals are unattainable (via anti-Semitism or any other means). Any sense of having achieved one or more of these benefits will rely on self-deception.

17. Sartre, *Anti-Semite and Jew*, 54.

18. Nagel, *What Does It All Mean?*, 100.

19. I am not claiming that this set of requirements is necessary in all searches for meaning. As mentioned earlier, some theists may well be content to believe that God gives their lives meaning without needing to understand how. Naturalists, of course, will make no reference to God at all, though they may still point to the value of understanding that meaning, perhaps as being partly constitutive of meaning itself. I have no interest here in adjudicating between these options. I merely wish to set up the approach that Danny seems take.

20. "Fuck you", of course, typically does not explain anything. "Fuck you" usually marks the end of meaningful dialogue, rather than playing a significant role in it. In this context, however, it may well have a place.

21. Note that Danny seems to suggest in this scene that "incomprehensibility" in religion would be acceptable. I suppose this could be cast in terms of human reason having limitations with respect to comprehending the divine. What Danny takes issue with consistently through the film is not that some elements of life are beyond his comprehension, but that he precisely comprehends them as ridiculous.

22. While earlier I claimed, with respect to Appiah's theorizing of racism, that in terms of Danny's explicit rationalizations of anti-Semitism he appears to harbor extrinsic anti-Semitism, at this point it would appear appropriate to gesture toward a hitherto unrecognized intrinsic anti-Semitism. Unlike the intrinsic racism envisaged by Appiah, in which one holds one's own to be worthy of more positive judgment than others, Danny's intrinsic anti-Semitism takes the form of holding his people to higher standards than others, resulting in a harsher judgment against them.

23. Nagel, "The Absurd", 720.

24. While Nagel suggests that absurdity is "one of the most human things about us: a manifestation of our most advanced and interesting characteristics," and a condition best met with irony (Ibid., 727), Danny is clearly less sanguine about it.

25. The theme of assimilating the Jews as a way of destroying them is explored in Sartre in his analysis of "the Democrat" in *Anti-Semite and Jew*, Chapter 2. In this case, however, the motivation seems to be a matter of erasing cultural differences, as opposed to quashing disruptive questioning.

26. Appiah, "Racisms", 7.

27. Sartre, *Anti-Semite and Jew*, 53–54.

28. It is interesting to note here that writer, Henry Bean, based the character of Danny Balint on a real person: a Jewish Ku Klux Klan member who was also "outed" as a Jew by a *New York Times* reporter. Bean, *The Believer: Confronting Jewish Self-Hatred*, 3–4.

29. Lester Hunt, "Motion Pictures as a Philosophical Resource," 403.

30. This is not to suggest that these films are without value with respect to thinking about racism. One need only turn to Lawrence Blum's excellent contribution to the present volume to see that this is not so, at least in the case of *Crash*, I think it undeniable, however, that both films deal with much more familiar "types" of racist, and thus

perhaps do less goading of the imagination regarding the possible natures of racists and their motivations.

31. My own view, which I hardly have the room to defend here, is that existentialist (or existentialist-style) notions, such as the threat of absurdity and how it can be implicated in the individual's struggle for identity with and against others, can provide important resources for analyses of anti-Semitism and racism. They cannot do so alone, however, They will be effective only when conducted in conjunction with third-person, historico-social approaches that provide accounts of the conditions within which far-from-atomistic individuals conduct their strivings from subject positions characterized as much by habituation of belief and action as they are by freedom and reason.

6

MELTING WHITES AND LIBERATED LATINAS

IDENTITY, FATE, AND CHARACTER IN *FOOLS RUSH IN*

PAUL C. TAYLOR

I.

IN THE WAKE OF THE GREAT DEPRESSION, the American writer Ralph Ellison found the meaning of democracy in the basement of a New York City tenement. He had gone there in search of signatures for a petition, only to find a group of soot-covered, dungaree-clad African-American working men. While taking a break from feeding coal to the building's furnace, the men were knowledgeably debating an unexpected topic: "which of two celebrated Metropolitan Opera divas was the superior soprano!"[1]

By the time Ellison came to write about this surprising debate, it struck him as entirely appropriate to America's unfinished experiment in democracy. The unlikely expertise of the boiler-room opera critics was the predictable fruit of a democratic culture, one that distributes opportunities for erudition and education widely and without regard for social class. Also, it was the natural consequence of a pluralistic society, one that has knitted its diverse elements into a complex and variegated tapestry. One could not understand America, Ellison argued, without first accepting two things: the internal complexity of the place, which kept its animating ideals and practices from being the property of any single group; and the fact that a responsible and authoritative critic of those ideals and practices might emerge from anywhere—even from the obscurity of a basement boiler room.[2]

These lessons provide a useful frame for an encounter with the film *Fools Rush In*. This romantic comedy is, in its way, an extended riff on essentially Ellisonian themes. It follows a Mexican-American woman named Isabel (Salma Hayek) and an Anglo-American man named Alex (Matthew Perry) as they conceive a baby, marry, grapple with their cultural differences, have their baby, divorce, and remarry. In all this, the newlyweds enact what Ellison calls "the most agonizing mystery sponsored by the democratic ideal . . . our unity in diversity, our oneness in many-ness." Ellison explains the mystery's "agony" in a passage that also supplies a passable précis of the film:

> [W]e cooperate and communicate across this mystery, but the problem of identity that it poses often goads us to . . . . acts of disaffiliation. So we seek psychic security from within our inherited divisions of the corporate American culture. . . . We stress our affiliation with that segment of the corporate culture which has emerged out of our parents'

past—racial, cultural, religious—and which we assume . . . . that we "know".[3]

The newlyweds withdraw from each other and return to their pasts in an act of marital disaffiliation that emblematizes Ellison's broader problem of identity. As with nearly all new marriages on film, and as in many multiracial, post-suprema-cist, pluralist democracies, the determination to repress and deny interethnic inter-connectedness leads to trouble. It goes hand in hand with the determination to shirk the burdens of self-creation and to forge a critical, authentic, and productive relationship to the sources of the self.

Fools Rush In joins Ellison in a long tradition, descended at least from Emerson, of transposing a familiar ethical burden into a definite sociohistorical context. John Dewey says that all ethical deliberation comes down to one question: *What kind of person shall I be?*[4] Sometimes, however, we raise the question of self-creation explic-itly, and, in places like the United States, in particular, by appeal to certain value-laden, socially prescribed options for forging a social identity. In settings like this, the relevant ethical question is not just one of self-creation, but also of the right relationship to one's culture and to oneself as an artifact of culture.

If Ellison's reflections help specify the film's Emersonian ethical agenda, they also clarify the challenge of taking the film seriously. Whatever its aspirations, *Fools* bears all the marks of an assembly-line romantic comedy, complete with such telltale signs of Hollywood manufacture as rampant product placement and fre-quent music-video montages. It is, as a consequence, apparently weighed down by unevenly developed characters, one of whom undergoes substantial change while the other seems to go nowhere; by a central relationship that thumps and clunks into view, after clunking noticeably at the outset; and by what seems to be a loss of focus or courage regarding the theme, which allows the reality of social difference to give way to some talk about fate and to the idea that, as characters keep saying, there are signs everywhere.

Here we need to keep in mind the lesson of the boiler-room opera critics. On Ellison's view, the possibility that valid criticism might emerge from obscurity should teach artists not to underestimate their audiences. In the same spirit, he might have warned audiences against underestimating authors, or their own ability to "aid the author in achieving the more complex vision . . . . that was im-plicit in [the] material."[5] Despite its lumbering first steps, and despite the dismis-sive first readings it might invite, *Fools Rush In* reflects with surprising depth on Ellison's problem of identity. And while this reflection may be implicit, it is se-rious enough to resonate with Deweyan thoughts on the dialectic of freedom and culture, with Emersonian reflections on the demands and uses of fate, and with Stanley Cavell's explorations of moral perfectionism and the comedy of remar-riage. Seeing how the film does all this is essential not just to crediting its tran-scendence of what seem to be failures of craft, but also, I would say, to seeing the film at all.

II. PRELIMINARIES: REBUKING REMARRIAGE
AND PRACTICING PERFECTIONISM

It may be useful to begin with a few words about the kind of film I take *Fools* to be, the kind of argument I take it to make, and the kind of interpretation I'll offer. I've mentioned that while the film seems interested in the problem of identity, it also seems to abandon that interest in favor of talk about signs and fate. An assembly-line Hollywood love story would not see this thematic bait and switch as an embarrassment. Love is about overcoming differences, these films always say. Furthermore, when the lovers are from distinct cultures, races, or regions, the distance between them becomes a chasm—or, as the iconography of this film routinely suggests, a canyon. Gestures at fate may simply mark one of the many differences between the characters, signaling their conflicting approaches to religion. This fate talk earns its place in the thematic foreground, Hollywood might say, because it so nicely sets up the appeals to destiny that inevitably appear in our love stories. ("I am your density," Marty McFly tells his eventual wife in *Back to the Future*, before correcting himself.)

As it happens, though, there are less formulaic ways to reconcile the two themes, even in Hollywood. Or, there are more interesting formulas. *Fools* is what Stanley Cavell calls a comedy of remarriage, and recognizing this fact makes available a constellation of meaning that greatly clarifies the relations between fate and identity, and between these metaphysical notions and our heroes' lives. Hollywood love stories also always say that lovers must find themselves before they can give themselves to or claim someone else. This Hollywood film reminds us that finding actually means making, that this making is an ethical project, and that social identities are among the resources and challenges that define this project.

According to Cavell, the genre of remarriage comedy self-consciously links the condition of marriage to broader philosophic considerations about social life, America, and the human condition.[6] The genre emerged in the 1930s, in films like *It Happened One Night*, and then, for reasons that we can't pause to consider here, retreated from prominence just after World War II (effectively ending with *Adam's Rib* in 1949). My sense is that remarriage comedy re-emerged in the late 1990s, more than a decade after Cavell's groundbreaking study, and that *Fools Rush In* was part of this second wave. It joins the Depression-era films, and such contemporaries as *My Best Friend's Wedding*, in self-consciously using the structure of the remarriage narrative to conduct philosophical inquiry.[7]

The name of the genre indicates its most striking feature. Other forms of romantic comedy tend either to make marriage a point of aspiration—a far-off divine event that the narrative haltingly but inexorably approaches—or to ignore it altogether. Comedies of remarriage, by contrast, begin with the condition, or the prospect, of marriage. When these films begin, two people are already married, or are about to be. Something then parts them before death does, at which point the narrative devotes itself to the question not of whether these two people will get married, but of whether they will remain divorced (often literally). The divorce may involve the film's protagonists, or it may disentangle one of the protagonists from someone else, thereby preventing a false suitor from blocking the heroes' path to each other. In either case, the central pair has its own separation to get over, and the road to their reconciliation is paved with a handful of characteristic devices. Eventually there is forgiveness, usually after some explicitly philosophical conversation educates one or both characters about their identities and desires. They marry, again.

Fools Rush In clearly fits the basic remarriage pattern. Isabel's musings about Chuy—whom, it is generally understood, she will marry—put marriage at issue from the outset, and she and Alex get married before the first act ends. From then on, the question is whether Isabel and Alex's inevitable divorce will stand, or whether their figurative "divorces" from their other suitors—Cathy and Chuy— will stand. They work this out with the aid of many of the familiar devices, including conversations about fate and destiny that lead, apparently, to some education. It will matter in what follows that this education, inherited from the duties of the woman's father in older forms of comedic drama, will involve moral authority figures lecturing the woman. (As Cavell notes, *The Philadelphia Story* consists almost entirely of people lecturing Katherine Hepburn.)

Reading *Fools* as a remarriage comedy also begins to locate the film's ethical argument. To be an interesting participant in the genre, Cavell tells us, is to add something new to the ur-text of the standard narrative. As it happens, none of the early comedies pay much attention to social identities apart from gender.

All of Cavell's protagonists are WASPs, as far as we can tell, and the films contain few explicit, and no extended, treatments of ethnic or racial difference. The only explicit treatments of racial difference involve a dubiously white workingman who swarthily mumbles his way through a scene in *The Lady Eve*, and a Japanese valet in *The Awful Truth* who declares "me ju-jitsu" before fighting with Cary Grant. Several of the early films do explore something like class divisions. Real poverty, however, to say nothing of class *politics*, is almost never in view, and never for long. Class in this world is what race is for Emerson—a limitation to be transcended on the way to embodying the spiritual promise of the American experiment.[8]

If the genre embodies a tradition of cinematic reflections on the meaning of America, then *Fools* offers a gentle rebuke to the homogeneity of that tradition. The rebuke begins with the imagined union of the central pair, but it develops further in ways that I mean to make clear in what follows. That said, the rebuke remains rather gentle, since it leaves in place so many of the other ideological constraints on the genre. For example, it refuses to question the generic insistence that the lovers be heterosexual and young, and it stays as close to home as possible in rethinking whiteness, going only as far as Mexico, instead of, say, to Africa. (If I am right about the second wave of remarriage comedy, other films will take up some of these issues.)

The very structure of the film, then, points toward an ethical argument—call it an argument in post-supremacist ethics. In its determination to highlight and correct an instance of social exclusion that grows out of, among other things, white supremacy, *Fools* embodies the same sensibility that animates much work on post-coloniality, feminism, critical race theory, and more. These critical approaches typically combine familiar norms of equality and autonomy with three additional convictions: first, that individuality is culturally mediated; second, that deliberations about justice, right conduct, and good character must be sociohistorically specific, not least by attending carefully and concretely to the role that existing institutions and practices play in the distribution and uses of power; and third, that when a society officially forswears identity-based privilege, responsible moral agents must excavate and confront certain nonconscious and unconscious fixations, assumptions, and biases. Social identities are key at each step here: they are mechanisms of cultural mediation, they arise from politically efficacious institutions and practices, and they are repositories of non- and unconscious psychic resources.

The film insists on the ethical dimensions of this post supremacist sensibility by developing its connections to a kind of moral perfectionism. The perfectionism I have in mind is not the political view that rejects neutralist liberalism, or the potentially elitist view that privileges the cultivation of some fixed set of virtues or traits. I am borrowing once more from Cavell, who says that the perfectionism he finds in Emerson and elsewhere "is not a competing theory of the moral life, but something like a dimension or tradition . . . that spans the course of Western thought and concerns what used to be called the state of one's soul."[9] Cavell goes on to name Aristotle, Kant, Mill, and Nietzsche as, at one moment or another, exponents of this tradition; then, in good Nietzschean or Emersonian fashion, he declines to offer a definition. He says enough, however, to indicate that he has at least two things in mind. One is the emphasis on the cultivation of character that cuts across the dominant schools of thought in ethical theory and that moves contemporary theorists to study utilitarian and Kantian forms of virtue theory as well as the canonical forms derived from Aristotle and the heretical form practiced by Nietzsche. The other is the emphasis on self-care and self-creation that shows up most clearly in the philosophical heresies of Nietzsche and Emerson. This approach refuses the consolations of moral codes; it instead imagines self-creation as a creative, perhaps aesthetic, and ongoing enterprise. Cavell has more than this in mind, and it would take a detour through Freud, Heidegger, and others to make sense of his view. All I have in mind, though, is the creative, dynamic, and open-ended approach to the formation of character that he finds in Emerson. The idea here is not that virtue requires the possession or cultivation of some specific set of traits. It is instead that something like virtue consists in continually posing Dewey's question—*what kind of person shall I be?*—and in taking the answers that emanate from one's culture not as dispositive but as suggestive, and perhaps as symptoms of a malady to be overcome.

Feminism provides the most famous expression of the connection between perfectionism, so construed, and post-supremacist ethics by insisting that the personal
is political. The idea, here as for Marx, Foucault, and others, is that political forces
work on and through individuals in ways usually quotidian enough to escape
notice, and that, as a result, the practice of self-scrutiny is essential to a properly
engaged politics. This stance translates easily into talk about forming character,
cultivating habit, or caring for the state of one's soul.

The mode of interpretation that depicts *Fools* as an exercise in post-supremacist
and perfectionist ethics actually models the self-excavation that is essential to both
enterprises. Both involve, as Cavell says, taking one's experience seriously. In the
context of reading film, this means taking seriously the degree to which viewers
of film are awash in a sea of shared meanings, and making those meanings explicit
by making one's own experience of a film articulate. This leads to a form of
reader-oriented transactionalism that treats authors, texts, and readers as participants in a joint cultural encounter, but uses readers to unlock the meanings that
ideological forces and formal conventions can covertly embed in authors and
texts.

So: I will read this film with the aid of people like Emerson, but not because I
believe either that director Andy Tennant had this in mind or that some ideal
reader would have it in mind. The film puts me in mind of such things, and following out these thoughts helps me account for the work the film seems to be
doing. This is in the first instance an impressionistic exercise, but it aspires to
intersubjective intelligibility because it assumes a kind of representativeness. I am
using the film not to sound my own depths, but to sound in myself the depths that
I share with others. I will appeal to conceptual resources that may resonate more
with me than with other readers. These appeals should still excavate and illuminate the meanings that constitute the shared culture that mass entertainments presuppose and that help constitute us as individuals. Chief among the meanings I
will consider are the ones that flow around and through notions like "race", "gender", and "nationality", all of which provide defeasible but powerful templates for
imagining one's self, one's prospects, and one's relationships.

III. "THE WHITE PEOPLE ARE MELTING"

Fools Rush In demonstrates its interest in the complexities of social identity most
clearly by having the parents of the central pair argue over the unborn child's religious upbringing. After complaining about the heat, Alex's father declares for
Presbyterianism, only to have Isabel's mother dismiss the idea that Presbyterianism is a religion at all. The fathers then escalate the dispute.

> MR. WHITMAN: This country was founded by people who were escaping
> religious persecution. The Whitmans were one of them.

MR. FUENTES: Sir, when the West was stolen from Mexico, the Fuentes family made a vow. That even though they took our land, they'd never take our culture.

MR. WHITMAN (*shouting, standing*): Culture? You call this culture? Guacamole and a ghetto blaster in the middle of a desert?

MR. FUENTES (also shouting and standing): Now you're offending Amalia's guacamole? What's wrong with Amalia's guacamole?

MR. WHITMAN (*still shouting*): In case you haven't noticed, the white people are melting out here.

(*Silence follows, as the mothers and children exchange bewildered looks.*)[10]

This marvelous last line makes as clear a claim to significance as anything else in the film. The idea of melting is doubly significant for students of the idea of America, and accordingly offers two ways of reading Mr. Whitman's odd exclamation. On one level, an image of passional redemption from a business-obsessed culture comes into view; on a second level, the familiar image of the melting pot, long the symbol of pluralist democracy in the US, materializes.

MELTING THE IRON CAGE

The first reading of Mr. Whitman's line specifies the work that Isabel is doing in Alex's life. She is melting his heart and thereby helping to redeem him from his fixation on work. Alex needs this redemption because he suffers from a kind of enervation that has long been associated with capitalism, especially in America.

Fools recommends this redemptive image of melting with a number of clues, beginning with Alex's religious commitments. Alex is Presbyterian, by his own

Figure 6.2

and his father's insistent declamation. He finds himself, however, unable to dispute Isabel's claim that this religion plays no role in his life. In his case, Mrs. Fuentes seems to be right: Presbyterianism is not a religion. What can it be, then? Nonpracticing but culturally committed Catholics and Jews are a familiar part of the U.S. social terrain, but there is no category like this for Protestants. What does it mean that the film insists on the Whitmans' religion, on it being specifically Presbyterian, and on its inertness in their spiritual lives?

We might take a cue here from Max Weber, who thought Presbyterianism provided the purest expression of the Calvinist impulse that he found behind American capitalism. Weber argues that the quest for material goods in modern capitalist societies has trapped the human spirit in an ascetic "iron cage". Capitalists have learned from Protestantism to make success in worldly affairs their highest priority, to take it as a sign of moral and spiritual rectitude. They have also learned, however, to curtail this quest for success by renouncing worldly enjoyments. Unfortunately, the original theological motivation for this union of striving and asceticism has dwindled away, leaving only a rationalized "pursuit of wealth, stripped of its religious and ethical meaning." So Presbyterianism is, in this sense, not a religion: it is instead the source for the stultifying but secular moral discipline—the protestant *ethic*—of capitalist America.[11]

Whatever Weber's shortcomings as a chronicler of capitalism's origins or essence, he successfully encapsulates a concern about America's capitalist culture that was already quite familiar by the turn of the twentieth century. The worry is that the culture churns out confined, repressed, joyless prisoners to the idea of material accumulation, figures like the lead characters in narratives from Herman Melville's novella, *Bartleby, The Scrivener* (1853) to John Patrick Shanley's 1990 film, *Joe Versus the Volcano*. By renouncing their desires and reducing themselves to cogs in a rationalized economic bureaucracy, these Bartleby figures become what Goethe teaches Weber to call "specialists without spirit" and "sensualists without heart."[12] They become, in effect, frozen: dead to—or alienated from, Marx and others would say—the vital world of emotion, beauty, and relationships. They cannot be redeemed until something or someone melts their hearts and reignites the vital flames of passion for life.

As an inhabitant of a screwball world, and as the sort of character fit to be animated by Matthew Perry, Alex Whitman cannot be as numb as Bartleby or as dour as Shanley's Joe. He is, however, definitely a "specialist without spirit." He testifies to his own spiritlessness by denying religion, fate, or destiny any role in his life. He is specialized in the sense that the multifaceted human person he might have been has instead become a single-minded seeker of business success. We see this in his indifference to food, interior design, religious community, and family life, and in his willingness to accept and repeat his friend Jeff's warnings against letting anything distract him from work.

Isabel appears in Alex's world to save him from the coldness of this life without "distractions". She makes this abundantly clear—she announces that she will "spice up" his colorless house, she recruits her large and noisy family to help deck the house out in tropical hues and religious icons, and she captivates him with an exhibition of simultaneous dancing and cooking. In all this, she may simply be expressing a deeper trait, one that in the world of Hollywood films specifically suits Isabel for this role. She is, as at least one reviewer of the film irritably noted, a hot-blooded Latina, whose destiny in a narrative like this could hardly be other than to revive the spiritually moribund white man.[13]

There will be more to say about Isabel's trajectory soon enough. Just now, the point is that Isabel's identity points us to the fact that Alex needs saving not just as an individual, but also as a white person, as someone for whom self-renunciation has become a defining cultural trait. Weber certainly had white people in mind when envisioning his secular Protestants. The connection between whiteness and Puritan renunciation goes deeper than this accident of history and sociology, however. There are plenty of reasons, and precedents, for thinking of whiteness as essentially bound up with ascetic self-denial. Scholars since Weber have told us that this link was quite explicit for most of the history of the country.[14] As a republican polity with a capitalist economy, the United States needed citizens with the capacities for self-governance and self-restraint. The dominant racial ideologies insisted that only white people—and only some of these, like the English, and men—were endowed with these virtues. This racial chauvinism made whiteness a necessary condition for proper citizenship, but it also made whiteness a burden, a disciplinary regime that consigned certain people to suffer the maladies that Weber connected to self-renunciation. The scourges of repression, joylessness, and spiritlessness became, to borrow and misuse a phrase, the wages of whiteness—they became the costs that white people had to pay in order to prosper and govern themselves. This is why African-American comedians have long parodied white people by feigning repression—as in Richard Pryor's comparisons of black and white mourners at a funeral, or in the stilted gait and speech that Eddie Murphy combined with "whiteface" makeup in his "White Like Me" skit.[15]

STIRRING THE MELTING POT

The first reading of "the white people are melting," then, leads us to a parable of the spiritual redemption of whiteness. Since at least the Surrealists, who hoped African "savagery" would help redeem European civilization, there has been a tradition of imagining whiteness as in need of nonwhite redemption. *Fools Rush In* joins films like *Bulworth* in the cinematic version of that tradition.

The second reading of the line makes Isabel's redemptive mission more ethically palatable. So far, her importance for Alex might lie in providing him with an opportunity for what bell hooks calls "eating the other."[16] This is what happens when someone uses a person of a different, "exotic" background as a means of enhancing his or her own experience. We might think here about sex tourism, with American men going to Thailand or European women visiting the Caribbean.[17] Hooks finds her paradigm cases in Flaubert's encounters with Egypt and, more colorfully, in the self-confessed dating habits of white male college students, some of whom she overheard talking openly about their plans to have sex with as many nonwhite women as they could. According to hooks, the students saw sex as "a way to confront the Other, as well as a way to make themselves over. . . ." In contrast to a history of sexual exploitation for the sake of racial domination, "These young men see themselves as non-racists, who choose to transgress racial boundaries within the sexual realm . . . so that they can be acted *upon*, so that they can be changed utterly."[18]

To his credit, Alex seems never to have been moved by this sort of instrumental exoticization. As it happens, the evidence for this is entirely negative. For example, it does not occur to Alex that his parents will mistake Isabel for a maid. Neither he nor his friend Jeff uses Isabel's social identity to frame their praise for her physical virtues—Jeff calls her "the one with the body," not, as one might expect of the Jeffs in American film, a "hot tamale". In these ways, the film refuses to show Alex "eating the other," leaving room instead for us to consider how her presence in his life forces an overhaul of his identity. Here again, she causes him to melt, but this time in the sense that implicates the idea of the melting pot.

The melting pot metaphor underscores the acculturating dynamics involved in turning a collection of immigrant groups into a nation. When the expression was coined, the idea was originally that different ethnic groups would melt together into a single American populace, or that the individual members of these groups would see the traits that distinguish them melted away in the cauldron of Americanization. This would then leave behind only a common, homogenized American identity that all citizens could share. The originating context for this idea remains its most common and natural referent—the assimilation and Americanization of European ethnic groups in the late nineteenth and early twentieth centuries.[19]

Of course, the narrative of America as a molten mixture of immigrants leaves out a great deal. It ignores the limits of the homogenizing model, both as an account of how acculturation actually happens and as an image of how it should happen. More to the point, in its standard uses, it ignores the people that the model never fit particularly well. The participants in the immigrant drama of American mythology were white people, whose cultural differences from America's "native" whites were relatively easy to submerge beneath the imperatives and allures of shared racial identity. It is true that these intraracial differences were also racialized, which is to say that there were worries about the degree to which certain "probationary" white people—Irish, Italians, Eastern European Jews, and so on— could fit into and contribute to Anglo-American civilization. The politics of immigration, the horrors of the Holocaust, and other forces, however, enabled these peoples to become, by and large, fully white by the 1960s. Nonwhite peoples, by contrast, generally did not benefit from these whitening pressures; were often excluded from the national narrative of the melting pot; and, as a consequence, were, and too often still are, not thought of as real citizens.

This racial nationalist vision of American identity has been under assault for quite some time, by activists and scholars working in the wake of the 1960s rights revolutions and in the tradition of earlier thinkers like W.E.B. Du Bois and José Martí. *Fools* leans toward joining these critics in a critical reconstruction of the idea of America. Isabel tells the story of her great-grandfather participating in the building of the Hoover Dam, which links an ordinary worker from Mexico to the building of a U.S. national landmark. A bit later, Mr. Fuentes complains about the western United States having been stolen from Mexico, a remark that highlights something the film works throughout to dramatize. By imagining an entire family of Mexican-descended American citizens, a family that asserts as old and as good a claim to the land as the Mayflower-borne Whitmans, the film reworks the idea of America to include Mexicans not as immigrants, interlopers, or newcomers, but as co-founders—as what Du Bois called "co-workers in the kingdom of culture."[20] We might think in this spirit of the film's determination to unite these two old American families, one Mexican and one Anglo, in marriage. It is as if Latin America and Anglo America, what Martí called "Our America" and "the Other America,"[21] have suffered a rupture, a divorce—call this "the Mexican-American war." And in the idiom of remarriage comedy, a divorce cannot stand.

White people are melting, then, in this second sense: Just as the boundaries that separated white "races" from each other in the early twentieth century melted away, the boundaries separating the late twentieth century's whites from others are melting. Just as before, peoples who think of themselves as separate will rediscover their shared contributions and commitment to the American project. What better way to symbolize this than with a marriage, and a baby?

IV. "I MAKE MY OWN CHOICES": CULT, CAGE, AND DOMESTICITY

If the foregoing is right, then Alex begins to become a fit suitor for Isabel—he begins what the genre of remarriage depicts as his education—by learning the lessons of post-supremacist ethics and of moral perfectionism. In keeping with the perfectionist emphasis on holistic self-cultivation that linked Weber to near-contemporaries like Emerson, Marx, and Charlotte Perkins Gilman, he learns to balance work with love, family, and, in ways we've yet to explore, spirituality. In keeping with the post-supremacist injunction to treat social formations as objects of historical analysis and cultural criticism, he learns to think of Mr. Fuentes' "West" as part of America and of people like the Fuentes family as coworkers in the kingdom of American culture. He is able to learn all of this because he sees Isabel not just as an individual, but also as an extension and expression of her family and culture, in keeping with the post-supremacist emphasis on social identity.

Isabel's lessons are harder to isolate. She seems not to confront the complexity of the post-supremacist condition. Her accommodation to it seems not to involve much in the way of education at all.

Isabel seems not to grow because, unlike Alex, she seems not to reach a new accommodation with the sources of her self. In some ways, this is because she needs no education. She is fully aware of the *mestizo* roots of American culture, and so she has no need to join Alex in working toward an expanded racial and national identity. In addition, her acceptance of what seem to be ethno-racial stereotypes—of, for example, the hot-blooded Latina—points less to the need for her own enlightenment than to her recognition that the stereotype crudely reflects an important reality: that her culture does in fact tend to eschew Weber's asceticism, and that it can as a result serve as a corrective to the overly Anglicized, or Protestantized, sense of American identity that the Whitmans represent.

In other ways, though, Isabel's lack of growth might suggest an imperviousness to education—as, for example, in her complete acceptance of gender-specific social roles. Her presence enriches Alex's home life and provides a counterbalance to his work in precisely the way that the nineteenth-century ideology of separate spheres required. Every day, like clockwork, Alex returns to his public life in the workplace, while the domestic sphere that feminism invites Isabel to deconstruct or escape instead becomes her habitat. We see her cook, clean, and wash clothes, all in her husband's house. We see her beautify this house and then populate it, first with herself, then with a dog, and throughout with the promise of their child. We see her going to church and otherwise insisting on religion, in accordance with her womanly obligation to cultivate morality and spirituality. (We even see her pray for her husband's career while he is away pursuing it.)

While Alex's career remains in the foreground, nothing comparable appears among Isabel's priorities. During one of their arguments about where to live, Alex says, "My work is in New York." Isabel responds, "My *life* is here." We see her at work only once, and this after hearing her tell Alex that it is not part of her "real life". She is "really" an art photographer, a vocation that makes her job merely an expedient, and a much less effective one than a well-paid and supportive husband. As if to underscore this asymmetry, we see Isabel with her camera or in a darkroom only twice, and this briefly, during montages, while Alex's work life structures the entire narrative. Hers is not a career but an avocation, one that, after her marriage, recalls the image of the pampered wife as dilettante.

The film completes Isabel's consignment to the cult of domesticity by doubly objectifying her. First there is a focus on her appearance. A point of view shot invites the viewer to join Alex in covertly watching her dance. As we've seen, Jeff invites us to think of her as "the one with the body" and compares her to the impossibly proportioned animated character Jessica Rabbit.[22] While the film's opening scenes introduce Alex in a business suit, they introduce Isabel in a flimsy and revealing wrap (to the delight of the young boys who share the scene with her). In addition to this focus on the outer surfaces of her body, there is a second focus—on its inner workings: Isabel's physicality is always under consideration, and it is essential to the plot at crucial moments. Her irresistible need to use the bathroom brings them together, and then her pregnancy reunites them. We get to see her sit on the toilet, and insist on Alex's presence while she does it, two times. (It is tempting to add here that the pain of childbirth recalls Isabel from her overrationalized resistance to Alex's entreaties, and it wrings from her an apology and a profession of love. There will, however, be another story to tell about this.)

With respect to Isabel's aspirations, her daily life, and her narrative function, what ought to be her education seems to involve simple domestication. She does not even have to be educated, or indoctrinated, into this. She falls into it naturally, as if born to it.

At this point, it is important to notice that the film means for us to take seriously a subtle, but crucial, detail about Isabel's situation. Unlike her nineteenth-century predecessors, she has not simply fallen into her separate sphere. She has chosen it, and we are supposed to wonder whether a cage remains a cage when it is chosen.

Isabel's determination to choose for herself is the key to understanding her character. The film presents her throughout as a free spirit. She breaks up with the person everyone thinks she will marry. She regularly travels, alone, across state and national boundaries. She is an independent-minded artist, hard at work on the sort of extended and so far unremunerative project that makes parents despair of their children's prospects. She makes unpopular choices—about keeping her baby and perhaps upsetting her family, about concealing her baby and upsetting her husband—with minimal hesitation. She is difficult and confrontational, while Cathy, her luckless competitor for Alex's affections, is solicitous and agreeable—and alone. (Though it may be that the difference between Isabel and Cathy is that Cathy is too solicitous, and betrays her feminine role by chasing Alex; Isabel, by contrast, lets the man chase her.)

Isabel's insistence on choice is also the key to her education. She begins her most momentous trip, the one that finally reunites her with Alex, after saying to her grandmother, "I make my own choices now." She has been making choices throughout, of course, and occasionally declaring that she is doing so, as when she tells Alex "I choose to keep this baby." She comes to see, in the space of perspective and renewal provided by her grandmother's hacienda, that her choices have been inappropriately conditioned. Whether she is at this point in the narrative ready to achieve autonomy is an open question; but she has at least identified, for herself and for the audience, the focus of her education. She must learn to set aside fate, stop trying to read its riddles, and decide her future for herself.

Whether Isabel has actually or properly chosen her domestic cage will depend on what one takes choice to mean, and on how determined one is to submit the act of choice to ethical scrutiny. The right sort of feminist or social theorist will say that that the problem with the cult of domesticity is not that it was imposed, but that it is an invidious ideology, working behind the scenes to shape preferences and choices in unjust ways. On this approach, what looks like a choice must be located in a broader framework, and this framework must itself be subjected to ethical and political criticism.

If, as I've suggested, this film is a document in post-supremacist ethics, it should share this openness to ideology critique. It should, in particular, resist or frustrate the reading, call it a post-feminist reading, developed so far. On this reading, Isabel's determination to choose reflects the successful consolidation of the gains of the feminist movement. But it also reflects her refusal of the version of Weber's cage that, some say, imprisons women after feminism. After a generation of trying to be superwomen, the post-feminist says (in the words, I confess, of a critic) that women find themselves "unhappy, unfeminine, childless, lonely, and bitter."[23] A cottage industry of popular writing explores this problem, usually by reducing it to a tragic choice—*career or family?*—and by trying to combine "professional assertiveness and self-confidence" with "fairly conventional attitudes" about gender roles.[24]

So construed, post-feminism offers a highly tendentious diagnosis of life after, say, Betty Freidan. It represents the new opportunities wrought by feminism after 1960 as opportunities for individual women to assimilate into public institutions as they stand. It declines to call into question any of the implicit and explicit norms that still govern gender roles and family responsibilities—except the ones that keep women out of the workplace. Instead of questioning the social conditions that make it difficult, for men *and* women, to reconcile careers with family, it puts the problem at the feet of individual women and forces the tragic choice. Nevertheless, the view is not irrational. One could choose it, as Isabel seems to, and then work to preserve the pleasures and benefits of traditional femininity.

This post-feminist reading is in tension with the film's post-supremacist sensitivity to the problems of ideology, but not irremediably. The tension dissipates once it becomes clear that post-feminism illuminates not the argument of the film as a whole, but Isabel's trajectory alone. There are two reasons not to identify the film's argument with a thematization of post-feminism. First, there is the materiality of the document under scrutiny. This film is a Hollywood product, and as a consequence shares Hollywood's usual, though not universal, diffidence about "radical" ideas. It also, however, shares the entertainment industry's determination to reach as many, and offend as few, people as possible, which means that it was likely aimed simultaneously at multiple audiences, and submitted to focus group after focus group to verify its widespread acceptability. So it does, of course, prominently feature themes that are compatible with a media culture that routinely raises the question of post-feminism—career or family?—and that takes this question to be well-formed. It also, however, has multiple layers of inchoate meaning, which provide the resources for alternate readings or for alternate ways of projecting its unfolding narrative into its fiction-world future.

The second obstacle to identifying this film with one character's post-feminist path lies in its generic obligations. In ways that the multivocality of contemporary entertainment industry products surely facilitates, comedies of remarriage *insist* on the dynamism of their unseen futures. One point of these narratives is that their central pairs are embarking on something together, and that this shared undertaking will require continually renegotiating their identities along the way. I see no grounds on which to assume that Isabel's post-feminist sensibility will be exempt from this renegotiation. The film ends, in fact, with an image of incompleteness or of nextness that is as open-ended as the remarkable closing scenes of *The Philadelphia Story*, or of *The Awful Truth*—and trumps these by adding a newborn. Remember: we last see the characters isolated, together, at the edge of the Grand Canyon, in the sublimely empty desert. If anything is clear about these people, it is that they must go *somewhere else*. Add to this the newlyweds having declared their intention to move to New York, which will mark the beginning of a new phase in their relationship, unprecedented by anything we have seen in their lives on film.

All of that is to say that *Fools* means to foreground Isabel's acts of choice, and her growing recognition of the constraints on her past choices. Recognizing this allows us to specify the focus of her education and to resist the sense that her character remains static while Alex grows. This emphasis on choice privileges, and is most visible in, Isabel's embrace of the problematic behind so much "chick-lit" and its cinematic analogues. Its full significance becomes clear, however, only in light of the remarriage genre's orientation to an open and experimental future. This orientation points us, finally, in the direction of the film's deeper reflections on fate, to which we now turn.

V. READING THE SIGNS

Fools Rush In explicitly presents itself as a meditation on fate. The entire dynamic of the central relationship appears in germ in the first conversation between Isabel and Alex. This one exchange sums it up:

> ISABEL: I believe that your destiny has already been decided. You just have to read the signs.

> ALEX: I think if a guy gets hit by a bus, it's because he wasn't looking. Not because of some master plan.

Isabel believes in fate, and in the signs by which it declares itself. Alex, by contrast, does not. If we credit his response here, his alternative is a belief not simply in temporal and natural causes, but in individual agency. The pedestrian dies not because of a master plan, but also not because of something beyond his control, like a balky traffic signal or a drunk driver. He dies because *he* wasn't looking. In light of this idea, and of its consistency with the secular Puritan emphasis on terrestrial striving, call Alex's alternative a kind of self-reliance.

Isabel and Alex do not so much defend opposing sides in the struggle between fate and self-reliance as announce flawed initial views that they both will have to correct. The dispute is not internal to the relationship but to each character, where it serves as a sign that each is as yet unfit for marriage. When their educations are complete, both characters will believe something that they can capture in the words that we get used to hearing from Isabel. Believing in fate and signs, however, will not mean the same thing to either of them that it meant to the Isabel that Alex first met.

Early on, Isabel thinks of fate in a way that is morally problematic and disabling. Fate is for her an external agency that maps out the future from on high and that then waits for us to arrive at our preordained destinations. We see this in the scene of her meeting with Alex, when she lamely tells her friend Lanie that fate licensed her rejection of Chuy by breaking a piece of jewelry that he had given her. She goes on to tell Alex how fate has brought them there, to that very spot, and then jokes, tellingly, that fate wanted to shorten her wait for the bathroom. Later, when Alex asks her to marry him, the very next thing we see is the wedding, such as it is, with neither comment nor complaint from Isabel. It is as if she, or the film, has been waiting for this, as if his proposal was all that was needed to set things in motion. More than this, it is as if her agreement is a foregone conclusion, as if there is no place here for her agency. Finally, after Isabel announces and demonstrates her new indifference to fate, she says to her great-grandmother, "Now I make my own decisions," as if she has not been making decisions all along. In all these ways, she uses fate to evade responsibility for charting and implementing the life plan that has left her where she is. What she calls a belief in signs is actually bad faith, or a refusal of moral responsibility, and Alex is right to reject it.

Where Isabel is guilty of bad faith, Alex is guilty of fetishizing his independence, or of failing to see the deeper cultural and emotional forces at work behind his choices. The dominant discourses of whiteness make it normative and invisible, which turns the residents of New Canaan, Connecticut, into unencumbered individuals and turns other people into the bearers of culture. Weber and the rest tell us, however, that secular Puritanism is a cultural phenomenon and that Alex's alienation makes him not an abstract individual but a cultural artifact. His house and his life are colorless not just because he has chosen to work all the time, but because he belongs to a form of life that recommends this way of proceeding. (As Emerson says, "He looks like a piece of luck, but is a piece of causation.")[25] In addition, Alex fails to examine his choices for signs of heteronomy. Consider the road to his proposal to Isabel. First, at his house, he forces himself to say the right thing about the pregnancy, after betraying his true feelings in the spontaneous swoon of gratitude with which he met what he thought was her willingness to have an abortion. Then, on the way to her family dinner, he explains that his own family never meets this way and implies that this is just as well, given who or how they are. At dinner, after being visibly intoxicated by the warmth and vitality he finds in the Fuentes family home, he holds a baby and shares a passionate kiss with Isabel. This last happens after they cross the room in slow motion—a sure cinematic signal of the deliberative faculties being overwhelmed. All of this suggests that his choice, the choice that sets the narrative in motion and occasions Isabel's inarticulate acquiescence, is not autonomous but the product of what Emerson calls "unpenetrated causes".[26] This, like Isabel's silent assent, practically guarantees that a divorce is in the offing.

The turn away from these problematic approaches to freedom and fate begins in the third act, when Alex rediscovers the language of signs and fate. This happens after he returns to New York, alone, receives his divorce papers, and accepts an invitation from Cathy Stewart to join her parents and his own for a weekend getaway. On the morning of the trip, and the morning after a priest has told him, "There are signs everywhere," he sees, in quick succession: a chihuahua, a picture of the Grand Canyon, a Caesar's Palace sign, and a little dark-haired girl named Isabel. All of this shakes him, and though he makes it to the heliport from which the Whitmans and Stewarts are to depart, and though Cathy clings to him like ivy, he sends them away and runs in the opposite direction. This begins his pilgrimage to and from central Mexico to claim his wife. When he finally catches up to her on the dam, he declares his belief in signs and insists, over her protests, that she still believes in them, too. After they are reconciled and the baby is born, he wishes on a coin and hurls it into the chasm.

In the world of remarriage comedies, the pilgrimage, with its ample opportunities for risking reputation, safety, and dignity, is the test of Alex's newfound fitness as a suitor. His apparent embrace of destiny, in both word and deed, signifies that he has passed the test. He became fit, however, in New York, in ways that Emerson and Dewey can help make clear.

Emerson explores the gap between freedom and destiny in his essay on fate. He begins by recognizing the uneasy juxtaposition in human psychology of the two sets of ideas. "This is true," he says, "and that other is true. But our geometry cannot span these extreme points and reconcile them." Accepting both commitments as basic, and struggling to think through their simultaneous appeal, he offers a diagnosis. We invoke fate, or blame it, whenever we find ourselves limited by what seem to be immutable and inscrutable circumstances—when confronted by "facts not yet passed under the fire of thought." As one might expect from a thoroughgoing voluntarist and idealist, Emerson argues that intellect can turn these obdurate limitations into resources for action and insight. Floods and other natural disasters, for example, often strike people as evidence of fate's cruelty and indifference to us. When we discover what drives these events, though, we can locate nature's whims in a rational framework and perhaps subject them to prediction and control. In this way, "The mischievous torrent is taught to drudge for man," and we learn to harness the power of steam.[27]

So far this is a voluntarist's evasion of fate-talk, a way of reducing it to ignorance and a failure of nerve. By applying the same thinking to moral psychology, however, Emerson connects the idea of destiny to the cultivation of character. If fate is a name for what limits us, we have to recognize that the constellation of habits that makes us who we are is itself an element of fate. In this spirit, Emerson says, "A man's fortunes are the fruit of his character."[28] Characteristically, this statement points in several directions, some subset of which the "Fate" essay goes on to explore. Key here are the three respects in which this approach assigns character some causal efficacy. First, because our characteristic repertoire of habits has shaped our choices in the past, it shapes the present that our choices have helped make and with which we must contend. Second, this new present includes the present self, since character is subject to internal modification and is as a result an evolving "organization of habits" that is only "relatively stable".[29] Finally, because the habits that define the self are habits of perception and attention, the world that we experience is the world that character predisposes us to see and engage. In all these ways, "events grow on the same stem with persons."[30]

Alex's ability to see the signs testifies to an alteration in his habits of perception, which in turn testifies to a deeper alteration in his character. The Alex who married Isabel the first time would not have been moved by his experience on the way to the heliport. The so-called signs—two advertisements, an ordinary dog, and an ordinary little girl—are not all that out of place in New York City, that Alex would say. He would blame his interest in them on the principle of selective perception. His recent experiences, he would say, simply prepared him to notice things that would have been there in any case but that he simply, in the past, would not have cared about. This is, however, precisely the point—Alex's time with Isabel has quite literally made him someone else, someone who sees the world differently. He refuses to board the helicopter because he accepts the testimony of these signs. Or, put in a more obviously naturalistic idiom, he accepts the testimony of his newly selective awareness of ordinary coincidences, which tells him that he is no longer made for the life that Cathy offers him. He refuses to board because he accepts, and takes responsibility for, the self that his choices have brought into being.

This is a parable of the kind of self-scrutiny and self-ownership that come with the forms of perfectionism that we find in Emerson and Dewey. These forms of self-cultivation insist on taking experience seriously in the moral life. This means, among other things, that they emphasize the ethical burden of self-creation, of connecting moral deliberation to the task of caring for the state of one's soul; and that they take society seriously, in ways that the parable also reflects. Dewey and Emerson both insist, for different reasons, that the moral self is a social self, and that living ethically means achieving a kind of critical perspective on the social underpinnings of one's character. For Emerson this is a matter of self-reliance, or of nonconformity; for Dewey it is a matter of critical intelligence, or of reflective morality. Both have in mind, however, the failure to live what Heidegger might call an authentic life.

Alex's conversion figures this line of thinking in ways that draw on the conventions of remarriage comedy. In this genre, it is not enough for potential partners to have grown up together, as Isabel says of Chuy and Cathy says of Alex. They must, to borrow Hegel's language, achieve a mediated immediacy. Their intimacy must not be the natural connection of people who happen to have been reared together, like brother and sister. It must be the hard-won intimacy of people who have recognized their separateness and found a new ground for relatedness. In keeping with the requirements of the genre, Alex refuses the incestuous immediacy that Cathy offers him. (Just as Isabel refuses Chuy.) At the same time, however, in the same moment, he refuses the secular Puritan life from which Isabel has liberated him, the life that his parents and the Stewarts still represent. Cathy represents this life above all, as evidenced by the lingering point-of-view shot that finds her smiling and languorously awaiting Alex at the door of the helicopter. Accepting the future she literally puts before him, a future in which he and Cathy become copies of their parents and produce copies of themselves, would mean accepting an irresponsible re-immersion in the world that produced him. It would not be impossible to choose this life responsibly, which is to say, while accepting the burden of caring, critically and intelligently, for the state of his soul. The person he has become cannot do so, however, and briefly contemplated doing so only in a moment of weakness, when he was ready to evade the responsibility of navigating the present that his choices and experiences had made.

This Emersonian reading of fate allows Alex to embrace fate without contradicting his self-reliant, anti-theological bent. He can accept and even say that signs are everywhere, because he sees that they point to the Alex Whitman that has been and remains in the making. The fate that they signal is the structure of limitation that his past self, among other forces, has imposed upon his present, a structure that he can turn into a resource for the creation of his next self. He can, in addition, pay homage to the sources of this transformation by wishing on a coin, as Isabel would, in what one might call a gesture of piety. Isabel, with her coins and candles, gave him the conceptual resources to think of himself in this new way, and to recognize the changes that together they have wrought in his life. Wishing on the coin signifies and cements his embrace of this new orientation.[31]

Where is Isabel's education in all this? We have seen her embody the disabling account of fate. We also have seen that her abortive attempt to escape this ethical trap—"Now I make my own choices"—is not only false to the facts of her past but also a lie about her present. She still believes whatever she believed before, as evidenced by her attempt to wish on a coin on her last trip across the dam.

Notice that Isabel never makes this last wish: Alex interrupts her by leaping in front of her car. This intervention enables her to complete her education, just as the memory of her words enables him to complete his. He forces her to break with her old evasions the way she pretended to in central Mexico. Now she will have to take responsibility for her choices.

As further insurance that she will take responsibility, physical law—another level of fate for Emerson—intervenes, in the form of the baby. When Alex renews his claim to Isabel's heart by embracing fate, she responds by announcing that her water has broken. This might be a way of saying, again, that her will has no place here, that Alex's conversion speaks to her so primordially that nature itself, woman's nature, will decide for her. Notice the sequence of events, however. After Isabel's water breaks, she is not silent, as after his first proposal; instead, she is positively garrulous. She tells him she hates him, in the way pregnant women on film are wont to do. Then, however, she tells him that she loves him and needs him. This is what she did not say, or what we did not hear her say, when he proposed to her at the end of the first act. The baby has interrupted what might have been another hasty concession to the man's claim, or to the dictates of social convention. It has given her—or, perhaps, the film— the space not just to make her assent articulate, but also to preface it with an entirely warranted expression of dissatisfaction. We might say that childbirth has distorted her thinking and led her to embrace him when she otherwise might not. This is a woman, however, who has no trouble separating the sentimentality and physiology of childbearing from her preferences in a relationship. She has already broken up with Alex—in a hospital, while dealing with the pain of some prenatal complication. This permits us to see the pain of childbirth working to clarify her thinking rather than to distort it. It strips away the rationalizations she might otherwise marshal and makes her focus on what matters most to her.

VI. NATURE'S LOFTINESS

In the essay on fate, Emerson writes, " 'Tis weak and vicious people who cast the blame on Fate. The right use of Fate is to bring up our conduct to the loftiness of nature." Later, he explains what it means to aspire to the loftiness of nature: "[W]hen a strong will appears, it usually results from a certain unity of organization, as if the whole energy of body and mind flowed in one direction . . . There can be no driving force except through the conversion of the man into his will, making him the will, and the will him." In this way, we embody and emulate the directness of (the rest of) nature, which is undeterred in its projects by rationalization, self-deception, or self-doubt.[32]

Isabel and Alex complete their educations when they achieve this unity of organization. Having finally abandoned the evasions of bad faith and false consciousness, they have embraced the perfectionist vocation of self-creation. Isabel has learned not to cast the blame on fate, Alex has learned not to fetishize his individuality, and both now recognize the will as an agency in creating the circumstances that define and constrain the future. In addition, they emblematize for us the process of ethical criticism that distinguishes a critical and responsible engagement with the social forms that condition the project of self-creation. Alex's journey excavates hegemonic discourses of social identity and makes the film a companion piece to narratives of white redemption like *Dances With Wolves*. Isabel's journey involves a critical, post-feminist, mediated appropriation of its own hegemonic discourses, while also opening onto a future that promises to renegotiate her gender identity and obligations.

These different strains of thought come together in the very form of the film, in its commitment to the remarriage genre. As has been noted, *Fools Rush In* adds color to what has been an overwhelmingly white tradition, though it leaves the bourgeois and heterosexist biases of the tradition completely in place. It also adds a baby, which is, in a way, counter to the spirit of the enterprise. According to Cavell, the point of these usually childless films is to purify the discussion of marriage, so that the relationship can work out its justifications without appeal to external factors like the burdens of reproduction. If, as Cavell says, deviations from the basic storyline will receive compensation, as if to offset the missing feature by doing its work in a different way, what is the compensation for this intrusion on the private affair of marriage?

As one expects in contemporary media products, aimed as they are at different and sometimes conflicting markets and constituencies, the storyline of the baby has multiple functions. It reflects the reduced stigma of out-of-wedlock pregnancy, while also piling onto the hot-blooded—and fertile—brown-person stereotype that the film tries to appropriate and defang. At the same time, it also reflects the heightened insistence on the sanctity of marriage, or on family values, that marks the United States after Reagan. Perhaps most broadly, it symbolizes two familiar thoughts about the future of the United States: that the population will grow increasingly brown, thanks to trends in immigration, interracial mating, and Hispanic birth rates; and that the center of gravity in U.S. social life is moving increasingly to the west, to the land that was born from joining the old Americas of Mr. Fuentes and the elder Mr. Whitman.

Most important for current purposes, though, the layering of a remarriage narrative over a narrative of pregnancy and birth thematizes the stakes of moral perfectionism in ways we have almost touched upon. These two characters are quite literally confronted, at almost every moment, with the fact that their choices will bring a new person into being. Their choices have constrained this person's future horizons in ways that will manifest with the decisiveness of fate. These constraints will nevertheless leave room for creatively appropriating limits and causes in order to bring new futures, and new selves, into being. Whatever else ethical reflection and action is, it must take seriously the challenge of Dewey's question, *What kind of person shall I be?* This film, with its ever-present, steadily growing, but late-arriving baby, reframes the question. It asks, *What kind of person am I making?* It insists that this question is always relevant, and always connected to the burdens and resources of social identity.

NOTES

1. Ellison, "The Little Man at Chehaw Station," 519–520.
2. Ibid., 495.
3. Ibid., 507. It may seem perverse to treat this film, featuring this woman, as a riff on Ellison themes rather than on, say, Gloria Anzaldua's discussion of borderlands, or on María Lugones' discussion of world-traveling. I take it as an implication of Ellison's view that there can be sources of illumination concerning a Latina woman's experiences other than Latina theorists. Still, it would be perverse not to mention this

consideration, or to assume that Ellison, or Emerson, or Martí, will say everything on the subject that needs saying. *See* Gloria Anzaldúa, *Borderlands/La Frontera: The New Mestiza*; María Lugones, "Playfulness, 'World'-Travelling, and Loving Perception".

4. Dewey, "The Moral Self," 342.

5. Ellison, "Little Man", 502.

6. Stanley Cavell, *Pursuits of Happiness*.

7. Other participants in this revival include *My Best Friend's Wedding, Runaway Bride, French Kiss, Addicted To Love, Jerry Maguire, Intolerable Cruelty*, and, outside of Hollywood, Jane Campion's *Holy Smoke*.

8. On this aspect of Emerson's thought, see Cornel West, *The American Evasion of Philosophy*.

9. Stanley Cavell, "Moral Perfectionism", 355.

10. All dialogue quoted in this essay has been transcribed directly from the film.

11. Max Weber, *The Protestant Ethic and the Spirit of Capitalism*, 125, 182.

12. Ibid., 183.

13. See Rita Kempley, *"Fools Rush In*: Ay Caramba!"

14. E.g., Matthew Jacobson, *Whiteness of a Different Color*, and Ronald Takaki, *Iron Cages*. The argument of this section owes a considerable debt to these remarkable studies.

15. "Richard Pryor Live in Concert"; Eddie Murphy, "Saturday Night Live."

16. bell hooks, "Eating the Other," 31.

17. Klaus de Albuquerque, "In Search of the Big Bamboo."

18. hooks, "Eating the Other," 23–24, emphasis added.

19. Jennifer Harrison, "Melting Pot".

20. "This, then, is the end of [the American Negro's] striving: to be a co-worker in the kingdom of culture. . . . " Du Bois, *Souls*, 365.

21. Jose Martí, "Our America".

22. Jessica Rabbit is the female lead in the 1988 animated film *Who Framed Roger Rabbit?* Tellingly, her name has since been affixed in U.S. popular culture to Melyssa Ford, first and most voluptuous among equals in a new class of highly entrepreneurial and usually nonwhite video models, all of whom leverage popular visual culture's interest in their physical assets into multiplatform marketability.

23. Susan J. Douglas, "Manufacturing Postfeminism".

24. Susan Bolotin, "Voices From the Post-Feminist Generation."

25. Emerson, "Fate", 386.

26. Ibid., 379.

27. Ibid., 362, 379–380.

28. Ibid., 385.

29. Gregory Pappas, "Dewey's Ethics", 111.

30. Emerson, "Fate", 385.

31. This is piety in Santayana's sense: an expression of fidelity, as religion scholar Jeffrey Stout puts it, "to the sources of one's existence and progress through life." *Democracy and Tradition*, 20.

32. Emerson, "Fate", 374, 377–378.

"LIGHTHOUSES IN A FOGGY WORLD"

IDEALS IN FRANK CAPRA'S *MEET JOHN DOE*

SAMANTHA VICE

I N A SCENE THAT MARKS the *denouement* of Frank Capra's film *Meet John Joe*, the hard-bitten newspaperman, Connell, reveals to our good-hearted hero the machinations of D. B. Norton. Connell tells Long John, "I get mad for a lot of other guys besides myself. I get mad for a guy named Washington, and a guy named Jefferson and Lincoln. Lighthouses, John—lighthouses in a foggy world."[1] Tipsy, he declares that Norton's attempt to impose, as Norton himself later expresses it, "an iron hand, discipline" on the honest John Does of America makes him "sizzling mad". Norton and his fascist henchmen are "wolves waiting to cut up the John Does," and to snuff out the lights of decency, freedom, and democracy.

In this chapter, I want to look at the sentiments expressed in this scene and explored in the film as a whole: The nature of ideals—those "lighthouses" personified by Lincoln, Washington, and John Doe—and their relation to the moral life. The film deals particularly subtly both with the moral benefits of ideals and their potential dangers. Furthermore, I shall suggest that *Meet John Doe* is more than an illustration of my claims. Rather, the film *enacts* the relation to ideals that we have in the nonfictional world, and it is for this reason of philosophical interest.

There are not many accounts of ideals in moral philosophy, and the influential discussions tend to be critical.[2] A full account of ideals would need to answer such criticisms and explain the place of ideals within a larger normative theory. This paper has the more limited aim, however, of sketching out an account of ideals and indicating, through a reading of Capra's film, how they can give direction and energy to our moral pursuits. If successful, this would provide the outline of an answer to criticisms like those of Michael Oakeshott, that a moral life centered around the self-conscious pursuit of ideals would breed "nothing but distraction and moral instability."[3] I begin this task with an exploration of the nature and moral function of ideals.

I. IDEALS

Ideals belong to the class of value; they are things that it would be good that the world contain or good that we realize in our actions, characters, relationships, and institutions.[4] They differ, however, from other values in (at least these) two ways: The first is that they are a particularly fundamental kind of value, representing what we take to be of deep and abiding value. They provide us with standards by which we judge our conduct and lives as a whole, and by which we organize our actions and other values. It matters to the way we evaluate our lives whether we have lived up to our ideals; if we do not, then, in that respect, our lives are marred by failure.

This feature gives us one way of explaining why not all values are comfortably thought of as ideals. Order, efficiency, and discipline could certainly be values, if they are not tainted necessarily with D. B. Norton's fascism, for instance. But could we imagine drastically re-ordering our lives, or even sacrificing them for these values? Sacrificing oneself for "Justice" or "Freedom" or "Love" has a certain persuasive ring to it, sacrificing oneself on the alter of "efficiency" slightly less so. My point, however, is not merely rhetorical. If ideals are indeed to have an organizing and justifying role in our moral lives, they must be such as to demand allegiance from the best part of ourselves, the part responsive to an "idea of perfection," in Iris Murdoch's words,[5] and they must expand our moral vision in a way that encourages moral reorientation.

The second way in which ideals and values differ is that ideals are values that are not yet realized or that can never be fully realized in the actual world. As Willis Moore writes, an ideal is an "imagined construct of superior value," stimulated by the inadequacy of an actual world which nonetheless provides an intimation of how things could be.[6] Some ideals are inherently unattainable—call these "standards of perfection"; others are difficult to attain but can, with dedication, be achieved—call these "standards of excellence." As soon as ideals *are* realized, however, they cease to be ideals, while yet remaining values. Examples of attainable ideals include many personal career or vocational ideals: being a good teacher, an excellent doctor or parent, or honing to the best of one's ability some difficult skill. Examples of inherently unattainable ideals include values that have built into them a requirement of perfection. Despite the inevitability of failure here, the striving to even approximate unattainable ideals matters morally. *Meet John Doe* shows us that failure to reach perfection in the realm of ideals is not always outright moral failure.

These two features distinguish ideals from other values, but there are differences within the class of ideals as well. Some ideals, for instance, can be specified in great detail, and if one achieves something that is not quite complete in those details, one has failed to reach one's ideal. The ideals most discussed in philosophy and public life, however, tend to be very general, ideals whose specification is, at least within certain limits, up for discussion. Justice, peace, democracy, neighborliness, compassion, and equality can be given different interpretations by those who are sincere in their pursuit of them. The generality of these ideals is part of their power, for different people can unite around them without necessarily agreeing on the details. Particular interpretations, of course, often have a communal history and force that play a central role in the self-understanding of a culture, but we can all more or less grasp the concept of justice, say, even if we do not agree on a particular conception of it.[7] We are disagreeing about the same thing. It is with these more general values that I shall for the most part be concerned in this paper.

It should be clear from the discussion so far that ideals are values that can be personally motivating. People are inspired to act and reorder their lives in the light of ideals. Clearly, however, ideals do not play this personal role for everyone. On the one hand, we say that a person "has" or "holds" an ideal when we wish to indicate that ideals play a personally motivating and guiding role for her. On the other hand, we don't usually admit that ideals are not ideals when particular persons are not moved by them. All the same, ideals must present us with a good that it is possible and reasonable to be moved by, even if not everyone is so moved. Justice, peace, and the end of poverty, racism, or slave labor are ideals, and ought to be recognized as such even by those who do not orient their lives around their achievement. In *Meet John Doe*, we see the moral change that occurs when people do take up ideals that they have only abstractly recognized before.

In sum, ideals have a complex relation to conduct. They (can) *motivate* us to act in certain ways; they *justify* those actions, and they *structure* or *govern* our actions and plans, providing us with hierarchies of importance and methods of organization. More globally, the achievement of, or progression toward, ideals can be a constituent of a meaningful life and one's overall verdict on one's life will be to a significant extent dependent upon one's success in the realm of ideals. And finally, ideals present each person with limits on their actions: there are certain things that a person who holds to an ideal will never do (or do only under dire duress). Harry Frankfurt writes that a

> person's ideals are concerns that he cannot bring himself to betray. They entail constraints that, for him, it is unthinkable to violate. Suppose that someone has no ideals at all. In that case, nothing is unthinkable for him; there are no limits to what he might be willing to do.[8]

We often discover what has ideal value for us by discovering what it is we cannot bring ourselves to do—as Long John Willoughby discovers that he cannot knowingly act as Norton's political puppet.

Connell's lighthouse metaphor, which I quoted at the start, is instructive for understanding the moral role of ideals. (To be more precise, Connell uses the image to describe the people who embody particular ideals, and I will return to this a little later.) Like the sun in Plato's *Republic*, ideals illuminate the world for us. They give us a kind of moral vision that allows us to see our way and, if we pay attention, to negotiate the dangers of a morally treacherous world. They also allow us to see the terrain more generally: they do not only light up our immediate steps, but illuminate the lay of the land. Ideals thus show us the broader and deeper moral picture, and by marking what is for us of most importance, they structure and guide the plans we make for our lives.

We can pursue the metaphor of the lighthouse a little further by noting that ideals can, in a sense, be extinguished. They require from us a vigilance that we may not always sustain, and they require for their ongoing efficacy that we recognize a need for them. By this, I do not mean that their existence or their value depends on each individual recognizing them, but only that their usefulness and power for us does. Ideals, I said earlier, are values that it is possible and reasonable to adopt as personally motivating; if they lose such personal resonance (as perhaps has happened to ideals of chivalry or humility), they lose their power to move us to action. Lost ideals do not cease to be ideals, but they cease to be effective in our lives and that is (almost) as effective as their not existing at all.

It should already be clear, then, that central to *Meet John Doe* is the moral efficacy of ideals. The film was released in 1941, and although the war in Europe is never explicitly mentioned, the dangers represented by Norton are clearly meant to be understood within its context.[9] Within the political and social framework of the movie, Norton threatens the same political ideals under threat in war-ravaged Europe. Ann Mitchell's creation, John Doe, starts out by exhorting people to remember decency, neighborliness, and love; by the end of the movie, these interpersonal ideals are shown to be intimately connected to political and moral ideals like freedom, democracy, and justice. The film shows on the one hand, that those more quotidian ideals, like neighborliness, are equally threatened by Norton's power, and on the other hand, that unless people are moved by love, decency or neighborliness toward those in proximity to them, those grander moral and political ideals upon which the greatness of America rests will be easily replaced by the fascistic values of Norton and his blackshirts. A small indication of the change that the John Doe clubs are bulwarks against is suggested at the start of the movie when the *Bulletin's* motto, "A Free Press means a Free People" is chiseled off and replaced by a motto for the *New Bulletin*, "A Streamlined Newspaper for a Streamlined Age." Freedom is under threat from market values of order and efficiency, which Norton will use to increase the circulation of his mouthpiece and thus further his own political career. When Norton says that Americans need "an iron hand, discipline," the ominous image of what he means is that of his black-clad motor corps doing their stiff maneuvers, a reminder of Mussolini's Fascism.

So the ideals for which John Doe stands are the values of the ordinary citizen and a decent polity. They are the values for which Lincoln, Jefferson, and Washington stood, and they represent, for Frank Capra, what is great about America.[10] If citizens can be roused out of their complacency, and if they try sincerely to put these ideals into practice, America will be rejuvenated. Capra is wholehearted about this, despite—in the midst of—being less sanguine about our ability to *be* clear-sightedly moved. What is not so obvious, however, is the role of exemplars for the moral power of ideals, and this the film explores in a nicely subtle manner. John Doe, Lincoln, Washington—all represent in their own persons these ideals. Yet, while understandable and often benign, such embodiment of ideals is not unproblematic. As we shall now see, a large part of the tragedy in *Meet John Doe* is caused by a confusion between the man and the ideal he represents. It is at this point, too, that the particular virtues of film for this topic become apparent.

II. THE EMBODIMENT OF IDEALS

Because ideals are often such general and abstract values, with little specification *per se* about what that means or how it would look in reality, they often gain resonance only when we meet them *in* someone. It happens often enough that we are inspired to take up a cause because of a particular person. We come to identify a person with an ideal, and through that person we learn how the world might be enriched if an ideal were to be realized. It seems, then, that we need to see ideals in our own, human, terms. The most powerful example of this is certainly the figure of Christ, God literally embodied for us. In a less complex way, John Doe, Mother Teresa, or Nelson Mandela embody the abstract ideals of neighborliness, justice, charity, or forgiveness. Of course, many people can represent the same ideals for us; embodiment can take various forms, and this generosity allows us to hold together without too much tension different interpretations of the ideal. This feature of ideals gives them an elasticity and endurance that makes them responsive to changing circumstances.[11] Let us now see how this embodiment works in the film.

Most obviously, Ann Mitchell chooses the name "John Doe" to represent both the "typical average man" and what he represents: decency, hard work, social cohesion and neighborliness, family values, and political and moral integrity—values that are in opposition to big business, corrupt politics, and a lack of sympathy in public and private life. The film, recall, opens with images of crowds, babies and work—the life of "everyman". The fact that Ann's fake story gets such a swift and overwhelming response shows how people can be affected by a personal stand—the story of one "little punk", an ex-minor-league baseball player and "disgusted American citizen," who is prepared to do something to express his disgust. Ann correctly maintains that if the *New Bulletin* can find itself a "real" John Doe, the story will run and run. John Doe is a living representation of what is best about America; in him, the citizens see their moral potential, and that both chastens and invigorates them. This double effect of chastening and invigorating is, I think, another central feature of all ideals. In the light of ideals we see both our shortcomings and the realization of what we could be—if not perfect, at least a great deal better.

It is one of the ironies of the film that a deception comes to have the moral high-ground and it is partly this irony—in yet another twist—that gives Norton his power to destroy the movement. Ann starts to believe in her own hoax when she writes John Doe's radio speech, inspired by her father's diaries, in which there is "something simple and real, something with hope in it." Rather than writing yet another "complaining political" speech, she writes a paean to every John Doe: "simple and wise . . . . inherently honest but . . . [with] a streak of larceny in his heart . . . . the world's greatest stooge and the world's greatest strength." John Doe represents all at once her father and his ideals. For Long John, the change to believing in the fundamental goodness of the deception's goals occurs when the folk of the John Doe Brotherhood Club tell their stories of moral rejuvenation, showing him what he has achieved. Later, when Long John tells Ann his curious dream (in which, significantly, he is her father), he refers to his dream self as "the real me, John Doe," showing how far Ann's words of advice to him at the radio speech have settled into him: "If you'll just think of yourself as the real John Doe."[12]

Ann still has her moments of doubts. At one point, she wearily tells Long John that "what we're handing them is platitudes, things they've heard a hundred times." He, however, realizes that by embodying the ideals expressed in these platitudes he has given them new vitality and motivating power. Ideals *do* often sound platitudinous. This is partly because they are values whose force and history goes deep; partly because they are often general in scope—as we have seen, it is this range that gives them much of their power. All this is as it should be, but what has to be fought against is no longer seeing their value. By giving a human form to ideals, John Doe revitalizes them, encouraging people to restructure their lives around them. They once again see the ideals as they are realized in an admirable person.

Iris Murdoch has explored the moral role of attending to something better than our own selves. She writes that "so long as the gaze is directed upon the ideal," we "*grow by looking.*"[13] John Doe becomes a visual representation of the ideals, one on which the ordinary folk can focus. His image is constructed partly by the "hunger" of the people themselves and partly by the media, which literally manufacture his history and feed the public what it thinks the public will respond to. As his image is spread across newspapers, it becomes more and more iconic. Much of the rise of the John Doe phenomenon is tracked in the film through fast-paced cuts and fades between newspaper headlines and photos (and his fall from grace is similarly presented). However dubious its construction and origin, though, the image of John Doe thereafter provides an object of attention that takes people away from petty concerns.

Much of the film's power in this regard is a consequence of the casting of Gary Cooper as Long John Willoughby. In fact, the cultural significance and construction of film stars is paralleled in the film by the *New Bulletin's* creation of John Doe and by the cultural significance he then acquires. Gary Cooper brings already a familiar aura and character to the film, which is then matched by the construction of John Doe. Cooper's rangy, slightly uncomfortable form and serious good looks really do provide an image of plain, hardworking goodheartedness. His mere presence thus makes it entirely believable that Long John Willoughby can find himself comfortable in John Doe (and his capacity for imaginative engagement is evident in the game of baseball he plays in his hotel room). Another important irony of the film is that, in a sense, the deception is no deception at all, because Long John really *is*, at heart, himself a John Doe. According to Capra, so was Gary Cooper. He writes of the actor in his autobiography that "[e]very line in his face spelled honesty. So innate was his integrity he could be cast in phony parts, but never look

phony himself . . . [He] embodied the true-blue virtues that won the west: dura-
bility, honesty, and native intelligence."[14] By casting a man who was becoming a
screen icon,[15] Capra brought to the film an already powerful sign of American
values. As a visual "type",[16] and by virtue of the cultural meaning that surrounded
Cooper already, the figure of Long John/John Doe is a visual representation of the
movie's concerns. Both Gary Cooper and John Doe in their persons combine the
"exceptional with the ordinary, the ideal with the everyday," as has been said about
film stars in general.[17]

Pre-eminently, if not essentially, a visual medium, film is for that reason
also particularly suitable for exploring the relation between ideals and personal
embodiment.[18] That is, there is a particularly apt and close connection between
the plot and message of this particular film and the typical medium and tools of
film itself. That we see our ideals represented in certain people is both shown by
the film in the double physical presence of Gary Cooper and John Doe, and is
part of the film's point. As already suggested, the physical presence of the actors
and the already accumulated meanings they bring with them to a role constitute
a crucial dimension of our engagement with film characters. Murray Smith
reminds us that

> the process by which we evaluate characters and respond to them emotion-
> ally is often framed or informed by our evaluation of the star personae of
> the stars who perform these characters. Star "charisma"—the elusive appeal
> that stars possess, often deriving from their embodiment of central social
> concerns in a particularly intense or compelling way—can obviously be used
> to direct our sympathies.[19]

Both the audience of the film, and the characters within the film, respond favor-
ably to the subtle and complex physical presence (natural and choreographed) of
the actor and the narrative's hero.

What then, is the film's relation to the philosophical investigation of ideals presented so far? I do not wish to claim that the film is philosophy, or itself philosophizing—to claim so would make any narrative out of which one can garner
philosophical insights a piece of philosophy, and this would require a fairly complex
argument to render plausible. In any case, however, we can make both a weaker
and a stronger claim about this film's relation to philosophy. The weak and probably uncontroversial claim is that the film provides an illustration of what I have
discussed, making vivid and concrete a rather abstract discussion of value. In principle, that discussion could have progressed without the excursion into film, or
with another carefully chosen (subtle and complex) example. Despite this admission, we can still think that the role of this film is not entirely accidental or negli-
gible to the claims about value I have been making, because the connection
between its form and content is too close. *Something* significant, it is plausible to
think, is added or revealed in this connection, and it is just here that the film has a

philosophical significance beyond that of mere illustration. Just what is this stronger significance?

I shall use the term "enactment" to refer to a stronger way that film can exemplify a point. Enactment has two features: first, the use of the illustration as an integral part of the content and aim of the narrative; and second, the *performance* of this content and aim. Regarding the first feature, we can note Karen Hanson's point that while examples are often used to make or support or destroy a philosophical point, exemplification itself also "can *be* the point."[20] In *Meet John Doe*, exemplification is at least part of the point. As we have seen, ideals find exemplification in the figure of John Doe (and, to a certain extent, in Gary Cooper) and it is part of the point and story of the movie to show us this at play, unfolding in time before us. This leads to the second condition: We see performed, not just described, our relation to ideals; we see the nature and construction of that relation that mimics, in recognizable time, how it is outside the fictional world.[21] Performance, whether on stage or screen,[22] is the living out of possibilities, and, sometimes, actualities; we forget much about the power of both screen and stage if we forget that the story is enacted in time before audience members who recognize something of their own selves and human predicaments in what is unfolding. In viewing *Meet John Doe*, we see in nonphilosophical, nonabstract terms the relation to ideals that this paper has explored. In sum, because the film enacts the relation to value that has been explored philosophically, it moves beyond mere illustration of the philosophical point.[23]

The difference between enactment and the more usual illustration is therefore twofold: First, the act of illustration itself is part of the goal or point of the narrative. That is, one of the aims of the narrative *just is* the intentional act of illustration itself. In this film, the John Doe phenomenon illustrates certain claims about our relation to value and this illustration is itself part of the film's content and point. In this particular case, too, the visual medium adds to the power of the claim that we recognize or see ideals through people. In contrast, with a "mere" illustration, the act of illustration itself is not an integral part of the point of the narrative. Second, the narrative is performed in time before an audience—whether that audience is present at the time of the original performance, as with stage productions, or present at a recording, as in film.[24] An example could, in contrast, be visual and not itself essentially time dependent (though, of course, viewing it will be), or it could be presented as a summary or be sketchy in the details, like many philosophical thought experiments. Of course, not all narratives will contain this stronger kind of exemplification, and, in fact, the first condition will probably be rarely met within classical Hollywood cinema (and so Capra's film is unusual). It remains, however, one way (and there will be others) in which a film can be of interest to philosophy beyond the provision of convenient examples.

It is, finally, plausible to think that enactment provides some ground for accepting the claims that can be gleaned from it. Insofar as the performance of the claims is attractive and credible, and something of the human predicament is persuasively presented, and insofar as the sincerity or tone of the performance is not undercut by devices such as irony, satire, or pastiche, then we have a reason to accept, if not the truth, the *prima facie* credibility of those claims. Successful enactment will bring normativity with it. In the case of *Meet John Doe*, then, that we experience the enactment of a plausible story about how ideals can gain force through embodiment, is enough to give some support to what we might think of as the embodiment thesis (further support, of course, is provided by the philosophical work of this paper). This is weightier support than that provided by a "mere" example because, as I have hoped to show, the connection between the content of the film and the claims about enactment is closer than that between the typical example and what it illustrates. We can reject an illustration as inappropriate or unhelpful and still hold to the claim; to reject the illustration of the embodiment thesis as implausible or poorly thought out or actually impossible is, also, I think, to reject the claim, or at least to cast serious doubt on it.

I have argued in this section that *Meet John Doe* enacts one relation we can have to value—our attraction to an ideal in the physical presence of a person. This relation, however, carries with it risks as well as moral benefits. The film suggests generally, and quite plausibly, that it may be easier to care deeply about something concrete and particular: the kindness in *this* person, justice in *this* particular court case, *this neighbor's* need. Right action becomes easier to discern when we focus on particular people around us, and certain extraordinary people can be exemplars of values. In this respect, our tendency to focus on particulars and to see ideals through people is morally helpful, and part of our deeply rooted responses to what is attractive in others. There is a danger, however, that we will confuse the ideal with the person, and this we see explored in the film, in a way similar in form to the exploration of embodiment. While defending the importance and functioning of ideals, therefore, the film at the same time balances this with an awareness of the moral dangers raised by a mistaken view of their nature.

III. THE DANGERS OF EMBODIMENT

Briefly stated, the danger in the embodiment of ideals is that we can confuse a limited human being with an abstract ideal of perfection or excellence. *Meet John Doe* shows that while the embodiment of values is understandable and often morally helpful, our own frailties tend at the same time to undermine the force of ideals. People are fallible, our heroes have feet of clay, and when they fail us we dismiss the ideals for which they stood as well. Like the embodiment thesis itself, this danger is enacted successfully within *Meet John Doe*, and so there is some reason to consider it in our thinking about the ethical role of ideals. We see Norton using this confusion, and the "typical average" folk falling prey to it when, at the terrible finale at the stadium, they dash their own progress and their own redemption in a fit of pique.

The "typical average" folk sincerely respond to what John Doe stands for because they recognize it as part of their own implicit conception of good character and good citizenship. As soon as the ideal is divorced from its representative, how-ever, they lose their focus on the real end of the John Doe movement, and reject as fake its ideals as well as its origins. In this, they represent, I think, our common moral state, and *Meet John Doe* makes a general point: Just as John Doe represents what is best about ordinary lives, so the crowd at the John Doe rally shows how easily we are swayed and how far we are from living in accordance with ideals we in some sense recognize. What we see concretely before us usually has greater power over us than the abstract ideals that are given form in the particular, and unless we can make ideals themselves an object of our moral attention, we will be forever prone to this mistake. In this, we are like Plato's sight lovers, imprisoned frustratingly in the cave of appearance, requiring some "turning of the soul," some *metanoia*, before we can see reality.[25] The scenes at the rally act out this failure, as Long John's humiliation is staged before crowds that refuse to recognize the real object of their desires.

In light of all this, the moral status of the deception in *Meet John Doe* proves complex. Starting out as a way for Long John to get his "wing" fixed by Bonesetter Brown, Ann to retain her job, and Norton to increase his power, it quickly gains a significance that is morally independent of the fact of its being a deception. The deception *is* wrong, and at least some of its original motives are certainly so, but the connection between the fact of deception and the values that it espouses is accidental. That is, the values have a moral force that has nothing at all to do with their origins in deception, and the moral task is precisely that of separating them from human fallibility.

Just as the people forget, with Norton's encouragement, that what John Doe stands for is not reducible to the character or even the existence of Long John, so they forget that while the John Doe movement might have had murky origins, they were attracted to it because it represents something true and something they need—Long John tells Ann that he and the people are "hungry for something" that the movement satisfies. We might only realize how hungry we are when faced with some particular desirable thing, but (at least in this kind of case) the real object of our desire is the value, not the particular object. This is shown by the fact that our desire remains even when its putative object disappears.[26] In the context of the film, the story takes off before Long John even assumes the public role of John Doe, and there is no indication at the end that the people are less "hungry" than before. They are attracted by John Doe's stand before meeting him, even if the public prolifera-tion of his image then strengthens their attachment. As we have seen, it is certainly important that Long John is personable and charming; it is understandable that at-traction to an ideal should be confused and mingled with attraction toward his person. After all, Ann chooses Long John from the array of down-and-outs pre-cisely because of his looks, reminding us once again of the essentially visual origins of the people's attraction. The mistake is understandable, but no less a mistake.

This is more than the obvious point that an ideal belongs to a different category to a person, that of course a person isn't what she might represent. The—only slightly deeper—point is that ideals are *normatively independent* of their mouth-pieces. Their normative force is not exhausted by the attractive qualities of their representative or spokesperson. The consequence of this is that we have *no reason at all* to reject an ideal because we have lost faith in the person espousing it. Long John Willoughby himself realizes the independence of the John Doe movement from his own person. Confronting Norton before the rally, he declares that the John Doe movement is "bigger than whether I'm a fake, it's bigger than your ambitions, and [with a jab at Ann] it's bigger than all the bracelets and fur coats in the world." This, possibly, is the central message of this unashamedly didactic film.

That ideals are normatively independent of people is still not a very deep point, but the frequency with which we get muddled here is significant, and that the related logical mistake of confusing person and argument has its own name is indicative of its ubiquity. In the light of the role that I am giving to ideals in the moral life, moreover, the confusion has real practical import. If ideals have a role in structuring and grounding our ethical pursuits, and if we often espouse an ideal because of a person, then the fact that we just as often confuse ideal and person has potentially negative effects for our moral lives, in spite of the obvious helpful-ness of embodiment. We are pulled in different directions here: As finite, embod-ied, and social creatures for whom interpersonal relations and attractions are deeply part of a meaningful life, we quite naturally are responsive to the good we perceive in and through others, and we are quite rightly responsive to aesthetic and aretaic excellence. At the same time, the causal relation can go both ways: Some-times we come to embrace an ideal *because* we first see it embodied and enacted in a certain person. We may or may not then come to see its normative indepen-dence. Sometimes—as I suggested was the case in *Meet John Doe*—we are drawn to the person because we already hold to an ideal and see it reflected in the character and deeds of a remarkable person. In this second case (and if, in the first case, we recognize later the independence of the ideal), we see the other side of our natures: the side responsive to what is *not* finite and limited, that is attracted by an "idea of perfection." The moral power of ideals and our responsiveness to them can some-times be in tension with the inevitability of attraction toward people and generate confusion between ideals and their representatives.[27]

The tendency to confuse people and ideals can be exacerbated and made even more morally troubling by cynicism, which is a major concern of the film. Exploring this will show us a further dimension to our relation to ideals and sug-gest the importance of ideals for a healthy social and political culture.

IV. CYNICISM

The tendency to believe that people are never purely motivated, that everyone has a price, is shown in *Meet John Doe* to be corrosive of political, civic, and personal virtue. This is so, in varying degrees, for all the cases of cynicism we meet in the film: the pernicious, manipulative cynicism of Norton; the humorous and disdainful cynicism of Long John's fellow-hobo, the Colonel; and the self-destructive cynicism displayed by the "average folk" when they learn of the hoax.

What is most disturbing about Norton is not his manipulation of others for his own political ends, but rather his manipulation of something genuinely good for vicious ends. As Long John says when he confronts him, Norton is "deliberately killing an ideal that's made millions of people a little bit happier . . . It may be the one thing capable of saving this cockeyed world. Yet you sit back there on your fat hulks and tell me you'll kill it if you can't use it." Norton uses the basic virtue of the John Does of America and their potential for moral progression simply for his own private and vicious use. This cynicism is particularly sinister, as it turns what is best about people against their own end of moral improvement. It is here that the need to focus clear-sightedly on the ideal rather than the person becomes most pressing, both for individual virtue and for the virtue of the polity.

My reading of *Meet John Doe* has concentrated so far on the individual and social elements of the film, but Capra's suspicion of politics and politicians is of course central. It is noteworthy that politicians are not welcome in the John Doe clubs. The film manifests a deep suspicion of politicians, and the models we are given (the malicious conniver, Norton; the ineffectual small-town mayor; and the self-interested city mayor) are hardly inspiring. Their polite slighting by the clubs sets up a stark distinction between the ordinary folk and their supposed representatives. While the world desperately needs reminding of the political values that are under threat in Europe and, according to Capra, in America, *Meet John Doe* shows the moral inadequacy of politicians to deal with the threat and to provide stirring moral direction. This, it seems, must come from the ground, from a hobo like Long John Willoughby; power and money cannot do it. Moral conversion, too, is a matter for the individual soul or for small, neighborly groups, rather than people *en masse*. Norton, of course, realizes that groups are easier to manipulate; that is one reason to support a mass rally. At the end of the film, Bert Hanson tells Long John: "We're with you, Mr. Doe. We just lost our heads and acted like a mob." People are not at their best in crowds—easily enthused by something good, but just as easily turning vicious. Ideals, the film suggests, are best understood, sustained and acted upon in small-scale rather than grandstand arenas.

The film's suspicion of politicians does not, however, translate into a generalized cynicism, although Capra is obviously tempted in that direction.[28] Blanket cynicism is shown to be a mistake, as much by the film's depiction of the Colonel as of Norton. A wonderful creation by Walter Brennan, the Colonel sees most people as "heelots", corrupted by the material world, out to take care of themselves, masking self-interest with high-sounding platitudes. His response to John Doe's exhortation to "tear down the fences" is, "Tear down all the fences! Why, if you tore one picket off of your neighbor's fence, he'd sue ya!" In his tirades against the heelots, he hits one mark and misses another. He is on the mark about the dangers of populism and politics, the tentacles that inevitably entangle those who are part of the material world of power and possessions. But he is also off the mark. The behavior of the heelots, and that means just about everyone, provides him with continual evidence, he thinks, to dismiss the very possibility of genuine adherence to ideals, and to ideals themselves. His cynicism about the self-interested motives and acquisitiveness of ordinary folk prevents him from seeing that a phenomenon like the John Doe movement really can change people for the better. His insight into the motives of certain people thus exists side by side with moral short-sightedness about others. Give the "typical average man" an empowering and attractive image of moral change, and he can be moved by it. While the dangers of manipulative cynicism lie in its disrespect and harmfulness, the moral dangers facing these cynics lie in their lack of faith in the redemptive potential of people and a willful inability to interpret people in any other way than as self-interested. Capra argues through his film, however, that this kind of hope is precisely what is essential if the world is ever to improve.

The Colonel's cynicism makes him prone to that confusion of embodiment and ideals that has been explored. His theory of human nature leads him to dismiss the possibility of un-self-interested action and, furthermore, makes him reject the notion of ideals at all. As I have suggested, though, just because people are weak at times says nothing so far about whether there are such things as ideals or about whether people have the capacity to be moved by them. The Colonel's certainty makes him, through most of the film, immune to the kind of hope the film advocates for political and personal progress. There are, however, cracks in the Colonial's cynicism, showing just how hard it is to maintain a flawless distrust. For all his antisocial resilience, he is a good friend to the naïve Long John. He cannot see Long John as himself a heelot; to do so would be contrary to friendship. So he comes to the rally—maybe to support his friend, maybe because despite himself he is moved by it. In the end, he, at least, can keep distinct his friend from the heelots, as he can also keep distinct his friend from John Doe.

Hope is also what the ordinary people find through the John Doe movement and then lose in their moral confusion. The most fundamental reason for their confusion and loss is also cynicism, and it is part of Norton's political genius to use this. Cynicism here exacerbates that natural tendency to confuse person and ideal, earlier explored, and gives it an added moral dimension. The people are used to being disappointed—in their neighbors, in their politicians, in themselves. This makes them expect the worst and it makes them furious when, after having let down their guard, they discover they were moved by a deception—that they were "suckers". D. B. Norton knows that this is precisely what their reaction will be and uses it as blackmail against Long John. In the terrible scene at the stadium, Long John is publicly humiliated, watching everything he believed in and stood for disintegrate. In vain, he tells them, "Listen, John Does, you're the hope of the world," appealing to the part of their natures that first responded to his message. As Ann says in despair later, "He was so all alone." The people's reaction is just grist to the cynic's mill.

It should be clear enough how intimately cynicism is connected to the dangerous confusion between ideals and persons. Because we are already prone to the confusion, cynicism easily finds a footing.[29] People we are morally attracted to *do* fail us; politics and our institutions disappoint us. The cynic uses this as evidence that no one is ever non-self-interestedly motivated—that ideals are never untainted or purely followed. This generalization is unfounded, however, and cynicism is in a fundamental way antithetical toward the very notions of moral fellowship and progress. It is a different kind of irony now, that a film—trading as it does in images and the ephemeral, making use of stars whose weighty signification is partly of the industry's own making, constructing a myth as part of its story-line—can remind us that cynicism is confused and trades in confusion. Capra's film tells us that cynicism relies on the same confusion between ideals and people that causes John Doe's fall from grace. The image of John Doe has its morally rallying effect; but we need then to disentangle ourselves from mere images and turn our attention to what they stand for, the task that Bert Hanson and his neighbors finally achieve.

Because cynicism makes us so suspicious of each other, it also makes us blind to the real moral effort and progress that is guided by ideals. If we are suspicious of our ability to be moved by ideals, they will have no hold over us. Our response to ideals will simply collapse into judgments about people, and because people are fallible, our ideals will very quickly lose their force. We can see here how cynicism feeds on and exacerbates the natural tendency to confuse people and ideals. So we needn't insist that humans are naturally *wicked* to realize that we are certainly morally muddled, prone to self-centered rationalizations and the confusions that *Meet John Doe* so aptly depicts. If this is the case, however, the remedy is to focus more diligently on ideals, not to reject them. They provide stable, independent standards toward which moral striving aims, and attracted by them, we can change ourselves and our lives in their light.

V. CONCLUSION: AN IDEALS-BASED MORALITY

In the course of this paper, I hope to have suggested a role for ideals in the moral life. I have not argued that ideals are necessary for living a moral life; a kind of nonreflective moral decency is certainly possible given the right upbringing and, probably, a benign environment. For reflective, well-intentioned agents in an obdurate and complex world, however, living morally is typically a risky, uncertain project in which one easily becomes lost. The problem is only exacerbated at the level of politics and civil society. For this kind of agent, in this kind of world— and this is most of us—the guiding, structuring, and attention-focusing role of ideals becomes almost certainly beneficial. This remains true despite the possibility that, by misunderstanding the nature of ideals, we might also confuse them with the people who remind us of them. The moral life requires just such a struggle against this tendency. A more ambitious claim about our relation to ideals has been lurking beneath much of the paper, however. Besides their instrumental role in guiding the moral life, our attraction toward ideals says something deeper about us. We are creatures, as I said earlier, who are both limited and can sense and long for some perfection beyond ourselves. The desire for progression is dependent upon a recognition of inadequacy in the light of something greater, which we can—however dimly—sense the power of. This inadequacy, I have suggested, is not necessarily felt as enervating.

Worries remain about our capacity to meet the demands of ideals. According to J. O. Urmson, a moral code should not be "too far beyond the capacity of the ordinary men on ordinary occasions, or a general breakdown of compliance with the moral code would be an inevitable consequence."[30] Additionally, Michael Oakeshott complains that, "When the guide of conduct is a moral ideal we are never suffered to escape from perfection."[31] Putting aside the debate over the boundary between the obligatory and supererogatory, *Meet John Doe* shows, I think, that such worries are exaggerated. The reason the ordinary folk fail morally is not because John Doe demands too much, but because they confuse the man with the ideals. In any case, ideals demand from us not perfection in one stride, but an intense, engaged project through a life of moral progression; it is each small step that is important. The impossibility of escape from perfection thus needn't be destructively demanding. While we sense our immense distance from the ideal, to accept an ideal is to acknowledge it as good, to feel its motivational power, and to acknowledge the standard it legitimately sets. We may become disheartened by our own failures, to be sure, but *to the extent that we accept an ideal*, this cannot be our lasting state.

In a fine paper, David Norton writes that "[m]oral thought and moral life require their upper reaches if they are to enlist human aspiration lifelong," and it is precisely a characteristic of ideals that "they are capable of enlisting the full measure of human aspiration."[32] In making moral requirements minimal in the sense of being simple, straightforward and easily met, the effect of modern moral philosophy is "to afford to moral life little space for aspiration; it is a small room with a low ceiling and not much of a view."[33] If I am correct that it is a deep feature of human life that we be attracted to—at least—improvement, then this kind of minimalism does us a disservice. We *will* fail to meet the demands of ideals, but the appropriate response to this inevitable failure need not be harsh censure; it can, rather, be self-assessment and continued, improved effort. The psychological claim that the more we expect of ourselves and others, the less we will in fact achieve morally, is implausible, as individual and communal behavior in times of emergency, upheaval or plain unhappiness often demonstrates, and as we see in *Meet John Doe*.[34]

In conclusion, I am not claiming that Capra is aware of or explicitly making in my terms, all these claims I have gleaned from *Meet John Doe* about the nature of ideals and the moral life. The trouble his ending gave him is an indication that his spirit was, in fact, far less hopeful than the final product makes out. What I do hope to have shown is that his film—taken as an autonomous whole independent of his own misgivings—indicates how a practical, rejuvenating morality could be centered around the pursuit of ideals if they are clearly seen and kept separate from humanity. This morality is viable both politically and personally—indeed, as I have suggested, part of the message of the film is the interrelation of these dimensions.

I also argued that the film, through its intentional enactment of the embodiment thesis, does philosophical work beyond that of providing a replaceable or dispensable illustration. This performance need not have been intended by Capra in any of the philosophical terms I have used in this paper, but in choosing the plot and actors he did, the paper's claims about the dangers and benefits of embodiment are performed before us. The claims are made more vivid, certainly, but more than that, they are worked out in a way that mimics our own troubled relation to ideals. And insofar as the film expresses and makes sense of these often unarticulated relations, we find in it some independent support for the claims that, through philosophical work, were made in this chapter.

The ending that Capra eventually chose provides a fitting conclusion for this discussion. The final impression is that of hope in ordinary people being able to improve themselves if their vision and possibilities are enriched. Ann reminds Long John that "if [his ideal is] worth dying for, it's worth living for." The echoes of Christ's resurrection are obvious and made explicit by Ann, when she calls Christ the "first John Doe." In one image, we have brought together humanity's weakness and potential for redemption if given something great to aspire toward. The final line of the film is given to Connell: "There you are, Norton! The people! Try to lick that!" Pessimism about our capacity for moral muddles and self-betrayal is here finally allowed to rest in a necessary faith in the goodness of ordinary people.

NOTES

Thanks to Ward Jones for helpful comments on earlier drafts, and to participants of a graduate course on film and philosophy.

1. In quoting from the film, I have relied on Tim Dirks's "Review of Meet John Doe."

2. For representative criticisms: Isaiah Berlin, in *Two Concepts of Liberty* and Michael Oakeshott, in "The Tower of Babel" were critical of desiring perfection and attempting to instantiate incompatible ideals. In "Saints and Heroes," J. O. Urmson worried that setting the bar of duty too high would literally demoralize us.

3. "The Tower of Babel," 74. Because my concern is not to offer a theory of right and wrong or the limits of duty, Urmson's worries in "Saints and Heroes" about where to set the boundary between the obligatory and the supererogatory can legitimately be set aside.

4. Much of what I say in what follows is in agreement with Abraham Edel, "The Evaluation of Ideals," Willis Moore, "On the Nature and Justification of Ideals," and Doret de Ruyter, "The Importance of Ideals in Education."

5. See "The Idea of Perfection" and "On 'God' and 'Good,'" 61–62, both in *The Sovereignty of Good*.

6. "On the Nature and Justification of Ideals," 112.

7. For the distinction, see John Rawls, *A Theory of Justice*, 5.

8. Harry G. Frankfurt, "On the Necessity of Ideals," 114.

9. The film's reticence about the war (which America had not yet entered) gives it an inward and patriotic character that is, perhaps, in conflict with the universal values it advocates. An alternative reading is that the obvious background of the war forces us to generalize the values that are shown in the film as typically American.

10. Authorship in films is a contentious issue. In *Meet John Doe*, however, it seems safe to make claims about the intentions of the director, producer and co-writer, Frank Capra (his fellow writer was Richard Presnell, Sr.). In his autobiography, *The Name Above the Title*, Capra writes explicitly of his intentions in making the film (see, e.g., Chapter 16) and as the very title of the autobiography, as much as the text itself, reveals, he was very concerned to be recognized as the maker of his films. On authorship in films, see Paisley Livingstone, "Cinematic Authorship".

11. I am here disagreeing with Oakeshott, who writes that an ideal-dominated morality has "little power of self-modification; its stability springs from its inelasticity and its imperviousness to change. It will, of course, respond to interpretation, but the limits of that response are close and severe" ("The Tower of Babel," 69). This feature also goes some way toward answering Oakeshott and Berlin's worry about the incompatibility of values.

12. There is irony here, too, as Ann also declares of John Doe, "I think I've fallen in love with him."

13. *The Sovereignty of Good*, 31. Also see 54–56.

14. *The Name Above the Title*, 182–183.

15. Hubert Cohen suggests that by selecting actors "who themselves were in the process of becoming icons," Capra "called into his shadow-play the tallest shadow in American political and folk history—that tall, lean, slow-speaking, humble figure of unimpeachable integrity, Abe Lincoln" ("Review of *Orson Welles* and *Frank Capra: The Man and his Films*," 64). And cf. Bordwell, et al.: "the selfish pitcher John Willoughby becomes the rustic idealist John Doe because Willoughby was, in latent form, Gary Cooper to begin with. We discover the Gary Cooper persona afresh, even while knowing that it was there before the start." (*The Classical Hollywood Cinema*, 14).

16. Cooper seems to fit the type of the "Good Joe", in the typology developed by O. E. Klapp. See Richard Dyer, *Stars*, 53–56.

17. Edgar Morin, quoted by Dyer in *Stars*, 25.

18. Much of the power of film generally has to do, however obscurely, with its being a visual medium. Noël Carroll suggests that it is precisely because it consists of "*pictorial* representations" that film is "generally accessible to mass, untutored audiences" ("The Power of Movies," in *Theorizing the Moving Image*, 80).

19. *Engaging Characters*, 193.

20. "Minerva in the Movies," 396.

21. This is not to deny the various narrative devices used to shorten, lengthen, skip, or otherwise distort time. The time of events in the plot very rarely keeps time with the performance itself. Audiences, however, are for the most part literate and

comfortable in such narrative devices and conventions and so these manipulations do not feel alien.

22. While stage or screen performances are the most typical kind of performance, performance in my sense is not restricted to them. Visual art with a strong kinetic and narrative element may also qualify. While it is true that reading may demand imaginative engagement with the unfolding of character and events over time, and the act of reading is itself time bound, I wish to restrict performance in my sense to the (at least) *visual staging* by performers before an audience. This would include so-called performance art.

23. In his discussion of illustration in philosophy, Tom Wartenberg's claim that *Modern Times* "involves the complete visualization of Marx's metaphor [of machine-like, dehumanized workers], a visualization that makes that metaphor more concrete" is similar to, though perhaps weaker than, mine (Wartenberg, "Beyond *Mere* Illustration," 28).

24. There are certainly significant differences between stage and screen performances, but none are relevant to my point here. On this see Stanley Cavell, *The World Viewed* (enlarged edition.), Chapter 2, especially 25–29.

25. See *Republic* 518 c–d.

26. At least, this is often what is going on; we can admit without losing the point that sometimes we just *are* enamored with the object not the ideal.

27. To avoid misunderstanding, this is not the problematic Platonic claim that we should "ascend" (i.e. progress) from love of particular persons to love of the abstract Good. I am not making a claim about the nature of love or attraction more generally, but only about ideals and their relations to remarkable people.

28. Capra set out to "convince important critics that not every Capra film was written by Pollyanna" (*The Name Above the Title*, 303). The five different endings that Capra shot for *Meet John Doe* leave very different impressions on the viewer in this regard. One ending had Long John committing suicide; another showed attempts by Ann and Long John to revive the clubs snubbed by the folk; another had Norton undergoing a rather unbelievable conversion. The ending finally chosen was in fact suggested to him in a letter from a fan, signed simply "John Doe" and was, he says, "the best of a sorry lot, but *still* it was a letdown" (ibid., *The Name Above the Title*, 305).

29. My claim is not that the tendency toward confusion *per se* is already cynical. We can be noncynically confused. Certain kinds of cynicism, however, rely on this more fundamental confusion.

30. "Saints and Heroes," 212.

31. "The Tower of Babel," 69.

32. "Moral Minimalism and the Development of Moral Character," 185, 192.

33. Ibid., 185.

34. Further worries about moral "rigorism" are expressed by George Orwell, "Reflections on Gandhi," and Susan Wolf, "Moral Saints".

8

LA GRANDE ILLUSION
AS A WORK OF ART

PETER GOLDIE

I. INTRODUCTION

JEAN RENOIR'S MASTERLY *LA GRANDE ILLUSION* is set during the First World War. In the film, an aristocratic French staff officer, de Boeldieu (Pierre Fresnais), asks a pilot officer called Maréchal (Jean Gabin) to take him over German lines in order to clarify a certain smudge on an aerial photograph that he has been inspecting—perhaps it is a sign of enemy activity. They are shot down and captured. Immediately after, they are stylishly entertained at lunch by their German captors, commanded by von Rauffenstein (Erich von Stroheim), before being sent to a camp as prisoners of war. After many failed attempts to escape many different camps, they are finally sent to a remote castle, Wintersborn, from which no one so far has ever escaped and which, coincidentally, is run by von Rauffenstein. Rauffenstein is so badly injured that he can no longer fly a plane, and being in charge of Wintersborn is now all that is left for him to do for his country. He renews his acquaintance with de Boeldieu, with whom he has much in common. The prisoners make a plan to escape that involves de Boeldieu causing a distraction while Maréchal and a Jewish prisoner, Rosenthal (Marcel Dalio), climb down the wall of the fortress with ropes that they had secretly made. As he foresaw and even planned, de Boeldieu is shot and fatally wounded by von Rauffenstein, acting with deep regret out of a strict sense of military duty. Maréchal and Rosenthal manage to get away. Exhausted, they hide for a few days in a farmhouse belonging to Elsa, a German farm woman (Dita Parlo), who takes them in out of sympathy. She lives alone, with just her young daughter for company, after her husband and all her brothers have been killed; she points out their photographs on the wall and enumerates with sad irony and bitterness the battles in which they died: "Verdun, Liege, Charleroi, Tannenberg—our greatest victories." Maréchal and Elsa have a brief romance, and he is reminded of his past life, but Maréchal and Rosenthal have to leave, and, finally, they make their way through the thick snow to Switzerland and safety.

In its detail, which any sensitive viewer will observe, the film is replete with sentiments, brilliantly evoked, that are both against war and against the nationhood that drives war making.[1] Renoir himself said, "Because I am a pacifist I made *La Grande Illusion*."[2]

I want to argue that this reading of the film, while correct as far as it goes, fails to do justice to the film's depth. First, it fails to do justice to the importance of what the film shows about the role of class, as I will understand this term. Renoir shows how class separates people of a nation from each other; and he shows how it unites people of the same class across nations, in what Renoir has called "horizontal connections" or "horizontal relations". Second, this reading fails to recognize the bleak thought beyond this—that certain capacities or characteristics of human nature might be universal or pancultural, but not uniting. Specifically, Renoir shows how three such capacities can even be a force for disunity: the capacity for language, the capacity for ingroup cohesion (where class is one kind of group) and for conflict among groups, and the sheer capacity for aggression.

I close with a discussion of the relationships between *La Grande Illusion*, philosophy, and art. I suggest that this great film is best thought of as a work of art, which is simply *showing* us, in wonderfully fine detail, a small fragment of human life that illustrates certain aspects of human nature. In this respect, I will suggest, Renoir's great film resembles the paintings of his father, Auguste Renoir: its cognitive value lies in its capacity to show us, through illustration, truths about human nature, and not in its capacity (which some other films might deploy) to put forward claims or to provide arguments for a conclusion. That *La Grande Illusion* is art, and not argument, in no way detracts from its having this value.

II. UNITED AND DIVIDED: THE HORIZONTAL AND THE VERTICAL

There is a massive gulf between the two French officers, Maréchal and de Boeldieu. Maréchal, a mechanic before the war, is completely at a loss in his efforts to understand the aristocratic de Boeldieu, as are the other French officers ("Can we trust your pal the Captain?"[3]). Sense of humour, interests outside prison camp, style, and manner of speech all make for division rather than unity under the banner of liberté, egalité, and fraternité—a banner that was supposed to express the abandonment of all these differences and the attainment of unity of all French people as fellow citizens. "There is a wall between us," says Maréchal to de Boeldieu as he helps him wash the white gloves that he will wear as he diverts the German guards while the escape takes place. Maréchal asks, as just one example among many of his failures to understand, why de Boeldieu does not use the familiar *"tu"* in addressing him, instead of the more formal *"vous"*. When de Boeldieu replies that he also uses *"vous"* when addressing his wife and his mother, Maréchal is baffled into silence ("Alors . . . "). Gloves, English tobacco—"Everything separates us."

On his side, De Boeldieu is not only conscious of his separateness from his fellow-officers—he is also proud of it, and he never hesitates to point it out to the others ("You have the instincts of a shop girl"). Although he is proud of his separateness, however, he feels that, more than a hundred years after the French Revolution, his class is finally dying out, to be "merged" into all the others. He remarks regretfully that his class will soon not even be distinguished from others by its maladies: "The pox used to be our privilege, but we've lost it. Like so many others. Everything is popularized: Cancer and gout aren't working-class diseases, but they will be, believe me." It is in large part because of this that he, in effect, arranges his own death at the hand of von Rauffenstein; there is now nothing left to live for.

When we turn to von Rauffenstein, it is clear that he is in a similar position to that of de Boeldieu; he, too, has no like-minded souls among his fellow officers. Not once do we see him in anything like a civilized conversation with them; all he does is bark out orders. Even his room expresses his solitariness and self-contained austerity, with just a single geranium in a pot on the windowsill—the only flower in the whole fortress.

When de Boeldieu arrives at the remote castle, von Rauffenstein sees at last a man with whom he has, as he already knows, so much in common—someone of his own class. This was established right from the start, in their very first conversation at lunch, just after de Boeldieu and Maréchal had been shot down: "I knew a Boeldieu in Berlin, a Count de Boeldieu." "Ah yes, my cousin, Edmond de Boeldieu; he was a military attaché." And then in English from von Rauffenstein: "He was a marvellous writer," and de Boeldieu replies, also in English: "Yes, he was a good author." Just a few words, and everything is established that needs to be established between them: they are of the same class.

In the prison camp, de Boeldieu and von Rauffenstein realize further that they have socialized in the same milieu—horseracing, Maxim's in Paris, and so on—and they even find out (to von Rauffenstein's evident surprise and slight irritation) that they both knew a girl called Fifi from Maxim's. It seems, also, that they simply *know* when to slip effortlessly into English, depending on the topic of conversation. Most of all, each of them bemoans the loss of their "function" as a class, and, finally, von Rauffenstein is able to say that he envies de Boeldieu his early death. Their last conversation exquisitely expresses their regrets at the lost past: "I am not the one to be pitied; for me it will all be over soon. But you'll have to carry on." "Carry on a useless existence." "For a commoner [*un homme du peuple*], dying in war is a tragedy. But for you and me, it's a good way out." "I missed my chance." And then, immediately after de Boeldieu is pronounced dead, von Rauffenstein cuts off the head of the geranium as the snow falls outside. The man who has just died—a Frenchman whom, out of duty, he first captured and later shot and killed—was his only friend.

Returning to Maréchal, he, too, finds unity within his class and across nationality. At the first conversation at lunch, while von Rauffenstein and de Boeldieu are talking, he strikes up a conversation in French with the German officer who is seated beside him, and quickly establishes that they were both mechanics before the war—it was as a mechanic in Lyon that the German officer learned his French. One gets the clear impression that their lunch would have been a very jolly affair if it had not been interrupted by the arrival of a wreath for a French officer who had been killed in combat.

Later, after Maréchal's escape from the fortress, he finds his natural habitat when he and Rosenthal are taken in and sheltered by Elsa at her lonely farm. The child, the farmhouse, the simplicity of the tasks, even the smell of the cow are all perfectly familiar to him. ("You smell like my grandfather's cows—a good smell. You're a cow from Würthenburg and I'm a working man from Paris. But we can still be pals.") He seems more at ease than at any other time in the narrative—exemplified by that marvellously expressive gesture of picking up the wood axe as he strolls past and banging it back into the chopping block.

What is this notion of class that can divide people of one nation and unite people across nations? The term "class" as I mean to use it here is little more than a placeholder for a cluster of things shared with certain others—a shared range of interests, of experiences, of memories, of ways of dressing and eating and speaking, and even of diseases, according to de Boeldieu. A class boundary in this sense is not simply an economic matter, nor is it a necessarily impenetrable barrier, as, for example, one might be excluded from the *noblesse* simply because of one's ancestry. Still, it is practically impenetrable for all that, given how great the differences are—and indeed given how class differences tend to be welcomed and even exaggerated by its members in ways that exclude others—a point to which I will return.

With this notion in place, can we not see a message of hope in the film's portrayal of shared classes that can unite people across national boundaries? Indeed, according to Renoir, the important connections in the social world are "horizontal" rather than "vertical"—by shared class rather than by shared nationality. As Renoir put it, "If a French farmer found himself dining with a French financier, those two Frenchmen would have nothing to say to each other. But if a French farmer meets a Chinese farmer they will find any amount to talk about."[4] Are these horizontal relations between farmer and farmer, aristocrat and aristocrat, mechanic and mechanic, able to provide what Renoir called *un terrain d'entente*[5]—something which can form a ground or foundation of understanding between people as fellow human beings? As such, a *terrain d'entente* need not amount to anything grander than Orwell's much-discussed experience in the Spanish Civil War of deciding not to shoot at a Fascist who appeared in his line of fire with his trousers down:

> At this moment, a man presumably carrying a message to an officer, jumped out of the trench and ran along the top of the parapet in full view. He was half-dressed and was holding up his trousers with both hands as he ran. I refrained from shooting at *him*. It is true that I am a poor shot and unlikely to hit a running man at a hundred yards, and also that I was thinking chiefly about getting back to our trench while the Fascists had their attention fixed on the aeroplanes. Still, I did not shoot partly because of that detail about the trousers. I had come here to shoot at "Fascists"; but a man who is holding up his trousers isn't a "Fascist", he is visibly a fellow-creature, similar to yourself, and you don't feel like shooting at him.[6]

Perhaps, then, Renoir is suggesting in *La Grande Illusion* that if horizontal relations, properly appreciated and borne in mind, can similarly provide a *terrain d'entente*, then national disagreements would be less likely to degenerate into warfare, pointlessly pitting the mechanic Maréchal against the German mechanic, and the aristocratic de Boeldieu against the aristocratic von Rauffenstein. So,on this reading, Renoir's idea is that there is a unity here, if only horizontally, *within* classes, from which a peaceful coexistence can be built.

I believe that Renoir's thinking goes deeper than this reading so far suggests, and that its tone is darker. To begin with, horizontal unity within a class certainly falls short of the sort of unity one might hope for among all of humanity, perhaps of the kind given voice to in Kant's various formulations of the categorical imperative, in which what unites us is our rational nature. From this perspective, being united horizontally within a class is surely no better *a priori* than being united vertically within a nation. More than that, however: Renoir sees that horizontal unity has problems of its own. Horizontal unity with others is contingent upon there *being* such others, at least within one's immediate environment. In other words, it is possible to be isolated.

There are three notable figures in the film who are in this position. First, there is Demolder, the "intellectual", the avid student of the Greek poet Pindar; Pindar, he says, "means more to me than anything, more than you, the war, my life." Demolder is universally mocked for his obsession ("Poor old Pindar!," says von Rauffenstein), and even for his intellectualism itself; when he complains about the Russians setting fire to the books they are sent (they had expected food), he cannot be taken seriously. Second, there is the strange figure of the black Senegalese prisoner who says only one thing in the whole film. In the scene (just after the Pindar scene), Maréchal and Rosenthal are putting together a map of the surrounding land, and the Senegalese is working at a table nearby on what is a stunningly footling task, which seems to involve making some kind of a model out of heated plastic. He finishes and then approaches Maréchal and Rosenthal to show them with pride his picture of "Justice prosecuting Crime," commenting that it came out well. They each give a cursory "yes" and return to poring over their map. The Senegalese goes away dejected, and this is all we hear from him throughout the entire narrative. Third, there is Rosenthal, the rich son of the banking family. His Jewishness is never forgotten ("I never could stomach Jews," says Maréchal in despair as Rosenthal's injured foot is holding up their escape), although his splendid food parcels are welcomed by all the prisoners. There is a very poignant moment when Maréchal is returning to his comrades from his solitary confinement. They all joyfully gather round him, with the exception of Rosenthal, who stays in the background, tearfully preparing a feast for Maréchal. It is also only his charm and tact that enable him to disguise his solitariness in the presence of Maréchal's and Elsa's meaningful glances.

So these three figures find themselves, as a contingent matter, isolated horizontally. Having kindred spirits elsewhere in the world is cold comfort indeed, especially when one is a prisoner of war. In a sense, then, de Boeldieu and von Rauffenstein were lucky: at least they had each other; the intellectual, the black, the Jew—they had no one.

Thus far, then, we seem to be no further forward in finding the *terrain d'entente* of which Renoir spoke. Where can we go from here? Another possible route is to look within human nature, to what is universal among *all* human beings. Here, I think, we find the real pessimism of this film, in its brilliant illustration of certain deep difficulties with this aspiration: it shows that what is universal in human nature can serve to divide us rather than to unite us, to set human being against human being. I will argue that Renoir in *La Grande Illusion*, through recurring themes, sets out to illustrate how three kinds of universal characteristic militate against the possibility of a future without nations and without war. So the hoped-for *terrain d'entente* will turn out to be a chimera—an illusion. Only towards the end will we begin to see some hope—hope in art itself.

III. UNITED AS HUMAN BEINGS?

The first universal characteristic of humans is the capacity for language. But while having language may be something we all share, there remains the fact—a contingent one perhaps, but a fact nevertheless—that what each of us has is *a* language, and that our language is just one among many languages, at least since the Tower of Babel.[7] With different languages, we are faced with failures to understand each other, so that, in spite of their horizontal connections, the French farmer and the Chinese farmer will not be able to communicate over their dinner. The film is replete with carefully drawn examples of such failures to communicate.[8] A few will suffice. There is the sad moment when Maréchal can no longer stand his solitary confinement. His guard comes in to comfort him, saying a few kind words in German, which Maréchal cannot understand. Maréchal shouts out "Get off my back! I can't take it any more! I've had it! . . . I want to hear a voice." And then, more calmly, "I want to hear a *French* voice; I want to speak *French*." The guard sadly leaves him a harmonica and some cigarettes, and goes out of Maréchal's cell, realizing that he cannot help because he cannot speak French and thus cannot express his sympathy in a way that Maréchal will understand and appreciate. There is another occasion, when Maréchal is unable to understand what Elsa's little daughter is saying—the "international" Rosenthal has to translate; even the simple sentence "Lottie has blue eyes" is a struggle. Then there is the moment when the departing French prisoners fail to communicate to the arriving English prisoners that there is a tunnel. There are many more such failures of communication: we all speak *a* language, but there are many languages, so being language-speaking creatures is not the basis for a *terrain d'entente*. In other words, the characteristic is universal but not uniting.

The second universal characteristic of us humans that Renoir illustrates in *La Grande Illusion* is, if anything, even more problematic. This is the universal tendency toward cohesion within the group and toward dislike of, and conflict with, "outsiders", with those who belong to other groups. We have already seen this in the horizontal unity between those with the shared interests of their class—the exclusive, and excluding, way of talking of von Rauffenstein and de Boeldieu, for example. We also see it in the unity of the British and French prisoners against their German captors after Maréchal announces the capture of Douanment from the Germans; we see the brilliant absurdity of a British officer, dressed as a woman cabaret dancer, singing *La Marseillaise*, facing in all seriousness the German officers in the audience. Later, we see it in the other direction, when Douanment is recaptured, with German soldiers celebrating late into the night. Jim Hopkins has argued that this tendency, to "ingroup cohesion and outgroup conflict," appears in individual aggressive motivations as "two sides of the same evolutionary coinage." As he puts it, the tendency "gives rise to a series of psychological and social phenomena, ranging from transient enjoyable rivalries involving one's home town or team, through serious corporate competition, to the intractable destructive hostilities of feuds, tribalism, bigotry and racism, nationalism, intolerant aggressive religious fundamentalism, individual paranoid psychosis, and disputes among schools of psychology. However we moderns think ourselves guarded against such modes of thought, the roots remain active."[9] He cites not only support from evolutionary theory, but also from Freud:

It is always possible to bind together a considerable number of people in love, so long as there are other people left over to receive the manifestations of their aggressiveness . . . In this respect the Jewish people, scattered everywhere, have rendered most useful service to the civilizations of the countries that have been their hosts; but unfortunately all the massacres of the Jews in the Middle Ages did not suffice to make that period more peaceful and secure for their Christian fellows. When once the Apostle Paul had posited universal love between men as the foundation of his Christian community, extreme intolerance on the part of Christendom towards those who remained outside it became the inevitable consequence . . . Neither was it unaccountable chance that the dream of a Germanic world-dominion called for anti-Semitism as its complement; and it is intelligible that the attempt to establish a new, communist civilization in Russia should find its psychological support in the persecution of the Bourgeois.[10]

The alarming consequence, then, is that what binds the group together, vertically or horizontally, by nation or by class, has its inevitable correlate in the rejection of the "other", of the stranger, of the barbarian (so called because he was incomprehensible), and generally of the person who is "not like us." Again, what is universal divides us rather than unites us. And Renoir's *La Grande Illusion* amply illustrates this: the Germans and the French, the Russians, the English, the upper classes and the working classes—each "ingroup" holds itself together in part through uniting itself against the "outgroup".

The third universal characteristic of us humans that Renoir reveals as a source of disunity is already part and parcel of the second, although it is found elsewhere too: sheer aggression, expressed in part in our delight in warfare and in its trappings and paraphernalia. Freud often pointed out how keen we are to deny this,[11] but still, it is a fact that we—perhaps one should say *mankind* here rather than humankind—are aggressive animals.

Where, though, is the aggression in *La Grande Illusion*? There are no scenes of violence in the film, apart from the shooting of de Boeldieu, and this is portrayed in a very aseptic way, certainly with no aggressiveness on the part of von Rauffenstein. Even the knocking out of Maréchal while he is in solitary confinement takes place off screen. There is one scene, however, that I consider to be central to the film's whole narrative, in which the human appeal of aggression is evoked by Renoir with wonderful subtlety and clarity. The scene surrounds the still I have chosen from the film. It begins in the courtyard of the first prison camp, where young recruits are on parade; "Poor boys", says an old lady as she sees them through the gates of the prison. Inside the camp, Maréchal, de Boeldieu, Rosenthal and the other prisoners are in their dormitory overlooking the courtyard, preparing their clothes for the concert. As they hear the marching of the young soldiers in the courtyard growing louder and louder to the sound of pipes and drums, the prisoners' attention is drawn to the window. The camera, located outside the window, pans from one prisoner's face to the next as they look down.[12] De Boeldieu says, in his supercilious way, "I have a horror of pipes." "Still, it gets to you," says Demolder, the intellectual. Then Maréchal says bitterly, "It's not the music, it's not the instruments, that gets to you; it's the sound of marching feet (*le bruit des pas*)." For a moment they are all silent at the window, deep in thought, as the noise outside increases further. We have the clear sense that Maréchal, along with his fellow prisoners, not only feels the psychological appeal of the sound—an appeal grounded in our universal aggressive nature—but that he also resents it. It may be boys (poor boys) "playing at soldiers," as de Boeldieu observes, but the militaristic noise—*le bruit des* pas—inexorably reaches beyond the confines of any particular language to achieve universal appeal—not least to the charming and congenial characters of *La Grande Illusion*.

What is illustrated in this film, then, is that we are universally possessed of three characteristics that tend to pit us one against the other rather to unite us: having a language, having the tendency to ingroup cohesion and outgroup conflict, and, simply, aggressiveness. It is these three sources of disunity that the film appeals to as the grounds of our devastatingly dysfunctional tendency to war making, and not (or not only) to nationhood; nationhood, rather, is an expression, a manifestation, of these universal human characteristics.

IV. *LA GRANDE ILLUSION*, PHILOSOPHY, AND ART

What is the relationship between these ideas and *La Grande Illusion*? I could say simply that I myself am brought to think of these ideas about human nature through seeing the film. I have, however, already committed myself to more than that—namely, that Renoir set out to *illustrate* these ideas in the film. In the context of some rather extravagant claims made on behalf of the role of film in philosophy, and of philosophy in film, however, this seems very modest, and perhaps unduly so. Could I not go further than this, perhaps to claim that these ideas are to be found in *La Grande Illusion* as "theories", or even that these "theories" are *argued for* in the film?[13] Briefly, my reply is this: whether or not some films make, and argue for, philosophical theories, *La Grande Illusion* is not to be numbered among them. Let me explain why.

Sometimes, works of fiction, films as well as novels, may specifically raise philosophical concerns or make philosophical claims, with or without specific arguments for these claims. No doubt Tolstoy does this in *War and Peace*, especially in its closing stages. In film, it might well be true, as Thomas Wartenberg argues, that Chaplin's *Modern Times* "could be both an illustration of a philosophical theory and yet also a site of deep thinking on the mechanisation of the human under capitalism."[14] The philosophical theory that Wartenberg has in mind is, of course, Marx's theory of the alienation of the worker. These examples may indeed be supporting evidence for the claim that novels and films *can* make and argue for philosophical theories, but no one, of course, would be so rash as to argue that *all* novels and films do this, or that they set out to do this; each work has to be considered individually. I see no good reason to think that this is so in the particular case of *La Grande Illusion* (any more than in, say, Kingsley Amis' *Lucky Jim* or in Jane Austen's *Persuasion*). Unlike in *Modern Times*, there is no symbolism, no argument, explicit or implicit, in support of *theories* (such as Marxism) or *claims* (such as that capitalism alienates the worker). No doubt Renoir would himself give some kind of an answer to what his film is "about"; indeed, I have mentioned his remarks about *un terrain d'entente* and about horizontal and vertical relations. There is, however, a world of difference between, on the one hand, philosophical claims and arguments being part of the explicit or implicit content of a film, and also illustrated by the film in order to support the claims, and, on the other hand, a film whose content is, simply, a narrative about particular people at particular times. We can say, perhaps, that the film illustrates the "claims" that I have been making here, just as long as this is not taken to imply that the film itself is making or arguing for these claims. Even to give the title "claims" to the ideas that *La Grande Illusion* illustrates seems to me to be a misnomer. (Imagine someone saying "Renoir is making four central claims in *La Grande Illusion*.") Renoir was, like his father, Auguste Renoir, an artist. His interest, like that of his father, was in the particularities, in observing the fine detail of the particular lives of particular people at particular times.

A film that illustrates—that "merely" illustrates—important truths about human nature can still be profoundly interesting philosophically, and it can, moreover, be a source of significant cognitive value. Let us consider for a moment Auguste Renoir's *La Loge*. This is a painting of a couple at the opera. She is seen in all her finery sitting in their box, in the foreground of the picture, gazing wistfully towards the stalls. The man is toward the back of the box, his face partially hidden by the binoculars though which he is inspecting the audience. Now, James Young has persuasively argued that traditional artworks (of which *La Loge* is one) are illustrative representations.[15] Such representations do not, he says, have cognitive value through providing rational demonstrations as philosophy does, or through providing evidence to support hypotheses as science does. Rather, illustrative representations provide what Young calls *illustrative demonstrations*—a kind of showing—and thereby they can "open perspectives on objects so that audiences may achieve a fuller understanding of them."[16] *La Loge*, then, has cognitive value because it *shows* the loneliness of the human condition—a loneliness that is made even more stark by the glamor of the two characters' clothes and by their glittering surroundings. Comparably, *La Grande Illusion* has cognitive value because it provides an illustrative demonstration—because it shows profoundly interesting and important truths about human nature.[17]

Let me reach finally for Joseph Conrad to bring out a little further what I mean—to his wonderful Preface to *The Nigger of the "Narcissus"*. Conrad says that the artist, like the "thinker" and the scientist, "seeks the truth," and he "makes his appeal." The artist does so in a quite different way than the thinker and the scientist, however. The passage is worth quoting at some length:

A work that aspires, however humbly, to the condition of art should carry its justification in every line. And art itself may be defined as a single-minded attempt to render the highest kind of justice to the visible universe, by bringing to light the truth, manifold and one, underlying its every aspect. It is an attempt to find in its forms, in its colors, in its light, in its shadows, in the aspects of matter and in the facts of life what of each is fundamental, what is enduring and essential—their one illuminating and convincing quality—the very truth of their existence. The artist, then, like the thinker or the scientist, seeks the truth and makes his appeal. Impressed by the aspect of the world the thinker plunges into ideas, the scientist into facts— whence, presently, emerging they make their appeal to those qualities of our being that fit us best for the hazardous enterprise of living. They speak authoritatively to our common-sense, to our intelligence, to our desire of peace or to our desire of unrest; not seldom to our prejudices, sometimes to our fears, often to our egoism—but always to our credulity. And their words are heard with reverence, for their concern is with weighty matters: with the cultivation of our minds and the proper care of our bodies, with the attainment of our ambitions, with the perfection of the means and the glorification of our precious aims.

It is otherwise with the artist.

Confronted by the same enigmatic spectacle, the artist descends within himself, and in that lonely region of stress and strife, if he be deserving and fortunate, he finds the terms of his appeal . . . He speaks to our capacity for delight and wonder, to the sense of mystery surrounding our lives; to our sense of pity, and beauty, and pain: to the latent feeling of fellowship with all creation—and to the subtle but invincible conviction of solidarity that knits together the loneliness of innumerable hearts; to the solidarity in dreams, in joy, in sorrow, in aspiration, in illusions, in hope, in fear, which binds men to each other, which binds together all humanity—the dead to the living and the living to the unborn.

It is only some such train of thought, or rather of feeling, that can in a measure explain the aim to the attempt, made in the tale which follows, to present an unrestful episode in the obscure lives of a few individuals out of all the disregarded multitude of the bewildered, the simple and the voiceless. For, if there is any part of truth in the belief confessed above, it becomes evident that there is not a place of splendour or a dark corner of the earth that does not deserve, if only a passing glance of wonder and pity.[18]

The artist, then, does not plunge directly into "ideas" or into "facts" in order to bring to light truths; instead, the artist appeals to our shared emotional responses (delight, wonder, a sense of beauty, of pain, of fellow-feeling), through "presenting", or what I have called *showing*, an episode in the lives of men; and thereby certain ideas can be illustrated. Just so did Conrad himself weave his spell in his great novels and short stories; and just so does Renoir in his *La Grande Illusion*. More than this, Conrad is suggesting that, in art, we can find a universal characteristic that truly unites all humanity, a true *terrain d'entente*, namely the capacity to appreciate, and have shared emotional responses to, great works of art and to the truths that they illustrate, through which we can come to appreciate "the subtle but invincible conviction of solidarity that knits together the loneliness of innumerable hearts." At last we have found, in art, a source of universality and of unity—like a glimpse of sunlight amid the encircling gloom. And this glimpse is there, to be found, in Renoir's great work of art, *La Grande Illusion*.[19]

NOTES

1. Accordingly, I am surprised by James Kerans' remark that " . . . *La Grande Illusion* is not always consciously and immediately recognizable as a pacifist film . . . " ("Classics Revisited: "La Grande Illusion," 11). Even the original poster for the film was explicit in its pacifism, and the title of the film was drawn from the 1910 anti-war book of the same name by Norman Angell, the Nobel Prize winner.

2. He made this remark in a postscript to the film in 1938. I owe this reference to Kerans, "Classics Revisited", 10.

3. All dialogue quoted in this essay has been transcribed directly from the film.

4. Cited by Peter Cowie in his discussion of *La Grande Illusion* in The Criterion Collection: www.criterionco.com.

5. Referred to by Kerans, "Classics Revisited", 14.

6. In his "Looking Back on the Spanish War". 158

7. The regret here, if there is one, ought not to be that we do not all speak the same language—English or French, say—or otherwise one will fall into the trap of the woman at Versailles spoken of by Voltaire: *"Je ne suis pas commme une dame de la cour de Versailles, qui disait: c'est bien dommage que l'aventure de la Tour de Babel ait produit la confusion des langues; sans cela tout le monde aurait toujours parlé Francais."*

8. Jeffrey Triggs has a very helpful discussion of the role of language in *La Grande Illusion* in "The Legacy of Babel."

9. "Conscience and Conflict," 225, 229.

10. *Civilisation and its Discontents*, 305. I have added to Hopkins' citation.

11. For example, he says, it is a truth "which people are so ready to disavow," Ibid., 302.

12. To see how the faces come together prior to the moment of the still, it is best to watch the sequence in slow motion: the movement is both balletic and yet entirely natural.

13. The following issues are discussed in a number of papers in *The Journal of Aesthetics and Art Criticism* 64:1, 2006.

14. "Beyond *Mere* Illustration," 30.

15. In his *Art and Knowledge*. I discuss Young's claims about the cognitive value of conceptual art in "Conceptual Art and Knowledge."

16. *Art and Knowledge*, 80.

17. Jenefer Robinson gives a similar kind of account of how we can learn profound truths about human nature from novels, as part of what she nicely calls a sentimental education; see her *Deeper than Reason*, Ch. 6.

18. Conrad's Preface to *The Nigger of the "Narcissus"*. I discuss this passage in my "Towards a virtue theory of art."

19. Thanks to Stewart Wood, to Ronald de Sousa, and to the editors for comments and suggestions.

9

A "*CRASH*" COURSE ON PERSONAL RACISM

LAWRENCE BLUM

THE FILM *CRASH* IS A powerful portrayal of a range of moral issues related to personal racism. The film's wide array of storylines concerning several different racial and ethnic groups raises issues of personal stereotyping, prejudice, racial humiliation, wielding of racial power, and racial and ethnic insensitivity and misconnection. *Crash* is structured in such a way as to engage in a kind of moral education with its audience—calling our own stereotypes, prejudices, and other unwarranted racial assumptions to our attention, then leading us to question them. At the same time, as a totality the film conveys some morally problematic messages about race and racism.

Crash was a striking cultural phenomenon of the year 2005. An independently produced and distributed film, made on a tiny budget by Hollywood standards ($7.5 million), it opened in early May of that year and grossed $180 million worldwide. The film was widely and on the whole well reviewed. It was much talked about for its unusual frankness about race in the United States.[1] Quite a few of my students, both high school and college, told me I had to see it. By the end of the year, when films from earlier in the year are generally forgotten and ignored in the round of yearly awards, *Crash* had won or been nominated for several significant ones[2] and, most strikingly, had been nominated for several major Academy Awards, including Best Picture, Best Director, and Best Screenplay.

Crash put on the big screen an array of racial situations seldom seen in American film.[3] The film depicts the racial diversity of America crashing against one another. There are blacks, whites, Latinos, and Asian Americans; reflecting post 9/11 America, there are also "Middle Easterners" and, reflecting its Los Angeles setting, the Middle Easterners are Iranians. There are about fourteen main characters and several important secondary ones. The film is in the mold of Robert Altman's *Short Cuts* (itself modeled on his earlier classic, *Nashville*), and Paul Thomas Anderson's *Magnolia*, both set in Los Angeles, with multiple interweaving of stories and characters. Some commentators have decried the implausibility of a particular character from one scene showing up in another, but all of the films of this form ask the audience to suspend disbelief of this sort. The important issue is whether the characters' behavior is realistic and compelling in the scenes in which they are placed, and in this regard *Crash* largely succeeds.

I. TYPES OF PERSONAL RACISM IN *CRASH*

Crash depicts a remarkable range of types of personal racism—racism on the part of individuals in interaction with other individuals. There are racist fears based on stereotypes—a housewife thinks that because her Hispanic locksmith has a tattoo and wears his pants low-slung he will sell the key to the lock he has just installed in her house to his friends. There is the demeaning or ridiculing of others based on ethnicity, race, or immigrant status—several characters mock the accents of Asians; a gun shop owner insults and derides a Middle Eastern man by linking him with terrorism ("Yo, Osama! Plan a jihad on your own time.") There is racial hypocrisy—a district attorney, in order to ingratiate himself with the black community, exploits a cop-shooting by falsely portraying the victim as a hero. There are powerful portrayals of white people using their social power to demean blacks—a white TV producer compels his black director to reshoot a scene, implying that the black director is out of touch with whether a black character's accent is appropriate. (The film's central example of racial humiliation is described in detail below.) Several characters confuse or are unable to distinguish one ethnicity from another—thinking Iranians are Arabs; Koreans, Chinese; or Salvadorans, Mexicans. Many more examples could be given.

II. RACIAL STEREOTYPES

Crash is particularly powerful in prompting a questioning of racial stereotypes, and this aspect of the film bears more detailed discussion. The idea of "stereotype" refers to two distinct things, especially in the context of filmic representations. The more common use refers to a "cultural" stereotype—that is, an image familiar to most persons in a given society that links a racial or ethnic group to a particular characteristic (blacks as lazy, Jews greedy, Irish as drunks, whites as racist, and so on). (In this chapter, I will discuss stereotypes only of racial and ethnic groups, although virtually any social group can be a target of stereotype.) Construed as generalizations, these stereotypes are always false or at best misleading; this is one feature distinguishing stereotypes from valid generalizations.[4]

A second meaning of "stereotype" in relation to film refers to a character in a group who not only possesses a group-stereotypic characteristic (as in a cultural stereotype), but in whom this characteristic is, in the film, the only salient characteristic. This is a "one-dimensional" stereotype. The two types of stereotype differ in that a character conforming to a cultural stereotype might still be a three-dimensional character with many attributes other than the stereotypic one. Sometimes, however, simply having a character who corresponds to a cultural stereotype can be problematic, even if the character is three dimensional, because it reinforces a damaging cultural image of a particular group.

Thus, films can help to undermine stereotypes in two quite distinct ways. One is to have characters in a stereotyped racial or ethnic group who do not possess the attributes in the stereotype; an Irish person who does not drink, for instance. The other is to have characters who do possess the stereotypic attributes but are three-dimensional characters who possess a range of human characteristics other than and in addition to the stereotypic one.

III. CHALLENGING STEREOTYPES: EXPLORING
THE "VIOLENT YOUNG BLACK MALE" STEREOTYPE

Crash challenges stereotypes in both ways. A straightforward example of the cultural stereotype kind is an Asian couple who is initially a target of sympathy, in part because the woman is the butt of racist ridicule and the man is hit by a car—but also, I think, because of the "model minority" stereotype that Asians are hard working and law abiding. Then, near the end of the film, it is revealed that the Asian couple are smugglers of illegal Asian labor for sweatshops. The "model minority" stereotype is challenged through setting up an expectation based on that stereotype, then defeating it.[5]

The film's most extended and complex challenging of racial stereotypes, in both the cultural and the one-dimensional form, concerns a particularly potent and damaging stereotype—that young black males are dangerous, violent, and to be feared. Challenging stereotypes fully requires recognizing two distinct moral truths about them. One is that all stereotypes and stereotyping are bad and wrong. The other is that some are worse than others. They can be worse for several different reasons—the degree to which the attribute in the stereotype is socially or morally disvalued (being violent is more disvalued than being a good dancer, and both are stereotypes of African Americans); the historical associations of some stereotypes being more negative or more culturally embedded than others (blacks as unintelligent [a centuries-old stereotype, originating in racial slavery] vs. whites as bland); or because, in context, some stereotypes contribute to ill treatment of the group in question more than do others. Among at least the first and third of these, the "violent young black male" stereotype is a particularly damaging one. It deleteriously affects young black males' ability to find employment, receive respectful and appropriate treatment in schools, and be treated with appropriate civic regard in public spaces.

Sometimes, in trying to identify what is wrong with this particular stereotype, people say that every person should be treated as an individual, not as a member of a group. Others deny the generalization that black men are any more dangerous as a group than any other group of males. Both of these responses are well-intentioned yet importantly false or misleading. It is a fact that black males commit a higher percentage of violent crime than males of other groups in the United States in proportion to their numbers, even though it is also true that black men are discriminated against with regard to arrest, trial, and sentencing, so that the large gap in incarceration rates for violent crimes is not solely a reflection of commission of violent crimes.[6]

Suggesting that people should be looked at only as individuals and not as members of groups is also ill-founded advice. People are individuals and members of groups, and they need to be acknowledged as both, not solely as one or the other. In an early scene in *Crash*, two young black men, good friends, emerge from a restaurant in a white area of Los Angeles. One of them, Anthony (Chris "Ludacris"

Bridges), decries racist treatment at the restaurant (a form of public disparagement to which blacks are indeed subject), while his friend, Peter (Larenz Tate), is not so sure. A well-off white couple, Rick and Jean Cabot (Brendan Fraser and Sandra Bullock), is approaching them. Jean clutches Rick's arm; Anthony sees this and points it out to Peter, complaining about the stereotype of young black men as dangerous or thugs. The stereotype is thus challenged. Anthony is correct to complain that the way he and Peter dress and comport themselves should not lead a passerby to be afraid of them. The film audience is distinctly encouraged to recognize and question this stereotype, which the filmmakers can assume is held at least to some degree by almost all American viewers, because Anthony calls attention to it and because we think he may be right that Jean Cabot's actions are an unwarranted response to it.

Yet, it then turns out that Anthony and Peter are thugs. They have guns and they carjack the Cabots' car; nor is it their first time doing this sort of thing. The film has set us up to question the cultural stereotype that young black men are dangerous, yet in this case, the stereotype holds true.

As the film proceeds, the story line of the two carjackers engages with the second type of stereotyping—not recognizing attributes in the character other than the stereotypic one. No doubt, for many viewers, once Anthony and Peter are revealed as thugs, the culturally salient image of the dangerous young black male kicks back in, displacing the questioning of the stereotype in which the viewer may have already engaged, and thus setting up a set of expectations of these young men as moral reprobates and unsavory characters all around. Some of Anthony's and Peter's later behavior does comport with the latter image; but some does not. Anthony turns out to have a set of moral principles related to his particular pro-black outlook on the world. He will not rob black people, for example.[7] He is critical of blacks whom he sees as preying on the black community. The audience is not meant to approve of Anthony's particular political principles, but the fact that he has them is not what one expects of a "thug".[8] It does not fit the stereotype. Anthony is also shown to be somewhat capable of moral growth and change. Later in the film a black man, Cameron Thayer, an important moral presence in the film, criticizes Anthony (in regard to his carjacking) as shaming black people ("You embarrass me. You embarrass yourself," he says to Anthony). Anthony is shown as taking this exchange to heart. In a late scene, he is in a position to sell a group of smuggled, illegal Asian workers slated for sweatshop work to a (white) acquaintance of his. Anthony refuses to do this, and he sets the smugglees free. (This action seems meant also to express a connection, recognized by Anthony, between blacks as former slaves and the slave-like condition of the Asian smugglees.)

Even more than Anthony, Peter also defeats the viewer's (again, especially the white viewer's) stereotypic expectations of black thugs. He is a sensitive, likable, and thoughtful young man. He comes across more as a nice boy who went astray than as a thug, which is just to say that film gives him a human complexity that the deeply rooted "black thug" stereotype in which it initially places him denies. While both characters conform to the cultural stereotype of a dangerous young black man, they also are both shown to possess a range of human traits other than and often at odds with that stereotype.

Earlier I said that a film can help to challenge stereotypes through showing individuals who do possess the stereotypic characteristic attached to their group as fully realized, three-dimensional characters. It would be a stretch to say that *Crash* manages this in the case of Peter and Anthony. The film is juggling many characters, and none of them really come across as full individuals. So the stereotyping is challenged in the sense of showing characteristics, such as moral principledness or thoughtfulness, seen as contrary to violence and dangerousness, but not in the sense of a fully individualized, three-dimensional character.

There is one further way that films can have nonstereotypic characters from a given group—to have a range of different characters from the group in question, some of whom do not possess the stereotypic attributes, even though some do. *Crash* succeeds in this regard with respect to its black characters; in addition to Anthony and Peter, there are three other major black characters (the Thayers [discussed below], and officer Waters [Don Cheadle]) all of whom, while shown with human frailties, are sympathetic, decent, and basically honorable people who are largely free of black stereotypic attributes.

How successful is *Crash* in its various challengings of the "violent young black male" stereotype? We can assess this only in relation to what one can realistically expect of a film in the challenging or undermining of stereotypes. I mentioned briefly that cultural images held as stereotypes are characteristically resistant to challenge. Seldom do people simply abandon their stereotypes in the face of evidence to the contrary; this is part of the power of stereotypes and part of why they are so pernicious. Even in classroom situations with a captive audience over a stretch of time, fully undermining students' stereotypes is a difficult business. Still, one of the ways to effect this result is precisely to challenge them with contrary evidence; film is in a position to do this because of the power of its visual image. *Crash* goes a bit beyond merely presenting counterevidence (of the three forms mentioned—a group member not possessing the stereotypic characteristic in question, three-dimensional characters from the group in question, and a range of characters from the group, some of whom do not possess a given stereotypic characteristic), because it also explicitly calls attention to stereotyping on the part of its characters, for example, Anthony's doing so with respect to Jean Cabot and, I have suggested, on the part of its audience by priming stereotype-based expectations and then defeating them.[9] That having been said, it is "just a movie," and many viewers can dismiss its "evidence" against various stereotypes in a way that would not be so easy to do if that evidence were an encountered, flesh-and-blood individual counterstereotypic member of a stereotyped group.

IV. THE TOTALISTIC CONCEPTION OF RACISM

In line with its exploring the psychic complexity of stereotyping, *Crash* frequently goes beyond merely depicting forms of personal racism, or other race-related wrongs, to show that the human attitudes underlying them have a psychic complexity frequently unrecognized in discussions about racism. One familiar image of a racist person is that he thinks or behaves badly in every interaction with members of the group against whom he is racist; he might restrain his behavior for fear of sanction or disapproval, but his thoughts and feelings toward the group are in all instances prejudicial or stereotypic. Let us call this the "totalistic" conception of (personal) racism. If Jones, a white person, is racist against Latinos, then he acts or thinks badly toward all Latinos on all occasions. *Crash* is helpful in showing that personal racism seldom operates in this totalistic way. People have many ways of exempting certain subgroups or individuals from their racism toward the larger group, seeing them as exceptions yet without dislodging the prejudices toward the group itself. An obvious example of this is when a particular black person is regarded as "not really black" by someone for whom this individual does not comport with her overall prejudiced or stereotypic image of blacks. A slightly different form of nontotalistic racism is when an antipathy toward the group kicks in only when certain other characteristics are also present; for example, someone may be respectful and comfortable with older black people, or with black women, but not with younger blacks, or with black males.[10]

In addition, in much popular discussion, someone who is viewed as "racist" will be assumed to be a virtual moral untouchable. *Crash* appreciates the complexity of human motivation, both in relation to racial matters and more generally. People who exhibit racial prejudice may be sympathetic or even morally admirable in other respects; more generally, racial prejudice is routinely shown in an admixture with other qualities, as so often happens in life.

A small example of this nontotalistic racism is the wealthy housewife Jean's racist distrust of her Hispanic locksmith, Daniel (Michael Peña). While this distrust is entirely despicable within the film (reinforced by the fact that she voices her prejudices in his hearing), it is also true that earlier the same evening, she has been mugged and her car hijacked, by two young black men (described above). Jean is understandably on edge. Her insensitive husband patronizes her and completely misses why she might be anxious about her sense of security in her house, an anxiety that expresses itself in racist fears about the locksmith. Her racism is mixed in with these other feelings.

OFFICER RYAN AND THE THAYERS: RACIAL VICTIMIZATION AND HUMILIATION, AND A FALSE RESOLUTION

Two central storylines in *Crash* exemplify this moral complexity of nontotalistic racism particularly well. In an early scene, two white officers, Ryan (Matt Dillon) and Hanson (Ryan Philippe), in their police cruiser, are supposed to be looking for a car, described over the police radio, that has been carjacked. Ryan is driving and, over Hanson's protests, instead follows a different vehicle in which he thinks he sees a white woman performing fellatio on the black driver. Ryan pulls the couple over. He sees that the wife, Christine Thayer (Thandie Newton), is a light-skinned black woman. The husband, Cameron Thayer (Terrence Dashon Howard), tries to mollify Ryan; in a cooperative spirit he accedes to Ryan's request for his license and registration, and, somewhat bemusedly and not confrontationally, laughs about how he is going to reach into his glove compartment to retrieve these items. (The reference here to stereotypes about black men reaching for guns foreshadows an important later incident, discussed below.)

Possibly irritated by Christine's defiance (she is also a bit drunk) and by Cameron's failure to pay what Ryan regards as due deference to him, Ryan orders the couple out of the car. After roughly slamming Cameron against the car, Ryan proceeds to feel Christine all over her body, and especially between her thighs, allegedly for weapons. The scene is lingered over, and the violation of Christine is compellingly and painfully rendered.[11] Christine challenges her husband to do something, but Cameron recognizes that any attempt he would make to protest Ryan's actions would likely cause him or them more harm. The film makes it clear that Cameron also suffers humiliation because a white man is violating his wife without his being able to do anything about it.

Ryan is portrayed as quite aware of this double humiliation, and as enjoying his power to cause it. It is a flat-out example of personal racism in several ways. He does not respect black people's civic rights, and he feels entitled to use his position as a police officer to victimize black people; he knows, at least intuitively, that his humiliation of Cameron is all the more demeaning to him because he, Ryan, is white, and Cameron is black; and he is incensed at the idea of a white woman sexually gratifying a black man. The film shows the damage this incident causes to the Thayers. Once at home, they quarrel about Cameron's not challenging Ryan's violation of Christine, and they trade stinging accusations of racial ignorance, lack of racial self-respect, and racial disloyalty. The damage to and crisis in the Thayers' relationship remains a presence throughout the film.

Soon after this incident, however, we are shown another side of Officer Ryan. His father has a painful and humiliating prostate condition, which has been misdiagnosed as a urinary tract infection. Ryan is shown tenderly and sensitively caring for his father. He is a caring and devoted son. At the same time, when Ryan tries to get help for his father from his HMO, the HMO's bureaucrat, a black woman (Loretta Devine), is very unhelpful. Ryan makes fun of her black-identified name ("Shaniqua Johnson") and, in a later scene, seems to attempt to play on her sympathies by telling her a preposterous story about how affirmative action ruined his father's life.[12] This scene gives the impression that Ryan is seething with resentments and prejudices against blacks, thus filling in a bit of the back story to his earlier despicable treatment of the Thayers. At the same time, we see that although entirely racist, Ryan is in certain respects a good person, in being a caring son.

In a later scene, about two-thirds of the way through the film, Ryan comes upon an accident with an upended car in danger of catching fire. He rushes to the scene, undeterred by the potential danger and showing himself to be a courageous professional in his line of work. Looking into the overturned car, he can hear a woman crying; he can see that she is suspended upside down in the car, but he cannot see her face. He struggles toward her and before he can see that it is Christine Thayer, she sees him and, in great agitation from her dangerous situation now compounded by the memory of this racist cop's violation of her the previous night, screams hysterically and resists Ryan's further trying to rescue her. "Don't touch me . . . please, somebody, anybody but you." Ryan is momentarily startled and we get the impression that he recognizes why Christine would be resistant to him. But as the scene proceeds, Christine's hysteria about Ryan is shown as irrationally jeopardizing her own safety. "Stop moving, lady, I'm not trying to hurt you," Ryan says. Christine's reaction and the difficulty it poses for his rescue effort overtake any focus on Ryan's understanding and recognition of the harm and despicableness of his earlier actions. The scene could have been constructed differently. Through words and facial expressions, Ryan could have been shown more defini tively and fully to recognize his previous racist treatment of Christine and how it was now harming his ability to carry out his role responsibility to rescue her.[13] But the film does not take this path.

Ryan proceeds with the rescue and carries Christine away, just before the car explodes, as she clings to him. Parts of the scene are shot in slow motion, and the encounter is lingered on more than any other scene in the film; a haunting song and score play prominently over the action, giving the scene a vaguely religious dimension and also marking it as special within the film. (The film takes place on Christmas Eve, and there are many crosses throughout the film.) As Ryan carries Christine, she looks up at him with intense gratitude; her resentment at his previous treatment of her has (understandably, given the situation) disappeared. When Christine walks away from the scene, she looks back at Ryan, again with gratitude and perhaps wonderment. Ryan's earlier momentary recognition of Christine as the woman he has previously victimized is completely overshadowed by the heroism of his rescue. The black woman's gratitude at her white savior has dwarfed both the damage to her and the white man's remorse at having victimized her.

Some viewers have seen this scene as the most powerful and significant one in the film. Mary Ann Johanson, the "flick filosopher", says, "There is one devastating moment in the film, a scene I don't imagine I will ever forget the power of, in which one character is suddenly confronted with the frangible humanity of someone he'd previous dehumanized in the basest way."[14] Ryan is confronted, indeed, but I don't think he learns what he needs to from this confrontation. The reconciliation in this scene mutes and distorts the damage of Ryan's racism. Reconciliation can be appropriate when the perpetrator fully acknowledges the wrong and harm of his racism, when he conveys this acknowledgment to his victim, and when she is able to forgive him. Ryan does not do this.

Ryan's rescue of Christine has become the signature scene in the film; images from it grace every movie poster I have seen. [See still, page 191.] It is the cover of the DVD. That the promoters of the film wish to emphasize racial reconciliation, rather than racial prejudice, division, and misunderstanding, as the film itself mainly does, is not surprising.[15] That framing, however, distorts the more challenging aspects of *Crash*.

The way the film plays, the rescue and Christine's gratitude seems to absolve Ryan of the moral wrong of his earlier racist behavior. In some sense, I think the audience is meant to think of him as cured of his racism. The totalistic understanding of racism mentioned earlier contributes to this implausible view. It implies that if Ryan rescues a black woman who hates him, then he cannot be racist. We saw, however, that while the film might have made Ryan see the error of his ways but did not, it is also true that a racist police officer can engage in a heroic rescue of a member of a group against whom he is racist without being any less racist for that. Ryan saw a life-threatening situation and acted appropriately; his professional ethic trumped his racism, and it should not be surprising that it did. There is nothing in Ryan's rescue of Christine that would lead one to think he would give up any of his resentments and hostilities against blacks as a group. It wouldn't be in the least surprising to see Ryan in the future using his police power to victimize other blacks. He can be, and is, a racist, yet he is also a good cop (in certain respects, though not in others), and a good son. The scene both depicts nontotalistic racism and also partially succumbs to a totalistic version of racism.

OFFICER HANSON: RACISM IN A WHITE NONRACIST

Another powerful illustration of the psychic complexity of personal racism is the portrayal of the rookie officer Hanson (Ryan Phillippe), Ryan's initial partner. Hanson is revolted by Ryan's treatment of the Thayers in the early scene, and he tries and succeeds in having himself transferred to a single-cop cruiser. In a later scene, he and some other officers come upon Cameron Thayer, whom they wrongly believe has stolen the car he is driving. Cameron becomes belligerent toward them. (His racial humiliations and tensions with Christine, mentioned above, have put him over the edge.) Hanson intervenes and tells his fellow (white) officers, who are possibly on the brink of seriously harming Cameron, that Cameron is a friend of his, and asks them to let Thayer's menacing behavior go with a warning.

Clearly, in part Hanson is doing penance for having been an unwilling but unprotesting accomplice to Ryan's earlier racist victimization of the Thayers. Hanson was genuinely revolted by his partner's racism. When he attempts to secure a transfer, he has to stand up to a higher ranked black officer who derides him for doing so.

In a later scene, late in the film but the same night as the incident just mentioned in which he has helped Cameron Thayer, Hanson is off duty, driving home, and he picks up a young black man (who turns out to be Peter, one of the carjackers) hitchhiking. Does Hanson do so because he is still feeling guilty about his earlier role in the Ryan/Thayer incident, and wants to help out a black man? Or is he feeling good about himself for helping Cameron out and thus feeling racially expansive? It isn't clear, but the possibilities help to speak to the complexity of Hanson's race-related motivation and attitudes.

Once in Hanson's car, Peter remarks on the country music that Hanson is playing on his car radio; he says that he is in fact writing a country song, and that he has been re-thinking his attitudes toward country music. (He and Anthony had a race-related exchange about country music earlier.) Hanson expresses skepticism about this. In response to Hanson's query about what he has been doing that evening, Peter says he has been ice skating. (We know from an earlier scene with Anthony that Peter likes ice hockey.) Peter notices a St. Christopher's figurine on Hanson's dashboard (we know that he himself is attached to this figurine, a fact for which Anthony has ridiculed him) and begins to laugh, seemingly at the irony and the coincidence.

Hanson thinks Peter is laughing at him and pulls the car over and orders Peter to get out, in a deserted spot. Peter unsuccessfully tries to calm Hanson down. What is going on in this scene up to this point? I have run across two interpretations. One is that Peter is indeed laughing at Hanson and mocking him by claiming "white" interests, such as ice skating and country music. This does not square with what we know of Peter, who seems sincere in his profession of interest in country music and ice skating. Moreover, in his scenes with Anthony, Peter unfailingly rejects both the sharp racial boundaries that Anthony is always drawing and the racial parochialism he espouses. He is the sort of character, we are led to believe, who likes what he likes and doesn't care if it is seen as white, black, or other.

A second possibility is that Hanson thinks, stereotypically, that a young black man, especially one dressed like Peter (the camera briefly shows Hanson seeing Peter's torn jacket and muddy sneakers) couldn't have such interests. He might well think that Peter is mocking him, even if he isn't. There seems to be something else going on as well, however. By claiming a common interest (in country music), and by laughing innocently (though Hanson perceives the laughter to be at his expense), Peter has crossed a boundary of racial comfort that Hanson does not realize he is invested in. Hanson is uncomfortable with the kind of familiarity toward him that this young black man (about his age) is edging toward. Hanson in some sense needs for there to be "white activities" and "black activities" so that he can draw a line between Peter and himself, between black and white. It is not that Hanson thinks blacks are inferior, but this is nevertheless an attitude arising from a segregationist history. It is a form of the idea that blacks have to be kept in their place, interpersonally if not socioeconomically.[16]

Hanson is not aware that he holds such attitudes. In an earlier scene, after Hanson has transferred from riding with Ryan, they run into each other. Ryan says to Hanson, in response to the unspoken reason for the transfer, "You think you know yourself. You have no idea." Hanson's encounter with Peter is clearly meant to illustrate Ryan's observation. Hanson tries and wants to be a racial good guy and does not realize his unconscious investment in racially problematic norms.

The fact that Hanson is not aware of his racial biases in no way renders inauthentic his earlier revulsion at Ryan's racism. What this does show is that some forms of personal antiracism are perfectly compatible with other forms of personal racism; these can coexist in the same individual. Hanson is the only white person in the film who genuinely tries to do the right thing in the racial domain of life, and the exposure of layers of racism in him is a depressing, if significant, revelation. Hanson's racism suggests that white people's attitudes toward blacks can be part of a collective unconscious with deep historical roots.

Hanson's unacknowledged racism turns out to be toxic. Peter stops laughing and tries to get Hanson to see that his remarks and behavior have been entirely innocuous; it is not clear to me whether Peter is fully aware of the racial subtext of his interaction with Hanson. He tells Hanson he wants to show him something that will make Hanson see that Peter's words and behavior should not offend him, and Peter starts to reach into his pocket. Hanson warns him not to, and reaches toward his own pocket. A gun goes off, but the camera has shifted to behind the car, and we do not see what has happened. A moment later, we see Peter dead, with his St. Christopher figurine in his hand. Hanson is horrified by what he has done; but he also tries to cover up evidence of his crime and takes no responsibility for it.

The scene is skillfully shot. In retrospect, it is obvious that Peter would be reaching for the figurine; he wants to show that he has been laughing and experiencing a kind of connection to Hanson because he owns, and indeed treasures, the same figurine Hanson has on his dashboard. And so, of course Hanson is the one who has done the shooting. The brief time lapse, however, allows the audience, especially, one might say, the nonblack audience, to be momentarily unsure who has shot whom—time for the stereotype that this young black man is pulling a gun to trump the viewer's knowledge that Hanson is an agitated cop with some unconscious racist attitudes who has a gun and probably believes Peter is reaching for his gun.[17] Again, *Crash* deals with stereotypes in a manner that both portrays the wrongness of the characters' stereotypes and stereotyping, but that also brings the viewing audience's participation in stereotyping into play in a manner that can lead us to recognize how we too are prey to it, and how harmful that can be.

V. THE "ALL RACISM IS EQUAL" PROBLEM

Crash is thus replete with a wide range of forms and aspects of personal racism and race relations in the United States in the early twenty-first century. Yet the film as a totality is in some important respects less than the sum of its parts. One respect is that by including so many different forms and modes of personal racism, *Crash* somewhat leaves the viewer with the impression that they are all of equivalent moral seriousness. To take three examples, the first two of much greater moral seriousness than the third: a young man is killed because of racial stereotypes and the transgressing of rules of interracial personal distance; a white cop violates a black woman in a deeply racist (and sexist) way; various people confuse one ethnic group with another—Iranians with Arabs, Chinese Americans with Korean Americans, and so on. These items obviously differ greatly in moral character, both in their consequences and in the underlying race-related attitudes, misunderstandings, and commitments they manifest. This is not to belittle the nonrecognition that, say, Korean Americans experience when people do not realize they are distinct from Chinese Americans. Such nonrecognition is not really at the same level of moral seriousness as racial violation, or racial hostility, hatred, or diminution involved in more serious manifestations of racial wrongfulness, however.

It is not that the film in any way positively asserts or directly implies that these distinct racial bads are equally significant. By its construction as a stringing together of so many "racial incidents" without clearly marking moral distinctions being made among them, however, it lends itself to this impression.

This conflation of differently valenced modalities of racial wrongs is quite familiar in public discourse about racism, and it is encouraged by several related tendencies. One is the indiscriminate use of "racism" as a catchall term for all forms of racial wrongs or mishaps, of whatever level of seriousness.[18] This use of "racism" helps to create (while it also reflects) a public insensitivity to the moral distinctions among forms of racial wrong, and *Crash* to some extent both draws on and plays into this insensitivity.

A related reason for this moral conflation is simply that Americans are not accustomed to talking about race, except within their own racial groups, and whites tend not to do so even within their own group. For many white Americans, almost any reference to race functions as a kind of red flag, discouraging further conversation or probing more deeply into the character of what is being discussed. As a result many whites are unaccustomed to thinking seriously about racial matters at all. One understandable consequence of this is that they have not developed the ability to make appropriate moral differentiations in the racial domain.

VI. THE "RACISM IS COLOR-BLIND" VIEW

One important aspect of a failure adequately to differentiate different moral levels among racial wrongs or bads is the view that a particular manifestation of personal racism or other race-related wrong—acting from prejudice, thinking ill of someone, demeaning someone, and so on—is equally morally problematic, no matter what the race of the parties to the transaction, whether done by blacks to Latinos, whites to blacks, or Asians to whites. Let us call this the view that "racism is color-blind."

Even leaving aside for the moment the matter of systemic racism (discussed below), the "racism is color blind" view seriously misrepresents the moral importance of racial asymmetries in personal racism. Being the target of racial prejudice is a very different matter for a member of a socially vulnerable, stigmatized, or marginalized group than it is for a member of a nonstigmatized, dominant, or socially accepted group—even when the prejudice itself is of the same psychological character in the two cases. White people can indeed be the target of racial prejudice and even racial hatred, and this is a very bad thing (a point denied by the misleading but popular view that only white people can be racist); but for an Arab American or an African American to be a target of such racial prejudice or hatred is, everything else being equal, substantially worse. For an Arab American to be hated by a white person typically and standardly invokes and makes psychically salient his or her sense of being stigmatized, of being socially marginal and vulnerable. The psychic damage to that individual Arab American is, then, typically substantially greater than that of a white person who is hated by an Arab American. The situations are not symmetrical. In this sense racial prejudice is not "color blind". Racial identities matter in personal racism.[19] The point that *Crash* wants to emphasize—that racial prejudice and stereotyping are not confined to any single racial group, but afflict us all—while true and important in itself, can readily be taken to deny these racial asymmetries.

At the same time, *Crash* does not go as far down this path of denial as it might have. For one thing, whites are always the purveyors of personal racism, never its victims; so *Crash* avoids the direct implication that racism against whites is on the same level as racism against people of color. Also, however, the film sometimes appreciates the special vulnerability of various nonwhite groups. Farhad (Shaun Toub), the Iranian shop keeper, is distrustful in a way that is destructive to himself and his family because (the film implies) he has often been mistreated by others, especially in the post-9/11 world, that is expressed most fully in his store being vandalized as part of a hate crime against him (but is also shown in the early scene of the racist gun store owner mistreating him).

More substantially, the damage done to Cameron and Christine Thayer by Officer Ryan's victimization of them early in the film is entirely race related, embedded in deeply gendered hierarchies of white domination and black subordination. Cameron is successful and well off; but his success has required compromises required by the structures of racial deference within which he is situated. The particular nature of Cameron's humiliation at the hands of the white producer, which pushes him over the edge emotionally, could only be experienced, in the United States, by a black man. That humiliation draws, at least implicitly, on the distinctive history of white domination of blacks in the United States. This thread of the film could not have played convincingly if the couple had been Asian or Latino (although perhaps in some parts of the country, possibly including Los Angeles, a Mexican couple could almost have stood in for the black one)—nor if the cop and the producer had been anything but white. There is no confusion about racism being color-blind here.

Again, this is a way that the film taken as a totality is misleading in a way that focusing on some of its constituent parts is not. The totality gives the impression of saying that everyone is prejudiced, everyone is racist, we're all in this together, and we're all similarly positioned with regard to this scourge. But this major story line of the film—Officer Ryan and the Thayers—exhibits a clear awareness of the specificity of racial subordination of Blacks by Whites in the United States.

Indeed, all of the most serious personal racism in the film is perpetrated by whites: Ryan's victimization of the Thayers; Hanson's unconscious stereotyping and racial boundary-drawing regarding Peter; Jean Cabot's assuming Daniel is a gang member; the white producer humiliating Cameron Thayer; the district attorney's assistant, Flanagan's, demeaning remarks about blacks; and the gun store owner's contempt for Farhad. The forms of racism on the part of the people of color are uniformly of less moral weight—Graham Waters, the black detective, can't remember which Hispanic group his associate and lover, Ria, belongs to; Anthony and Peter think all Asians are "Chinamen"; Shaniqua Johnson and Ria (separately) slur Asian immigrants and make fun of their accents. This quite appropriate differentiation in the perpetrators of personal racism goes unremarked upon in all of the reviews of the film I have read. And on only one viewing, it may very well be dwarfed by the "racism is color-blind" way of looking at the film.

VII. "EVERYONE IS RACIST": WE'RE ALL RESPONSIBLE, OR WE'RE ALL OFF THE HOOK

Another, though related, problem with *Crash* as a totality is suggested by its surprise win of the Academy Award for Best Picture of 2005, in a field of quality films (especially *Brokeback Mountain*, the clear favorite). Over the years, the Hollywood establishment has given different types of pictures the Best Picture award, but very seldom has it done so to a film that causes Hollywood viewers to reflect on their own shortcomings. This suggests, I would venture, that in the months leading up to the awards, the film was no longer (if it had ever been) seen by a large number of Academy voters as a searing portrayal of personal racism, but rather as a serious film that Hollywood could feel good about itself for creating. Some commentators even speculated that the film came to be regarded by Angelenos as a "feel-good" movie about multicultural Los Angeles.[20]

Part of what may have allowed *Crash's* more pointed and challenging dimensions to get sidelined in the public view of it relates to the way the film says that everyone is prejudiced, everyone is racist, everyone stereotypes, and so on. Such a perspective on personal racism can be taken in several quite distinct directions. One of them can certainly be quite salutary. If everyone is subject to the sorts of racial wrongs depicted in the film, then we can all recognize our shared responsibility for doing something about it. If no one is immune from such personal racism, then no one is exempt from the responsibility of trying to root it out. There is generally a greater stigma to being seen as "being racist" or doing something disapproved of in the area of race than in other domains of social existence—economic inequality, health care, global warming—that might equally require constructive public action. Self-righteousness and moral posturing often infect interchange in the racial area, inhibiting a collective exploration of solutions to problems. If all parties agree that "we are all racist," however, much of this moralism can be short-circuited, and we can get on with the business of honest conversation and constructive action.[21]

Unfortunately, however, the idea that we are all personally racist can also lead in a quite different direction. Especially if one focuses one's concern about personal racism on the agent's intentions and behavior, rather than on the harm of racism to its victims, the idea that everyone is racist can encourage the thought that each individual need not be overconcerned about his own racism. If everyone is guilty, then any given individual is no worse than anyone else. This unfortunate effect is also, in part, a byproduct of the way that a concern with being *seen* as "racist" so often becomes the individual's primary concern, at the expense of actual concern with the wrong of racism itself. In my experience, whites are especially prone to "letting themselves off the hook" when racial prejudice on the part of persons of color is brought to their attention. The moral outrage that should be prompted by the various racial wrongs and harms portrayed in the film is dampened by the thought that racism is, after all, only to be expected, since everyone is subject to it.

Thus, the idea that "we're all in the same boat" when it comes to racism can lead in quite divergent moral directions with respect to prompting an appropriate response to racism. On this point, a statement of the writer-director Paul Haggis about the film is quite instructive: "I hope that *Crash* succeeds not so much in pointing out our differences but in recognizing our shared humanity."[22] This is a fine sentiment; common humanity is something of which we need to be continually reminded, and a constant harping on racial and ethnic difference can blind us to common humanity. All this, however, has very little to do with this film, and with its genuine accomplishment. *Crash* takes as its context what, for Americans, are salient differences of race, ethnicity, and immigration status. It recognizes that those differences are a source of prejudice and other forms of misrelationship, and it shows the damage of those misrelationships. Haggis's counterposing of "pointing out differences" and "emphasizing common humanity" simply does not correspond to what the film is actually doing. The film does emphasize something importantly common to human beings, namely our capacity and proclivity for racial prejudice. Common racism, however, is not the same as common humanity, which in moral contexts generally refers to shared human characteristics that would naturally lead those who recognize them to feel more connected to other human beings, to care about them merely as human beings, and to have regard and respect for them. There is very little, if anything, in *Crash* that expresses common humanity in that sense.

VIII. INVISIBILITY OF SYSTEMIC RACISM

Finally, a serious limitation of the film is its confinement to personal racism, racism concerned with how individual persons treat racial others. That the film deals so much more extensively and complexly with personal racism than one virtually ever finds in mainstream films might blind us to the fact that the film is almost entirely silent on the institutional, structural, and systemic dimensions of racial inequality— and the history that lies behind such inequality. For example, there is no recognition that urban black crime, most closely exemplified by Peter and Anthony, might have something to do with poverty, poor schools, racial stigma, and a paucity of options. Indeed, criminals Peter and Anthony themselves are not clearly located in any distinctive economic position at all. Peter is at one point contrasted with his brother, Graham (Don Cheadle), emphasizing that Graham has made a success of his life, so, it is implied, Peter bears full and exclusive responsibility for the bad choices he has made. Whether or not this is a useful perspective on Peter, it is a very misleading general message about blacks' involvement in crime.

The treatment of the one character clearly depicted as a "lower-class black"— Peter and Graham Waters's mother (Beverly Todd)—is revealing of the film makers' skewed perspective on systemic racism. This character is one of the most unsympathetic and vilified in the film. For no apparent reason, she is resentful of Graham's success and implies that it is a sort of betrayal of her and Peter; she greatly favors her criminal son, Peter. The almost monolithic contempt shown in the film for Mrs. Waters, in contrast to the complexity of so many of the other characters, plays into a dominant and familiar image in the United States of the situation of lower-class blacks—that their misery is of their own making, that they are immersed in a cycle of dependency and that they do nothing to help themselves. (It is also sexist; see Note 31.) One review suggests that that the mother's resentment of Graham's success is an attitude that the film implies is part of what keeps blacks from improving their situation.[23] There is barely a hint in the film of the historical and social forces that have contributed to blacks' disproportionate immiseration, and that might well have some bearing on Mrs. Waters's life situation.

This largely absent wider world is, however, at least partially evoked verbally by Anthony's personal philosophy (discussed earlier), but the way this is done further contributes to sidelining matters of systemic racial injustice as serious concerns. Anthony articulates some vague sense of a white power structure, but Peter continually challenges Anthony's views as being too black-centric and paranoid. My sense is that the film as a whole tilts toward Peter's views more than Anthony's; while Anthony's political stance may help to humanize him, this does not mean it is to be taken too seriously in itself.[24]

It is important to put this criticism in an appropriate perspective. I am not saying that in failing to deal with systemic racial inequality the film fails to deal with racism—on the grounds that racism is something white people do to people of color.[25] The oft-heard view that, since racism can be engaged in only by the dominant group—that is, whites—people of color cannot be racist, they can only be prejudiced, seriously understates the harm and damage of racial prejudice and stereotyping and the actions to which they lead, as the film so powerfully demonstrates. Moreover, this view implies that Asians, blacks, and Latinos who harbor and express racial prejudices do not need to be too concerned about taking responsibility for this, since anything other than the proffered account of "racism" is implicitly consigned to the morally inconsequential.[26] *Crash* shows how morally limited such a view is.

The view that racism is solely about what white people do, and have done, to people of color is often linked to the historically accurate observation that Europeans essentially invented the idea of race to rationalize imperialist expansion, colonialism, and slavery.[27] Once racial categories have been created, however, even for this purpose, people's identities are bound up with them in complex ways (pride, solidarity, social self-understanding) that are no longer pure external impositions by dominant whites. Psychic and social space is thus created for members of every group to hold racist attitudes toward every other group. It is a kind of genetic fallacy to think that because whites created "race", every bad thing connected to race is the fault of whites.

The view that the elements of personal racism with which the films deals are not of great moral significance has been helped along by the account, given in some reviews and indeed by Haggis himself, that "tolerance" captures the subject matter of the film.[28] This is not to belittle intolerance as a social ill, but the aspiration and accomplishment of the film transcend whether people of different groups are able to get along with one another. A person who stereotypes another is not necessarily intolerant of that person. Officer Ryan's victimization of Christine, and the attendant humiliation of Cameron, are not matters of intolerance, and they are much more morally weighty than intolerance. *Crash* shows how personal racism harms people, making them unable to relate to one another in a human way. This goes far beyond tolerance as "getting along".

That having been said, a film that takes up the issue of race as a moral problem, but without dealing with the structures of racial inequality and the social processes that perpetuate it, is deficient in a way that a film that does not take up the issue of race at all is not.[29] Haggis has said, and repeats on the DVD commentary, that he was prompted to write the film by his having been mugged ten years before by two young black men who have become the characters of Anthony and Peter. Certainly many white Americans experiencing such an incident would have become hardened in their racism, and it is to Haggis's credit that he drew a somewhat sympathetic portrait of his muggers from this experience.[30] But the incident does not seem to have prompted Haggis to look very far beyond a Hollywood version of the world or of Los Angeles. Neither he nor his co-writer Bobby Moresco (or, for that matter, Don Cheadle, the producer), in their DVD commentary, express any recognition of systemic racial injustice or the need to understand it in order to grasp what is going on in the film.[31]

IX. CONCLUSION

Crash is a many-faceted exploration of personal racism—racism on the part of individuals in interaction with other individuals. Its many plot strands illustrate various forms of racial stereotyping and prejudice, and they show the damage caused by these forms of personal racism. It explores in a particularly powerful way the damaging stereotype of young black men as dangerous. Seldom has such a frank exploration of so many facets of personal racism been portrayed on the American screen.

The film, however, suffers from throwing together vastly different forms of racism, morally speaking, without marking moral distinctions among them. In addition, although a recognition of white power and black subordination permeates some of the central relationships in the film, the personal racism is not framed in a broader context of systemic and institutional racial injustice. In that respect, *Crash* is positively misleading if seen as a treatment of racial wrongs generally. While it should prompt some serious reflection on the many forms of personal racism, it goes almost nowhere toward pressing whites to recognize the structures of unearned advantage from which they continue to benefit.

NOTES

I am indebted to the many friends, family, students, and colleagues with whom I discussed, and often viewed, *Crash*. I want to single out for special thanks Lisa Gonsalves, Mickaella Perina, Emily Schatzow, Karen Miller, Susan Tomlinson, Judith Smith, Zary Amirhosseini, Lhakyi Lokyitsang, Harry Chotiner, and Laura Blum-Smith. I also wish to thank Ward Jones, Samantha Vice, and Harry Chotiner for excellent feedback on various drafts.

1. The Los Angeles police chief was reported to have seen the film three times and encouraged his deputy to distribute it in the department. The L.A. mayor, an Hispanic whose electoral victory depended on a multiracial coalition, was reported to love it. Cara Mia DiMassa, " '*Crash*' resonates in LA on race relations."

2. *Crash* won the Screen Actors Guild's "Best Ensemble Acting" award and the Best Picture award of the African-American Film Critics Association and the Black Film Association (for films with black-oriented themes). It was also nominated for several major Golden Globe awards.

3. Some Spike Lee films (*Do the Right Thing, Bamboozled, Clockers, Jungle Fever*) are a notable exception.

4. These brief claims about stereotypes are drawn from a much more extensive discussion in my "Stereotypes and Stereotyping: A Moral Analysis." My overall discussion of stereotypes in this article relies heavily on that one.

5. It is also possible, however, to see the final view of the Asian couple as exemplifying the cultural stereotype of Asians as devious and untrustworthy.

6. See Blumstein, "Race and Criminal Justice," and Loury, *An Anatomy of Racial Inequality*.

7. Later in the film, Anthony unwittingly violates this principle.

8. I owe to Lisa Gonsalves the idea that Anthony tries to guide his behavior by certain moral principles.

9. Although the film is particularly insightful and powerful in exploding the violent young black male stereotype, and others as well, its treatment of Farhad, an Iranian

shopkeeper, is itself stereotypical, both in the sense of displaying a cultural stereotype of "Middle Easterners" as irrational and violent (an association linked to terrorism) and in not supplying Farhad with a range of other human characteristics contrary to that stereotype. When Daniel, the Hispanic locksmith described earlier, comes to Farhad's shop to fix his lock, Daniel tells Farhad that his main security problem is not the lock, but the door. Farhad does not understand what Daniel is telling him; it is not clear whether his English is not good enough (somewhat undermining the film's apparent stance of sympathy with him in the earlier scene when he asserts his citizenship and his capability in English to the gun shop owner) or whether he is just so distressed and irrational that he cannot listen to Daniel properly. It is also possible that part of what is going on here is Farhad's prejudice against Hispanics; this would be in keeping with the film's larger themes, but there is no direct evidence that it is operating in this situation. (I owe this point to Zary Amirhosseini.) Farhad's shop is vandalized in a hate crime soon after, and, brooding on his losses (the insurance company will not compensate him since he left the broken door unrepaired), Farhad comes to blame Daniel. He finds Daniel's address and goes to his house, waits for him for several hours, then shoots him (and, accidentally, Daniel's little girl, who has run out to protect him) when Daniel comes home from work. Although Farhad is the target of racist treatment and of a horrible hate crime, and his purchase of a gun suggests that he has suffered threats and racism before, his actions are so destructive and self-destructive—so completely out of line with anything that might rationally benefit him—that his behavior does not seem accountable for by how he has been treated by others. Thus, it seems to exemplify a "violent Middle Eastern person" stereotype.

10. On the phenomenon of thinking about individuals in a group differently from how one thinks of the group as a whole, see Stephan, *Reducing Prejudice and Stereotyping in Schools*, 44. On group antipathy that only kicks in when other characteristics are present, see my discussion of "selective racism" in *"I'm Not a Racist, But . . . "* 30–31.

11. A scene of a white man sexually violating a black woman resonates with the sexualization of black women that has excused white men's abuse and violation of them throughout American history. See, for example, Roberts, *Killing the Black Body: Race, Reproduction, and the Meaning of Liberty*, 10–12; Hine, "Rape and the Inner Lives of Black Women in the Middle West."

12. Although Ryan's affirmative action story is ludicrous, it also reflects the kind of "urban legend" that white Americans have been known to tell themselves to rationalize their opposition to affirmative action. I assumed that the screenwriters, Paul Haggis and Bobby Moresco, were aware of this political role of such stories, and that they placed this one in the film for that reason. In the DVD commentary, however, Haggis talks as if the story were a true one told him by an angry letter writer (responding to a television show Haggis had written) about his own father.

13. Ryan has to reach across Christine to try to remove her seat belt and tells her he has to do so. In doing so, he also pulls her skirt a bit down her legs. Perhaps this aspect of the scene is meant to remind the audience, and Ryan himself, of his earlier sexual violation of her, and it may also be a way of Ryan trying to undo his earlier violation. Considering the deep-rooted sexualization of black women referred to earlier (see Note 11), however, it is not clear that this avoids yet a further sexual stereotyping of, and in a sense another sexual violation of, Christine.

14. *"Unleashed* and *Crash* (review)."

15. *Driving Miss Daisy,* awarded Best Picture of 1989, is only the most prominent manifestation of Hollywood's tendency to reward themes of racial reconciliation. Other recent exemplars are *The Green Mile* (1999), *Monster's Ball* (2001), and, further back, *In the Heat of the Night* (1967) and *Guess Who's Coming to Dinner* (1967).

16. I owe to Judith Smith the idea that Peter is violating tacit rules, in which Hanson is unconsciously invested, of appropriate black-white interaction.

17. It is not quite as simple as this, since the viewer also knows that Peter has a gun, or at least did in an earlier scene. I think, however, the audience is meant to realize, when the smoke clears, that Peter could not have acted the way he did if he were reaching for a gun; that would have made nonsense of the scene.

18. This feature of the term "racism" is explored in my *"I'm Not a Racist, But . . ."* and "What do accounts of 'racism' do?"

19. A fuller argument for moral asymmetries in personal racism is given in my *"I'm Not a Racist, But . . . ."* in Chapter 2, "Can Blacks Be Racist?"

20. Quite telling is that some commentators regarded *Crash* as the "conservative" choice compared with *Brokeback Mountain,* with its moving portrayal and condemnation of homophobia, set in a context in which the Western hero, a staple of "old Hollywood" screen icons, turns out to be gay. One commentator opined that *"'Brokeback'* took on a fairly sacred Hollywood icon, and I don't think the older members of the academy wanted to see the image of the American cowboy diminished." (David Cohen, quoted in David Carr, "Los Angeles Retains Custody of Oscar.")

21. I am grateful to Harry Chotiner for the idea that if everyone acknowledges that everyone is racist, then accusations of "racism" should not stand in the way of productive conversation about racial wrongs.

22. Quoted as part of an account given by Haggis as to how he came to write the screenplay (<http:www.network54.com/Forum/message?forumid=408205& messageid=1115659830>, last accessed 21 June 2010).

23. Joanne Laurier, "The essential things go unexplained."

24. Yet in the DVD commentary, Haggis says he agrees with some of Anthony's analysis. He specifically mentions Anthony's view that the white power structure deliberately wiped out radical and progressive black leaders of the 1960s and 1970s. This hardly constitutes the larger systems and institutions of racial inequity, however, and so does not count against the point made here. The other invocation of the larger context of systemic racial inequality is in the mouth of Flanagan, Cabot's assistant; here it serves the sole purpose of his cynical manipulation of Graham Waters into doing his bidding. Flanagan is so cynical and vile that any social analysis from his lips is entirely discredited, making it worse than if it had not been mentioned at all.

25. This view is taken in an article I have run across several times on the internet. Robert Jensen and Robert Wosnitzer, "'Crash' and the Self-indulgence of White America."

26. This view of "racism" and "prejudice" is criticized in my *"I'm Not a Racist, But . . . ,"* especially Chapters 1 and 2.

27. Jensen and Wosnitzer make this point, but it has been made many times before.

28. Haggis is quoted on the tolerance message of the film at <http:www. network54.com/Forum/message?forumid=408205&messageid=1115659830>, last accessed 21/06/10.

29. My claim that *Crash* fails to deal with the structures of racial inequality may seem inconsistent with my claim earlier that, especially in the portrayal of the Thayers' plight, the film does show an awareness of the way that even successful black people's lives are intimately bound up with structures of white dominance. The point there, however, was that the film was aware of the psychic character and costs of these structures. My point here concerns the material structures of dominance that most fully affect the lives of nonprivileged blacks and Latinos; it is these that are absent in *Crash*.

30. I am grateful to Harry Chotiner for this perspective on Haggis. Haggis says of the mugging, "That event, a collision of two worlds that normally don't intersect, forced me out of my complacency. I began considering the lives of my attackers. I became acutely aware of my urban isolation." (<http:www.network54.com/Forum/ mesage?forumid=408205&messageid=1115659830>, last accessed 21/06/10)

31. Although *Crash* concerns race and racism, it is impossible to overlook the film's sexism (a point to which I am indebted to Judith Smith). The male characters are on the whole much more complex, many-faceted, morally ambiguous, and interesting than are the female characters. The former often develop in the course of the film; the latter almost never do. On the whole, the film is more about the male characters than the female.

ETHICS AND PERSONAL RELATIONSHIPS

LOVE AND FRIENDSHIP IN THE BALANCE

THE CASE OF *JULES ET JIM*

KAREN HANSON

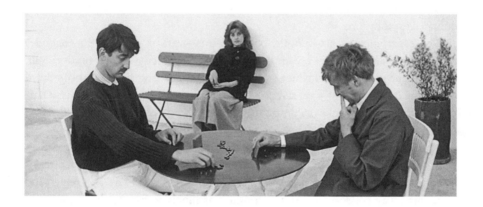

I. INTRODUCTION

THE FUNDAMENTAL QUESTION OF ETHICS—"How should life be lived?"—does not arise for all of us everyday, even if every day presents most of us with some large or small moral problems. What occasions the special reflection that is philosophical, and on what does reflection focus? Common sense? Common experience? Extraordinary experience and outstanding examples? The natural history of humankind or the uncommon humans who stand out from their kind? Perhaps the spurs to and the vehicles of reflection differ for different people, but we do have paradigm cases of ethical thought—Aristotle's *Nicomachean Ethics*, for example—and a history of texts of widely varying styles—compare, for example, Kant's *Groundwork of the Metaphysics of Morals*, Mill's *Utilitarianism*, and Nietzsche's *Beyond Good and Evil*—that exemplify and can shape our own explorations.

The experience of art—novels, poems, films—can of course also engender thought, but art is seldom meant to be didactic or directly argumentative. Still, there may be other ways in which some art can be placed in the context of ethical reflection. In this essay, I want to consider that prospect—the way in which a particular film might provoke or contribute to philosophical reflection on the conduct of life.

The film on which I will focus, Francois Truffaut's *Jules et Jim*, has an explicit narrative focus on questions about happiness and success in life, on puzzles about human relationships and obligations. That this film may be understood as in some way concerned with the conduct of life may thus seem obvious. But if it is obvious that the film is about the conduct of its characters' lives, it is not obvious how the film bears on our thought about the conduct of ours. I shall not argue that the film makes an argument about ethics or that it aims at rational persuasion for a particular point of view on the lives and life choices it portrays.[1] I do want to suggest, however, that the film can offer material for reflection and a depiction of ethical complexity that is as rich and compelling as a philosophical text.

We can best appreciate this point, I believe, if we bring a reading of some central philosophic texts to bear on a reading of the film—and bring the film to bear on our reading of those texts. The film takes friendship as one of its crucial themes, so it makes sense to begin this investigation with one of the fundamental philosophical texts on friendship, that found in the *Nicomachean Ethics*.

II. JULES AND JIM AS ARISTOTELIAN FRIENDS

Aristotle says that friendship is a virtue and a necessity of life. No one would choose to live without friends, he says, even if he had all other goods.[2] In poverty and other misfortunes, friends are of course a refuge. Even for the rich and powerful, however, friends are crucial. Prosperity is hollow, Aristotle claims, except as it provides opportunities for beneficence; and whom can we take satisfaction in benefiting if not our friends? The young can be kept from error and the old and the weak can be cared for by good friends. For those in the prime of life, friendship stimulates noble actions—"'two going together'—for with friends men are more able both to think and to act."[3]

Truffaut's *Jules et Jim* presents a friendship in, and across, the prime of life. The title characters meet as young men, around 1912, and the film follows their lives until just before WWII, observing not just the course of their friendship but also their prospects for love and happiness, for accomplishments and "noble actions". Jules is newly arrived in Paris when he and Jim meet, and Jules enlists Jim's help to secure an invitation to an art students' ball. Both men are contentedly living a bohemian sort of life; they are interested in poetry and literature and uninterested in money; they find that they can chat easily; and each discovers in the other "the best listener of his life."[4] Thus we are given a quick exemplification—and, in its attractiveness and plausibility, a substantiation—of the central tenets of Aristotle's theory of friendship: (1) there is no friendship for soulless things; (2) friendship is not merely good will nor even reciprocated good will; (3) friendships that are maintained only as the friend is useful to one or a source of pleasure are incomplete; and (4) perfect friendship is the friendship of good men, alike in excellence or virtue, who wish each other well, each wishing well for the other's sake. These perfect friendships are pleasant and useful, even if they are not predicated on pleasure and utility; and they are enduring, lasting as long as the principals are good—and virtue, according to Aristotle, is an enduring thing.[5]

III. A NEW AFFINITY—VOLATILE LOVE

How does friendship fit into a complete life? How does the perfect friendship of men fit into a life of love and family? Women come and go in these young men's lives, until Catherine arrives. Both men are moved by her, but Jules begins immediately to see her alone, and when he brings Jim back into the picture, Jules makes a prefatory stipulation: "Not this one, Jim, OK?" They become a threesome, with no diminution of the men's friendship, though Jules is in love with Catherine and wants to marry her, and Jim seems to feel the pull of her magnetism. These good men are able to sustain their Aristotelian harmony with one another; but what does Catherine bring to the ethical mix?

Certainly not harmony. Much later in the film, when Jules discloses the instability of his and Catherine's marriage, he tells Jim that, when things go too well,

Catherine begins to feel discontented, her manner changes, and she lashes out. She becomes a tyrant when she feels she is not being appreciated, and appreciation evidently involves more than sympathetic understanding and settled enjoyment of her company. The film's narrator says that Catherine believed that love, complete love, never lasted for more than a moment, though that moment could come again and again. She evidently expected love to be combustible—to break into flames at once purifying and destructive.

Jim has early evidence of this: When, at the start of their time as a threesome, Catherine decrees that they should go to the seaside together and asks Jim to come to her apartment to take her luggage to the station, she burns a pot of letters in his presence, catching her nightdress on fire. He quickly extinguishes the flames and discreetly cleans up the ashes. As they are about to leave, her last item to pack is a bottle of vitriol "for lying eyes." Jim is practical enough to warn her that the bottle will break and ruin her clothes and to inform her she can buy vitriol anywhere; but he is impractical enough not to question the import of her melodramatic rituals and the assertion that she "swore she would only use this bottle."

Linda Williams says that *Jules et Jim* "explore[s] the pitfalls of a triangular affair with the eternal feminine as its apex."[6] While it is true that Catherine is always the object of Jules' love, and for a time Jim is "her slave", so in love with her that "no other woman existed for him," there is also a time when Jim refrains from focusing on her, and there is a time when she leaves him cold, when his heart no longer leaps up at the sight of her. Yet Jules' and Jim's friendship endures. Is this dynamic best understood as a triangle? And in what sense is Catherine "the eternal feminine?" This description may be connected with a view of Catherine expressed by Jules when he has to acknowledge one of her periodic disappearances from home. He says she is a "force of nature," "guided by the conviction of her own innocence." When Jim says, with some wonder, "You talk of her as if she were a queen!" Jules declares, "But she is a queen!" If they are to speak frankly, Jules says, "Catherine is neither especially beautiful, nor intelligent, nor sincere, but she is a real woman—the woman we love and whom all men desire." While this is Jules' view, I'm not sure it should be ours.

IV. AN ARISTOTELIAN ALTERNATIVE TO VOLATILE LOVE

Does Aristotle's view of women and friendship help here? Because Aristotle believes there is a permanent inequality between men and women, he would not expect a perfect friendship possible between them, but he does think that men and women can have an abiding friendship, a friendship both pleasant and useful:

> Between man and wife friendship seems to exist by nature; for man is naturally inclined to form couples—even more than to form cities, inasmuch as the household is earlier and more necessary than the city. . . . [H]uman beings live together not only for the sake of reproduction but also for the

various purposes of life; for from the start the functions are divided, and those of man and woman are different; so they help each other by throwing their peculiar gifts into the common stock.[7]

There is royal rule in the household, according to Aristotle, but that is the rule of the father over the children. The woman in Aristotle's household is certainly not a queen, but neither is the man a king over her. Their relation is better understood along the lines of constitutional rule, each having a particular role suited to the natural, gender-divided virtues appropriate to each sex.[8] There is a soothing stability in the relationship Aristotle describes, but this comfort comes at the price of the permanent subordination of women. Catherine would seem unlikely to understand her virtue as realized in obedience,[9] and neither Jules nor Jim ever asks this of her. If none of the relations between the men and Catherine can be understood as Aristotelian friendship, how should their relations be understood?

V. UNDERSTANDING COMMUNITY

Stanley Cavell uses the language of anthropology in studying the relations among Catherine, Jules, and Jim, suggesting that the men may view her as a totem.[10] She does come to have the central role in defining their community, to be a force that delineates their kinship. The film lays the basis for the position she comes to have in the lives of Jules and Jim through the study of an image, a totemic statue. Near the beginning of the film, Albert, a character who is said to know all the artists who will be famous in ten years, shows them a slide of the statue with its beautiful, slightly scornful smile. Jules and Jim are so taken by this image that they travel at once to see it, in an open-air museum on an island in the Adriatic. They stare at it for hours, and the narrator says that if they ever met that smile, they would follow it. Catherine has the statue's smile, so their attention to her can seem another assertion of the bond between the two of them, but her capacity to absorb their attention goes well beyond her physiognomy.

Cavell, analyzing the force of the freeze frame technique in this film, says that it shows the images "private to the two men," confirming not only Catherine's identity with "the figure they first saw in her—the statue . . . come to life—. . . but also the fact that she is their creation, their greatest work as artists, the one on which they could stake their lives."[11] Within the film, however, it is Catherine who sets up those images, dramatizing herself and insisting the focus be on her, even if she has to command their attention through a hard slap on Jules's face. (Her self-avowed linkage with Napoleon—underscored by her embrace of a small statue, a bust of Napoleon—proved too subtle an intervention to get the men's attention at this point. They are playing dominoes in silence, and she is on the sidelines, talking; so she marches ahead with combative action, and the Napoleonic link is reduced to the role of foreshadowing.)

Cavell does note that:

The woman will not be the statue, the totem of their community, but she will be watched, and not merely when they want to see. And she is right—not alone as a woman but as a totem. Even if she is their creation, their success is that she is alive and separate, that there is community among them (community: not just marriage, not just desire, nor just comradeship, because there are three).[12]

It is true that there is community among them, but the character and the ties of that community must be pondered. The men's friendship comes before this community; and marriage, desire, and comradeship are multiply inflected in the course of the construction and erosion of this community of three.

I take it, contrary to Cavell, that Catherine's independence is not the men's success, that is, that it is not a success to be attributed to them, that she is not their creation. It is not merely that she dramatizes herself—though she does do that, and it seems Jules and Jim are not her only audience. (Albert himself also moves from appreciation of the statue to sustained engagement with the woman.) She reinvents herself and puts her inventions to the test. (That last, putting a self-presentation to the test, is her own description of her foray into the streets, disguised as a young man. Jules and Jim are then said to be moved by the success of her disguise, "as if by a symbol they did not understand."[13]) It is not merely that Jules takes her to be a "force of nature," forever doing something irreparable, wreaking havoc. It is her egoism—testified to, in different ways, by Jules, Jim, and Catherine herself—the way in which she is placed, by herself, at the center of the universe, that precludes her being a product of these two men. She is not just their totem, the image that defines and cements their kinship.

Catherine repeatedly asserts that she counts. She counts in the sense that *she* must be reckoned—consider the scene in which Jim says, "We love each other, and our love is all that matters," and Catherine responds, "No, because *I* count too, and I, I love less"—and she counts also in the sense that she engages in counting and wants to balance out the score. For instance, in considering Jules' marriage proposal, she says that while he has known few women, she has known many men, and thus, "It might even out—perhaps we'd make a good couple." She is forever acting to "even things out." When Jules' mother offends her before the wedding, and he does nothing, she takes up with an old lover in order to punish him and so wipe the slate clean for their new beginning. When Jim is slow to return to her in Germany, straightening out his work in France, but also saying good-bye to his long-time lover, Gilberte, Catherine takes up again with Albert, saying, "Albert equals Gilberte" and "We must start from scratch."

There is something contractual about her attention to an evenly balanced starting point. Her relationships seem to be understood less in terms of the organic teleologies of Aristotle and more in terms of the autonomous individual of modern moral philosophy.[14] She assumes that the parties to a contract—say a marriage contract—must be free in order for consent to be meaningful, but the conditions of freedom are strangely abstract. This could also be said of the initial conditions of freedom in the social contract theories of Rousseau, Hobbes, and Locke, for example, but Catherine's operationalizing of these conditions highlights an oddity.[15] Catherine's ground rules for the commitments of erotic love involve shedding or overcoming or erasing past emotional ties, obliterating them through this process of getting even. For most people, the escapades that are undertaken to get even would count as further entanglements; they would bring additional erotic and moral baggage to a couple's prospects for love. She sees the commitment to love as an utterly fresh start.

The combination of stringency and laxity in the moral personality implied by Catherine's theory may seem untenable, but is it any more peculiar than the moral metaphysics of a variety of social contract theories? These philosophical accounts of the ties that bind typically begin with stipulations that the parties to the contract must be in some crucial way free and self-interested, though the defining characteristics of the self and its interests—surely at least in part a product of an individual's past, his or her history of interactions with others—are to be ignored or overcome. There is generally some requirement of formal equality, so that everyone counts, and counts the same. If it is not to the point to ask of the social contract theories, "Could this ever happen? Could these initial conditions ever be realized?," why does it—if it does—seem appropriate to wonder if Catherine's conditions can be productively realized?

We shouldn't be put off this question by the fact that often Catherine seems not to play fairly. In the famous early scene of the foot race, when she is dressed as a man, it is Jules who is doing the counting—"one, two, three," to signal the start—but Catherine sprints away on the count of "two", leaving the men behind. When they catch up at the finish line, Jim protests, "Thomas, you cheated!" and Catherine calmly responds, "But I won." In a later moment in the film, revealing the problems in their marriage, Jules says to Jim that Catherine believes that the world is rich and that one can cheat a little. "She asks the Lord's forgiveness in advance, certain that it will be granted." Still later, Jules ruefully summarizes Catherine's motto: "In a couple at least one party must be faithful—the other."

If we can assume that Catherine is, or might be, faithful to her view of the requirements of love, however, what does the film tell us about the viability of these arrangements? Near the end of the film, Jim summarizes the hopes and the failures of Catherine's aspirations. He says that, like Catherine, he believes that, in love, the couple is not ideal: "You wanted to invent something better, refusing hypocrisy and resignation. You wanted to invent love from the beginning . . . but pioneers should be humble, without egoism." Is it her egoism that has "made a mess of everything"? How would humbleness have helped? How could she have refused resignation and hypocrisy if she were not willing to act on her passions as they stirred and to abandon the pretenses of love once ardor had cooled?

Of course, if great emotion can be expected to wax and wane, and if we cannot expect perfect synchrony in the turnings of two hearts—as the crossed correspondence sequence in the film so aptly illustrates—it is difficult to see how this re-invented love can function to hold a community together. Indeed, it doesn't in the film. Jim has apparently come closest to matching Catherine's swings of passion—Jules says, "Your love fell to zero, then rose to a hundred again with that of Catherine. I have never known your zeros . . . . or your hundreds"—but Jim and Catherine still hurt each other and those around them. Neither can hold the other, and, within the whirlwind of their love, even the friendship of Jules and Jim suffers.

Should love have been expected to hold a community together? Both Plato and Aristotle suppose affection serves as the basic glue of society, though in Plato's *Republic* erotic ties are deliberately dampened, and family ties are spread widely but thinly, in order to guard against the disruptive force of passions, against the strife of jealousy, the likelihood of favoritism and partial loyalties. But Aristotle compares Plato's arrangement to a little bit of sweetening in a large glass of water, and he insists that the strong ties of a couple, with children and a household, should serve as roots for the organic growth of the polis.

Aristotle's account of the couple's bonds is alarming to the modern ear, however: The woman by her nature has inoperative or deficient rationality, and therefore she cannot be a perfect friend to the man. While there is a biological basis for the linkage of this couple, their friendship is inherently imperfect, because of the woman's defective rationality. This view of Aristotle's cannot be easily excised, and his account thereby "updated", because without this identification of the essential deficiency of the household's relations, there is nothing to motivate the man's drive toward "full development" in politics. He is driven by the inadequacy of his connection to his wife to connect with other men in conversations about justice, goodness, etc. Jules and Jim were, of course, able to have those conversations apart from their involvements with women, and their involvement with Catherine at times impairs the most satisfying elements of their friendship.

Moreover, neither Aristotle nor Plato considers—neither expects in the context of ties of friendship and love—the volatility of utterly free choice and the willfulness of the strongly self-interested agent, the agent essentially defined by self-interest. That is a picture best aligned with social contract theories, but it is worth noting that contract theories do not then rely on love as the bond that secures a community. One is instead bound through the contract, obligation arising as a result of free and *rationally* self-interested choice.

Does Catherine's attempt to live by new laws contain a coherent notion of obligation? There is, again, one clear contract that is repeatedly at issue for her—marriage. She marries only Jules, but she considers marriage to Albert, and she plans to marry Jim. What is her *understanding* of marriage; what are her hopes and expectations?

VI. MARRIAGE AND CHILDREN

It must be noticed that, for all the film's—or the film's dialogue's—identification of Catherine with the forces of nature and emotion, her aspirations are often explicitly characterized—constituted—as epistemological, if not exactly as rational. Does she understand the ideal marriage as a meeting of minds, a mutuality that involves perfect knowledge, each of the other?[16] It's true that when Jim and Catherine are beginning to act out their attraction, in the long walk and talk at night in the woods, it is important to her that he *remembers* everything of their shared history; but when he says he understands her, she says she doesn't want to be understood. She wants to *know*, but her attitude toward *being known* is more complex. When, near the end of the film, Jim summarizes her story and the story of their relationship, he says:

> in a novel you lent me I found a passage you had marked. It was about a woman on a ship who gives herself in imagination to a passenger she does not know. That struck me as a confession on your part. It's your method of exploring the universe. I have this lightning curiosity too; perhaps everyone has. But I control mine for your sake, and I'm not convinced that you control yours for mine.

Additionally, when Jim is trying to explain Catherine to the caring, ever faithful Gilberte, he says:

> Listen, Gilberte, you see . . . . once Catherine wants to do something, so long as she thinks it won't hurt anyone else—she may be mistaken, of course— she does it for her own enjoyment and to learn something from it. That way she hopes to become wise.

And what looks as if it might simply be the natural consequence of love and marriage—having a child—seems to have, for Catherine, the status of a *proof*, something with definitive epistemological force. Her relationship with Jules is at its best when she is pregnant with his child, and there is evidence that he has known her carnally, evidence not only in the fact of her pregnancy but also in the character of his letters to her, which she finds beautiful. (The letters abandon interest in her soul, abandon "belief" in it, and fix on her body and their child—Jules says their "son"—growing inside her body.) Once Catherine has given birth, however, one might say that the natural consequence of love and marriage has been realized, and she seems to regard this as a conclusion, as if the final step in a proof, now a proof that she has fulfilled her contract. What many would see as a beginning, she sees as a full stop. She once again sees herself as free.

Having children with Jim would be a proof of *their* love. (Albert's willingness to take on the (already existing) child as part of marriage is a proof that his marriage proposal is serious, but it's a shadow of the central dynamics, appropriate to his secondary—tertiary—role.) When Jim and Catherine have difficulty conceiving, Catherine thinks of this as failing a test. The pregnancy that then results from their unhappy night at the railway hotel (as Jim is being "exiled") is debated in both epistemological and metaphysical terms. Jim doubts her pregnancy and says their farewell cannot have succeeded "where love failed." In any case, if she is pregnant, he doubts he is the father; he has, he claims, "every reason for doubt." Catherine tells him that "so many unbelievable things are true. . . . Your love is a part of my life; you are living inside me." When a miscarriage ends the pregnancy, however, Catherine and Jim's love is also aborted. The interest in and failure to produce children punctuates the last conversation Jim and Catherine have as a pair. She cries for the beautiful children they might have had and accuses him of not wanting them. He denies this, but he has already made it clear that he intends to try to have children with Gilberte. Gilberte's having his children is connected (by Jim) with an image of marriage as growing old together.

That is a prospect Catherine sought, too, but more impulsively, with Jules, when she was in desperate need of the comfort of his unconditional love, as a balm after a flare-up with Jim. It is already clear, however, that a smooth and quiet old age, with their child and the uncomplicated pleasures of grandchildren, would not sustain her. Children are important to Catherine—as a proof of love, as the fulfillment of a relationship or vow—but her life is not nourished by the tasks of nurturing a child once that child is separate from her. Although the scenes with "la petite Sabine" are idyllic, and Catherine shows gentle warmth, comfortable intimacy, courteous solicitousness, and some authority with the child, the thrilling highs and depressing lows of motherhood are not on view. For all we see, Catherine could be a favorite visiting aunt.

Indeed, the child might do well to regard Catherine as a visitor, a visiting relation, because she seems to come and go. When she "took back her liberty" after "giving" Jules a child, she actually left them *both*, husband and child. She describes that affair as a great holiday, but not serious, because the man was too young, but, "He was there, free as air . . . and so was I." "Free as air" is not a self-description that would occur to most new mothers of babies or toddlers. On subsequent absences, it's noted that she leaves "without explanation"—to, presumably, anyone. At the time of Jim's first arrival in Germany, Jules feels Catherine is about to leave again, because things are going too smoothly.

One might suppose that, from a child's point of view, an orderly and harmonious household would be a blessing and the departure, without explanation, of one's mother would be profoundly disturbing. Catherine seems to consider these possibilities not at all. In her walk in the woods with Jim, she notes that at some point in her holiday, with the too-young lover, she found "to [her] surprise" that she missed Jules' indulgent ways and that her daughter "drew her like a magnet." Catherine is attracted back—but whether her daughter has been yearning for her, whether her daughter has needed her or been injured by her absence, seems not to be a part of Catherine's reckoning. Now, furthermore, she is hinting—both to Jules and, in their talk, to Jim—that she is poised to leave again, perhaps with Sabine, perhaps not.

An account of the right conduct of life might or might not linger on the prospects and responsibilities of having children. The Aristotelian and Platonic accounts of community quite naturally assume that some attention must be paid to a proper arrangement for the continuation of the community, to provisions for the next generation, and to a normative understanding of relations between parents and children. Social contact theorists, on the other hand, have a harder time attending to the dependent status of the young and to the idea that there are fully human—and very demanding—creatures who yet lack full rationality and the power of autonomous choice.

The little Sabine is shown sweetly interacting with the various men in her mother's life: her father, Jim, Albert. In the happy idyll at the chalet, as Jules, Jim, and Catherine have freshly, optimistically re-arranged the terms of their community, they and Sabine play a game of making funny faces, "the village idiot," around a table that symbolizes the village. It is said that Catherine invented the game after learning that in the village below their chalet, she, Jules, and Jim were called "the three lunatics." The film's narrator says that Sabine was very talented at the game, good at making them laugh. She is a *fourth* in the game, however; the village, conventional society, regards only the trio of adults as the lunatics. She has fun now, as part of this game, but does she really have a viable role, if this game of living outside the old rules persists?

The film doesn't have an answer. From this moment on, Sabine virtually disappears from the film. (There is one additional long-shot sequence showing the four walking across a bridge and around a lake, skipping stones, while the narrator discloses that Jim is imagining the children *he* and Catherine would have: "They would be tall and thin and would suffer from migraines.") There is a reference to Sabine in the explanatory comments made by the narrator at the very end of the film, after Catherine has deliberately killed herself and Jim by driving off a ruined bridge. The narrator says, "They left nothing behind them. Jules had his daughter."

This narration is part of a final sequence (the recovery and disposal of the bodies) remembered by Stanley Cavell, in *The World Viewed*, with these thoughts: "Upon cremation, the bones of love remain, the gender indistinguishable except in size. As Jules and the child walk away hand in hand, the last words tell us Jules is 'relieved'."[17] In fact, however, the film does not show Jules and the child walking away hand in hand. Apart from the relevant functionaries, Jules is alone with the coffins at the crematorium, and with the caskets of ashes, and as he walks from the cemetery. It is he alone who must discreetly attend to the remains of Catherine's burned-out love.

Cavell says in the preface to *The World Viewed* that he was working from memories of movies—not scripts, moviolas, tapes, or DVDs—and he offered a confession that, "A few faulty memories will not themselves shake my conviction in what

I've said, since I'm as interested in how a memory went wrong as in why the memories that are right occur when they do."[18] If it is possible to ratify a confession by experiencing the substance of its creed, then I can lend specific support to this faulty memory. Though I have seen this film scores of times over the course of decades, I sometimes have a memory, a sense, of the final shot that Cavell describes. The film's narration—"They left nothing behind them. Jules had his daughter"—perhaps contributes to the false memory, but it may also be that we long to see an affirmation of a tie, an unbreakable human relationship, instead of the lonely, solitary figure walking from the cemetery.

This ending wouldn't, however, make narrative sense: twenty years have passed since Sabine was that little child. At the time of these deaths she would be a young woman, about the age of Jules, Jim, and Catherine when they met.

But how would she have grown up in the tumult of her mother's life? How would her independence, her own erotic life, impinge and be impinged upon by her parents' design for living? Cavell's memory suggests that Catherine was able to leave the issues of *this* bond, the matter of the responsibilities of continuing parenthood, to Jules, that *that* allowed her practice of departures: "With the child, Jules knows he can keep faith; and the woman knows this, she could always count on it. It is the affinity he would himself have selected. Patience and nurturance, the requirements of motherhood, were always his manly virtues."[19] Sabine is lucky for that, but what if there *had* been offspring of Jim and Catherine? Jim shared with Catherine the capacity for a love shifting "from zero to one hundred and back," that "lightning curiosity" about new erotic encounters, the interest in moving on. Their children would indeed have needed luck.

VII. A PERILOUS PERFECTIONISM

Catherine at one point says, "I'm not very moral," and yet she, as well as Jules and Jim, surely represents allegiance to some version of what Cavell delineates as perfectionism. Jules, Jim, and Catherine are shown as bohemians at the beginning of the film—young people still developing their talents, interested in the arts and literature, in culture. They do not embrace an Aristotelian sort of perfectionism, however; they do not accept a settled view of "the good life" or a particular picture of the social arrangements that will allow for the full development of their human potential. They, especially Catherine, may seem to be stirred by the Nietzschean perfectionist question, "How can your life, the individual life, retain the highest value, the deepest significance?" and the seductive Nietzschean promise, "There exists in the world a single path along which no one can go except you: whither does it lead?"[20]

Catherine surely does not engage in utilitarian hedonic calculations, and she does not hesitate to break a variety of moral rules. Her life is instead guided by the power of attraction, by her best understanding of what is pulling her forward.

She rejects the constraints of duty. Her moments of moral reflection do not take up the question, "What is the right course of action?," but rather, and explicitly, "Have I lost my way?"[21] She has confidence in her inclinations expressed in aesthetic terms, in her rejection—even destruction—of what disgusts her.

At the beginning of the relationship of Jules and Catherine, Jules tells Jim that Catherine "ignores the average and teaches those she is drawn to." ("Teaches what?" Jim asks. "Shakespeare!" This is lighthearted, but it seems to suggest a Nietzschean commitment to following an attraction to individual and cultural excellence.) The point at which Catherine and Jim openly begin their sexual relationship is finessed by a pretext that Catherine insists on reading, or rereading, Goethe's *Elective Affinities*, which Jules has lent to Jim. We can see why both Catherine and Jim are interested in this tale of passion, the decoupling of marriage and love, and the force of natural attraction. At the end of the film, however, in her middle age, there is nothing, no one she is drawn to, no affinity that seems compelling. She seems to have nothing to teach and no way to learn, and she is stuck in joyless repetition.

Cavell sees Catherine as keeping the faith of this once so attractive community even in that final act, the plunge to death. I am less inclined to a hopeful analysis. It seems to me that Catherine cannot find a next self to inhabit, and she has no satisfaction in stasis. The path she has found through her life reached a dead end, and so complete was her commitment to that path that she had no alternative routes to fall back to, no way to go on. Jim seemed more nearly correct when he had summed up his and Catherine's despair: "It is noble to want to rediscover the laws of humanity; but it is much easier to conform to existing rules. We played with life and lost it."

Jules may have had, as he put it, "an unfortunate tendency to specialize"—in his intellectual work and in love—but he was not without an admirable flexibility. When he is disclosing to Jim the weakness of his marriage, and he says that he is gradually renouncing his claim to Catherine and to everything he has hoped for in life, it is a terribly sad moment. *Some* capacity for renunciation and forgoing may be necessary even in better, even in the *best* circumstances, however. Jim says that for Catherine's sake he controlled his urges, the sudden attraction to others that a member of any couple might feel; but he was not convinced that she ever did the same for him, and he links her unwillingness to do so, to be "without egoism", to the failure of their attempt to pioneer new forms of love. The film repeatedly suggests that Jim and Catherine are, in matters of erotic fire, "evenly matched", yet Jim is able to control that "lightening curiosity" for the sake of Catherine, and he is able to worry about and attend to the feelings of his friend, Jules, even when on fire for Catherine. This seems an appropriate form of renunciation, as does the personal control of self required in parenthood. One would hope—expect, demand—that a parent would be able to control himself or herself, to forgo some self-gratification, if care for a young child demands it.

VIII. CONCLUSION

The narrator at the end says that the friendship of Jules and Jim "had no equivalent in love. Together they found amusement and satisfaction in mere trifles; the discovery of their differences did not lessen their affection." Is it *obvious* that such a friendship *could* have no equivalent in love? It is from a perfectionist mood that one can hope that is wrong. Jules, Jim, and Catherine did not find a sustainable balance for their community—the failure to account adequately for the next generation is the clearest lapse—as clear, upon reflection, as the plunge into premature death—but that is not proof that their ambitions for a new form of life were mistaken.

Is there anything that could be "proof"? Would we reject their ambitions because they did not comport with the view of marriage and household arrangements described by Aristotle—the man ruling, the wife finding her virtue in obedience—or the family arrangements proposed by Plato—the communal family, without strong erotic ties between couples or particularized ties of affection to a son or daughter, the whole older generation a collective parent to all the youth? Jules, Jim, and Catherine did not solve the problems of love, friendship, and children but neither did Plato, Aristotle, or the social contract theorists, or, for that matter, Kant, Mill, or Nietzsche. Still, all may help us as *we* give thought to these issues.

Catherine's willfulness and assertions of self are welcome corrections to the story Aristotle tells of relationships between men and women. The ecstasy of the erotic passions that propel the narrative of Catherine, Jules, and Jim is seductive enough to make Plato's restrained and always rational communities seem boringly unattractive and unlivable. Yet Catherine's incarnation of modern autonomy and free choice, while politically and sometimes personally magnetic, is also troubling. Her abandonment of her daughter and the pain Catherine occasions for all the film's principals are striking and should cause us to wonder about the problems we ourselves may have if we try to insist on our autonomy and on a contractual basis for our living arrangements, given the deep—the abiding as well as the accidental, unexpected—contingencies of life. And even if we are thrilled by the intimations of Catherine's perfectionism, we should recognize that the bracing call to self-trust embedded in a bold perfectionism must be modulated by an understanding of the relational nature of the self, the ties of responsibility—to children and others—that may define our lives.

Jules et Jim does not provide a moral guide or a set of ethical object lessons, but it does keep moral problems *alive* for us, and it presents these problems to us in a particularly compelling fashion. We see what may seem an ordinary story—a story some read as "a triangular affair," eternal—with characters and events that are at once common and extraordinary. These are not great historical figures being portrayed, but the characters of this film, animated by those actors, are singularly fascinating, and we are in a position to contemplate them in the silence that makes room for thought. Our conditions of viewing—our experience and memory of the film—allow, at once, both absorption and distance. We are not in the thick of life, of these lives, but in this film masterpiece, there is something like the fullness of life. At the same time, as it is a film we are watching, there is narrative coherency and closure, as there isn't, really, in life. There is a complete object here, available for thought. One is reminded of Ludwig Wittgenstein's adversion to "Indian mathematicians" offering just a picture, with a proof that consists in the instruction: "Look at this."[22] The picture alone can, Wittgenstein says, change one's way of looking at things. So can some films. Can we ask any more from our ethical reflection?

NOTES

1. Nor will I address issues connected with identifying the filmmakers' intentions and their views on the conduct of life. Part of what I hope to suggest is that concentration on the film alone, the experience of seeing the film, can offer material for reflection that is, in its peculiar combination of immersion and distance, both like and yet constructively unlike the thick of our everyday life. The film is, of course, a product of intentional choices, as much of our everyday experience is not; but the transparency of the photographic basis for this film, and the fact that the camera recorded human beings, even if human beings acting a script and under the guidance of a director, gives us what can be seen as a "slice of life." I want to focus on what that slice might provoke us to think about our own lives, not on the (equally compelling) question of who produced this slice and why.

2. Aristotle, *Nicomachean Ethics* (ed. Jonathan Barnes), Book VIII, 1155a ff.

3. Ibid., 1155a 15.

4. According to the film's narrator. (The quote is a translation of the narration. Quotations of dialogue and narration from the film are, throughout this essay, based largely on Nicholas Fry's translation, *Jules and Jim, a Film by Francois Truffaut*, with occasional modifications based on my own viewing and translation.)

5. Aristotle, *Nicomachean Ethics*, Book VIII, 1155b 28–1156b 18.

6. Williams, *Oxford History of World Cinema*, 491.

7. Aristotle, *Nicomachean Ethics*, Book. VIII, Ch 12, 1162b 16–26.

8. Aristotle, *Politics*, Book I, Chapters 12 and 13.

9 Ibid., Chapter 13, 1260a 23–24.

10. Cavell, *The World Viewed* (enlarged edition.), 138–139.

11. Ibid., 138.

12. Ibid., 139.

13. Film narrator.

14. Natural egoism, of course, also underlies natural autonomy in some influential accounts of the social contract. Compare Hobbes' understanding of man's nature, as inherently self-interested, and the declarations of value Hobbes believes the autonomous person makes: "Whatsoever is the object of any man's appetite or desire, that is it which he for his part calleth *good*; and the object of his hate and aversion, *evil*; and of his contempt, *vile* and *inconsiderable*. For these words of good, evil, and contemptible, are ever used with relation to the person that useth them: there being nothing simply

and absolutely so; nor any common rule of good and evil, to be taken from the nature of the objects themselves; but from the person of the man. . . ." *Leviathan*, Part One, Chapter 6, 48.

15. The oddity is highlighted, not created, by the film. The puzzling character of the freedom that is supposed to precede the social contract is given an explicitly paradoxical formulation in the opening sentences of Rousseau's *The Social Contract* ("Man was born free and everywhere he is in chains") and is highlighted by Hobbes's contention that, apart from being bound to a sovereign in a social contract, people freely pursuing their own interest will live with no industry, no culture, no knowledge, no letters, no arts, but with "continual fear, and danger of violent death" (*Leviathan*, Part One, Chapter 13, 100). Locke's sunnier view is equally perplexing: "Men being. . . . . by nature, all free, equal, and independent, no one can be put out of his estate, and subjected to the political power of another, without his own *consent*. The only way whereby any one divests himself of his natural liberty, and *puts on the bonds of civil society* is by agreeing with other men to join and unite into a community. . . ." (*Second Treatise of Government*, Chapter 8, 58). The initial conditions of these social contracts—Catherine's fresh starts, or the classical theorists' real or hypothetical states of nature—are *all* enigmatic.

16. This would also underscore her modernity. She does not see marriage in the organic terms that shape an Aristotelian account of the growth of community. She is instead, in her romantic adventures, a Cartesian knower, seeking proof of other minds.

17. Cavell, *The World Viewed*, 141.

18. Ibid., xxiv.

19. Ibid., 141.

20. Nietszche, *Untimely Meditations: Third Essay: Schopenhauer as Educator*, Sec. 6, 162, and Sec. 1, 129.

21. See Cavell's *Conditions Handsome and Unhandsome*, especially xxix–xxx and 1–30, for a sketch of this understanding of moral perfectionism.

22. Wittgenstein, *Philosophical Investigations*, Sec. 144.

SOPHIE'S CHOICE

TORBJÖRN TÄNNSJÖ

I. INTRODUCTION

THE FILM UNFOLDS AS THE ASPIRING AUTHOR Stingo arrives in New York City from the South and begins his acquaintance with his neighbors, Sophie and Nathan, in a Brooklyn apartment just after World War II.[1] Sophie emerged alive from Auschwitz at the liberation of the camp. An ordinary Polish Catholic citizen, she ended up in the camp for trivial reasons—she stole a ham. After a first, short visit to Sweden, where she made a failed attempt to kill herself, she arrived in the United States and has been taken care of by an American Jew, Nathan, who is obsessed with the Holocaust. Nathan saved Sophie's life, we are first informed, by taking medical care of her when she was suffering from severe anemia. He has made her "bloom like a rose." From the very start of the film, however, we sense that there is something wrong in their relationship. Stingo first listens to Nathan and Sophie making love in the apartment above his own in a manner that makes his lamp swing, only, in the next moment, to hear them quarrel, with Nathan leaving Sophie, saying that he needs her "like death". It soon surfaces that Sophie and Nathan are living in a relationship characterized by obsession, self-destruction, and lies. These lies are eventually exposed, one by one. Sophie's father was not the courageous person he is first presented as being; he was an aggressive Polish anti-Semite. Nathan is not the famous scientist he pretends to be, but a psychotic (schizophrenic) liar, haunted by his paranoid visions. Additionally, Sophie's background is not only tragic. Not only has she accidentally ended up at Auschwitz, not only has she lost her son in the camp—she has also made a very problematic choice. In the crucial penultimate scene of the film, where the *peripati* of the drama takes place, Sophie informs Stingo of the choice she actually made. It is a choice that, once all the lies and deceptions surrounding it are gone, turns out to be inconsistent with continued life on Sophie's part. Lined up in the queue leading to Auschwitz, and provoked by a sadistic guard keen on testing her Catholic faith, Sophie decided to sacrifice one of her children—her daughter, Eva—in the (vain?) hope that this would mean that her other child—her son Jan—as well as herself, could survive.

After telling Stingo about this choice, Sophie spends a night with him. Stingo takes advantage of her to have his first sexual experience, without in any way understanding the gravity of the situation. "My lust was insatiable," he comments afterward.[2] This is so in spite of the fact that Sophie has mocked him and his belief that, if only he learns the truth, he will understand and forgive her. There is no forgiving, Sophie implies.

Consequently, the next morning, Sophie leaves Stingo, who had hoped for a life back in the South together with her, and returns to Nathan, only to seek death in a suicide with him in which their deaths are brought about by cyanide (an ingredient in Zyklon B, the chemical used in the gas chambers). The use of cyanide sends a message. It is as though Sophie is "correcting" the choice she once made at Auschwitz. She now seeks the very death she then escaped.

The film presents the viewer with many challenging moral problems. I will discuss several of them. My intention, however, is not merely to use the film as an illustration of a moral conundrum, to be discussed in philosophical terms. My aim is more ambitious. I want to try to use philosophy to make better sense of the film. I want to use philosophical analysis in an attempt to explain Sophie's decision to seek death together with Nathan. Why she sought death is the central problem in the film. Sophie is the only true character, played with outstanding skill and clean intuition by Meryl Streep. Stingo has not yet developed any character when the film starts, and he does not do so while the story of the film unfolds. He is there only to exercise a catalytic effect on Sophie and Nathan and to communicate what happens. Nathan, if we can distinguish between a "personality" and a "character"—when a personality is a biologically given fact and a character is something we develop through education and training—is a person more or less without any character whatever; he is in the grips of his—sick—personality. So it is Sophie we want to understand. Sophie's actions and choices are what we want to explain.

To explain an action is to rationalize it, that is, to render it rational by the lights of the agent. That is why explanations of actions provide understanding of them. Here, I want to make sense of Sophie's suicide. In particular, I will try to see if there is any way of making *philosophical* sense of it. Otherwise, it seems to me, we cannot understand it at all.

I will discuss three hypotheses. First of all, I will consider the hypothesis that Sophie did something terribly and obviously wrong when she sacrificed her daughter, Eva. Or, even, that she did something wrong before she ended up in the concentration camp. Perhaps she is lying when she claims that she was innocent. Her father and her husband, who was a disciple of her father, were anti-Semites, but she was not, she claims. Suppose she is lying? Would that render her suicide rational? Second, I consider the hypothesis that Sophie was presented with what has been called a moral "dilemma", either in the form of what I will call a "tragic moral choice" or in the form of what I will call a "moral conflict". Perhaps she could not help acquiring guilt, or perhaps remorse was the only appropriate attitude to take with respect to her choice. Finally, I will turn to the hypothesis that there was something terribly wrong with Sophie's character, rather than with her action (her choice). Perhaps the problem with her action (her choice) was not that it was wrong. It was right, all right, but a virtuous person should not have been able to do the right thing in a situation such as this one. Perhaps her action was an example of something we can call "blameful right-doing". I submit that this is the hypothesis that makes best sense of her choice.

Before going into this, I need to make a short comment on the problem of truth in fiction.

II. TRUTH IN FICTION

A piece of art presents the reader, viewer, or listener with a reality, and even, in some cases, with a complete world. In music, it is a reality that is actually presented to us. We can listen to it and relate to it. In literature and film, it is a fictitious "reality", This reality is presented to us as actual, it is there, and we can relate to it. We can ask questions about it. We can hold opinions about it. We can speculate about it. Of course, the author of a novel puts forward sentences, expressing propositions. It is as though the author describes the world. These propositions are made true, however, not by facts in the actual world, but by facts in the *fictitious* world. As a matter of fact, these sentences help *constitute* the fictitious world, rather than merely describe it. An additional reality is created. When it has been created, when it is "there", there is nothing more that can be added by the author. The author has no privileged position with regard to the interpretation of the work.

So there is such a thing as truth in fiction. For example, in the film *Sophie's Choice*, it is true that Nathan suffers from paranoid schizophrenia; it is true that Stingo, Sophie, and Nathan share a certain landlady; it is true that her name is Etta Zimmerman; and it is true that the color of her apartment house is pink. All these truths, however, are truths *in the film* or, rather, truths *in the fictitious reality constituted by the film*.

Moreover, it is typical of *realistic* film and literature, of which *Sophie's Choice* is an example, that we hold the principle of bivalence to apply to it.[3] We can thus rely on the law of the excluded middle. In a realistic piece of art there are no truth-value gaps. The fictitious world presented in the film is *constituted* by what is presented to the viewer in the film, in combination with facts in the actual world, but the fictitious world as such *transcends* our evidence.[4] This is not so in all films, novels, and screenplays. It would be absurd to apply the principle of bivalence to Goethe's *Faust*, for example. When it is appropriate to apply it, we may speak of realistic art. It is clear that *Sophie's Choice* is realistic in this sense. The film is made in such a manner that, even if there is no evidence available to us in the film, we feel that a question such as, "What was really going on in Sophie's head when she made her choice?" makes sense. Even if Sophie's motivation is not clear to us, we are allowed to speculate about it. We assume that there is a fact of the matter. That is why it makes good sense to ponder whether Sophie made the right choice. We can learn from the film in the same manner that we can learn from actual experiences in our lives. We can learn by posing and trying to answer psychological questions.

In *Sophie's Choice*, there are many truths that are obvious to us. We can trust our senses. What we see happen, happens. Moreover, because of a not very subtle narrative technique, we also know a lot about the past in the film. When Sophie tells us about what happened in the concentration camp, we can trust her words. The reason is that we are *shown* what happened, in black and white flashbacks that remind us of old newsreels. There are, however, some facts about the past about which we cannot be certain. Sophie gives the impression that she never shared her father's anti-Semitism. This is in no way shown in black and white. Is it true? It is impossible to tell for sure, given the evidence we can access in the film. Yet, since the film is realistic, we know for sure that it is true *or* false.

In the film, one historical person in particular, Rudolf Höss, is present. Are we, in our attempts to understand the film, allowed to use our historical knowledge about Höss? Yes, we are, and it is crucial to understanding the film that we do. Of course, we realize that the short episode of his encounter with Sophie never took place in reality, but he the person has lived. We are allowed to infer from what we know about the historical person what kind of character the fictitious one exhibits. Höss' warm feelings for his family are exhibited in the film, but his callousness is neither described nor shown. We, however, as viewers, know about it very well. We are never told in the film that he developed Zyclon B, but from the historical records we know about it. We know that he wrote:

> The gassing was carried out in the detention cells of Block 22. Protected by a gas mask, I watched the killing myself. In the crowded cells, death came instantaneously the moment the Zyklon B was thrown in. A short, almost smothered cry, and it was all over. . . . I must even admit that this gassing set my mind at rest, for the mass extermination of the Jews was to start soon, and at that time neither Eichmann nor I was certain as to how these mass killings were to be carried out. It would be by gas, but we did not know which gas and how it was to be used. Now we had the gas, and we had established a procedure.[5]

Sophie does not know this. Here we have an advantage over Sophie. She knows Höss only from her own experience. She gets the impression that she can manipulate Höss in order to save her son. We know that her attempt is bound to fail, and this knowledge is crucial to our understanding of her actions in the camp.

III. DID SOPHIE MAKE THE WRONG CHOICE?

The title of the film indicates that Sophie made a choice, but this has been questioned. When one views the penultimate scene of the film, one gets the impression that eventually, after having tried to avoid making any choice at all, Sophie does make a choice. In this terrible scene, we view how a sadistic prison guard, when he finds out that Sophie is a Catholic, wants to put her faith to a test. Christ says that you should leave your children behind and follow him, he claims. So he offers Sophie a choice. If she sacrifices one child, he will allow the other child to survive. Is this a genuine choice? No, claims Phyllis Deutsch:

Both Styron and Pakula evidently believe that the decision Sophie made to relinquish her daughter actually constituted a *choice*. In fact, Sophie had *no choice* in the matter. Choice presupposes a range of options in a context of existential freedom. Sophie's decision did not take place under such conditions. She made a *selection* within a narrowly defined context of competing evils; in such a context, choice is impossible.[6]

This is not convincing. Even in terrible situations, we may be left with some choice. Sophie is in a terrible situation, but there are still at least two options left to her. So, at least on a superficial understanding of what we see (later I will complicate this, but this has nothing to do with the severity of Sophie's situation), she eventually does make a choice. At least, she takes a kind of action. By sacrificing one of the children, which is something she definitely chooses to do, Sophie tries to save at least one of her children rather than sacrificing both as well as herself.

Granting, then, that Sophie did make a choice at the camp, the following explanation arises for her later suicide: she realizes that she made the wrong choice. If we approach the question from a simple utilitarian point of view—and judge her action in terms of its potential consequences—it is at least hard to give any convincing reason why her action was not, after all, the right one. She tried, in vain, to avoid the choice; when forced to make it, she made it. We do not know whether it actually saved the life of her son, but for all we know it may have saved him (note that this kind of speculation makes sense since it is a realistic film, and the question is not settled by any evidence presented to the viewer). It is hard to see any point, in the circumstances, in sacrificing both children. Even if, as a matter of fact, both children died, the choice probably did save Sophie's own life.

Could a heroic refusal on her part have taught the guard a lesson? It is hard to come up with any plausible speculation to this effect. It is also hard to see of what use her effort would have been. He would probably have stuck to his business. Would it have inspired other people in the line to resist, if she had resisted (and sacrificed herself and her children)? Again, this is hard to believe. On the contrary, the fact that she and both her children would have been killed would probably have made the other people in the camp, once they saw or heard about it, *less* inclined to resist. Certainly, a revolt of all the prisoners, together and at the same time, may have had some good effects. Some prisoners may have been able to escape from the camp, and some of them may have survived, but coordination of their actions in this way was not possible. That is a tragic fact.[7]

Moreover, once the critical choice has been made by Sophie—once her daughter, Eva, has been killed and her son, Jan, saved (for the moment)—she goes to great lengths to save her son permanently. Because of her Aryan looks, her manipulative character, and her perfect German, she obtains a position as secretary to Rudolf Höss, the commander of Auschwitz. She humiliates herself and uses her position in an attempt to seduce Höss and to convince him to save the life of Jan by making Jan part of the *Lebensborn* program. This program, initiated by

Heinrich Himmler, brought children with Aryan looks to Germany for adoption. Sophie's attempt fails because Höss does not keep his word. With the help of historical hindsight, we know why her attempt failed: she underestimated Höss' callousness. Her underestimation of his callousness was not unreasonable, however, given the knowledge she had been able to acquire about him. Furthermore, for the first time in her life, in this difficult situation and somewhat unexpectedly, I must say, she also takes a truly brave action. In order to help the Resistance, she makes an attempt to steal a radio set from one of Höss' children. She is exposed by the child to whom the radio set belongs and cleverly succeeds (by fainting) in gaining some sympathy from the child, who then does not report her to her parents. So from a utilitarian point of view, there is little to complain about in Sophie's actions.

If we are going to explain Sophie's suicide on the basis of the wrongness of her action, however, we need to show that *she* took her choice to be the wrong one. I have just argued that her choice was not wrong from a utilitarian viewpoint, but Sophie herself was not a utilitarian, she was a Catholic. Catholics share the view with utilitarians that we ought to make the world a better place, of course, but they do not think that the end justifies the means. There are ways of making the world a better place that we are nonetheless not allowed to take. Catholics adhere to the Sanctity of Life Doctrine, putting a strict ban on killing. We are not allowed to kill, according to this doctrine, even if killing means that we make the world a happier place.[8] Did Sophie, by agreeing to choose between the children, and by giving away her daughter, violate this ban on killing? This is not obvious. First of all, only the *active* killing of innocent human beings is strictly prohibited. It is compatible with this doctrine that we allow some people in poor countries to starve to death while we are living comparatively high. Allowing death to come about in this way does not amount to any kind of prohibited killing. By giving away her daughter, Sophie did not kill her. Others performed the actual killing of the daughter. *They* are responsible for it.

Of course, even giving someone away to someone else who will kill her may be wrong, according to Catholic ethics, even if it is not a case of murder. Note, however, that even some kinds of *active* killing can be morally warranted, and even required, according to this ethic. If the active killing is not intended, but merely foreseen, it may be permitted. For example, it may be morally permitted to give a patient a painkiller that kills her, if the intention is to kill the pain, not to kill the patient. The death of the patient is then merely a foreseen but not desired consequence of the action. Provided there is a reasonable proportionality between the good at which one aims (the patient's being free of pain) and the bad one foresees (death is hastened), it can be morally acceptable to give the lethal dose (provided there was no other way to keep the patient free of pain, of course).

We can run the active/passive and the intended/merely foreseen distinctions together, and we see that it is only one combination of them that is prohibited by the Sanctity of Life view here described:

KILLING	Death intended	Death merely foreseen
Active	FORBIDDEN	TOLERATED
Passive	TOLERATED	TOLERATED

Figure 11.2

What is strictly forbidden, according to the Sanctity of Life Doctrine, then, is only the active and intentional killing of an innocent human being. Sophie is certainly innocent of this. Even if it is also wrong (although not murder) to hand over a person to a killer, this is probably only wrong, according to the doctrine, if the intention is that the person should be killed. If not even active killing, without intent, is immoral, then handing over someone to a killer without intent that the person be killed can hardly be wrong; this is what Sophie does. When she hands over her daughter she foresees that the daughter will be killed, but this is not something she intends. If she could stop it from happening, she would do so. She hands her over in order to save the life of her son. So there is a reasonable proportionality between the evil she foresees (the death of her daughter) and the good she aims at (the survival of her son).

Of course, Sophie may feel guilt about the very fact that there is a concentration camp. She may blame herself for having ended up in the situation she did, arguing that, somehow, she shares responsibility for the Nazi atrocities. She may be lying to us (and Stingo) when she claims that she did not share her father's and her husband's anti-Semitism. Even though there is no way of telling if she is lying, I have the impression that she is lying. Why would she have held any opinions about the Jews very different from the ones held by her father and husband? We are shown a short visit she pays to the Ghetto, but it is hard to believe that this visit could have worked as an eye-opener to her if she were not already critical of her father's views. There is no evidence to indicate that she was critical of him before she typed a talk for him in which he put forward his anti-Semitic views (a talk she claims she made a mess of, but this is not something we, as viewers, are *shown*). Furthermore, when approached by the guard at Auschwitz, she cries out, in openly anti-Semitic terms, "I am a Christian. I'm not a Jew; neither are my children. They are racially pure." That does not show much, of course. Who would not try to save his or her skin in a similar manner in the circumstances? Let us assume, though, that, uncritically, she shared her father's anti-Semitic views. When she tells Stingo she did not, she lies. Would this mean that she was guilty of the existence of the concentration camps? Would this mean that she could feel such collective guilt that it made her continued life hopeless? This is very far-fetched. Many people share this kind of collective guilt, but few find it difficult to go on living, even if they become conscious of it. Political naivety may be a sin, but it is not, according to the Catholic faith, a deadly one. What are we otherwise to say of Pope Pius XII, who did not, even *after* World War II, clearly dissociate himself from the Nazis?

It seems, then, that neither from a utilitarian nor from a Sanctity of Life perspective is what Sophie does wrong. Or, at least, it is in no way *obvious* that she does the wrong thing, let alone that she does anything that is *outrageously* and *terribly* wrong. It is far-fetched to assume that she could not go on living because of what she had done. For all we (and she) know, she may well have done the right thing.

IV. MORAL DILEMMAS: TRAGIC CHOICES AND MORAL CONFLICTS

Perhaps the situation was more complex than I have so far admitted. Perhaps it was such that it was impossible to do the right thing. Perhaps Sophie faced a moral dilemma in the form of a tragic choice or a moral conflict.

Did Sophie face a moral dilemma? In one sense of this expression, she clearly did. She faced a *hard* choice. I here intend to use the word moral "dilemma" to cover something different, however. To explain what I am referring to, I will use the words "tragic" choice and moral "conflict", and I will use them in a restricted and slightly technical sense. So here we need to clarify the problem. First of all, are there situations such that, whatever the agent does, she acts wrongly? If there are such situations, I will speak of them as situations presenting *tragic choices*. Second, can we come to face incompatible obligations? If we can—that is, if there are situations in which we have more obligations than we can fulfill—I will speak of them as situations presenting us with *moral conflicts*.

Are there tragic choices and moral conflicts? This question has both a logical and a factual aspect. Considering the logical aspect, I will argue that both the notion of a situation in which whatever I do I act wrongly, and the notion of a situation in which I face incompatible obligations, are conceivable. There is no inconsistency involved in their description. Considering the factual aspect, I will argue that there are situations in which we face conflicting duties, but that, as a matter of fact, there are no situations such that, whatever we do, we act wrongly.

Let us first consider the problem of tragic choices. I believe some would like to argue that this is the kind of choice Sophie faced. The utilitarian is wrong when claiming that, if all the options are (equally) bad, then the agent is permitted to act as he or she sees fit. On the contrary, they claim, in this situation the agent cannot help acting wrongly.

It may be tempting to claim, however, that such situations are not possible. For if all alternatives facing an agent are wrong, then what does this mean? If an alternative is wrong, does this not mean that there is something the agent should have done instead? If all the alternatives facing the agent are wrong, however, there is no such possibility open to the agent. Does this not mean that the very notion of a right and a wrong action loses its meaning? We seem to have taken the gist out of our notion of wrongness so that, when we say that all the alternatives facing the agent are, in the new sense of the word, wrong, this comes close to saying that, in the ordinary sense of the word, they are all right.

This manner of handling the problem is much too simplistic, however. Even if not all alternatives in a situation can be wrong, it can be true that, whatever the agent does, it is wrong. This can happen if the normative status of our actions depends on what we do in the following way: An action we perform may be wrong, but had we not performed this action, it may have been what we should have done. There are some normative outlooks allowing this. At least, there are two approaches famously leading to this result. One of them treats problems of vagueness in a manner resulting in the fact that, whatever we do in certain situations, our action is wrong. The other is an "actualist" attempted solution to some problems in population ethics. Could any such view lead us to the belief that Sophie faced a tragic choice?

Let us first have a look at the view on vagueness which gives rise to tragic moral choices. Suppose there is such a thing as well-being, and suppose the utilitarians are right in their insistence that we should always perform the alternative that maximizes well-being. Suppose furthermore, with Bentham, that only *noticeable* differences of well-being are of moral importance.[9] Suppose furthermore (plausibly) that the notion of how well we fare is somewhat vague.

To see how this can lead to tragic conflicts, consider a case in which some person wants to cross a lawn and I can decide how many people should be allowed to do so. Suppose I allow one person to walk across a lawn. She gains some time. The lawn is not damaged in any noticeable way. The person crosses the lawn and hence improves the hedonic situation of the world. Once she has crossed the lawn, however, it may be the case that, from the point of view of the situation that has emerged, another person also crossing the lawn will not have any noticeable effect for the worse, but instead will mean a slight noticeable improvement. So, had one person crossed the lawn, then a second person should have been allowed to cross the lawn, too. If this person, too, had crossed the lawn, however, it may well be the case that there was now good reason to return to the *original* position. For now, an extensive change for the worse has come about. When compared to the original position, the lawn has been damaged in a *noticeable* way, we may assume, and *many* people can see this and suffer from the sight. The damage to the lawn (or, rather, the effect it has upon the spectators) clearly outweighs the gains made by the two people who crossed the lawn. Remember, once we have again reached the original position, in which no one crosses the lawn, we ought to move to a situation in which one person crosses the lawn, and so forth. The explanation how this can be possible has to do with the assumption that "better than" is vague. There are differences in regard to betterness that surface only indirectly. According to the evaluative assumption made by some hedonists, these indirect differences don't matter—only noticeable differences do.

This description is consistent, and it implies that, whatever action is taken is wrong, but it also implies that the normative status of the alternatives facing the agent is dependent upon what the agent actually does. A moral view with this implication may seem strange, but it is not inconsistent.

In population ethics, we come across views with similar implications. Some people claim that an action cannot be wrong unless it wrongs someone and that only actual people—that is, people who live, have lived or will, as a matter of fact, come to live—can be wronged. Then, however, we can end up in situations in which, whatever option we choose, we choose a wrong option. Suppose I cannot help but conceive a person, but I have a choice as to whom I will conceive. If I act in one manner, a certain individual, Sara, will live. If I act in the other manner available to me, Hagar will live instead of Sara. Irrespective of how I choose, my choice is wrong, since the person who will come to live will have a terrible life.

Suppose I conceive Sara. She complains, "Why did you do this to me? It would have been better if I had not existed!" I have to concede that I should not have conceived her. Had I not conceived her, however, I would have conceived Hagar. Does this make my decision to conceive Sara all right? No, it does not, since, in the world in which I conceive Sara, Hagar does not exist. She has no right to any complaint, then. So what if, instead, I had conceived Hagar? Well, in this world, Hagar is actual and can make a valid complaint. In this world, I should instead have conceived Sara (who is not around to complain). The upshot is that, whatever choice I make, I make the wrong choice. This is truly tragic.

Tragic moral choices are conceivable, then, but do they really exist? I think not. I do not think that there is any plausible moral view that implies that they do. The views indicated above make sense, but they are not morally acceptable.

Be that as it may, it is hard to see how we could describe Sophie's choice as an instance of any such tragic choice. There are no problems to do with vagueness involved in her choice, and both her children were actual people, living in the actual world. Her choice is "tragic" in the more mundane sense that, whatever she does, the outcome is bad. She faces a hard choice. It is likely, however, that the outcome will be better if she sacrifices one of her children than if she does not. Perhaps the boy had a better chance to survive in the camp. Then the choice reached by Sophie may even have been the optimal one. It was right to sacrifice one of the children, and it was right to sacrifice the girl. So I see no way of describing her choice as a truly tragic one.

So, did Sophie face a moral conflict? Did she face more duties than she could fulfill? Remember that we have reserved the word moral "conflict" to cover such cases. The most straightforward suggestion here would be, of course, that she has an obligation to save her daughter and an obligation to save her son, but she cannot fulfill both of them. But this is not convincing.[10] It would mean that her action would be wrong, irrespective of what she did. If this is how we describe her situation, we should merely mean that the obligations here facing Sophie are of a *prima facie* nature, and, granting that, it is reasonable to ask which one of them, in the situation, takes precedence over the other. Any plausible moral view should provide an answer to this question.

Here is a simple example of a genuine moral conflict, however: I ought to invite a person to dinner and settle a dispute with her. If I invite her, however, I will, as a matter of fact, quarrel with her, even though I can abstain from doing so. Thus, I ought not to invite her. Both these obligations seem to be real. Both these obligations are strict (absolute) ones, not merely *prima facie* obligations. Each obligates me to do something I can do, but I cannot fulfill both of them. For, certainly, I cannot both invite her and settle the dispute with her and not invite her. So I seem to be facing one obligation too many in the situation.

Once again, I see no logical problem in acknowledging moral conflicts of this kind. I have discussed this case elsewhere so I will be brief.[11] I have both these obligations, and, for each of them, I can fulfill it (I have assumed). It is not because if I invite the person I cannot help quarrelling with her, that I ought not to invite her. I can avoid this, and this is why I ought to invite her and settle my dispute with her, we have assumed. But the fact is that I *will* (voluntarily) quarrel with her, if I invite her, and that's why I ought not to invite her.

At the root of moral conflicts of this kind is always some kind of moral weakness together with a temporal aspect. It is because, as a matter of fact, if I put myself in a certain situation in which, further on, I will behave badly, that I ought not to put myself in this situation. This does not mean, however, that I *should* not put myself in the situation *and* behave correctly. Could Sophie be facing a genuine moral conflict of this kind? Such conflicts are not only logically possible, I submit that they exist in real life. We face them over and over again, and such conflicts may be proper sources of feelings of regret and guilt. If, in the example, I do not invite the person, I do the right thing. Yet, I may feel guilt, not because of this decision, but because of the truth of the counterfactual proposition: if I had invited her, I would have quarreled. Yet for all that, it is hard to see any way of interpreting Sophie's predicament in these terms. So, I conclude that Sophie is not facing a moral conflict.

One could perhaps argue that since she eventually killed herself and since her son was probably killed anyway, it would have been better if she had refused to concede to the guard and she and both her children had been killed at once. This would have saved both her and her son unnecessary suffering. The structure of her situation was this: She should have tried to save Jan and then gone on to live a good life. Since, as a matter of fact, she was going to kill herself, however, she should not have saved Jan. If this description of her normative situation is correct, her awareness of this kind of conflict cannot *explain* why she kills herself. For the conflict is generated by her decision to kill herself. If she had not killed herself, then the conflict would not have existed in the first place.

It seems, then, that Sophie probably did make the right choice, or at least not a choice that was in any *obvious* way wrong, and she was facing neither a tragic choice nor a moral conflict. So why can she not live with her decision once she acknowledges it? Is there something wrong with her personality? Or, is there some aspect that has so far been left out of the moral diagnosis? I think there is one more element to investigate, an element stressed in particular by virtue ethics, but that is of interest to all moral outlooks.

V. BLAMEWORTHY RIGHT-DOING

It becomes clear in the film that there is one thing Sophie fears: If she goes on with her life together with Stingo, she may become a mother again. She does not see herself as capable of being a good mother. Why not? She seems to believe that when she sacrificed her daughter, she exhibited a trait of character that is incompatible with being a good parent. Is she right about this? Should a good parent be incapable of making the kind of choice she made? What are we to expect from a good parent, then, in a situation like the one Sophie faced? Should we require of a good parent that he or she not be capable of sacrificing one of her children in order to save at least one of them?

This may seem like a plausible claim to make. Few parents have to make this kind of choice, so a capacity for making it would be of little avail. If parents in general were capable of making it, what kind of relationship would they have to their children? It is hard to believe that a good parent should be able to make this kind of choice. The readiness to make it could hardly be hidden from the child; it would surface in everyday situations involving the child and parent and the child could never feel secure in its relation to his parent.

Is this to hold on to a much too ideal notion of what it means to be a good parent? After all, parents have had to sacrifice their children in many poor societies, in more mundane circumstance than the ones facing Sophie. When there has not been enough food for all the children, some have had to go. In particular, infanticide has been a common practice in most civilizations. There is little evidence to indicate that this has had a devastating effect on the relationships between parents and children.

No child can feel threatened by a practice of infanticide, however, since when the child is old enough to feel fear it is too late to kill it. Sophie's choice is different. She chooses between two children who are capable of feeling fear. The despair felt by her daughter, Eva, when she is handed over by her mother to the guard, is unmistakable and truly heartbreaking. By handing over her daughter to the guard, Sophie shows that all the time she took care of her children, she has been a person *capable* of making this kind of choice. Is this terrible?

Upon reflection, I think it is. Of course, one may want to argue that the readiness to sacrifice one child in order to save the other is a manifestation merely of one's unwillingness to *abandon* one's children. The fact that a parent is prepared to give up one child in order to save the other, rather than have both sacrificed, should not be seen as a threat, even if it is sensed and acknowledged by the child.

I cannot help feeling, however, that this might be an awkward readiness to exhibit in a well-ordered, affluent society. This readiness may be functional in times of crises—and, certainly, if you want to escape alive from a concentration camp like Auschwitz, it is functional—but the very same readiness is problematic once you have escaped. If your choice is perceived to be one between, on the one hand, death, and on the other hand, a life together with Stingo, raising children in the American South after World War II, belonging to the white middle class, then the realization that you have this capacity may strike you as deeply problematic. You may indeed come to think that you have not ever been, nor could you ever become, a good parent, so death is the only reasonable option. In particular, you would never be able to tell your new children, truthfully, exactly what happened to their siblings in the past.

Moreover, Sophie's choice to sacrifice the daughter rather than her son may well reflect an even more obvious aspect of her being a poor parent. Did it not show, after all, a secret preference on her part for the son over the daughter? Did it not reveal a sexist or emotional bias of a strictly forbidden kind? Well, if it did, Sophie's suicide makes even better sense. We do not want a parent to be capable of making a choice, even if it is the right one, based on those kinds of reasons. At least, we do not want a parent living in reasonably decent circumstances to be able to make this kind of choice.

Sophie herself may have felt that she entertained a kind of bias that *clearly* signifies that she is (beyond repair) a bad mother. Not only was she a racist, she was sexist as well. By acknowledging this, she may have thought that she acted from an immoral character, or at least from a character inconsistent with the kind of life Stingo could offer her. Then, by her own lights, to seek death was the only reasonable action available to her.

Did she make a choice at all, though? Perhaps there is some room for doubt here. Even if it is clear that she made a decision to sacrifice one of her children in order to save the other, it is less clear that she actually made a choice *between* her children. This point is different from the one made above by Deutsch. The point is not that it is impossible to make a choice in difficult circumstances. This is possible, and it often happens. The point is rather that Sophie did not choose *between* her children.

One could here avail oneself of the distinction between choosing and picking developed by Edna Ullmann-Margalit and Sidney Morgenbesser. When we choose, the outcome of our action can be explained with reference to our beliefs and desires. When we pick, no such explanation is applicable. Our capacity to pick is what saves us from the predicament of Buridan's ass which, placed exactly in the middle between two stacks of hay, starves to death since it cannot make any rational decision to start eating one rather than the other. Could we perhaps claim that while Sophie chooses to sacrifice one of her children, she just *picks* her daughter?[12]

This interpretation is at least consistent with what we see. It all happens very quickly. Once she has conceded to the demand made by the guard, and hands her daughter over to him, it may well be that her sacrifice of her daughter is not really the result of any choice. Perhaps it cannot be rationally explained by any conscious or unconscious desire to sacrifice her daughter rather than her son.

Here we must speculate. It is indeed possible that, by sacrificing her daughter rather than her son, she made no choice whatever. According to this speculation, she *decided* to sacrifice one of her children rather than the other, but *picked* her daughter. Yet even the decision to sacrifice one of the children, even if one of them was then just picked, may have been one decision too many, a decision incompatible with the traits of character one should expect from a good parent. At least, this may be how Sophie herself conceived of the matter—she was not ever capable of becoming a good parent.

Perhaps a piece of psychological evidence is missing. Why need Sophie become a parent at all? Why need she choose between death with Nathan and life in the South with Stingo? Why is she stuck in this narrow realm of binary choices: Eva versus Jan, Stingo versus Nathan, life versus death? Why can she not break out of it? Why can she not go on with her life on her own? These are thoughts that are bound to arise for a contemporary viewer of the film.

A sad fact about Sophie, as we know her, is that her entire life seems to have taken place in relation to men. First, she is dependent upon her father. She then marries one of his disciples. Probably she shares, or is at least sympathetic to, their anti-Semitic political views. Then comes the episode with Höss, in which she tries in vain to seduce him, in order to save her son. Eventually, she lives with Nathan. She contemplates a life with Stingo. She seems to be incapable of living a life of her own. Moreover, as was noted above, we sense a manipulative trait in her character. She faints twice in the film. The first time, as we have already noted, is when she has attempted to steal a radio set at Auschwitz. One of Höss' children has detected her and is prepared to inform on her. She saves her life by fainting and gaining trust from the child. The second time is when she has recently arrived in New York. She faints in a library, at the feet of Nathan, who takes care of her.

Is this merely coincidental? One gets the impression that it is not. Sophie is both manipulative and dependent. Something is lacking in her personality. She cannot live on her own. We do not know why, but this surfaces in the film as a brutal fact. Part of the explanation is the time in which she lived, we may conjecture, but perhaps there is something further to the explanation of this fact, something that escapes us. Given the fact that she is incapable of living on her own, however, and given her realization that she cannot ever become a good parent, her suicide does indeed make sense.

VI. CONCLUSION

I submit that the best way of making philosophical sense of Sophie's choice is to see it as a case of blameful right-doing. By doing, in the situation, the right thing, or, at least, not clearly doing anything wrong, Sophie exhibited a trait of character we do not expect to find in a good mother. She had ended up in a situation in which a good parent is not supposed to be able to do the right thing. She had been prepared to sacrifice one of her children in order to save the other. She may even have held a preference for one of her children and acted from it. This is not what we expect from a good parent. Her choice to commit suicide, even if we cannot fully explain it, makes sense when viewed from her own subjective perspective and given her personality as we know it.

Sophie could not go on with her life. As we are invited to conceive of her situation, a decision to do so would have involved another choice. She would have had to choose Stingo over Nathan. She would have had to choose life over death. She would have had to choose a Southern life raising new children over no life at all. She was not, however, equipped for such a life. In particular, she could not ever become a good parent.

Once she realized the true nature of her choice at Auschwitz, and the light it was bound to shed on her character, she had no option. She had to commit suicide. We can thus rationalize her action; we understand why she did kill herself. If we had been in her shoes, we would have done the same.

NOTES

1. The film is based on the book of the same name by William Styron, first published in 1979. I will not make reference to the novel in my attempt to understand what is going on in the film. All dialogue quoted in this essay has been transcribed directly from the film.

2. The fact that he takes advantage of Sophie does not mean that she does not take advantage of him. In her relationships with men, during the entire film, she acts in a manipulative manner. She seduces Höss in order to save her son, she uses Stingo in order to reach a better understanding of the true nature of her choice at Auschwitz and, eventually, she uses Nathan when she seeks death. So perhaps she uses Stingo for sexual reasons as well. Why is she manipulative in this manner? A psychoanalyst would seek the answer in her relationship to her parents in general and to her father in particular, but all this is left in the dark in the film. There is no way of telling why.

3. I borrow this use of the term "realistic" from Michael Dummett. See his essay on realism in *Truth and Other Enigmas*.

4. The number of theories about truth in fiction is legion, but I doubt that that any single theory is true of all fiction; there are so many ways an author can create a fictitious world, and it is not likely that any simple theory is true of all of them.

5. Quoted from his autobiography in "Hoess: Death Dealer at Auschwitz," at http://www.auschwitz.dk/hoess.htm, accessed October 15, 2006.

6. Deutsch, *'Sophie's Choice'*.

7. The theory of oppression here alluded to is often called the "gunman" theory, or the "double correlation" theory. If it has application anywhere, it does apply to the situation in a concentration camp. See for example Russell Hardin, *One for All*, about this theory.

8. An authoritative statement of this doctrine can be found in *Sacred Congregation for the Doctrine of the Faith: Declaration on Euthanasia*, Vatican City, 1980, reprinted in the appendix of Torbjörn Tännsjö (ed.), *Terminal Sedation: Euthanasia in Disguise?* In the book, different attempts by different authors are made to interpret the Sanctity of Life Doctrine. In my own contribution I defend the interpretation I here rely on.

9. I think Bentham held this view, but I have not found any passage to quote in support of this claim. I did myself defend it, and the view I here characterize, in "The Morality of Collective Actions." I now believe this was a mistake.

10. For a defense of the idea that such conflicts are real, see Martha Nussbaum, "Comment", in Judith Jarvis Thomson, *Goodness and Advice*. For a rejection of this view, see Judith Jarvis Thomson, "Reply to Commentators," in the same book.

11. Cf. my "Moral Conflict and Moral Realism" and *Hedonistic Utilitarianism*, 41–43, about this.

12. Ullmann-Margalit and Morgenbesser, "Picking and Choosing."

DANGEROUS LIAISONS

LOVE, LETTERS, AND LESSONS IN SEXUAL ETHICS

JOSEPH KUPFER

I. SEXUALITY AND PERSONAL IDENTITY

THE STEPHEN FREARS 1988 FILM OPENS AND CLOSES with the same image: the Marquise de Merteuil (Glenn Close) looking at herself in her dressing-room mirror. At the end, however, the self-satisfied smile she earlier sported is replaced by a broken, despondent expression as she removes what now appears to be thick gobs of makeup. We are reminded of the theatricality of Merteuil's behavior throughout the film by the greasepaint, suggesting that her performances on the stages of society and the boudoir have been brought to a close. What happened in between the two shots to reverse the noble woman's fortune?

The apparent cause of the destruction of Merteuil's social career is that she has been exposed as calculating and cruel. While the machinations of social and sexual intrigue may be understood by her peers to be *comme il faut*, publicly aired vice is not acceptable. *Dangerous Liaisons* further suggests that Merteuil has ignored or flouted a deeper truth about the importance of sexuality in a good life. Within the film's nimble and witty portrayal of its protagonists making a social sport of sex is a view of sexual interaction as a defining dimension of human nature. The role of sexuality in our self-definition is borne out by the social demise of Merteuil and the literal demise of Vicomte de Valmont (John Malkovich), her paramour-ally-combatant.

Because sexuality is a defining dimension of human nature, it has ethical import. I use the term ethical in the broad sense of being concerned with living well, because ethics includes all manner of right action. Besides contemporary emphasis on duties, rights, and rules, we need to reflect on interpersonal relationships and moral character.[1] Friendship, for example, is ethically important because it contributes to a fulfilling life. Why else would such self-regarding character traits as moderation, perseverance, and self-knowledge be considered moral virtues, or envy, sloth, and ingratitude thought to be moral vices? These character traits are morally significant because ethics includes taking into account the impact of our behavior on our own well-being. Of course, sexual behavior typically affects other people as well, and with moral implications.[2] But the emphasis of the film is on the self and how sexual behavior contributes to or detracts from the goodness of the life the individual leads.

The film presents a rich conception of sexual ethics grounded in four related determinants of personal identity: intimacy, integration of personality, harmony between personality and body, and intrinsic valuation. Although this conception is fairly elaborate, I believe the detailed analysis of the film that follows its outline will support it. The intimacy that is the concomitant of sex with someone we truly care about involves sharing our personality as well as our body; consequently, personality and body are harmonized in ideal sex. In addition, the elements of our personality—desires, emotions, and thoughts—are themselves integrated when we focus on our lover. We are focused on our lover because we value the sexual interaction intrinsically, as part of a relationship that is prized for its own sake. *Dangerous Liaisons* presents this as an ideal of human sexuality by the contrast it draws between Valmont's manipulative sex and his caring, intimate sexual relationship with Madame de Tourvel (Michelle Pfeiffer). After articulating the salutary view of sexuality, we will understand more clearly the film's depiction of what happens to people who are habituated to uncaring (careless) sexual affairs. First, then, to the question of intimacy.

Sexual interaction encourages intimacy, psychological as well as physical. As Robert Solomon observes, sex is not just a medium for intimacy, it breeds intimacy, promoting the exchange of ideas as well as bodily sensations.[3] When we give the other person sustained, intense physical access to us, we reveal ourselves psychologically. We are encouraged to complement physical closeness with personal involvement because we are embodied beings, experiencing the world through our bodies. Consequently, when we present ourselves sexually to another, we invite psychological redefinition along with physical awareness.

Sexual interaction draws us into communion with another person, the sharing of our whole selves. Genuinely caring sex is especially intense precisely because focus upon the lover integrates different aspects of our personality: desires, emotions, and thoughts. Since sex is physical, our personality and body are also united. Because we care about our sexual partners, we desire them in their individuality. We desire to experience them physically, know them through their bodies, and please them by means of our bodies. Our sexual desire, then, is integrated with our emotions, since we desire what we care about. C. S. Lewis contrasts sex as a simple appetite, lust, with sexual desire engendered by love: "Without Eros [romantic love] sexual desire . . . is a fact about ourselves. Within Eros it is rather about the Beloved."[4] The physical pleasure we give and receive is informed by affection. Emotion both moves us to sexual communion and is in turn developed by it.

Moreover, emotions and desires are in harmony with our thinking, since our thoughts are about our lovers, what they are experiencing with us. We are cognitively absorbed with our sexual partners, thinking about their desires, pleasures, emotions, and what they are thinking. Since these aspects of their personalities are physically expressed, our bodies are entwined in our thinking. The harmony of desires, emotions, and thoughts is not unique to sexual interaction, but sex adds to this harmonizing a physical dimension. The integration of our personality occurs through our bodies: intense, sensuous, and total. Thus, we experience our persona as whole and as one with our corporeality.

This unity of self is achieved in response to another individual who is, ideally, experiencing a similar integration of self. The integration of self is therefore socially generated, in contrast, say, to those moments of personal integration that we find in rewarding but solitary work. It seems plausible to claim, then, that in loving sex, our integrated personality is one with our bodies and that we in turn are attuned to the other person. The communion between lovers is complete even as it completes the unification of each of its members.

Recall that integration of personality and harmony of personality with body take place only because we are giving our full attention to our lover. The attention occurs because we value the sexual interaction as part of the relationship that we prize intrinsically, for its own sake. Because we value the caring relationship for its own sake, we value its constituents, including sex, in this same intrinsic manner. The film sets such intrinsic valuation off against the instrumental value that Valmont and Merteuil place on their sexuality and, ultimately, on themselves and other people.

The film implicitly criticizes two competing conceptions of sexual ethics, conceptions that remain popular today. Although contrasting with one another, the two views are alike in subordinating sex to other ends, thereby valuing it solely in its instrumental capacity. The first conception can be understood as the conventional-virtue view of sexual morality. As sex is to be confined to marriage, the basic sexual virtues are chastity (before marriage) and fidelity (during marriage). In cultures in which this conception prevails, it typically applies chiefly to women, giving rise to the infamous double standard in sexual conduct.

Dangerous Liaisons subtly subverts this conventional outlook by framing it within a market attitude toward women and their sexuality. The value of a woman as a social commodity is determined by men and so depends upon her sexual purity and fidelity to her husband—otherwise, she is tarnished. The film makes its most overt attack on conventional sexual attitudes through its merciless caricature of Mme. de Volanges, the worried mother of an eligible young woman (Cecile). The conventional-virtue view of sexuality, however, informs the entire story, for it motivates the two seductions that Valmont pursues, and these drive the story's plot. Valmont sets out to defile the purity of Cecile and destroy the marital fidelity of Mme. de Tourvel.

The film more explicitly rejects a second view of sexual ethics, one that provides a stark counterpoint to the conventional-virtue conception. According to the view of egoistic hedonism, our own pleasure is the standard of good sexuality.[5] As long as we are maximizing our enjoyment, our sexual behavior is morally permissible, even advisable. The film criticizes such a conception by dissecting the sordid lives of the libertine protagonists, Valmont and Merteuil. As Lewis says, without romantic love, sexual desire is a fact about ourselves. Valmont and Merteuil personify the self-absorption that characterizes egoistic hedonism.

Dangerous Liaisons implies that the extremes to which Valmont and Merteuil go, including manipulation and deception, are the practical extensions of self-serving hedonism. Such hedonists are naturally inclined to manipulate and deceive others in order to achieve their own pleasures. Consequently, the pleasures to be derived from sexual behavior need not be confined to the body, but can encompass a wide array of pursuits. That is just what we see in the characters of Valmont and Merteuil, who not only adopt the egoistic hedonistic perspective on sexuality, but revel in it with a vengeance.

II. LOVE, LETTERS, AND INTRINSIC VALUE

We treat our sexuality as a thing apart—as a mere means to such ends as revenge, dominance, and bodily pleasure itself—at our own peril. The story shows why we must eventually pay for playing fast and loose with such a central dimension of personal identity. The price is fragmentation of self and unhappiness. If Solomon is correct, and sex breeds intimacy, then what must sexual experience be like for someone whose persona is habitually divorced from its bodily expression? Because sex so naturally instigates intimacy, sex without emotional engagement inhibits the impulse to disclose ourselves. Sex is likely to be experienced as exclusively physical or mechanical, and, in Valmont's case, a matter of technical virtuosity. Without the context of a caring relationship, sexual encounters will be insulated from our personalities or only connect with small portions of them.

Such alienation is what we infer about Valmont because his personality is not in harmony with his body. As his body goes through its technically adroit paces, Valmont's desires, emotions, and thoughts are preoccupied with things besides his lover. Moreover, the elements of his personality are not themselves in tune with one another, since Valmont is not fully attending to the lover of the moment. For example, while seducing Cecile de Volanges, Valmont appears detached and dispassionate. His sexual desire seems disconnected from emotion—which might be revenge (against a third party), pride (in conquest), or hopefulness (in anticipation of future pleasure). Nor are Valmont's thoughts focused on his lover, since she means nothing to him; they leap ahead to how this occasion, or affair, fits into his larger plans. As a result, his thoughts are also disconnected from his desires and emotions.

Valmont's uniquely joyous reaction to lovemaking with Tourvel indicates that his previous sexual experiences have all been truncated. Valmont has never enjoyed the full integration of his person in his sexual dalliances and has been alienated from his body. Clearly, Valmont has been habituated to depersonalized, manipulative sex. Using sex as a means to various ends has built obstacles to the expression of emotion and to the healthy risks inherent in the mutual disclosure of personality. Discovering the full depths of sex takes Valmont by giddy surprise, filling him with wonder, and upends his complex relationship with Merteuil.

For most of the story, we watch as Valmont and Merteuil scheme to achieve their tawdry ends by controlling less experienced individuals. These two are the master players, moving pieces on a societal chessboard as they joust and spar with one another. The field of their maneuverings is sex: seduction, satisfaction, and betrayal. Essential to the games of Valmont and Merteuil is language, and letters emerge as a telling motif. Letters written and read, letters intercepted and circulated.[6] In the film, letters parallel sexual embodiment and intersect with it.

As a parallel, letters physically present our personalities, just as our bodies do in sexual interaction. Both letters and bodies can be used and misused in intimate communication, to truly express ourselves or to misrepresent what we feel and think. Both the written word and the physical touch can deepen a relationship or seduce and control the other person. Letters communicate by means of formal language, even as we express and question with the body's informal language during sex. Moreover, as physical objects, letters have a life of their own, persisting beyond the spoken word.[7] Once out of our hands, they can confirm or contradict what we otherwise do and say. Then, too, our bodies may also reveal aspects of us that we cannot control or do not realize we are disclosing.

In the story, letters also intersect with the sexual encounters and intrigue of the characters. Letters are the means of arranging affairs, sabotaging relationships, and violating sexual trust. If bodies, especially in their sexual capacities, are the capital goods of the social world of Merteuil and Valmont, then letters are the currency that secures these goods. In the hands of this pair, letters are more valuable than gold, giving them information about and power over their prey. Although Valmont and Merteuil use letters to make sport with people, the written word exerts power over them. This is most dramatically portrayed at the story's finale, when letters precipitate Valmont's fatal duel and the social downfall of Merteuil. Instead of examining the role of letters in the story as it unfolds, I will gather together the film's various deployments of written communication at the end of the discussion.

As mentioned, *Dangerous Liaisons* illustrates the difference between instrumental and intrinsic valuation. Valmont and Merteuil use their bodies and language merely as the means to whatever purposes they may have, including revenge, dominance, and gamesmanship. While physical pleasure may be one such purpose, the body is nonetheless valued instrumentally, just as it is when we eat or drink to satisfy a desire. Such instrumental use contrasts with treating our bodies and language as part of the fabric of a meaningful, loving relationship. Sexual and linguistic intercourse are not simply means to a relationship of care and love. Rather, they are inherent to such relationships as contexts of intimacy and as such are valued for their own sake. Consequently, when Valmont sincerely interacts with Tourvel, he values his powers of expression as part of their interpersonal communion, not merely as physical devices to be put to some arbitrary use. Tourvel enables him to be at one with his body by focusing his desires, emotions, and thoughts on herself.

These are the lessons I argue that *Dangerous Liaisons* offers us and that Valmont learns. The philosophical views I ascribe to the film result from interpreting what we see and hear in the film's story; the ethical perspective on sexuality in particular, help make sense of what occurs. These generalizations about human nature enable us to explain what happens in the story, such as Valmont refusing to seduce

Tourvel or purposely wounding himself in his duel. The film endorses the views I offer in the sense that the story it tells lends itself to explanation by means of them. Whether the story is well-explained by the interpretation I offer must finally be decided by reference to the content of the story and its meaning. The discussion that follows, then, simultaneously seeks to organize and make sense of what takes place in the story and (thereby) justify the larger philosophical claims I attribute to the film. If successful, the interpretation should enhance our cinematic appreciation as well as deepen our moral understanding.[8]

III. WOMEN AS SEXUAL PROPERTY

The film begins with the latest sexual scheme being hatched between Valmont and Merteuil. Merteuil wants Valmont to deflower Cecile de Volanges (Uma Thurman) in order to exact revenge upon Merteuil's former lover, Bastide, who has left her. By presenting Bastide with a bride (Cecile) who is damaged goods, Merteuil can exert power over him and, by avenging her perceived humiliation, salve her wounded pride. Valmont only agrees when Merteuil sweetens the deal: If Valmont also seduces Madame de Tourvel, Merteuil will resume her amorous relationship with him.

As Mme. de Tourvel is a woman famous for her virtue and happy marriage, Valmont is excited by the prospect of moving her to "betray everything that's most important to her": God, virtue, and the sanctity of marriage. Valmont proceeds to his aunt's estate, where he knows that Tourvel is visiting. We realize just how clever and ironic Valmont is when we see his strategy for seducing the lady of virtue: to attack her through virtue itself. Announcing his desire for moral improvement, Valmont pays a poor peasant's taxes to forestall his eviction and then pretends to hide his magnanimity.

Even as he savors the irony of undermining Tourvel's virtue by the tactic of appealing to it, Valmont himself is ensnared in the inverse irony. Pretending to become more virtuous under Tourvel's influence, Valmont does indeed become a better person. Merteuil seems the first to realize that Valmont is truly falling in love with Tourvel. A close-up of Merteuil captures her understanding of Valmont staring, enraptured, at Tourvel during a musical performance. The sincerity of Valmont's interest disturbs and angers Merteuil. She is losing control of him and the situation. The subordinate plot involving the seduction of Cecile de Volanges now begins to take shape. Cecile's mother, Madame de Volanges (Swoozie Kurtz), has been tattling on Valmont to Tourvel, arming the woman of virtue against the rake's charms. Because despoiling her daughter will deeply wound Mme. de Volanges, the vindictive Valmont finds the job that much more attractive.

What makes *Dangerous Liaisons* philosophically interesting is that it raises important questions about our sexuality and provides the outline of an answer to them. The questions concern the bearing of sex on intimacy and personal identity, and extend to loss of control over our feelings. The opening and closing shots of Merteuil suggest that the tale is hers, but Valmont is the one transformed by the story's events. In lofty terms, it is he who is saved (in part from himself) and who gains genuine self-knowledge and, with it, knowledge of human nature. Valmont comes to appreciate that he has squandered his sexual energy playing self-destructive games instead of using it to deepen a loving relationship. The manipulative liaisons that Valmont habitually forms are dangerous because they alienate him from himself and obstruct his capacity for true intimacy. On the other hand, his loving liaison with Tourvel is dangerous because it jeopardizes Valmont's entire way of life once he sees it for the shallow thing it has been.

The film undermines the conventional-virtue understanding of sexual propriety. Valmont can find it worthwhile to seduce Cecile or Tourvel only because each has social value on the basis of her sexual purity. Cecile is valued as a prospective bride because she is a chaste virgin, and Tourvel is taken to be a good wife because she is sexually faithful to her spouse. The sexual morality that defines the status of each woman reflects patriarchal control of women and their reproduction. It is in the interest of the husband, prospective or current, to be assured that his wife's offspring are actually his. To guarantee rightful heirs to property, women in turn are treated as the property of men, and their sexuality is controlled by a conventional morality that reinforces patriarchal authority. The ethics of sexual exclusivity makes the value of sex instrumental—to male power and self-worth. Perhaps Tourvel succumbs to Valmont's wooing because he gives her genuine attention rather than treat her simply as so much chattel.

There next occurs a turning point during which Valmont demonstrates that a change has after all been wrought in his character by Tourvel. Valmont tells Tourvel that he is leaving his aunt's estate soon because he wants something deeper in their relationship. When he confronts Tourvel in her room, she confesses to loving him. Valmont kisses her. She cries, grabs his leg, and asks for his help.[9] Valmont carries her to the bed, undresses her, and then . . . he pauses. He starts to leave and tells Tourvel's maid that her lady is ill. Leaving Tourvel longing for him, Valmont has treated her with care and gentleness. Lest we think that he is totally reformed, he hisses with reptilian brio as he passes Mme. de Volanges in the passageway. Valmont the predator has some life left in him yet.

IV. THE MANY IRONIES OF TRUE LOVE

Consider what the change in Valmont signifies. The film prompts us to ask, why—why does Valmont lose his way, in fact, lose control of himself and his heart? First, we have the evidence that Valmont's feelings for Tourvel are genuine and strong. Shortly after declining the golden opportunity to seduce Tourvel, Valmont tells Merteuil, "I love her. I hate her. My life is a misery." That his relationship with Tourvel is uniquely fulfilling is confirmed later in the story. Valmont's rhapsodic description of making love to Tourvel and his dying words attest to the transformative nature of his affair with her. It is reasonable to infer that his sexual experience with Tourvel is central to the happiness that Valmont enjoys for the first time.

The film indicates that Valmont truly loves her, valuing her intrinsically and not simply as the means to a further end. Sex is for the first time in Valmont's storied erotic career embedded in a context of mutual affection. In naively giving Valmont complete access to her person as well as her body, Tourvel has unintentionally, tenderly lowered Valmont's own guard. Because someone he cares about has made herself genuinely vulnerable to him, Valmont stops playing a role. He is opened to gentler emotions that (he discovers) are more enjoyable than the sex act itself, especially when the primary purpose of sex had habitually been to dominate others. Perhaps Valmont is able to respond honestly to Tourvel's earnest self-exposure only because he has, in fact, begun to change. Only because he is becoming more virtuous—more caring, genuine, and open—is he able to respond with his whole self. Valmont is starting to become the very person he has feigned to be.

But might Valmont not have felt something similar when, in earlier days, he and Merteuil were lovers and, according to her, made each other happy? Here *Dangerous Liaisons* implies that their relationship, even at its best, could not permit the self-disclosure and vulnerability that Valmont now enjoys with Tourvel. Seasoned-game players that they are, Valmont and Merteuil could not truly trust one another and allow themselves the requisite vulnerability. Only an unpracticed heart, such as Tourvel's, can have the gentle strength to penetrate Valmont's calculating sophistication, opening him to genuine emotion and its expression.

The film suggests that sexual intimacy has the potential to complement and complete a communion engendered in nonsexual interaction. Sex that is whole-hearted and nonmanipulative is unscripted, leaving us open to the other person's desire and response. In so doing, moreover, we are open to discover new things about ourselves and, in the process, to define ourselves in unforeseen ways. At its best, our personality is woven through our sexuality; our sexual behavior is shaped by our desires, emotions, and thoughts, since they refer directly to the person with whom we are making love.

To illustrate how Valmont and Merteuil use their sexuality as an instrument to achieve such varied goals as revenge, one-upmanship, or yet other sexual favors, consider someone with a talent for poetry who writes advertising jingles. Her talent is not integrated with the rest of her personality; her poetic interests, deepest emotions, and most substantial thought are not being realized through her talent for writing. In the same way, Valmont and Merteuil's sexual behavior is disconnected, alienated from the most definitive aspects of their personalities. They treat their sexuality merely as a means to ends external to it.

When sex is a medium for sharing our selves to create communion with another, however, its function is internal to it. It is valued as part of what is intrinsically good—the personal relationship and the activities that develop that relationship. It is just because sexual interaction holds out this promise of enriching a genuinely caring relationship that Valmont is caught unawares by his involvement with Tourvel. Thinking he was in complete control, at any moment able to simulate the appropriate feelings or turn on his charm and wit, Valmont's sexual involvement with Tourvel calls forth an emotional response that overwhelms him and delights him in its forcefulness. Because Tourvel gives herself so fully and trustingly to him, Valmont is drawn out of his calculated playacting. What Valmont revels in is the uninhibited self-expression that he had never before experienced sexually.

The overall form of the film is irony. Manipulating less experienced individuals, Valmont and Merteuil end up wrecking their own lives. Then, too, Valmont tricks himself and becomes enamored of Tourvel even as he seduces her by his trickery. A more poignant irony underlies the fact that Tourvel is seduced because she thinks Valmont will kill himself unless she becomes his lover. Although his suicidal threat is a ruse on Valmont's part, Tourvel's sexual acquiescence does indeed lead Valmont to suicidal complicity in his fatal duel. Further irony lies in the fact that Valmont pursues Tourvel in the hopes of rekindling his liaison with Merteuil. Yet Valmont's revived affair with Merteuil never materializes, ironically enough, because of his love for Tourvel. The liaison with Tourvel, initially motivated simply to reprise Valmont's coupling with Merteuil, ends in Valmont discovering genuine love and his death.

V. VULNERABILITY VS. ARTIFICE

When Valmont arrives to tell Merteuil of his conquest of Tourvel, he is like a schoolboy, yelling "success" as he runs up the stairs to her boudoir. He has lost his usual self-awareness, so much so that he reveals too much to Merteuil, saying that his experience with Tourvel "had a kind of charm that I don't think I have experienced before." Unless he is intentionally trying to provoke Merteuil, Valmont fails to notice that her face is closing in on itself. Valmont gushes on, "Once she'd surrendered, she behaved with perfect candor." Here he touches on the disclosure of personality—desires, emotions, and thoughts—so essential to intimacy. The experience, moreover, is characterized by mutuality, as Valmont reveals his persona as well. Valmont describes the experience as "total mutual delirium" that, he adds, "for the first time ever with me outlasted the physical [sexual] pleasure itself." For the delight to outlast the physical pleasure, it must be fueled by more than just bodily sensations. Because Tourvel was astonishing, Valmont continues, "I ended by falling on my knees and pledging her eternal love."

Merteuil's face continues to fall and her head sinks lower and lower. Valmont says that for several hours, he actually meant his pledge. Crestfallen, Merteuil offers only a subdued, "I see." Valmont seems oblivious of the impact he is having on the woman whose affection and sexual attention he wishes to renew. The obliviousness is itself, of course, incriminating. Consequently, Merteuil proceeds to deny Valmont his sexual reward for seducing Tourvel, reminding him that he must still produce the agreed -upon letter from the lady to confirm his success. Letters are wed to sex in the story since they are often about sexual relations, used to achieve sexual intimacy, or to serve sexual betrayal or incrimination. Although the letter that Merteuil demands will truthfully attest to intimacy with Valmont on the part of Tourvel, its use will be a betrayal of her trust and love on the part of Valmont.

Merteuil then suggests that she and Valmont may have to forget the whole deal because she feels taken for granted, especially since Tourvel is so "astonishing!" Valmont protests that Merteuil misunderstands him and that they have always been frank with one another. In other words, he assumed that Merteuil would not be jealous, especially since Valmont is further betraying Tourvel with his painstaking revelations to Merteuil. Here, however, Valmont underestimates himself and the true depths of feeling of which he is capable and that Merteuil has perceived.

There then occurs the most open and honest exchange between the erstwhile confederates. After telling Valmont that he is indeed in love with Tourvel, Merteuil asks, "Have you forgotten what it is like to make a woman happy? And to be made happy yourself?" Almost musing aloud, Merteuil says that she thinks they once loved each other, "And you made me very happy." Valmont responds, "I want to come home," by resuming their suspended love affair. He kisses her neck and her eyes close in a near swoon. Valmont breaks the spell he has just delicately cast, however, conceding that he is infatuated with Tourvel. He then utters the fateful, damning words, saying that although the infatuation will not last, "It is beyond my control." Indeed, we have just seen how out of control Valmont is in expounding on the wonders of making love to Tourvel.

At this, Merteuil's dreamy smile sags into an angry frown and her eyes go cold. She removes herself to another room, symbolically, behind an imposing door paneled with mirrors. The prominent positioning of the bank of mirrors in this scene reminds us that both Merteuil and Valmont conceal themselves behind attractive appearances, appearances created by means of and vouchsafed by their images in mirrors (even as they are male-female images of each other).[10] The auxiliary motif of mirrors will be examined shortly. Merteueil is obviously shaken as she steadies herself against a wall to regain her composure before presenting a sunny face to one of her other lovers. Valmont will be made to pay for daring to love another woman in a way denied Merteuil herself.[11]

As we soon learn, "beyond my control" will become the catch phrase for Merteuil. She will insist that Valmont use it to lacerate Tourvel when he ends their relationship. The phrase underscores the loss of control in love, as we cannot keep from thinking about our beloved and wanting to be with her. Then, too, in the transports of sexual abandonment, we do indeed lose control. More significantly, we allow the beloved control over us, even enjoy it because we trust her. Valmont is experiencing such loss of control for the first time, and finding it pleasant because it occurs within the protection of a loving embrace and a caring gaze.[12]

The loss of control over our response can be delicious because it is a concomitant of unguardedness. Valmont, for example, need spend no energy concealing his true feelings, thoughts, or desires. Neither dissembling nor simulating something he is not, Valmont is completely himself and at ease because complete. His body and mind are in harmony and all aspects of his personality are united through making love to Tourvel.

Letting down his guard and entrusting himself to the personality of another is new and exhilarating for Valmont. He and Merteuil have always been in control of others because they are in control of themselves. As seducers, control is their stock in trade, and this is why their own relationship must ever be uneasy, even at its best. How can two people so practiced in the techniques of artifice and control, and who know this about each other, ever genuinely cede power to the other person? Only a naif, such as Tourvel—trusting and loving, and trusting in her love—is capable of disarming the likes of Valmont.

Since Valmont's effusions over his romance with Tourvel seem to be spontaneous expressions of his true feelings, we might consider here how the film highlights artifice and the artificial throughout the story. Our first exposure to the protagonists is of Merteuil, and then Valmont, being powdered, primped, and put together by their respective retinues of servants. They inspect their images in mirrors and are satisfied that they have been properly costumed for the social and sexual worlds in which they deftly maneuver. The language that Merteuil and Valmont (in particular) use is filled with irony and figures of speech, and riddled with a cleverness crafted to amuse themselves. In short, their speech and manner match the finery with which they adorn themselves.[13]

As noted, mirrors form a supporting motif, one that elaborates the theme of artifice and artfulness. Mirrors help Merteuil and Valmont prepare for their appearances on the Parisian stages: public (opera), semi-public (social gatherings), and private (drawing rooms). Mirrors signify the realm of appearances, confected by painstaking design for self-centered purpose. Indeed, the opening shot of the film is taken over Merteuil's shoulder, her face seen as she sees it—reflected in a mirror. Mirrors also indicate deceit, as when Merteuil stealthily disappears yet a second time behind the door paned with mirrors on her way to a secreted lover after again dismissing Valmont and his amorous interests.

In contrast is the more direct way Valmont can comport himself with Tourvel. His beloved reflects him more truly than mirrors do. Tourvel's eyes supplant the mirrors he and Merteuil have depended upon to create the appropriate appearance. When we are with our beloved, concern for appearance would be to please and delight our partner, not control her. Replacing mirrors with Tourvel's loving gaze reinforces Valmont's loss of control with her, for he no longer needs to make himself over for the purpose of manipulation. Valmont can see himself as Tourvel perceives him—as the compassionate, tender man who is reforming himself for Tourvel by means of her love.

The film explicitly epitomizes artificiality in Merteuil's very being. When Valmont asks her how she "invented" herself, Merteuil replies that she listened and observed what people were trying to hide, "I practiced detachment . . . I became a virtuoso of deceit." Such detachment and deceit, of course, lie at the heart of what is so corrosive in the sexual behavior of Merteuil and Valmont. Valmont is ecstatic when sex with Tourvel is unencumbered by the self-conscious artifice demanded by detachment and deceit. For Merteuil, morality itself is studied in order to "learn how to appear." Like mirrors, morality is useful to her only for crafting an appealing image.[14] Merteuil has purposefully created her persona, making herself into an artificial creature, and we wonder whether she could even know now what she truly feels, desires, or values.

VI. HEARTBREAK AND DEATH

As a foreshadowing of Valmont breaking off his affair with Tourvel, we watch him toy with her. Valmont intentionally lets Tourvel see him with a courtesan in his rooms, giving the courtesan money only to tell Tourvel that the money is for the woman's charitable works! To Tourvel's objection that he is philandering, Valmont astutely points out that he knew Tourvel was coming up since she was, after all, announced. Valmont has to grin when he says that the courtesan does a great deal of charity work and then tells Tourvel that she has even done some secretarial work for him. The latter is a joke we share with him as we earlier saw Valmont use the woman's derriere as a desk on which to write to Tourvel herself! Tourvel succumbs to her need to have faith in Valmont, saying to him, "I want to believe you." When she holds his head against her, we see a genuine melting in Valmont. He replies that he does have to apologize for being insensitive (for allowing Tourvel to see the other lover) and closes his eyes in what appears to be sincere remorse.

Next, Valmont tells Cecile's music teacher and suitor, Chevalier Danceny (Keanu Reeves), that in his absence he (Valmont) has had to do more improvising than an Italian actor. Valmont is giving Danceny to believe that he must improvise in order to keep the love affair between Danceny and Cecile alive and hidden. We know, however, that Valmont is ironically alluding to his own seduction of Cecile and their subsequent coupling. Here again, we have a fine example of Valmont's wit employed to entertain himself (and Merteuil), but in so doing, the film encourages our affection for him because he entertains us as well. Surely we laugh with him when Valmont later describes Cecile's miscarriage as more a "refurbishment" than an illness. Combined with his unvarnished enthusiasm for Tourvel, Valmont's humor endears him to the audience.[15] This is important because it enables us to feel sorry for him when he foolishly cuts short his newfound happiness.

Danceny himself serves a mediating role in the story. He mediates Valmont's relationship with all three of his lovers: Cecile, Merteuil, and, finally, even Tourvel. Since Danceny loves Cecile, he challenges Valmont to a fatal duel upon learning that Valmont has besmirched his beloved. Yet, Danceny has already allowed himself to be seduced by Merteuil, ostensibly the object of Valmont's affections. Last, Danceny delivers Valmont's dying message to Tourvel as she lies on her own deathbed. In yet another of the film's ironies, then, the butt of Valmont's mockery plays a vital part in his death and its vindication, while inconspicuously providing the film with a reinforcing narrative thread, woven through the affairs of the more central characters.

The story reaches its climax with a bitter confrontation between Valmont and Merteuil, followed by Valmont's complicit mortal wounding. The seeds of the confrontation are sown by Merteuil reasserting control over Valmont. After a thinly veiled reference to his description of his infatuation with Tourvel as beyond his control, Merteuil insists that Valmont break with Tourvel if he wishes to regain Merteuil's sexual favors. Since Valmont has already shown Merteuil the letter from Tourvel to him attesting to his compromise of her, Merteuil is clearly adding another condition to their amorous agreement. Valmont is momentarily taken aback, pausing and blinking as Merteuil's demand fully registers.

In the following scene, Valmont enters Tourvel's room, drops to his knees, and, pressing his head to her midriff, calls her his angel. He proceeds to tell her that he's bored; after all, their affair has been going on for four months. Valmont tells Tourvel that his boredom is "beyond my control." He says it angrily, perhaps angry at giving up control to Merteuil. We are left to wonder why he accedes to Merteuil's demand—to collect his sexual reward from her, or because his old habits of seducing and abandoning have reclaimed their dominion? He utters the telling phrase while looking in a mirror, as if to convince himself. Yet Valmont's mirror-looking ironically suggests his lack of self-reflection and, with it, lack of appreciation for what his relationship with Tourvel actually means to him.

Valmont is returning to his reliance on artifice and the mirrors that evidence it. In looking at himself in the mirror, Valmont is turning his back on the image of himself reflected in his lover's gaze. He is being dishonest with Tourvel and himself. His rejection of Tourvel and what he is with her is accompanied by a return to Valmont's former self: manipulative and artificial, relying on the appearance mirrors can confirm instead of the sense of himself elicited in loving relationship with Tourvel. Yet Valmont cannot go back to his old ways easily. His breakup with Tourvel is heavy-handed but ragged.

When he next says "beyond my control," responding to Tourvel's perplexed protestations, Valmont falters. The telltale phrase comes out jerkily, breathily. He says it again, with a stammer. Valmont's loss of his customary fluidity in speech suggests that he lacks conviction, that he does not wish to end his affair with Tourvel because what is truly beyond his control is his feeling for her, including his newly awakened tenderness. As if to steel himself to the faithless task, one that betrays his genuine love as well as Tourvel's trust, Valmont tells her that a woman he adores insists that he give Tourvel up. Tourvel shrieks, "Liar! Liar!" pleading with him to stop saying that his loss of interest is beyond his control (he utters the phrase no fewer than nine times!). Leaving her room, Valmont himself seems shaken and breathless, hardly the aftermath we should expect of the callous Casanova that Valmont has prided himself on playing.

When Valmont straightway informs Merteuil that he has ended his affair with Tourvel, Merteuil proposes the real reason for Valmont's termination of the affair—that he was ashamed of loving Tourvel and being laughed at. She concludes by observing that vanity and happiness are incompatible—this would be still another area in which love involves loss of control. When we love, we give up control over what other people think of us or our beloved. The happiness that comes from loss of power over one's heart is incompatible with worrying whether the world finds us foolish.

A terrible row ensues, one that dooms them both. Merteuil says that she will not be pushed around by Valmont, who demands that Merteuil reciprocate by breaking off her affair with Danceny. Valmont slaps her, and the struggle for control is joined. Valmont tells Merteuil that Danceny is not coming that evening because he will be with Cecile. Given the choice between Merteuil and his beloved Cecile, Danceny did not hesitate to choose the younger woman. Merteuil glowers and Valmont futilely and foolishly demands his sexual payment.

When Merteuil declares that she is better "at this" (sociosexual combat), Valmont replies, "It is always the best swimmers who drown." We are invited to speculate that perhaps the best swimmers swim until they are out of their depth, or they underestimate the strength of the current, even as Valmont has underestimated the pull that Tourvel has exerted over him. The scene ends with the pair agreeing to a war, presumably one involving the pawns in their game: Tourvel, Cecile, and Danceny.

The nature of the warfare is confirmed in the voice-over of Merteuil's letter to Danceny informing him that Valmont has seduced Cecile. This precipitates the duel between Danceny and Valmont, which we watch taking place in fits and starts, lurches and lunges, against a pristine, snow-covered background. Valmont soon has Danceny down, at sword's point, but he pauses, recollecting a moment of lovemaking with Tourvel. *Dangerous Liaisons* uses this recollection to initiate a series of fugue-like cuts between scenes of the duel and shots of Tourvel's ultimate decline in a convent bed.

Strolling about, Valmont again thinks of passionate moments with Tourvel until he and Danceny close, separate, and we revisit Tourvel, who is being bled by knife -cutting—a pointed parallel to the largely ineffectual blades of the duel. Then the swordplay resumes, only to cease as the two men seem exhausted. Valmont rests by a wall. He reaches a decision as the swelling violin music suggests Tourvel. Valmont drops his sword, runs at Danceny, and impales himself on the younger man's blade. Advising Danceny to be careful of Merteuil, the fatally wounded Valmont gives Danceny her letters, which Danceny may choose to circulate. Valmont asks the young man to tell Tourvel that he cannot explain why he broke with her and that "since then, my life has been worth nothing." He continues, saying that "her love was the only real happiness that I have ever known." We then get a long shot of the tableau in the snow of Danceny, Valmont, his blood, and his servant.

The film concludes by juxtaposing the reactions of Tourvel and Merteuil to news of Valmont's death, followed by the destruction of Merteuil's social existence. Learning of Valmont's death from Danceny, Tourvel gives stage directions, "Enough. Draw the curtains," and turns onto her back to die. We next hear a piercing scream before seeing Merteuil burst into her dressing room, grief-stricken at word of Valmont's end. She sweeps the makeup and paraphernalia of her cosmetic art from the table, scattering and smashing the tools of her trade, and then yells her servants out of the room.

We directly discover that Merteuil's attempt to continue her high-flown social life has been posthumously sabotaged by Valmont. For Danceny has indeed circulated Merteuil's self-incriminating letters, to devastating effect. When Merteuil enters her box at the opera, the music stops, all eyes turn to her; she looks around and freezes. A cascade of "boos" descends on her; she turns, staggers, and leaves. Back in her dressing room, a shot is held of her sitting immobile, almost lifeless. Unlike in the film's opening shot, we now see her face head on, as it is, not reflected in a mirror. With her heavy makeup, Merteuil looks like a mime. Absently, she wipes at the thick greasepaint, powder and lipstick, and a single tear runs down her cheek.

VII. THE ENDURING POWER OF THE WRITTEN WORD

The storyline is straightforward enough. A pair of devious members of the nobility are undone by their own scheming and need for control. Their conspiracy turns to competition when Valmont's heart betrays him and he discovers the joys of true love. Along the way, Valmont and Merteuil take their revenge on the likes of Cecile's mother (Mme. de Volange) and fiancé, only to have Cecile's beloved Danceny come between them—first as Merteuil's young lover and Valmont's challenger on the field of honor, and later, as the agent of Merteuil's social downfall. If the film is in many ways an old-fashioned morality tale, it is nonetheless a thoughtful one.

Among the many ways the film provokes thought is by offering the written world of letters as a literary counterpoint to the sexual world of social intrigue. We see that letters are not only the means of communicating over distance and time, but that they are also a major source of information, to be perused and used for advantage. As with contemporary telephone and e-mail, letters afford outsiders entrance to what individuals believe to be private communication. In the end, letters can make public these private communications.

By paralleling the give and take of letters, honest and manipulative, with the exchanges of sexual intimacies, sincere and seductive, the film gets us to think about letters and sexuality together. Both are physical embodiments of our inner natures. We express ourselves, whether truly or artificially, by the tangible means of words on a page and bodies in sexual connection. By their means we give ourselves over to other people and thereby take risks, often unawares.

Valmont, for one, does not realize that in playing his sexual games he is nevertheless presenting his self to another individual, subjecting himself to another's desires and touch, feelings and thought. Consequently, he is unprepared for the impact of Tourvel's bodily expression on his personality, and not simply on his body. Finally, personality and body are not as easily kept apart as Valmont and Merteuil have assumed. Just as the predatory pair have made their bodies do their mind's bidding, so too has Valmont's body had power over his psyche.

The same is true of letter writing. Whether or not we are aware of it, giving linguistic shape to our thoughts and feelings, even for the purpose of dissembling or deceiving, delivers a portion of who we are into the control of other people. This is most obvious in the case of the public circulation of Merteuil's letters by Danceny. It is also true, however, of Valmont when he mockingly and cleverly writes to Tourvel in order to triumph over her. For things said solely for effect have a way of reverberating within us and altering what we truly think, feel, and want.

Letters and sex are also more explicitly interwoven throughout the film, reciprocally affecting each other. First, letters are written, read, and purloined for sexual purposes. For example, Valmont blackmails Tourvel's maidservant to bring him all of the lady's letters in order to know her mind as well as to learn who is warning her against him. It is also by means of letters that Valmont arranges with a priest to reconnect with Tourvel, and then to seduce her, after their separation. Valmont writes to Tourvel to woo her. For her part, Merteuil tells Cecile that she can write to Danceny provided she shows both sides of the correspondence to Merteuil. Merteuil wishes to monitor their affair to facilitate the deflowering of Cecile—if not by Valmont, then by Danceny.

Second, the letters of Valmont and Merteuil describe and betray their sexual affairs. Most obviously, Valmont gives Merteuil the letter of love Tourvel writes to him and Merteuil betrays Valmont by writing Danceny about Valmont's affair with Cecile. *Dangerous Liaisons* offers many other instances of the sexual nature or use of letters, however. Valmont, for example, dictates Cecile's letter to Danceny while the pair lounges naked together, and he uses the courtesan's bare rear end as a desk on which to write to Tourvel. Here the deception is not merely in the content of the letters, but in the circumstances in which they are written!

The film emphasizes letters as physical objects: to be saved and shared, poached and revealed. Merteuil repeatedly reminds Valmont of the written evidence he must produce of his seduction of Tourvel, saying explicitly, "I need it in writing." Then, too, a dying Valmont gives Danceny Merteuil's letters as evidence of her treachery and to destroy her social standing. Conversely, the film employs letters to cinematic effect, to punctuate what we see on screen with a voice-over of the relevant missives being written and read. The film thereby reminds us that the effect of letters continues long after they have been read.

Letters help bind together the social, emotional, and sexual aspects of the characters' lives. They course through the film like a river of words whose currents sometimes speed the characters in desirable directions but often set them adrift or swamp them altogether. As with the language of sex, the linguistic turns of the letters and the letters as artifacts carry more weight than the characters seem to realize.

The film is itself framed by letters. As the opening credits conclude, we see a pair of braceleted hands (apparently Merteuil's) open an envelope to reveal the title of the film. Implicit in the closing shot of a shattered Merteuil listlessly removing her makeup are her conniving letters to Valmont, which Danceny has made public. We are given to surmise that all the social and sexual comings and goings that take place in the story are governed by the movement of mail. Even as Merteuil's arch and artful letters come back to haunt her, so do Valmont's love letters to Tourvel prove more truthful than he realized when he wrote them.

NOTES

1. The last two decades have seen academic philosophical discussion turn more seriously to questions of virtue and character, returning to the major ethical interest of the ancient Greeks and Stoics.

2. Indeed, much of the moral criticism of prostitution is based on the harm prostitutes do to themselves or to the lack of self-respect they show themselves. For non-sexual examples of ethical concerns that revolve about self-harm, think of the debates about recreational drug use and gambling.

3. Robert Solomon, *About Love*, 212.

4. C.S. Lewis, *The Four Loves*, 136.

5. Hedonism is the theory of value that defines pleasure as the only intrinsically good thing and pain as the only intrinsically bad thing. Egoism is the theory of moral obligation that claims that we ought to promote our own good, any other obligations are derived from duties to ourselves. When combined, the two positions yield the view that each person is obliged simply to pursue his own pleasure.

6. In thematizing letters, the film bears the stamp of its origins in the eighteenth-century epistolary novel *Les Liaisons Dangereuses*, by Choderlos de Laclos.

7. Here the film may be making veiled self-reference. As with letters, movies leave a more or less permanent record of human thought, emotion and desire.

8. We can then take the general moral claims about sexuality, personal integration, and intimacy and see whether they are true in the real world. If they are true or at least cogent, then the philosophical interpretation of *Dangerous Liaisons*, and film in general, can lead us to a more complete understanding of human nature as it actually is and not simply as it is presented in movies. The question of how film can present philosophical views about real life obviously requires more attention than space here permits. I address it more fully in *Visions of Virtue in Popular Film* and Noël Carroll argues persuasively that fictional stories in literature and film can provide analogs to

philosophical thought-experiments ("The Wheel of Virtue: Art, Literature, and Moral Knowledge").

9. Tourvel's imploring echoes Valmont's earlier feigned plea for her help in becoming virtuous, saying, "Tell me how to behave."

10. Merteuil leans against a wall just as Valmont braces himself with a wall after breaking off with Tourvel and then, again, just before running on the sword of Danceny at the duel's end—with images of Tourvel in his head.

11. Merteuil presently writes Valmont that when she returns from her sojourn the pair will have one last night together. They will regret that it's to be their last, "But then we shall remember that regret is an essential component of happiness." Merteuil once again reminds Valmont that he must still produce the evidentiary letter from Tourvel.

12. The healthy form of relinquishing control to another should be distinguished from the sort that involves the desire for danger. In the latter case, the individual delights in risking harm (of various stripes) by delivering himself into the hands of an uncertain partner.

13. Here *Dangerous Liaisons* itself, with its sonorous operatic score and sumptuous sets, joins with its protagonists in lavishing attention on appearances.

14. Just as Merteuil regards morality simply as a matter of appearance and social status, so do conventional morals reflect and reinforce the social order in their sexual strictures. Mertueil's studied use of moral norms to gain social acceptance echoes the sexual morality that values a woman's chastity and fidelity in order that she be acceptable to men with social standing and power.

15. Viewers may be taken aback at first by the casting of John Malkovich in the role of Valmont, the irresistible rake, as Malkovich is not especially good-looking. Yet, because he is nonetheless convincing in the role, we learn that matinee-idol looks are not necessary and that charm, wit and attentiveness—perhaps with an admixture of riskiness—are more important to the art of seduction.

JUSTICE, MERCY, AND FRIENDSHIP IN *THE THIRD MAN*

JULIA DRIVER

Now the city's divided into four zones, you know, American, British,
Russian and the French. But the centre of the city, that's international,
policed by an international patrol, one member of each of the four powers.
Wonderful. You can imagine what a chance they had, all of them strangers
to the place and no two of them speaking the same language.

—*The Third Man*, from the opening narration (American release version)[1]

THE THIRD MAN OPENS WITH an American man arriving in Vienna shortly after the end of WWII. He is a writer of formulaic western novels—the sort with heroes, albeit imperfect and often reluctant, who stand up for a code of values in the rough, harsh wilderness. He needs money. He has come at the behest of his friend, who would like to offer him a job writing for a charity. Since this man is out of work, he accepts the invitation, only to find on arrival that his friend has died in a strange hit-and-run accident. The American is Holly Martins, and his friend is Harry Lime. It is their relationship that underlies the plot of the film *The Third Man*. They are friends—at least, each considers himself the friend of the other. In the years since the war began, however, circumstances have changed considerably. Those changes, and Holly's growing recognition of them throughout the course of the film, test the friendship.

This friendship provides one of the central themes of the film. The audience sees the clash of ethical norms, such as justice and loyalty, Holly confronts in evaluating his friendship with Harry. One of the central virtues of friendship is loyalty. Loyalty is a virtue that is partial as opposed to impartial, in its focus. Friends expect loyalty from one another, and loyalty is not something one expects as due from strangers or mere acquaintances. Justice, on the other hand, is impartial. It would be unjust to treat a person differently in some important respect, just because he was not one's friend. Judges, for example, are called upon to recuse themselves from cases involving friends because of the concern that they cannot be truly impartial in such case. And justice demands impartiality. Cases of conflict can arise, then, especially when one has a friend who is doing something unjust, that ought to be stopped. It is exactly this sort of conflict Holly struggles with in the course of *The Third Man*. My claim is that Holly reaches a kind of balance. One natural viewing of the film is that he is rejecting friendship with Harry. I don't believe that is fully true. In the end he does not altogether abandon his friendship with Harry Lime. One of my claims in this paper is that friendship can survive vice, a claim that would be denied by an Aristotelian. Further, in the case of Holly Martins and Harry Lime, the lingering friendship explains exactly how the film ends.

The Third Man also represents—along with *Casablanca*, in my opinion—a kind of movie that seemed particularly inspired by the events of WWII and the war's nihilistic underpinnings. Many wanted to offer a response to the moral nihilism they saw represented by the Nazis and represented by the failure to consider human beings as deserving of moral respect. Of course, the voice of nihilism in *The Third Man* is Harry Lime, who has no political allegiance to the Nazi party. Still, he is the one who doesn't appreciate the value of human life. In the famous Prater Ferris wheel speech, when he is trying to explain his actions to Holly Martins, he notes, looking down on the people in the amusement park:

> Look down there . . . . would you feel pity if one of those dots stopped moving forever? . . . If I offered you £20,000 for every dot that stopped—would you, really, old man, tell me to keep my money?

It may be, however, that to the extent that Harry represents any moral perspective at all, it isn't so much a nihilist perspective as a kind of moral elitism, rejecting conventional morality. In the same speech he seems to argue that his ruthlessness is important because it is only through strife and conflict that human greatness is achieved:

> In Italy, for thirty years under the Borgias, they had warfare terror, murder, bloodshed, but they produced Michelangelo, Leonardo Da Vinci, and the Renaissance . . . In Switzerland, they had brotherly love. They had 500 years of democracy and peace, and what did that produce? . . . . The cuckoo clock. So long, Holly.

One is expected to hate Harry Lime, while at the same time admiring his charm and his cunning. At the end of the day, however, it is, in my opinion, the nihilistic interpretation of what Harry is about that wins. He is not striving for human greatness. He is striving for more money.

I. BACKGROUND

Holly Martins arrives in Vienna naïve. He is the not-so-bright American who, with a sense of true justice and entitlement, proceeds to investigate on his own his friend's rather mysterious and sudden death. He is dismissive, at least initially, of the British authorities in the city who have control of the Lime investigation. He believes the officer in charge, Major Calloway, does not take the odd circumstances of Harry's death seriously enough. He aims to show Calloway that there's more to

Harry's death than the authorities are accepting. Holly Martins, however, is operating in a city that doesn't resemble anything he could be used to.

Vienna after the war is a devastated city. Neighborhoods contain the rubble of
bombed, destroyed buildings. The infrastructure has been gutted by the war—
there is nothing like normal commerce. As the opening narration indicates, it is
also a mess in terms of legal administration. The city is controlled by four powers,
and authority is divided into four sections. The authorities in each of those sections were working to sort things out in the city to their advantage, and the most
feared of those authorities were the Russians. The screenplay for the film was
written by Graham Greene, who fully exploited this in the film's plot. Newspaper
reports at the time *The Third Man* was being planned and written reported Russian
kidnappings of "displaced persons" in Vienna. Interestingly, however, Carol Reed,
the director of the film, resisted the American producer's instructions to portray
the Russians more unfavorably.[2]

For the residents of Vienna, what resulted from the division of authority was a
chaotic mess of regulations that served to facilitate a sizable black market in goods
and forged papers. At first, Holly believes Major Calloway has some kind of ven-
detta against Harry for simply participating in the black market, which would
make him no different from almost anyone else in the city. Calloway, however, is
not after Harry for trading cigarettes for eggs.

Since the city was divided into sectors, each under the control of a different
authority, black market criminals made use of a mode of crossing sectors that
helped keep them hidden. Criminals frequently used the sewers in Vienna, since
they allowed fairly free travel between sectors. They allowed people to bypass the
maze of checkpoints above ground. This too, would figure into Greene's script.[3]

The seeming arbitrary division of authority in a city that had been severely
damaged during the war probably hampered attempts on the part of the residents
of Vienna to rebuild the community. In *Humanity*, Jonathan Glover has written of
how a sense of community can help underwrite our sense of humanity to fellow
humans. One of the devastating effects of World War II, and the years immediately preceding the war in Europe, was that in many communities the feeling of
shared values and shared commitments was lost. The Nazi contribution to this is
well known. Glover discusses how in Vienna the Nazi's engaged in campaigns of
humiliation, and much worse, against the Jewish residents—forcing them to scrub
sidewalks, and to clean latrines with sacred artifacts.[4] And these acts were a pre-
lude to other horrific atrocities.

Another Viennese case that Glover mentions is that of a Jewish man who had
lost a leg as a result of a World War I wound. He had fought beside his coun-
trymen in that conflict and been severely wounded in the process. In Nazi-
controlled Vienna, as elsewhere, Jews were forced to wear identifying yellow
stars. When this man fell down on the sidewalk and could not get up, no one
stopped to help him. Glover writes, "For three hours he asked passers-by to help
him, but they all left him there. He broke his wrist when he finally managed to

raise himself."[5] As Glover notes, the Nazis often relied on a process of "distancing" to blunt natural human reactions of sympathy and concern for others. "Distancing" is visible in Lime's Ferris wheel speech. He is standing up over all the little unrecognizable people, the "dots" that simply stand for a certain number of pounds. They are like figures on a balance sheet, to be erased, and then filled in with something else.

These kinds of cases illustrate how, in Vienna, as elsewhere in Nazi-controlled Europe, human beings had been treated as less than human. Populations had been made complicit in this rejection of humanity. This is where Holly Martins finds himself at the film's opening. This is the precarious moral space occupied by the four powers and their competing claims to authority. It is also the space in which Harry Lime had made a home.

II. THE FILM

At the outset in the film Martins is presented with a mystery—Harry Lime has been killed, it seems, in a hit and run accident just as the authorities—and particularly, a certain British Major Calloway—were displaying a keen interest in his activities. The authorities seem unaware of the significance of conflicting evidence in the case—particularly the report of a "third man" at the scene of the accident, someone who was left out of most of the eye witness testimony. This fuels Holly's pursuit of justice for his friend Harry.

Major Calloway makes an effort, ultimately successful, to expose Harry Lime's moral failures to Martins. He explains how Lime was betrayed by his accomplice in the theft of penicillin, a man named Joseph Harbin, who has very inconveniently disappeared. Calloway is convincing, so convincing that Holly loses heart in his pursuit of the truth about Harry. He goes to Harry's former girlfriend, Anna, and tells her about Harry, but Anna seems barely moved. Or, barely moved in the right direction:

HOLLY: Seventy pounds a tube. He wanted me to write for his great medical charity . . . . Perhaps I could have raised the price to eighty pounds for him.

ANNA: Oh please, for heaven's sakes, stop making him in your image. Harry was real. He wasn't just your friend and my lover; he was Harry.

HOLLY: Well, don't preach wisdom to me. You talk about him as if he had occasional bad manners. Oh, I don't know, I'm just a hack writer who drinks too much and falls in love with girls—you.

ANNA: Me?

HOLLY: Don't be such a fool, of course.

ANNA: If you'd rung me up and asked me were you fair or dark or had a moustache, I wouldn't have known.

HOLLY: I am leaving Vienna. I don't care whether Harry was murdered by Kurtz or Popescu or the third man. Whoever killed him, there was some sort of justice. Maybe I would have killed him myself.

ANNA: A person doesn't change because you find out more.

This segment of dialogue is extremely important to understanding the shift in Holly's views about Harry Lime. Numerous reviews of the film have noted the connections between the typical Western plot and this film. References to Holly's Westerns populate the film. Here, Calloway makes it explicit:

CALLOWAY: I told you to go away, Martins. This isn't Santa Fe. I'm not a sheriff, and you aren't a cowboy. You've been blundering around with the worst bunch of racketeers in Vienna, your precious Harry's friends, and now you're wanted for murder.

MARTINS: Put down drunk and disorderly too.

CALLOWAY: I have.

Like the Western hero, Martins feels he needs to set things right, at least a little. When he finds out about Harry's crimes, he's ready to leave and to leave Harry's possible murderer alone. He even acknowledges a kind of rough justice in what has happened to Harry—the kind of rough justice one sees in a culture lacking stable authority. Vienna is then like the lawless wilderness; Holly, the hero who must reluctantly take matters into his own hands; Harry, the villain; Anna, the woman who has been left bereft by the villain's perfidy; and so on. Major Calloway views Holly as an American caricature, prone to idealizing Wild West values. One of the film's many ironies is that Calloway needs to rely on Holly's independent sense of justice to finally snare Lime.

In the above segment of dialogue between Holly and Anna, Holly brings in the theme of *rough* justice. A distinction can be made between justice proper and "rough" justice. When a person has been accused by the authorities of a crime, that person will go through a process—like a trial—in order that guilt or innocence be determined, and then also that a fair sentence be imposed if the person is found guilty. The outcomes of the process—that is, the finding of guilt or innocence, and the sentencing—are independent of the process itself. Thus, we can make a distinction between procedural justice and outcome justice. Procedural justice occurs when the correct, legitimate procedures have been followed in determining guilt and/or sentencing. Outcome justice occurs when the correct finding and/or the correct sentence have been imposed. Rough justice occurs when the just process or procedure is bypassed, and a finding and sentence are imposed independently of the legitimate procedure. Rough justice can be compatible with outcome justice, but not with procedural justice.[6] In iconic western novels—such as *The Quick and the Dead*—when somebody wrongs you, and there's no effective authority to appeal to—rough justice is what's left.[7]

Maybe, Holly begins to think, death was what Harry really deserved. Those watching this scene in the film for the second time will appreciate its prescience. Holly will kill Harry. When Holly does kill Harry, however, it does *not* conform to the rough justice model. He will not kill Harry because he thinks Harry deserves to die. This view of their relationship seems to run counter to another natural viewing of the film, one discussed by Noël Carroll.[8] Carroll maintains that Holly kills Harry Lime because their friendship has been utterly dissolved by Holly's knowledge of what Lime has done. Carroll sees the representation of the friendship as Graham Greene's counterexample to the E. M. Forster claim that "When loyalty to a friend conflicts with loyalty to a cause, one ought to choose in favor of the friend."[9] I agree, in a limited way, with Carroll's claim that Holly violates Forster's maxim. When Holly informs Calloway of Harry's faked death, and when he agrees to set Harry up at the end of the film, in *those* instances he chooses loyalty to his duty as a human being. This is not the choice he is making when he shoots Harry, however. Carroll is mistaken in his more expansive interpretation of Holly's betrayal. Harry is trapped. Harry is doomed whether Holly shoots him or not. There was certainly betrayal, but, at the very end of the film, *how* the betrayal was fully realized was influenced by norms of friendship. We will explore this further, later in the essay.

After leaving Anna, Holly finally finds Harry—or, rather, Harry finds him. Harry cannot resist spying on Anna and Holly. One of the most brilliant scenes in the film is his being discovered, lurking in a doorway, by Anna's cat and, subsequently, by Holly himself. At that point Holly knows the truth about Harry and about the supposed accident. It was a fake, and Harry himself is the third man. Holly informs Calloway that Harry is still alive. He also tries to meet with Harry— and they do meet, at the amusement park where Harry delivers the infamous cuckoo-clock speech. This is a major climactic scene in the film.

Calloway's exposure of Harry's true character to Holly forces Holly to re-examine his loyalty to Harry. Holly has to weigh the value he places, personally, on his friendship against the harm Harry has done and might continue to do. He also has to weigh how a betrayal of Harry to Calloway could help to balance the moral books a little bit by neutralizing Harry's own betrayal of Anna. Holly's decision against Harry ultimately leads to another climactic scene—the scene in which Harry flees the authorities through the sewers of Vienna, only to be shot, and die, in them.

No documentary on *The Third Man* would be complete without these scenes. One reason is that these scenes focus on the pivotal relationship—friendship— within the movie, and they raise issues surrounding the moral norms one associates with friendship. Harry Lime is Holly Martins' friend, an old friend from school, and someone Holly has looked up to as a kind of charming facilitator. The shock to Martins comes when the charm is seen not as a sign of Harry's virtue anymore. Either Harry has changed, or, more likely, transplanted to an entirely different context, his amorality has been amplified. His smooth, confident disregard for the "dots" below is devastating, and one can see in Holly's face during the scene atop the Ferris wheel, a transformation in his view of Harry.

Holly's reached a point at which he needs to make a practical decision about what to do. What are the limits of friendship? Holly resists evidence of Harry's evil because he is Harry's friend. When he first agrees to help Calloway, it seems he does so primarily out of affection and pity for Harry's former girlfriend, Anna. He agrees to exchange his cooperation for their influence in helping Anna evade the Russians. Since she is a Czech citizen, the Russians have claimed her. Anna wants none of Holly's help, however, at least under those circumstances. She does not want her freedom to be bought with Harry's life. Ultimately, she tries to prevent Lime's capture. She is the figure bound by unconditional romantic love, love that does not engage in critical reflection of its object. Her line "A person doesn't change just because you know more" seems to justify unwavering love—Harry is who he is, she loves him, and if she finds out horrible things about him that may affect whether she would stay with him, that does not affect the love itself and her desire for his well-being. She seems to think that she can only change her feelings for Harry if Harry himself changes, not if her knowledge or her perception of Harry change. It is almost as though her view of love is that when one loves, one loves the person's essence, somehow, and not anything having to do with his properties, or qualities. Thus, when one's perceptions of the person's qualities changes, that's irrelevant to love. As Holly notes, however, it's not that Harry is simply afflicted with "occasional bad manners"—he has killed innocent people. This isn't a superficial quality, like hair color. The magnitude of his wrongdoing does speak to something of Harry's very nature. Even more so, his own approval of his actions, his lack of remorse, his personal betrayal of Anna and others, his attempts at justification of the deaths he has caused—Greene piles it on, and, even so, Anna remains firmly the romantic, uncritical heroine who chooses love over humanity.

Anna warns Harry as he steps into the café to meet Holly. She mocks Holly as a "police informer". Again, it isn't that she's unaware of the extent of Harry's crimes. She simply doesn't give them the weight they warrant—at least, if justice is taken seriously. She hasn't, at least as far as we can tell, gone through the struggle that Holly has.

The café scene marks the beginning of the film's extraordinary ending. Lime tries to escape the authorities, and Holly, by running through his familiar haunt—the sewers. This is a Harry we haven't seen before, truly desperate to escape Calloway. A murderer, Harry faces prison and execution. In the end, as Harry clutches at a sewer grate, trapped, it is Holly who shots and kills him.

The film's final ending is as its beginning—at Harry Lime's funeral. Calloway gives Martins a lift from the cemetery. As they are driving down a long stretch of road, Holly sees Anna walking behind them. He insists that Calloway stop and let him out. He would like to wait for Anna, to walk with her. Calloway is skeptical, but does as Holly wishes. Yet, on the long stretch of road framed by tall trees, Anna walks determinedly by Holly. She doesn't stop, she doesn't look at him. Holly remains in place, lighting up a cigarette as the film closes.

The ending is bleak and uncompromising. It's interesting that in Graham Greene's initial plans for the script, Holly and Anna leave the funeral together, reconciled.[10] It was David Selznick, the American producer, who insisted on the bleak ending. He felt strongly that Anna's love for Harry had to be so deep that there would not have been any room for Holly.

III. FRIENDSHIP

One of the central struggles of the film is Holly's internal struggle regarding what he ought to do about his friend Harry. It is usually taken to be central to friendship that friends care for each other, and they want what is good for each other. Friends are loyal to and supportive of one another. Aristotle believed that there were instrumental friendships based on utility and pleasure, but he also thought that the best sort of friendship involved two virtuous persons who helped each other reinforce their good traits—so that they were, in some sense, mutually dependent on each other. If one friend wavered in his virtue, then that would provide some reason to end the friendship. The friendship then might constitute a threat to the virtuous person's continued virtue.

One of the often noted shortcomings of the Aristotelian account, however, is that it doesn't recognize a deep friendship even when the friends, or one of the friends, is lacking in virtue.

> To be friends with one another on the basis of pleasure and usefulness is, accordingly, also possible for bad people, just as it is for good men with bad, and for one who is neither good nor bad with any kind of person at all. But it is clear that good men alone can be friends on the basis of what they are, for bad people do not find joy in one another, unless they see some material advantage coming to them.[11]

There are many modern writers on friendship who find Aristotle's view plausible. Nancy Sherman, for example, articulates an Aristotelian picture in which the best friendship—between virtuous individuals—is necessary for our happiness as human beings.[12] The value of friendship in its best sense is not instrumental—rather, it has intrinsic value, value in and of itself. It seems at least initially plausible to also hold that the sort of friendship that has intrinsic value is the best sort of friendship.

While it seems true—in fact, almost trivially true—that the *best* friendship is one that exists between the virtuous, it doesn't follow that this is the only kind of deep and strong affection, or friendship, that is not instrumental. Further, this very plausible view that the best sort of friends are those who are virtuous rests on an ambiguity that will be explored later in the essay.

Their friendship might be characterized as one of mutual dependency—but not of the sort that Aristotle praised in the *Nicomachean Ethics*. Aristotle believed that perfect friends reinforced each other's virtue. They would even live together to benefit from each other's company and example. The sort of mutual dependency one sees between Harry and Holly, however, has more to do with each one lacking something he wanted, or believed that he needed. In school, Harry was the charming one, and that was where his talents for "facilitation" were being put to use. Holly depended on Harry for things like status and a kind of vicarious social standing. Harry depended on Holly, too—for an external source of respect and validation.

This is probably what prompts Harry to send for Holly, in fact. He needs that external source of approval very much in Vienna. The people who do seem to at least not disapprove of him in Vienna—people like his fellow racketeers Kurtz and Popescu—are not people he can respect. He would like to have back his uncritical friend, his source of emotional support. Anna, his girlfriend, would have assumed this role for a time. Even before Holly arrives in Vienna, however, Anna has become for Harry something he can bargain and deal with, something he can give to the Russians for protection. He needs Holly. This view of Harry Lime may be idiosyncratic—Harry is certainly a terrible human being, but terrible human beings do, sometimes, form affections of sorts for others. David Hume believed that sympathy for others was a universal sentiment in human beings. It could be countered by selfishness and malice, but it was there nevertheless. When a person's self-interest is in no way affected by the cruel or selfish act, his view was that all humans would feel some sympathy—the degree could vary dramatically, of course, but it is still there. How does this affect action? Hume writes:

> Let us suppose a person ever so selfish; let private interest have engrossed ever so much his attention; yet in instances, where that is not concerned, he must unavoidably feel *some* propensity to the good of mankind, and make it an object of choice, if everything else be equal. Would any man, who is walking along, tread as willingly on another's gouty toes, whom he has no quarrel with, as on the hard flint and pavement . . . We surely take into consideration the happiness and misery of others, in weighing the several motives of action, and incline to the former, where no private regards draw us to seek our own promotion or advantage by the injury of our fellow-creatures. . . . The degrees of these sentiments may be the subject of controversy; but the reality of their existence, one should think, must be admitted in every theory or system.[13]

One could certainly disagree with Hume's theory of human nature. One could also hold that Harry Lime is not the normal sort of human being. Harry Lime is some sort of sociopath, perhaps, someone who is so abnormal and twisted, psychologically, that he really does lack any fellow-feeling, to the point at which he is even incapable of personal friendships. I don't see his characterization in *The Third Man* to be like this, however. The film is set in the aftermath of WWII, in a Vienna of the horrors described in the previous section. One of the shocking and pro-foundly disturbing aspects of the war and the events leading up to it was the reve-lation that ordinary people were capable of extraordinary evil when their own self-interest was at stake. Hannah Arendt notes that profound evil arose from the most ordinary of individuals. She notes that a psychiatrist who had examined the war criminal Adolph Eichmann found Eichmann's "whole psychological outlook, his attitude toward his wife and children, mother and father, brothers, sisters, and friends, was 'not only normal but most desirable'."[14] There were evil individuals who caused massive loss of life and yet who often had families and friends, and seemed to engage in loving relationships with others. This is one of the horrific features of the war that Arendt chronicles, and which many people had difficulty coming to grips with after the war. Who among those we know and love are capable of being Eichmanns? Of course, Harry Lime was not following anybody's "orders". He was, however, living in a city without a centralized authority, where sheer self-interest seemed a common standard.[15]

I view Harry Lime's character as evil. His profound evil does not make him, unfortunately, a totally abnormal freak—particularly when viewed in the context of World War II. Harry is capable of friendship and attachment to others. I think that this view is also supported by the events of the film itself. *Why* would Harry send for Holly Martins? Vienna was full of unemployed and desperate people. Why would Harry, otherwise, spy on Anna and Holly *himself*, rather than have one of his cronies do it? Why would Harry agree to meet Holly in the café after Holly has already betrayed him by revealing to Calloway that he is still alive? These events strike me as evidence that Harry had an attachment to, or an affection for, Holly. It was certainly not absolute and overridable. He would have killed Holly if that were the only way to save his own life, but he was willing to give Holly a chance that he would not have been willing to give others. Having said this, how-ever, none of my other claims in this essay hinge on the fact that Harry himself is capable of friendship. All that is necessary is that Holly is capable and considers himself a friend of Harry's. I do, however, just as a matter of interpreting the details of their relationship, believe that Harry Lime had some affection for Holly.

It is quite true that there are ways in which Holly's friendship with Harry is asymmetrical. Holly was the weaker of the two socially. He lacked Harry's wit and intelligence. In fact, these are the qualities that make Harry Lime a dangerous sort of anti-hero, someone of whom Plato would have deeply disapproved. Plato pro-posed that in the ideal state, censorship would be needed to keep poets from cor-rupting other citizens by portrayals that encourage damaging emotions.[16] His primary example is that of grief. In tragedies grief in suffering is encouraged, though, Plato notes, someone who so indulges in real life would be viewed by others with disgust, as unable to control his emotions. Attractive evil would pre-sumably have the same damaging impact. Perhaps Graham Greene and Orson Welles were thinking of the damaging impact of the *übermensch* ideology in Europe when they fashioned Harry Lime.

What Orson Welles does is convey beautifully Harry's fascination as well as his contempt for others around him. While being disgusted, and yet fascinated, by Harry Lime we also admire the performance. What Holly sees on the Ferris wheel is just an echo of that fascination. A world war has intervened and either hardened or utterly changed Harry Lime. His feigned pity for Anna, the damage he has done to others, his indifference, the casual threats aimed at Holly—these were all factors that intruded into Holly's deliberations.

Even though Harry had intelligence and social skills that Holly lacked, there was something in Holly that Harry responded to. Harry sent for him. He wanted Holly in Vienna working with him. I think that what Harry wanted was what was missing from his other relationships in Vienna. He wanted someone he could rely on, whom he could count on, someone *not at all like himself*—his old friend from America.

So, it was not a friendship between men of perfect virtue, nor a friendship between equals, as Aristotle understood that term, but it was a strong dependency, and affection—of the noninstrumental sort—that also characterized the friendship. For some friendships, the basis is one of sentiment. Friends care about each other. This attachment can flow through a variety of sources. In the case of Harry and Holly, it seems to have arisen out of a shared history before the war. Things like affection and a shared history don't account for what's really distinctive about friendship as opposed to other sorts of relationships, however. Jeannette Kennett and Dean Cocking argue that one thing that is distinctive about friendship is that friends are "directed" by each other's interests.[17] This certainly seems to feature at least in Holly's relationship to Harry. Holly is directed by Harry's interests. He comes to Vienna at Harry's invitation. He resists Calloway's claims about Harry until the evidence becomes extremely convincing. What of Harry? Does he allow himself to be directed by Holly? Less is presented in the movie that reflects Harry Lime's states of mind. Harry does agree to meet Holly at the café, however, and it seems unlikely that he would have made such an agreement under those circumstances with someone not his friend. At that point he would have been safer without Holly than with him.

The power of the sort of friendship between Holly and Harry has the same power as Aristotle's best friendship, but it has the power to produce viciousness rather than moral virtue.

> Friendship (as the ancients saw) can be a school of virtue; but also (as they did not see) a school of vice. It is ambivalent. It makes good men better and bad men worse . . . It will be obvious that the element of secession, of indifference or deafness (at least on some matters) to the voices of the outer world, is common to all Friendships, whether good, bad, or merely innocuous. . . . The danger is that this partial indifference or deafness to outside opinion, justified and necessary though it is, may lead to a wholesale indifference or deafness.[18]

C. S. Lewis focuses on the potential damaging effect of loyalty in friendship. Holly is on the edge. His attachment and loyalty to Harry could have made him get on the plane and leave Vienna, allowing Harry to escape justice yet again. Or, in helping the authorities as he did, he's forced into an act of disloyalty. Either way, he is doing something he doesn't feel right about, that is in some way bad. The question is, which alternative is worse?

Loyalty can involve a rejection of impartiality, and many moral philosophers have focused on this issue, using it to demonstrate that there is a facet to ethics that cannot be captured in an impartial system that requires individuals to treat all persons the same. This runs against the common assumption that impartiality is a crucial aspect of ethics, that, for instance, to be a just and fair person, one needs to be impartial and not display favoritism. Yet, one is not impartial with respect to friends, and that is considered entirely appropriate in a variety of contexts. Lewis, however, was noting that this kind of favoritism, and the shutting out of others, is one of the dangers of friendship. When both friends are flawed, they can exacerbate each other's flaws; when one friend is flawed, he can have a damaging effect on his friend's character. This is part of the background in *The Third Man*. The loyalty and partiality that Holly feels towards Harry at first leads to his shutting out Major Calloway. As other philosophers have noted, however, simply because some degree of partiality may be appropriate in friendship, this does not imply a wholesale rejection of critical reflection. It is the rejection of critical reflection, I think, that Lewis finds dangerous. Sometimes in being a good *friend* one is led into activities that are not morally good. Because of the ties of affection, and because of the willingness to be directed by one's friend, a constraint is imposed on critical reflection in friendship. It may be that in becoming friends with someone one already has made a choice to defer, to some extent, in order to keep the friendship going.

Others have noted the dangers. Kennett and Cocking have noted that the Aristotelian conception is overly moralized because of its insistence that friendship be morally good and morally enriching. They note that Gandhi, whose views on friendship were discussed by George Orwell, observed that friends are dangerous because one can be led by a friend into doing something wrong. Orwell writes, "The essence of being human is that one does not seek perfection, that one is sometimes willing to commit sins for the sake of loyalty . . . . "[19] Friends will often do things for each other that violate the norms of morality. It does not follow that because the norms of morality are violated, the norms of friendship are, as well. Kennett and Cocking discuss the case of a man who accidentally kills someone and then gets his friend to help him dispose of the body. In helping him, his friend violates the law in a variety of ways and harms the victim's family by lying to them.[20] He is a bad person, perhaps, but a good friend. In their view, a good friend need not be a good person. This picks up on the ambiguity that I referred to earlier. We use the word "good" in a variety of ways. Sometimes we mean that something is morally good, but other times we might mean that something is simply

good *of its kind*. For example, I may judge that Jimmy Carter would make a terrible evil dictator. He would not be a good evil dictator in the sense that he lacks
the necessary skills and dispositions to exemplify excellence within the kind "evil
dictator". This, however, has no impact on evaluating Jimmy Carter as morally
good—indeed, it may be that we view him as incompetent in the evil-dictator field
precisely because we view him as morally good. In the same way, to hold that
someone is a good friend does not commit one to the view that he or she is a morally good person.

In helping Calloway, Holly chooses to be a good person but to violate the norms
of friendship by betraying his friend. He views Harry as his friend, and there is
some evidence that Harry views Holly as *his* friend. What is crucial for my interpretation of the film, however, is simply that Holly is Harry's friend, even if the
relationship is not reciprocal, even if it turned out that Harry cared not a whit for
Holly. Holly is concerned about Harry's welfare, however, and it is this concern
that Calloway has to relentlessly undermine with the proof of Harry's disregard
for the value of human life.

This nonmoralized conception of friendship runs counter to the view one sees
adopted by writers inspired by Aristotle. These writers hold that to be a genuine
friend, one needs to be virtuous. Again, though, as Kennett and Cocking point
out, this Aristotelian view leaves too much out. Those who resist the view that
Harry Lime was Holly's friend, I think, may be appealing to the moralized Aristotelian conception. Harry is evil, and an evil man cannot be a good friend, or *any*
friend at all. My claim is not that Harry was Holly's good friend. He was, however,
Holly's friend, even though he was lacking in moral virtue. Holly was not a good
friend to Harry, either, but he was Harry's friend and acted on that friendship in
the end.

Another complicating factor has to do with Holly's own personal code of
ethics, which may be affected by his writing. He writes Westerns. The Western
genre is characterized by a code of ethics in which honor, loyalty, and redemption
are held in high regard. If one considers novels like *Shane* or *The Quick and the Dead*,
both icons of the genre, the Western hero is one, again, who fills a moral vacuum.
When Holly arrives in Vienna and begins to question the circumstances of Harry's
death and the police's seeming indifference, at first he must have felt that Vienna,
too, had become corrupt and morally empty. His job, at first, was to set things
right by Harry before leaving town.

The plot did not play out like the standard Western, however. Harry was the
bad guy, not a good man whose death had failed to be taken seriously by the police.
The "hero" is portrayed as a drunk who stumbles onto the truth. He doesn't get
the girl—but not for noble reasons. He doesn't get the girl because she doesn't
want him.

There was still the issue of redemption, and the Ferris wheel scene is pivotal for
that as well—it is there that Holly realizes that Harry cannot be redeemed. In
novels in which redemption is a theme, the "bad guy" has some goodness that

hasn't been utterly undermined, a sense of goodness that can lead to a change of heart at the end, and redemption. Holly wants Harry to give himself up for Anna, or at least not to actually sacrifice Anna. But the Ferris wheel scene makes clear this is not the ending of Harry Lime's story. There is no ambiguity left in the that scene, no hope that Harry has any bit of goodness left, and Holly's feelings of obligation toward Harry, to a large extent, dissolve. It may be that the crucial difference between Holly and Anna, who remains utterly devoted to Harry, is that Holly actually confronts Harry and is able to see his response. Anna never sees the Harry Lime of the Prater.

Through this debate it has become quite clear that even if one is partial towards one's friends, there are moral limits. Even though I ought to act in certain ways toward a friend in ways not owed to strangers—such as, perhaps, helping him move his furniture, or helping him with his homework, etc., it doesn't follow that proper loyalty demands one act in any way whatsoever to help one's friend. One shouldn't, for example, help one's friend violate the rights of others. Friendship, then, is subject to critical reflection. A friend can think about what a friend wants him to do and whether it is something that does or does not violate moral norms. A friend's immorality is reason to dissolve the friendship. It is Holly's first-hand witnessing of the effects of Harry's actions that leads to this critical reflection—he sees the damage Harry has done to innocent people and even to his own girlfriend, Anna. For Holly, the bond to Harry created by friendship is dissolving, but it is not utterly destroyed. This is important to understanding the movie's penultimate scenes.

In Holly we have a friend who is willing, though reluctant, to critically reflect on the friendship and, again reluctantly, reject that bond. In Anna, we have someone who loves Harry unconditionally, it seems, and is not able or willing to engage in that critical reflection. Anna hardly seems the paradigm of loving virtue. She is more of a vicarious moral monster—the sort of loving support that has encouraged and aided the morally compromised individuals we see throughout history. Critical reflection in romantic relationships is sometimes considered distasteful—indeed, it is sometimes considered completely unromantic. This really depends upon what the critical reflection is about. The moral character of the beloved is an appropriate object of such reflection. Even *if* one viewed love as something that appropriately resists such reflection, one could still consistently hold that acceptance should not. Anna is corrupt in continuing to accept and support Harry Lime after she knows what he is.

Throughout this essay I have maintained that Holly did not cease being friends with Harry. His disillusion with Harry weakened their connection. Holly felt he needed to betray Harry to try, in some small way, to set some of Harry's sins right. In setting Harry up he chose moral goodness over being a good friend to Harry, but this didn't mean that he was no friend at all to Harry. In the end it was friendship, and the pity this generated for Harry, that led Holly to shoot and kill Harry Lime as he looked at him trapped, chased down, in the sewers.

This was a scene that might well not have made it into the film. The Production Code censors initially objected to it since it looked like a mercy killing, and they were unwilling to let anything on the screen that seemed to condone such killings: "With regard to the ending of the story, Martins' shooting of Harry will be on a direct shouted order from Calloway, and there will be no flavor of either mercy killing or deliberate murder."[21]

Fortunately, though, Carol Reed ignored the censors on this point, and the scene remained. It is important to a full understanding of the relationship between Harry and Holly. Charles Drazin writes:

> Harry's death in the film would completely defy the censors' requirements. Wounded and cornered in the sewers, he gives his old school friend a piteous and pleading look. With a nod, he gestures to be put out of his misery . . . The mercy killing had to remain a mercy killing to be true to Greene's original intention. The moment in which a friend kills a friend contained so much of what the film is about.[22]

One *might* look at this scene and judge Holly to be engaged in a kind of "rough justice" of the sort that pervades Western novels. In this view, he is a good man in the wilderness faced with a difficult choice and forced to kill the villain who refuses to surrender. It is not that at all, however. It's true that Holly killed Harry so

Figure 13.2

that Harry could avoid the process of a trial and sentencing and then, very likely, an execution. Rough justice, however, generally occurs when people have no faith in a just procedure actually being available. There is either no working system of justice, or they think the system in place is corrupt. This, however, was not Holly's worry at all. Holly was doing this *for Harry*. He was not doing it out of a basic desire that Harry avoid the just procedures. He shot Harry because that's what Harry wanted. It was a mercy killing, and that mercy was prompted by friendship, not by hatred or rage. Holly betrays his friend out of duty, but kills him out of friendship.

NOTES

I would like to thank Ward Jones and Samantha Vice for their very helpful comments on an earlier draft of this paper.

1. This quotation has been transcribed from the film. All quotations to follow are taken from the screenplay, *The Third Man*, by Graham Greene.

2. Charles Drazin, *In Search of the Third Man*, 36–37.

3. Ibid.

4. On p. 340, Glover quotes from William Shirer's *Berlin Diary, 1934–41*, 92: "We had been told that the Jews had been made to scrub out the toilets with the sacred praying bands, the *Tefillin*."

5. Ibid, 338.

6. Some would deny this, arguing that rough justice is not justice at all. That is, it is necessary for an outcome's justice that it result from a just procedure.

7. Here is a characteristic section:

> *The stranger picked two slices of bacon from the skillet. Without looking up he said, "You ever kill a man, McKaskel?"*
>
> *"Kill a man?" McKaskel was startled. "Why, no I haven't."*
>
> *"You walk into that settlement with that gun an' you better figure on it."*
>
> *"I don't think . . ."— "*
>
> *"You walk into that place without bein' ready to kill an' your wife'll be a widow before the hour's gone."*
>
> *"That's nonsense. I'll go to the law."*
>
> *"Ain't none. Folks out here generally make their own."*
>
> *"I can use the rifle. I've killed a dozen deer . . ."*
>
> *"Was the deer shootin' back at you? Mister, that outfit figure on you comin' in. They want you to. Why do you s'pose they left all them tracks? They figure to kill you, Mister."*

From Chapter 1, *The Quick and the Dead*, by Louis L'Amour.

8. "The Wheel of Virtue."

9. As quoted in Ibid., 10.

10. Drazin, *In Search of the Third Man*.

11. *Nichomachean Ethics* (trans. Martin Ostwald), 1157a 15–19.

12. See, for example, her discussion at the beginning of "Aristotle on the Shared Life."

13. *Enquiries Concerning Human Understanding and Concerning the Principles*, 183.

14. *Eichmann in Jerusalem*, 25–26.

15. Both Joseph Cotten and Orson Welles had made movies prior to *The Third Man* in which a similar theme is present in the plot—the theme of evil discovered among loved ones; the theme that evil can be uncovered even in those who seem so totally normal, charming, intelligent, and attractive. In 1943, Alfred Hitchcock made *Shadow of a Doubt* starring Joseph Cotten as Uncle Charlie—an ordinary family's beloved uncle who turns out to be a serial killer. In 1946, Orson Welles directed and starred in *The Stranger*, playing Professor Charles Rankin, the respected member of a small Connecticut community who turns out to be a Nazi war criminal. In both of those films we have female characters quite different from Anna in *The Third Man*—agonized by the growing realization that the person they love is evil and yet choosing rejection in the end.

16. For example: "Can that praise in the theatre be right? To see a man behaving as one would not deem it right to behave oneself, indeed, as one would be ashamed to behave, to enjoy and praise the spectacle and not be disgusted by it?" (*Republic*, 250).

17. Kennett and Cocking, "Friendship and the Self." Kennett and Cocking also add that friends "interpret" each other, and allow themselves to be influenced by one another's interpretations. If Ann makes a comment about Sheila's lack of athletic prowess, Sheila will be inclined to take this seriously and reflect on this feature of herself—and perhaps change, but at least become self-conscious about it. Thus, she is being influenced by a friend's interpretation. I don't believe this analysis does the work that Kennett and Cocking wish in differentiating friendship from other relations of affection—for example, students are often directed by teachers and open to their interpretations. True, this is not characteristically reciprocal, but for Ann to be friends with Sheila it need not be reciprocal either (so, she may be Sheila's friend even if Sheila is not her friend). Further, the interpretation condition seems puzzling to me. Laving aside the issue of the exhaustivity of the account, however, Kennett and Cocking have focused on some important features of friendship and ones that shape the relationship between Harry and Holly.

18. C. S. Lewis, *The Four Loves*, in Neera Badhwar, *Friendship: a Philosophical Reader*, 46.

19. George Orwell, "Reflections on Gandhi," *Collected Essays* (London: Mercury, 1961), as quoted by Jeannette Kennett and Dean Cocking in "Friendship and Moral Danger," 278.

20. They take this case from the film *Death in Brunswick*; see ibid. 279.

21. Joseph Breen, Production Code administrator, as quoted in Drazin, *In Search of the Third Man*, 41.

22. Drazin, *In Search of the Third Man*, 42.

THE THIRD MAN

ETHICS, AESTHETICS, IRONY

DEBORAH KNIGHT

I. PRELIMINARY REMARKS

I EXPECT WE WOULD ALL AGREE THAT IN CONVENTIONAL fictional narratives we find characters, perhaps even heroes and villains, involved in actions that might merit praise or blame. We would therefore also agree that narrative fictions typically have an ethical or moral dimension, and that this will play a role in our engagement with and assessment of such narratives. Recently, some philosophers have argued that narrative artworks, notably narrative films, actually *do* philosophy, including moral philosophy.[1] This is not a position I endorse. I do not dispute that, from particular perspectives, narrative artworks might be seen to *illustrate* moral or ethical positions. Even so, that a film might illustrate a particular ethical position strikes me as considerably less interesting than interpretations of particular films and the ethical issues such interpretations might address or raise. I part company, methodologically speaking, with those who are interested in showing that particular narratives exemplify moral maxims. It does not add to our appreciation of, say, *Crime and Punishment* or, for that matter, to our appreciation of *American Psycho*, to treat these works as illustrations of the maxim that murder is wrong. My approach is to offer interpretations of films, rather than to treat given films as themselves making a contribution to general discussions in moral philosophy or ethics. The sorts of interpretations I have in mind frequently focus on ethical issues raised at the level of either cinematic content or cinematic form.

In this chapter, I will focus on what might initially seem a very specific issue, namely, the use made by Noël Carroll of Carol Reed's *The Third Man* as an illustration of a particular moral thesis about friendship. My argument has two parts. The first part questions certain assumptions Carroll has made about a position he calls "clarificationism", which he describes as *"one* of the most important and comprehensive relations of art . . . . to morality."[2] I will ask why Carroll thinks that *The Third Man* actually does what he claims it does in terms of clarifying for us our understanding of the concept of friendship. I should say in advance that I do not argue that clarificationism is not true, only that it is hard to see how the example of *The Third Man* shows that it is true. The second part of the chapter offers an interpretation of *The Third Man* intended to demonstrate that Carroll's focus on the ethical commitments of friendship is misdirected with respect to this film. A more rewarding way to think about *The Third Man*'s ethical implications must first highlight both the film's extremely self-conscious aesthetics and its essentially ironic perspective. Indeed, given that the film is an example of dramatic irony, one might anticipate that the concept of friendship is not so much clarified as ironized.

At the center of *The Third Man* are a naïve protagonist, Holly Martins (Joseph Cotten), and an unscrupulous villain, Harry Lime (Orson Welles). Friendship is not the real issue between them. If friendship is a reciprocal, rather than a one-way, relationship, then clearly we have a problem, since Martins mistakenly believes Lime to be his friend, whereas Lime is no friend of Martins. The film's ironic perspective allows us to pursue the implications of misapprehended friendship. In short, the narrative focuses on the potential costs of Martins' naiveté and his capacity for self-deception, and the assurance with which Lime exploits these failings. A central moral issue in *The Third Man* is undoubtedly raised by the figure of Lime, because he is at once charismatic and evil. Another, equally important, moral issue, however, concerns the consequences of misplaced loyalty, which is the situation in which Martins initially and unwittingly finds himself. Considering the film in terms of its ironic mode and its aesthetics will allow me to show why friendship is not the real issue here.

It may appear that this argument is too specific to be able to accomplish much with respect to the topic at hand, namely the relationship (or, possibly, the relationships) between ethics and films. I disagree. Any number of basic features of conventional narratives already bespeak the fact that ethical assessment is built into to our understanding and appreciation of narrative fictions. To name just three, consider the ethical status of individual characters. Then consider the ethical dimension of character action and interaction, whether leading to conflict or to the resolution of conflict. Finally, we have the nature of narrative closure, in which a course of events is resolved, for better or worse, from both an aesthetic and an ethical perspective. It seems that a better way of apprehending the ethical implications of particular films is not through testing general ethical questions against the film at hand, but rather by interpreting the film to see what cashes out, ethically speaking, from such interpretations. Let me start with a review of clarificationism.

II. CARROLL, CLARIFICATIONISM, AND *THE THIRD MAN*

Noël Carroll argues that one of the most important relationships between art and ethics is that art can help us clarify our ethical concepts and commitments. He further suggests that Carol Reed's *The Third Man* (1949)—or at least Graham Greene's screenplay for the film—provides an excellent opportunity to see clarificationism in action. Carroll claims that *The Third Man* allows us to clarify our understanding of the ethical commitments of friendship. Was it right for Holly Martins to side with the military police in trying to bring Holly's great friend, Harry Lime, to justice, or should Holly have remained faithful to his friend instead?

In "Art, Narrative, and Moral Understanding," Carroll argues that our engagement with narrative works of art "can deepen our understanding by, among other things, encouraging us to apply our moral knowledge and emotions to specific cases."[3] Indeed, through our consideration of specific narrative cases, Carroll argues, our moral understanding can possibly even be augmented.[4] More recently, in "The Wheel of Virtue: Art, Literature, and Moral Knowledge," Carroll shifts his focus somewhat by asking whether art, and in particular the narrative arts, can contribute to moral knowledge. His answer is yes, that literary—and by extension, cinematic—narratives might well be a "source of moral knowledge and education" if they can be seen to function like philosophical thought experiments.[5] To motivate the analogy, Carroll observes that "if philosophy uses [thought experiments] to produce knowledge, then arguably literature does too."[6] His argument goes: Philosophers of very different persuasions agree that we can learn from philosophical thought experiments because thought experiments encourage us to reflect upon, and thereby to clarify, important concepts. Carroll contends that fictional narratives also encourage us to reflect upon, and thereby to clarify, important concepts. Therefore, insofar as fictional narratives provide us with the same sort of opportunity for the development of conceptual knowledge as philosophical thought experiments, philosophers must conclude that we can learn from fictional narratives if we can learn from thought experiments. Whatever one might think about the possibility that narrative artworks can help us to clarify our concepts, including our moral ones, I will argue that Carroll is wrong if he thinks that narrative artworks are best treated as thought experiments.

To begin, the disanalogies between philosophical thought experiments and fictional narratives seem much more significant than their purported similarities. Perhaps the most immediately striking, although not in the end the most significant, disanalogy is that many philosophical thought experiments—for instance, John Locke's prince and cobbler, Donald Davidson's *Swampman*, or Hilary Putnam's *Twin Earth*—smack of fantasy or science fiction, whereas many critics who support the view that literature can be edifying concern themselves with classical realist texts, as we see for instance in Martha Nussbaum's numerous essays on the novels of Henry James as well as in much of the work of the late Wayne C. Booth.[7] It is easier to see *The Prince and the Pauper* (1937) as like Locke's famous thought experiment than to see James' *The Golden Bowl* as in any meaningful sense a thought experiment. While it is true that philosophical thought experiments are typically both fictional and narrative, they are very short examples of narrative fiction, frequently containing only a few episodes—for example, the prince and the cobbler before and after their brain swap. A second disanalogy is that the story aspect of philosophical thought experiments is strictly unnecessary to the conceptual point being illustrated, whereas how narrative fictions are presented is inextricably tied to what we value in them. The brain-swap scenario might be equally effectively illustrated by a ballerina and a sumo wrestler as by a prince and a cobbler, but swapping Mrs. Dalloway for Anna Karenina is only going to ruin the novel. A third disanalogy is that thought experiments focus our attention on concepts, whereas fictional narratives focus us on stories and the characters who appear in them.

Rather than focusing us on concepts, narrative artworks focus us on the development and interaction of themes, a point familiar to students of literature and one
that is emphasized, for example, by Peter Lamarque and Stein Haughom Olsen's
Truth, Fiction, and Literature. So, when viewing *Vertigo* (1958), we might reflect on
obsession as a theme, but not necessarily on the concept of obsession. In fact, it
might be more accurate to say that philosophical thought experiments focus us on
our *intuitions* about concepts, which is certainly not the primary function of most
literary works. A fourth disanalogy is that philosophical thought experiments do
not rely on our emotional engagement or on our desire for some narrative outcome rather than another—both of which are features of paradigm fictional
stories. We don't have a vested interest in what happens to the prince or to the
cobbler, whereas we do with what happens to Clarice Starling and Hannibal
Lecter, for example.

Paradigm thought experiments, such as the ones mentioned above, tend not to
resolve themselves. Their whole point is to challenge our intuitions about given
situations by illustrating how difficult it is to get clear about certain concepts, and
thus to provoke further debate. The project for us is to continue to think about the
challenge the thought example presents to us. What would be the case if the cobbler's mind were to take up residence in the prince's body? Just how would that
cash out? The question is open ended, and the answer is certainly not contained in
the narrative of the thought experiment, which offers no conclusion. Paradigm
narrative fictions, by contrast, traditionally do resolve themselves. Of course, we
can continue to discuss the work after we have finished watching or reading it, but
at that stage we are either engaged in something akin to criticism or something
like fantasy projection, for example, when we wonder whether Rick and Ilsa ever
meet again after the end of *Casablanca* (1942). While we can compare competing
interpretations, it is hard to see that this practice is congruent with dealing with
the upshot of different intuitions tested by a philosophical thought experiment. To
think about literary narratives involves thinking about such things as narrative
structure and genre, neither of which is relevant to philosophical thought experiments. Works of literature are best approached from what Peter Lamarque calls
the "literary point of view"[8]—that is, in terms of the sorts of interests that characterize our involvement with literature as an institution: for instance, our interest in
major themes and motifs, in the work's conformity to or departures from generic
conventions, and, more fundamentally, in the represented events themselves. So
here we find a fifth disanalogy: philosophical thought experiments are not produced in the context of the institution of literature, and thus our interest in them
is not consonant with our interests in literary works. Murray Smith offers another
way of putting this point: Perhaps there are both philosophical and artistic thought
experiments but they have different characteristics and different goals. Once these
differences are noted, one might legitimately suspect that "the thought experiment serves different purposes in philosophy and artistic storytelling, respectively."[9] Taken together, these disanalogies suggest that Carroll is wrong to believe

that fictional narratives ought typically to be treated as analogous to philosophical thought experiments.

Let me turn to Carroll's example of *The Third Man*. Or, I should say, to the example of Graham Greene's screenplay for *The Third Man*, which is really Carroll's focus, and to something that Carroll dubs "the Forster/Greene debate." Carroll reminds us of a 1938 essay by E. M. Forster entitled, "What I Believe." In it, Forster states that if he were presented with the moral challenge of deciding between his country and his friend, he hopes he would have the strength of character to choose his friend over his country. Carroll supposes that Forster has offered us a generalizable maxim for moral conduct, and thus he suggests that we can call the preference for friend over country the Forster Maxim (FM). Carroll asks us to compare FM with Greene's screenplay for *The Third Man*. Carroll's idea is that Greene's screenplay offers a counterexample to FM. In fact, Carroll claims that the screenplay of *The Third Man* functions as a thought experiment in which we get to reflect on— and reject—the truth of FM. As will be clear from what follows, I hold that treating *The Third Man* as such a refutation is to lose sight of what we should find valuable in the film.[10]

Carroll suggests that the test of clarificationism is not which concepts are clarified for members of elite groups such as moral philosophers or ethical critics of literature, but rather which concepts are clarified for "plain readers". It is "plain readers", Carroll conjectures, who might need to learn from *The Third Man* that Holly owes nothing to Harry Lime. Carroll's remarks here seem to grant "plain readers" not a lot of sense and also little understanding of the generic conventions and narrative structure of the film. Harry Lime's actions are explicitly depicted as evil, despite the fact that he is personally quite charismatic, so according to Carroll's account, it seems plain readers somehow miss this information. Still, it might be useful to think about what the group of plain readers amounts to. I'm not sure how many plain readers or viewers of either the novella or film version of *The Third Man* actually exist now, but the number of plain viewers of the film who are acquainted with the screenplay I would estimate to be nil. While I'm not at all sure just who would count as a plain viewer of *The Third Man*, surely it is obvious to any such plain viewers that Holly owes Lime nothing, and that he is therefore right in the end to help the military police in their campaign against Lime. The issue for me is not that Holly finally turns against Harry to help the forces of justice, but that he helps them reluctantly and with ulterior motives, a topic to which I will return.

Should we consider Forster's remarks to constitute a maxim comparable to, say, the Golden Rule or the Kantian maxim that we should treat others as ends, not means? If Forster's observation is not such a maxim, there is little point in constructing an argument to show that *The Third Man* proves the maxim to be false. To decide this question, we would do well to recall something about the political circumstances that formed the background for Forster's essay. Although keenly aware of the limitations of democratic government, Forster was nevertheless a committed democrat. He was writing in Britain in the year prior to the outbreak of the Second World War. In the context of a British ruling class of which many were alarmingly sympathetic to Hitler, to National Socialism, and, in some circles, to anti-Semitism, one can appreciate Forster's concern about having to make a decision between friend and country. Carroll neglects the highly charged atmosphere of 1938 Great Britain in his presentation of FM. In fact, Carroll treats FM as a straightforwardly generalizable, context-independent moral maxim. Surely the real question is whether it makes sense to treat Forster's remark as a maxim at all.

Recalling that FM is Carroll's way of formulating an idea he takes from Forster, this is how Carroll constructs the "debate". On Carroll's interpretation, *The Third Man* straightforwardly shows us that Holly Martins—the alcoholic American author of pulp Westerns who winds up in post–World War II Vienna—is right to choose against his friend, the notorious and utterly unscrupulous Harry Lime. The fact that Holly Martins makes the right choice with respect to Harry Lime, however, doesn't mean that *The Third Man* is a refutation of FM. *The Third Man* could be just as it is without any thought of Forster's alleged maxim and indeed without Forster having propounded any such maxim. For example, it is quite unclear how the film acts as a counterexample to the maxim that Holly should choose his friend over his country since Holly, like Harry, is American. Holly's dealings are primarily with the British occupying forces, and the ultimate benefactors of Holly's decision to help capture Harry are not only the British but the Viennese civilian population, which has been injured by Harry's black market activities. In the meantime, what seems to drop out of sight in Carroll's account is that Martins slowly comes to realize that Lime is not his friend. Consider the ominous time the two spend in a Ferris wheel compartment high over Vienna, where Lime implies, and Martins clearly understands, that Lime threatens to kill him. By the time he complies with the occupying forces, Holly has realized that Lime is no friend of his. What is striking is that notwithstanding this realization he helps only reluctantly.

Has Forster presented us with a maxim? Despite the rhetorical bravura of Forster's statement, there is no basis for claiming that it is intended to serve as a maxim for practical action irrespective of context. This should not surprise, since maxims aren't typically stated in the first person. All Forster says in his essay is that he hopes in difficult circumstances he would not betray a friend. Forster has reasons for his view, and his reasons concern what he takes to be the questionable moral basis of his own government in 1938. That said, Forster acknowledges in his essay that sometimes friends aren't true friends. Thus, he realizes that the commitment he is expressing requires unshaken faith in his friend, coupled with good reason to believe that his faith is not misplaced. Forster gives us no reason to think that one should be blind to one's friends' faults, especially their moral faults. Indeed, considering the circumstances in which he originally wrote, the clear danger that Forster anticipated was one in which he might be constrained by the state to act against his better moral judgment. The sort of situation Forster seems to

have worried about is one in which he would be compelled to side with a government committed to a morally dubious undertaking—such as appeasement, for
example—against a morally blameless friend. Forster is silent on the question of
whether one should choose one's friend over one's country if, for example, one's
friend was plotting the assassination of the prime minister or king, or involved in
espionage on behalf of the Nazis. I take this silence to mean Forster is concerned
about having to sacrifice a true friend for a false country. There is nothing in his
essay to suggest that one must chose a false friend over one's country. Thus, it
seems mistaken to claim that Forster is defending any maxim to the effect that in
all circumstances one should choose one's friend over one's country. It seems that
the scenario Forster imagines applies in specific cases, namely in cases where one
has justified faith in one's friend but where one does not have the same faith in the
decisions and motivations of the state. I conclude that there is no good reason to
treat Forster's remark as a maxim that is generally recognized to be universaliz-
able. Consequently I am not persuaded by Carroll that there is any debate between
Forster and Greene.

Arguably, Forster's original thought was not concerned with a decision between
someone who is recognizably a friend and a cause that is recognizably just—
although such a situation warrants serious moral reflection. Instead, Forster is concerned about blind support for a morally compromised state that might lead to
reckless abandonment of our genuine and deserving friends. Forster's careful and
nuanced vision of friendship is hardly what is at stake in *The Third Man*—we realize
at the outset that our protagonist, Holly, is himself incapable of the sorts of well-
motivated moral commitments Forster is talking about, and we learn in due
course that Harry Lime is someone quite untouched by the moral demands of
friendship. If we actually paid attention to the novella or to the film, we would
discover Greene's real thematic concern—namely, the potentially dangerous consequences of a naive and misplaced loyalty for a charismatic figure who is utterly
without moral conscience. Because Martins simply does not comprehend Lime's
mind and motives, the moral status of their "friendship" is entirely compromised.

III. AESTHETICS AND IRONY

Dramatic irony is a significant literary mode and thus one of the most central
aesthetic features of *The Third Man*. Unlike the other major literary modes—
tragedy, romance, and comedy—irony is a mode without a hero figure. A protag
onist, certainly, but the central figure will not be one whom we can admire. As
Northrop Frye argues in his magisterial *Anatomy of Criticism*, the ironic mode puts
us at a distance from the protagonist in at least two closely related ways. First, and
again this is a feature that distinguishes dramatic irony from the other key modes,
the audience is morally superior to the ironic protagonist (or imagines itself to be),
so our basic relationship is one of critical judgment. We see the protagonist's
weaknesses while the protagonist initially does not—and indeed, might never

manage to. Second, dramatic irony typically presents events to us with little explicit direction from author or narrator about how we should judge protagonists as events unfold.[11] Again, it is for readers and viewers of ironic works to assess the moral worth of protagonists and their actions. Dramatic irony has several distinguishable types, including variations, such as tragic irony and comic irony. Frye would place *The Third Man* in the category of comic irony, and in particular, as an example of the type of comic irony whose readers and viewers "can realize that murderous violence is less an attack on a virtuous society by a malignant individual than a symptom of that society's own viciousness."[12]

So let us try a different approach to *The Third Man*. Instead of treating it as a thought experiment dealing with the so-called Forster Maxim, let us think of it as a fiction film with its own particular aesthetic characteristics. Whether we want to focus on a theme such as friendship or a theme such as the one I have just suggested—namely, how the naïve Martins is manipulated by a morally bankrupt Lime—we cannot isolate these questions from the overall formal and thematic structure of the film, and thus we must pay due attention to the fact that it is presented in the mode of irony.

Produced jointly by British and American financing, *The Third Man* is a British *film noir* set in post-war Vienna that draws on both the *film noir* tradition of the American cinema as well as certain features found in British crime films of the post-war period. These features include the trope of the threatening world beneath an apparently calm surface, here represented by locations such as the sewers of Vienna, and by plot features such as the return of someone or something from the past that threatens the present, represented by Harry Lime. Finally, as is characteristic of *films noir*, the fictional world of *The Third Man* is one that features crime, the breaking or bending of laws, innocents caught in compromising or dangerous situations, and an underworld that pursues its own interests at whatever cost. The *film noir* world is one at least of moral ambiguity if not in fact one that operates almost apart from morality and law. This is the fictional world that Holly Martins becomes caught up in.

From the film's first frames, we find important clues about how we should understand what is going to unfold, clues that relate in large measure to the film's narrative tone, which is both ironic and self-conscious. Reed's inspired choice of Anton Karas's zither music for the film's score is the first thing to establish the film's tone. In due course we discover that the zither can convey a range of emotions—being by turns jaunty, alarming, haunting, poignant, ironic, and comic. But the so-called "Third Man Theme," which accompanies the opening credits and is repeated periodically throughout the film, is not one that suggests moral *gravitas*. Instead, it is cheeky and cheerful, and it functions as a musical metacommentary on the actions that are about to unfold, functioning in clear contrast to the purported suspense of the plot.

After the opening credits, a breezy voice-over[13] illustrated by a montage of documentary footage introduces us to post-war Vienna. The city is largely in ruins and divided into four zones, with a central section policed by members of all four occupying powers: America, France, Great Britain, and Russia. The joke is that the ordinary soldiers representing the four powers can hardly talk to one another except in what counts as their *lingua franca*—namely, a smattering of German. The voice-over speaker remarks that Vienna is not much worse off than other European capitals, hardly consoling news as we see bombed-out cathedrals and streets. Post-war Vienna, we are told anecdotally, is the "classic period of the black market." Moreover, the city is caught between the occupying powers and the racketeers—the speaker of the voice-over frankly acknowledges his own involvement in the Viennese black market. Just as breezily, he reminds himself that what he wanted to tell us was the story of Holly Martins, who arrives in Vienna from America "happy as a lark and without a cent." Holly's school friend, Harry Lime, has offered him a job and accompanied the offer with a plane ticket. Holly is about to discover that his great friend is being buried on the very day he arrives in Vienna.

This discovery plunges Holly into a mystery/suspense narrative in which he takes on the role of detective, without any adequate preparation, with the goal of discovering the real circumstances of Lime's death. In the various crime films that form the generic background for *The Third Man*, the figure of the detective typically enters a scenario *in medias res*, and Holly does as well. The detective's job is to figure out, from somewhere in the middle of the action, what has gone before and what the consequences will be. Indeed, this general situation is true also in films such as *The 39 Steps* (1935), where the protagonist, again not a detective, becomes inadvertently involved in a set of circumstances already well underway and is forced to figure out what has happened and why. In *The Third Man*, Holly deliberately takes on the role of amateur detective, questioning Harry's friends and associates, including the porter at Harry's flat; Harry's girlfriend, Anna Schmidt; and Harry's various alleged friends. Holly also raises questions about Harry's death with the head of the British military police, Major Calloway, challenging him to take seriously Holly's intuition that Harry has not died accidentally but, in fact, has been murdered. Now, the typical—and by that I mean American—*noir* detective is someone totally familiar with the underside of society, who has his own strong code of ethics, and who finally brings the wrong-doers to justice in the face of the general flat-footedness of the supporting police force, as we see, for instance, in *The Maltese Falcon* (1941). Here, by contrast, Holly, himself an American, is quite unfamiliar with the situation in which he finds himself, and he has little more than a simple code of ethics, which initially becomes apparent in his refusal to believe Calloway's suggestion that Lime was involved in black market activities.

From our earliest encounter with our protagonist, we realize that Holly Martins is in one sense the antithesis of the sort of Western heroes he writes about, since Martins has no heroic qualities whatsoever. Yet in another sense, he is quite like his heroes, who tend to see the world in black and white. The world of post-war

Vienna is a murky mix of greys, and Martins arrives without any sense of the complex economic, political, national, and criminal intrigues that are being conducted there. Nevertheless, he takes it upon himself to prove that his friend, whom he learns was killed by a passing car, did not die accidentally. Because of his relentless interest in what he believes to be the actual facts of Harry Lime's death—in particular, whether it involved a "third man"—Holly unintentionally discovers his seeming best friend's dark underside.

In the Vienna of *The Third Man*, it is next to impossible to be certain when your life is in danger or when you are just being whisked by pre-arranged taxi to the public lecture you have agreed to give on the topic of the modern novel—a topic that Holly Martins, who has been thus abducted, knows nothing about, although he is willing to tell an audience interested in James Joyce and the stream of consciousness novel that his primary literary influence is Zane Grey. The taxi "abduction" is a perfect example of the undercutting of what is initially presented as legitimate suspense. This theme is reprised at the end of Martins' lecture, when Harry's Romanian friend Popescu suddenly reappears with veiled threats directed at Martins as well as two henchmen who mean Martins no good. Here, too, suspense is undercut through plausible yet bizarre comedy, when Martins is bitten by a parrot in a dark room while trying to escape apparent danger.

The Third Man is a film that features any number of eccentricities, each of which contributes to the film's perspective of comic irony as well as its overall cinematic self-consciousness. The choice of the zither for the score is just our first hint of this. Reed also makes use of a unique, and indeed expressionist-inspired, *mise-en-scène*, emphasizing darkness and shadows both in interior settings and exteriors, features often identified with *noir* visual style. More than this, many shots are presented at a raking angle, another *noir* stylistic feature, suggesting at a minimum that whatever else is going on, things in Vienna are not in balance. The skewed camera angles, which Roger Ebert says "suggest a world out of order,"[14] begin when Holly, fresh off the plane, rushes up the stairs at Harry's flat only to be told by the building's porter that his friend is dead, that the mourners have just left for the cemetery, and that Harry Lime is now either in hell (the porter points upward) or in heaven (the porter points downward). The canted shots that Reed continues to use throughout the film function as a trope to illustrate the moral instability of the fictional world of *The Third Man* and the degree to which Holly is out of his depth in his efforts to exonerate Lime. The climatic meeting of Martins and the undead Lime on a Ferris wheel makes particularly good use of tilted angles, especially when Lime slides the carriage door open and Martins realizes it is to his advantage to take a good hold through the window so that he cannot be pushed to his death. That Reed skews the angle of these shots compounds our sense of just how off balance and dangerous the situation is. In the Ferris wheel scene we realize that Lime is at the center of much that is off kilter about the Vienna that Holly is trying to navigate.

In addition to its striking camera work and score, the film features any number of bizarre characters who contribute to its general conjunction of comic irony and moral uncertainty: the so-called Baron Kurtz, who carries a chihuahua about with him and smilingly wishes to offer Martins his advice; Dr. Winkel, who forever has to correct Martins' mispronunciations of his name but who, in response to Martins' questions about how Lime died, says he can "give no opinion" although he claims to have arrived at the scene just after Lime was run over; the Romanian Popescu, who cryptically remarks to Holly that "everyone ought to go carefully in a city like this"; Harry Lime's porter and his wife; Lime's girlfriend Anna Schmidt's babbling landlady; and Crabbin, the British propagandist working on cultural re-education in Vienna while trying to ensure that he doesn't have to introduce his female companion to his acquaintances. Post-war Vienna is a city in which everyone is prepared to bend the rules. This is true not only of the racketeers, but also of the police. Harry Lime knows immediately that Popescu is the person who can broker a forged passport for Anna, protecting her, a Czech, from the Russians who want to repatriate her. This is perhaps Lime's only example of bending the rules for a good reason, although, given that Anna is his lover, it is also self-serving. We also, however, see both Holly and Major Calloway doing what they can to help Anna. Even Calloway—the film's center of moral authority, persistently referred to by Martins as "Callahan"—is prepared to help Anna when it is discovered that her papers are forged, since Calloway's ultimate goal is to capture Lime, and he is willing, as Martins finds out, to pay the price asked—namely, safe passage out of Vienna for Anna. Yet Calloway is a crusty figure. After their first meeting, he dismisses Martins as "only a scribbler with too much drink in him." Calloway keeps trying to persuade Martins to go back to America, realizing that he is in over his head. Martins, by ignoring this good advice, discovers more about his boyhood friend than he had ever wanted to know.

Add to this Reed's splendid use of location to consolidate mood. In the ruins of Vienna, the streets are slick with rain and eerily deserted at night. Near the cemetery, the trees are virtually bare, dropping their final leaves. Looming shadows projected against the facades of buildings repeatedly suggest danger, and yet the apparent threat turns out to be a young child or an old balloon seller, deliberately undercutting suspense. At other times, a creature as innocent as Anna's kitten, washing its face in a doorway, reveals to Holly the location of Harry Lime, who is quite alive and hiding there. The three most important scenes that occur during the day are Lime's two funerals, which bookend the film, and the meeting between Lime and Martins on the Ferris wheel. These three scenes are emblematic of Martins' changing understanding of his "friend". Most of the rest of the film occurs at night. The upshot, thematically and aesthetically, is that nothing in The Third Man can be taken at face value, most especially the boyish face of Harry Lime himself, seller of cut-rate penicillin, which has killed many and filled a hospital ward with brain-damaged children.

Is *The Third Man* a film principally about friendship? The evidence counts strongly against this view. Near the beginning of the film, Calloway takes Martins to a bar and buys him a bottle of whiskey (Martins has no Austrian currency) in order to get information from him after Lime's first, and, as it turns out, false, funeral. Martins admits that the last time he saw Lime was a decade previously, in September 1939, which would be at the outbreak of the Second World War. Prior to that, Martins had only seldom seen Lime. Nostalgically and drunkenly, Martins says that Harry was the best friend he ever had, back in their school days, to which Calloway responds that Martins' version of this tale sounds like "a cheap novelette." The main things Martins recounts about his so-called friendship with Lime are that Harry was good at "fixing" things—for instance, cribbing for tests, and that later on, they got drunk together and Lime stole Martins' girl. Perhaps Martins admired Lime, or wished to be like him, or thought it good fun to spend time with him, but nothing about Martins' recollections gives any reason to think that a genuine friendship is at issue. Whatever the status of their former relationship, in the famous Ferris wheel scene Lime makes clear that he is prepared to kill Martins if necessary.

Does Martins eventually do the right thing? Is he somehow led to the correct moral reappraisal of his former friend, thus allowing him to act correctly? Certainly Calloway, by presenting Martins with all the details of the British military police's file on Lime, paints a persuasive picture of Lime as the despicable racketeer he truly is. Even then, however, Holly's motives are conflicted. He initially agrees to help Calloway capture Harry, but he is primarily influenced by the situation of Anna Schmidt, Harry's lover, who is in trouble with the Russian authorities in Vienna. Holly has decided to fall in love with Anna, in large measure because she was Harry's lover and thus the person best situated to reconnect him with (as he initially thinks) his dead friend. Also, of course, he desires Anna because Harry did, and to woo her away from Harry would be just deserts to the old friend who formerly seduced his own girlfriend. The first time Holly agrees to help Calloway capture Harry, it is a calculated action on his part meant primarily to help Anna. As Holly says, having seen all the evidence, Harry "deserves to hang." Still, he negotiates with Calloway, asking, "What price would you pay?" Calloway quickly replies, "Name it", and Holly names safe exit from Vienna for Anna. So, it is difficult to think of Holly as having acted morally after learning the details of Harry Lime's crimes, since he is primarily motivated by his sentimental attachment to Anna. Worse yet, Anna discovers Holly at the train station the evening she is about to leave Vienna. Curious, she leaves her train carriage to talk to him, and she realizes that he is about to sell Harry out in exchange for her ticket to Paris. She rips up her passport, saying, "If you want to sell your services, I am not willing to be the price." Rejected, Holly goes back to Calloway and refuses to help capture Lime. It takes a detour to the hospital, where Martins is introduced to young children who have received Lime's black market penicillin, before Martins tells Calloway, "You win", and "I'll be your dumb decoy duck." Hardly words spoken by someone of strong moral fiber. Martins' most promising effort to cooperate with Calloway against Lime was when Calloway might have been able to help Anna. In the end, his participation is noticeably unenthusiastic.

The final two major actions undertaken by Holly Martins in *The Third Man* show how little moral improvement there has been as a result of his adventures in Vienna. In the wonderful final chase sequence through the Viennese sewer system—which contributes both aesthetically and ironically to the film and certainly secures our metaphorical understanding of Lime as a "sewer rat"—Martins winds up holding a gun on Lime, who has been shot and seriously wounded by Calloway after Lime has shot and killed perhaps the most sympathetic character in the film, Calloway's sergeant. Martins catches Lime trying to escape up a metal staircase to a sewer hole. The two confront each other. Calloway has already told Martins to take no chances and to shoot Lime if he can. There is an exchange of glances between Martins and Lime. Lime seems to invite Martins to shoot him. There is a cut back down the sewer to Calloway. We don't see what happens, but we do hear a gunshot, and a little later Martins comes into view in the distance. The evidence suggests that Martins kills Lime, but only because he compliantly responds to Lime's facial gesture, which suggests that he wants Martins to shoot him. Even at this point in the film, given everything Martins knows about Lime, Lime is able to manipulate him. The final major action undertaken by Martins occurs as Calloway drives him away from the cemetery after Lime's second, and actual, funeral. Just as she did after the first funeral, Anna walks, alone, down the long road from the cemetery back to the city center. Calloway is trying to get Martins to the plane that will take him back to America. Martins, still besotted with Anna, persuades Calloway to drop him at the side of the road. Anna is a long way behind. Martins, as sentimental as he was when he arrived in Vienna, imagines that Anna will forgive him for helping the military police in their pursuit of Lime. As Martins gets out of the jeep, Calloway says, "Be sensible, Martins." Holly Martins jovially replies, "I haven't got a sensible name." In one of cinema's greatest extended takes, Anna continues down the street and toward the camera, finally walking straight past Martins without acknowledging him at all, before she passes out of the frame.

The Third Man is, among other things, a character study concerned with the moral weaknesses of both Holly Martins and Harry Lime,[15] not a thought experiment about the so-called Forster Maxim. Martins remains what he was at the start—clever enough in his limited, pulp-fiction way, sentimental, and lacking moral sophistication or seriousness. *The Third Man* tracks two main themes. One is Holly's discovery of Harry Lime's true nature, and his unwillingness to take a strong position against Harry and what Harry stands for. The other is Holly's inability to achieve full self-realization. At the beginning of the film, Holly is self-deluded about his relationship with Harry Lime, and at the end of the film, he is self-deluded about his relationship with Anna Schmidt. These twin themes support the view that *The Third Man* is ironic, and that a major part of the irony is that Holly cannot learn the moral lesson of his own experience in Vienna.

NOTES

1. Recently, there has been lively debate on this topic, with philosophers including Tom Wartenberg defending the view that fictional films do, indeed, philosophize, while others, including Paisley Livingston, suggest that we adopt the more modest view that some fictional films illustrate particular philosophical themes. See Wartenberg, "Beyond *Mere* Illustration" and Livingston, "Theses on Cinema as Philosophy."

2. Carroll, "Art, Narrative, and Moral Understanding," 319.

3. Ibid., 142.

4. Ibid.,.

5. Carroll, "The Wheel of Virtue," 7.

6. Ibid.

7. Consider Martha Nussbaum's *Love's Knowledge*, as well as her *Poetic Justice*. See also Wayne C. Booth, *The Company We Keep*.

8. Peter Lamarque, *Fictional Points of View*.

9. Murray Smith, "Film Art, Argument, and Ambiguity."

10. There are, of course, films and other narrative fictions that raise comparable questions and merit having those questions taken seriously. A recent example, *The Good Shepherd*, poignantly asks whether one should choose one's family or one's state—a theme that of course goes back to Greek tragedy.

11. Although, as I will argue in a moment, there are features of the style of Reed's film, for example the use of the zither in the score and the *mise-en-scène* of the film, that do give us a strong sense of the attitude we should take up with respect to Holly Martins. Still, this is not directly stated by the film.

12. Frye, *Anatomy of Criticism*, 48. Indeed, the novels of Graham Greene are the example Frye himself uses as illustrative of this sort of comic irony.

13. I am taking the British version of *The Third Man*, in which the breezy voice-over is spoken by an unnamed figure (and voiced by Carol Reed), as authoritative. In the American version, the introductory voice-over is rewritten so that it can be read by Joseph Cotten in the role of Holly Martins. The sense of detachment and irony of the British version is compromised by the substitution made for the American market. As the British version makes clear, the story we are about to see unfold is told by someone quite separate from the situation being recounted and thus by someone who is easily able to appreciate Martins' faults. Because Martins is the fictional speaker of the voice-over in the American version, we might think of him as a more sympathetic character than Reed intended.

14. See rogerebert.suntimes.com/apps/pbcs.dll/article?AID=/19961208/REVIEWS08/401010366/1023, last accessed 20 March 2008, or, more straightforwardly, search the Internet for Ebert "Third Man".

15. Frankly, here I should also include Anna, who has also been told by Calloway of Lime's black market activities. Despite what she learns, she still clings to the idea that Harry is worthy of her love. One thing in Martins' favor is that, however grudgingly, he does come round to the responsible moral position. An interesting note from the film: at the first, false, funeral, Holly scatters earth over the coffin, while Anna does not. At the second and actual funeral, Anna scatters earth while Holly does not.

MORAL INTELLIGENCE
AND THE
LIMITS OF LOYALTY

THE THIRD MAN AS PHILOSOPHY

THOMAS E. WARTENBERG

THE VERY NOTION THAT A fiction film could make a contribution to ethics will, no doubt, strike many readers as perplexing. Ethical insight, they might think, requires deep thinking about complex ethical situations in which one's commitments cut in different directions and even contradict one another. So, for example, I have a commitment to being loyal to my friends, but also to realizing a just social order. What happens if I find out that one of my friends is a terrorist who plans to kill many innocent people? Does this knowledge trump my loyalty to her? What about if I find out that a different friend once did something that I do not approve of, such as voting for a political candidate I think is abhorrent? Why might we think that this should not affect my loyalty to this friend, whereas my loyalty should be overridden in the former case? Clearly, accounts of such conflicts will require making subtle distinctions and carefully considering opposing views.

To continue the thought process I am imagining taking place in some of my readers, fiction films are just not capable of *that*. When we go to the movies, we are looking for entertainment, not enlightenment. Just think of the reaction film viewers at your local multiplex would have if, when attending a showing of a film titled *The Bottom*, they found themselves confronted with a film of the late John Rawls, the eminent moral philosopher, explaining why it was not permissible to adopt a social policy that did not advantage the least well off—those on the bottom. The flood of customers demanding their money back boggles the imagination.

I use this example to suggest how counterintuitive the idea of films providing us with moral insight seems to many. Still, I think that taking film and ethical knowledge to be antithetical is deeply misguided, for some films can—and *do*—contain important ethical insights. They do so by providing very specific and detailed examples that allow their viewers to understand the complexity of moral situations in a way that they previously might not have. For this reason, such films can make a contribution to philosophical ethics.

In what follows, I will use Carol Reed's 1949 film *The Third Man*, based on the screenplay by Graham Greene, as an example of a film that provides ethical insight. It does so, I shall argue, by illustrating an important idea in Aristotle's ethics that had not received sufficient attention at the time of the film's making. That idea is, as my title indicates, moral intelligence. The film shows us why it is important for a person to possess moral intelligence, what function it plays in their ethical life, and what is involved in its use. It explores this notion through a story about the limits of the loyalty that one owes to one's friends. And, in so doing, it presents some ethical insights.

I. THE CONCEPT OF MORAL INTELLIGENCE

The central ethical issue that *The Third Man* addresses is understanding how a person comes to have a correct ethical understanding of the specific situation in which he finds himself. The ethical requirements of any normal human life situation are quite complex. If I think about my own situation, there are a variety of different commitments that I could plausibly be said to have. Some accrue to me as a father, others as a husband. I'm also a citizen and a professor. Each of these roles brings putative commitments with it, not to speak of the general ethical commitments I have simply by virtue of my humanity.

So when it comes to acting, how do I decide what I should actually be doing? Should I spend my time furthering my own intellectual projects, or should I be helping my son do well in school or succeed in sports? What about fighting for the social order I deem desirable? These represent real choices that I must make. Is there any way for me to achieve what we might call "a morally perspicuous understanding of my situation" that will allow me to balance these competing demands?

The film's answer is that *moral intelligence* is required to assess one's situation in a morally perspicuous manner. Moral or practical intelligence is a notion developed by Aristotle in the *Nichomachean Ethics*. Intelligence might not leap to mind as an important ethical virtue, as would, instead, such traditional virtues as courage, loyalty, modesty, integrity, and truthfulness. Aristotle, however, thinks that intelligence is also a moral virtue: "For the agent they would call intelligent is the one who studies well each question about his own [good]."[1] In the terms I have been using, the person with moral intelligence is one who is able to achieve a morally perspicuous view of her own situation.

Aristotle argues that having intelligence requires more than simply knowing what moral commitments one has—it entails knowing how to assess their applicability in concrete situations. The example he gives involves the moral commitment to promoting one's own health, and what he points out is that general knowledge, by itself, is inadequate for making a considered judgment about what it makes the most sense to do in order to foster one's health:

> Nor is intelligence about universals only. It also must come to know particulars, since it is concerned with action and action is about particulars . . . . For someone who knows that light meats are digestible and healthy, but not which sorts of meats are light, will not produce health; the one who knows that bird meats are healthy will be better at producing health.[2]

Aristotle's point is that a morally intelligent person needs to know how to apply his general moral commitments in particular situations. It is not sufficient for a moral agent to know that loyalty is an important constituent of friendship—to choose an example that will be the focus of our discussion of *The Third Man*—she also needs to be able to accurately judge who her friends really are.

The notion of moral intelligence has received a good deal of attention as of late. Iris Murdoch, Martha Nussbaum, and Lawrence A. Blum, among others, have all argued for the importance of this notion in ethical theory, thereby correcting its neglect within contemporary ethics.[3]

In light of this, what can we say *The Third Man* contributes to this discussion in philosophical ethics? First, the film was made well more than a decade before the earliest contribution to this discussion of Aristotle's theory. So, the film makes its case for the importance of this notion more than a decade before philosophers first attempted its recovery. Second, the film provides a *concrete illustration* of Aristotle's claims about moral intelligence. This in itself can make a contribution to ethics, as I shall argue. Third, the film connects this issue with the role of art in modern times, with mass fictions. Again, this is an important claim that illuminates an issue in ethics (and aesthetics) that has recently been the focus of a great deal of attention. Finally, the film investigates loyalty as a moral virtue. In so doing, it raises the question of the role of loyalty in friendship, an issue that still has not received adequate attention within philosophical ethics.

These topics are only meant to serve as signposts for the argument that lies ahead. In it, I will show how *The Third Man* offers important insights about each of the issues just mentioned. It will be in virtue of this that I think we ought to acknowledge the film as making a contribution to philosophical ethics.

II. A CONFUSING SITUATION

The Third Man begins by throwing us willy-nilly into the milieu of post-war Vienna, presenting a series of newsreel-like clips accompanied by a voiceover in which a self-acknowledged black marketeer attempts to insinuate himself into our good graces. These clips depict post–World War II Vienna as a place in which things are not what they seem. People have to get by as best they can, and one cannot always use appearances to make accurate judgments. The anonymous narrator tells us what the city is like "now"—that is, after the war—claiming he had not seen it before. Now is the "classic period of the black market," he says, identifying himself as one of its players. "We'd run anything if people wanted it enough and had the money to pay."[4] He also explains the geopolitical realities of the city, describing how it has been divided by the four Allies into different zones, but the center of the city—where the action of the film takes place—remains shared by all of them and so is policed by an international force. He comments: "Wonderful! What a hope they had. All strangers to the place . . . . and none of them could speak the same language . . . . Except of course a smattering of German. Good fellows on the whole. Did their best, you know."[5]

This unusual opening sequence is unsettling because an unidentified voice speaks to us in what can only be called a confidential and confiding tone that presumes an intimacy for which there is no basis—as if we were conspirators in some deed the nature of which we know nothing about. The precise tone of the narration is difficult to characterize accurately. Since the narrator identifies himself as a black marketeer, he speaks with cynicism about the aims of the Allies, as if they did the best they could given their lack of knowledge about the city they were trying to control and their inability to even talk to one another. He characterizes the resulting situation in Vienna as one in which ethical principles have to take a back seat to necessity. In this highly fraught context, people need to do whatever it takes for them to survive, he asserts.

The film uses this unusual narrational style to raise the skeptical question that forms one of its foci: In a situation in which one lacks any secure basis for knowing whom to trust, how does one decide who is telling the truth, and how does one then settle on an adequate perspective for understanding what is taking place? When the narrator condescendingly judges that the Allies were good fellows on the whole—"Did their best, you know"—what is the basis for his judgment? How should we assess it? In doing their best, what did they let happen that they shouldn't have? Is he just being ironic and, if so, how should we then take his claim? These are all questions that create an atmosphere of ambiguity and give some urgency to the film's philosophic investigation of how one can achieve the correct moral perspective for viewing a situation, especially in complex moral situations, when it appears that the usual ethical rules do not apply.

This atmosphere of pervasive uncertainty continues throughout the body of the film and is achieved through a variety of cinematic techniques. Among the film's many superb expressionist elements is the use of a slightly titled camera to record many scenes, especially those involving conversations. By having us look at its world slightly askance, the film not only registers its central character's distrust, but also it distances us from the conversations it so depicts, keeping us a little off balance and dubious about the veracity of some of the characters. The film here achieves a cinematic equivalent of skepticism, deploying a visual analog of doubt.[6]

This sense of uncertainty, the lack of a secure perspective from which to assess competing claims about what is taking place, is not something that exclusively affects the film's audience, for its main character, at least in the sense of the one whose actions the camera follows for most of the film—Hollis Martins (Joseph Cotten)—also suffers serious confusion.[7] Martins is a penniless writer of cheap Western novelettes who has come to Vienna because his old friend Harry Lime (Orson Welles) has offered him a job and sent him a plane ticket for the flight. The film follows Martins as he arrives in Vienna and goes to Lime's apartment only to discover he has just missed his friend's funeral service. Clearly taken aback, Martins has to figure out exactly what to do now, for here he is, nearly broke, brought to a foreign city by a friend who has unexpectedly died, with no clear agenda other than understanding what's going on.

Things will get worse for Martins before they get better, for he will find his friend suspected of being a criminal. Even now, however, the film has created an atmosphere of doubt and uncertainty, both for Martins and its audience, about what is really going on in Vienna. This sets the appropriate context for its investigation into the question of how an adequate moral perspective on one's situation is achieved.

III. ACHIEVING CERTITUDE

Martins achieves his first settled moral perspective on his situation—albeit on the basis of what we later come to recognize are mistaken inferences—as a result of his encounter with Major Calloway (Trevor Howard), the officer in charge of the British military police in Vienna. Calloway gives Martins a lift back into town after Lime's burial and suggests they go for a drink. As Martins gets drunk, he tells Calloway how much Lime meant to him: "Best friend I ever had," he slurs.[8] Lime had, it seems, filled an important void in his life: "Never so lonesome in my life till he showed up."[9] Calloway's response—"That sounds like a cheap novelette"[10]—is rude and unsympathetic. After all, Martins has received a real shock, and we therefore have some sympathy for him and his plight, especially because the film is structured so that our access to the events in its narrative is nearly always through Martins. Although we will come to see him as a gullible and incurable romantic, at this point we lack sufficient evidence for making this assessment of him.

We are therefore taken aback by Calloway's repeated baiting of Martins. When Martins opines that Lime's death as a result of being run over by a car was "a shame", Calloway retorts, "Best thing that ever happened to him," and goes on to explain why: "He was the worst racketeer who ever made a dirty living in this city."[11] When Martins responds by conceding that Lime could have been involved in minor black marketeering—and admission we were prepared for by the film's initial newsreel-like sequence—Calloway counters that Lime's illicit dealings involved murder and not just the petty racketeering Martins has in mind. When he then dismisses Martins as a "scribbler with too much drink," Martins responds by accusing Calloway of not taking Lime's death seriously but only using it to solve crimes he is too lazy to investigate. Once again, Calloway's contemptuous response emphasizes Martin's profession as an author of popular fiction: "Going to find me the real criminal? It sounds like one of your stories."[12]

Although we may only realize it retrospectively—or, more likely, in subsequent viewings—Calloway has been baiting Martins for a reason. As Lime's friend, he is a suspect in his death. As a result of Martins' responses, Calloway has already dismissed him as innocent of knowledge of Lime's crimes. Because we don't yet know whom to believe about Lime—Was he a good person or a wicked criminal?—we remain uncertain about how to assess Calloway's accusations against him, a doubt the tilted camera accentuates. Martins' excessive drinking, wallowing self-pity, and precipitous but ineffectual attempt to slug Calloway all temper our initial sympathy for him. Still, we lack sufficient grounds for deciding whether this means his view of Lime is mistaken and Calloway's is correct.

Martins, however, has also been sizing up Calloway. Annoyed by Calloway's suspicions of Lime, he questions Calloway's motives, accusing him of trying to save himself work by using Lime as the patsy for his unsolved cases: "Pin it on a dead man."[13] When Calloway continues on in the same vein, Martins mimics the aggressive tone of Calloway's comments: "Why don't you catch a few murderers for a change?"[14]

These sarcastic comments do not only register Martins' obvious disdain for Calloway, they also subtly establish an important, if very ordinary, moral commitment that Martins has—he believes that murderers should be caught and punished, and he is contemptuous of Calloway for failing to live up to his moral responsibility to do so. What we recognize as an investigator's strategy for determining the guilt or innocence of a suspect, Martins takes at face value. At the same time, Martins also reveals another important moral commitment he has, his loyalty to his friend Lime. Faced with accusations about Lime's conduct and despite any specific knowledge of what Lime has been doing in recent years, Martins defends him and is even willing to take a shot at Calloway to defend his friend's honor.[15]

What seems remarkable about all this is that, given that Martins is a writer, he is so inept at interpreting Calloway's motives for baiting him. The film, however, is quick to suggest that Martins' profession is precisely the reason why he is so oblivious—he uses the plots of his own "cheap fictions" to provide him with a moral perspective in which both Calloway and he have clearly defined, albeit trite, roles to play. This emerges when, a moment later, he addresses Calloway's assistant, Sergeant Paine (Bernard Lee), a fan of Martins' writing. "Did you ever read a book of mine called *The Lone Rider of Santa Fe*?" he queries. When Paine says that he hasn't, Martins tells him, "It's a story of a man who hunted down a sheriff who was victimizing his best friend . . . I'm gunning just the same way for your Major Callahan," misremembering Calloway's name for the second time.[16] Because one of his pulp novels employs roles appropriate in his imagination to Calloway, Lime, and himself—corrupt cop, innocent but persecuted best friend, lone crusader for justice—Martins finds the novel's perspective easy to use as a way of getting some clarity on his very perplexing situation.

So, early in the film, Martins has been established as both a loyal friend to Lime and a person committed to murderers getting their due. As we shall see, the film uses a conflict between these two moral commitments as the vehicle for its investigation of moral intelligence.

IV. THE INADEQUACY OF FICTION AS A MORAL GUIDE

Before moving in that direction, however, the film takes a critical look at Martins' use of the character structure of his own fictions as a means of establishing his own moral perspective. As Nöel Carroll has pointed out, a fictional work of art can provide a variety of moral roles that function as templates for interpreting one's experience.[17] As we have just seen, the film presents this as precisely how

Martins handles the uncertainties he faces: He perceives his world through the fictional characters and scenarios articulated in his own "cheap novelettes". That hackneyed popular fiction provides a stunted moral perspective for its audience is one of the important philosophical claims made by this film.

The Third Man develops its critique of Martins' popular fiction-inspired point of view more fully in a subsequent scene, when his bungling investigation into Lime's death results in the death of an innocent person. Martins, who has precipitously gone off to discover Lime's murderer, finds inconsistencies in the testimony of the eyewitnesses to the event. His persistent questioning induces the porter of Lime's building (Paul Hoerbiger) to admit that he saw a *third man* carrying Lime's body from the middle of the road, despite the testimony of Lime's associates Popescu (Siegfried Bauer) and Baron Kurtz (Ernst Deutsch) that they were the only ones present. When Martins reveals the porter's testimony to Popescu, we suspect him of making a grave error, for Popescu is clearly part of a plot to obscure the truth about Lime's death—a suspicion confirmed by the porter's subsequent murder. When Martins himself is suspected of being the murderer, it also becomes apparent that he has unleashed forces that he is ill equipped to deal with effectively and that this threatens him and those with whom he has had contact, with dreadful consequences.

At this point, the problems that the film sees with a certain type of popular fiction emerge clearly. It is critical of such works for presenting a romanticized worldview that renders its aficionados incapable of exercising moral intelligence because they rely on simplistic and stereotyped moral schemes. This is more than simply a problem for those people, according to the film, for their misperceptions can result in real harm being done to others. Because "cheap fictions" stunt the moral intelligence of their readers, the film takes a dim view of this type of popular fiction.

Although the secondary literature on the film stresses the interest that both its producer, Michael Korda, and its director, Carol Reed, had in post-war Vienna, I can't help but see the film as here also reflecting on a broader issue posed by the war itself: How can an evil person convince basically decent people to support his endeavors?[18] Why don't these people see evil for what it really is and oppose it? Although there have been many proposed answers to this question, I think *The Third Man* puts forward an interesting alternative suggestion. Despite its not being a complete account of the rise of fascism, its depiction of how deficient moral intelligence, fueled by pulp fiction, can aid the triumph of evil strikes me as a contribution to our understanding of evil's ability to command people's loyalty.

V. PROVIDING THE EVIDENCE

Martins' presence has now become more than a mere nuisance for Calloway, who has been trying unsuccessfully to get Martins to leave Vienna. The film includes the running joke of Martins inevitably failing to catch the plane for which Calloway repeatedly provides him with a ticket. Because Martins is now causing others to be harmed, it is imperative that Calloway get him out of harm's way before he precipitates further disasters. The problem is that Martins won't leave Vienna as long as his perspective on his situation remains unaltered. Calloway therefore has the task of getting Martins to alter his assessment of his situation, and this can only happen if Martins rejects the adequacy of the interpretation he has made of his own situation through the lens of his own fiction. Only then will he be able to revise his views of both Lime and Calloway, seeing neither the former as an innocent victim nor the latter as a corrupt cop.

To achieve this, Calloway decides to show Martins exactly what Lime has done, what crimes he is guilty of. This will justify Calloway's contempt for Lime as well as, he hopes, make Martins reject his unquestioned loyalty to his friend. At the same time, it marks a crucial element of the film's depiction of the process that results in Martins having a more adequate and morally intelligent assessment of his situation.

Calloway explains to Martins that Lime has committed the crime of selling diluted tubes of penicillin on the black market for huge profits. At first, Martins doesn't see the significance of Calloway's revelation, dominated as he is by his pulp-fiction-induced suspicion about the major and his character. As a result, he pooh-poohs this new information, reiterating his disgust at Calloway for his supposed failure to even try to apprehend Lime's murderers: "Are you too busy chasing a few tubes of penicillin to investigate a murder?" Calloway patiently explains that, while there is a murder here, Lime is its perpetrator, not its victim. Many people were treated with the doctored drug—"Men with gangrene legs . . . . women in child birth . . . and there were children, too," Calloway tells Martins. He continues, "They used some of this diluted penicillin against meningitis. The lucky children died . . . The unlucky ones went off their heads. You can see them now in the mental wards."[19] When Martins counters that Calloway has still not shown him any *evidence* of Lime's crimes, Calloway resorts to "a magic lantern show."[20] He has Sergeant Paine project photographic slides onto a screen, slides that include, among other things, pictures of Lime with his collaborator, Joseph Harbin, a medical orderly who, we later learn, Lime has killed and substituted for himself in his coffin to prevent the man from being a witness against him. These images, together with some actual physical evidence, convince Martins of Lime's guilt. "How could he have done it?" Martins asks incredulously, to which Calloway cynically replies, "Seventy pounds a tube."[21]

How does viewing Calloway's evidence against Lime affect Martins? First of all, it radically alters his view of Lime, for he can no longer maintain his preconceived image of his former friend. Seeing what Lime has done, for that is how the show impacts Martins—it lets him see *with his own eyes* evidence of Lime's guilt—diminishes the hold of the pulp-fiction-induced perspective according to which Lime is a good friend being persecuted by a corrupt cop. Martins is no longer able to reactively dismiss Calloway's perspective, for Martins now has seen evidence that shows that Lime is a murderer as well as a black marketeer. Seeing the actual evidence of Lime's treachery dislodges Martins' blind faith in his own assessment of Lime's actions and character, one based on an array of characters derived from his own pop fiction.

I italicized the words "with his own eyes" in the last paragraph to emphasize the film's presentation of a series of photographs as able to constitute evidence of Lime's treacherous actions. The film thus juxtaposes photography and popular fiction as alternative sources of moral conviction. Whereas the film presents pulp fiction as lacking the means to provide a morally perspicuous assessment of Martins' situation, however, it characterizes Calloway's magic lantern show in very different terms—its use of photographs provides the evidence of Lime's crimes that Martins demands and that play a role in his dawning acknowledgment that Lime was not really his friend and thus might not deserve his loyalty.

How does the slide show have the power to provide Martins with the evidence he requires? Although it is tempting to describe this as a scene of instruction, I want to emphasize how similar Calloway's role is here to that of a film director. That is, he has carefully arranged a series of visual images to produce a specific effect in its beholder, Martins. And that—together with the fact that "magic lantern show" is an oddly appropriate way to describe film itself—suggests that the film is here allegorizing film and photography as an alternative to pulp fiction as determiners of moral perspectives. The reason that film and photography are superior to fiction, according to the film's view, is that they allow us to see the evidence that supports a particular perspective in close-up and with attention to detail, to foreshadow the terms that I will introduce more carefully in a moment.

VI. LOYALTY AND FRIENDSHIP

The Third Man emphasizes the beneficial effects of Calloway's magic lantern show in the following scene, when Martins appears—drunk again when his view of the world has been challenged—at the apartment of Anna Schmidt (Alida Valli), Lime's former lover. Once more, self-pity has overwhelmed him, although this time it is also fueled by his unrequited love for Schmidt.[22] What's important for us, however, is his reassessment of Lime. He tells Schmidt, whom Calloway has also told of Lime's treachery, that he is no longer so sure of who Lime is: "I knew him for twenty years—at least I thought I knew him. I suppose he was laughing at fools like us all the time."[23] Schmidt grows impatient with Martins for saying that Lime might have brought him to Vienna to enhance the profitability of his illegal penicillin sales: "Oh, please, for heaven's sake, stop making him in your image. Harry was real. He wasn't just your friend and my lover. He was Harry."[24] Martins, who is not really listening to her but is continuing his own line of thought, tells her that he now sees Lime's death as in some way righting the wrongs he had done: "Whoever killed him, there was some kind of justice. Maybe I'd have killed him myself."[25] Once more, Schmidt counters, this time telling Martins that Calloway's information shouldn't affect their sense of who Lime was: "A person doesn't change because you find out more."[26]

The film's presentation of Schmidt and Martins as having different reactions to Calloway's revelations begins its depiction of an alternative to the array of morally tinged roles that Martins has used to understand his situation: maligned friend, corrupt cop, crusading writer. In particular, the film will present Schmidt, Martins, and Lime as characters with different understandings of the relationship between friendship and loyalty.

Friendship is a topic that has been discussed by philosophers at least since Plato, but it is Aristotle who offers a systematic account of its role in his *Nichomachean Ethics*, where he claims that having friends is one of the components of a good life. More recently, Lawrence Blum has developed Aristotle's claim, arguing that friendship entails a concern for the good of the friend.[27] Surprisingly, however, there has been little philosophical discussion of whether a friend is committed to being loyal to his or her friends. This is an issue that *The Third Man* investigates in detail and about which it makes important suggestions through presenting what Nöel Carroll has termed a "virtue tableau"— that is, an array of characters who embody a particular virtue, here loyalty to a friend, in differing ways.

In this scene, the film highlights the differences among its characters' views about how loyal one must be to one's friends. As we have already seen, the film initially presented Martins as loyal to Lime in the face of Calloway's jibes. Now, however, the information Martins has received as a result of Calloway's magic lantern show causes him to reassess his loyalty. In particular, the brutal murders that Lime has committed cause him to doubt that his supposed friend really deserves his loyalty. In a foreshadowing of the film's dramatic penultimate scene, he even imagines himself as the agent of Lime's justifiable death. Deeply in love, Schmidt remains completely loyal to Lime despite the new information she has gotten. Her refusal to re-evaluate her loyalty to Lime might even seem slightly pathological—a refusal to give up her own sense of loss—and it marks her as lacking in moral intelligence.[28]

Even though Martins has begun to acknowledge the limitations of his earlier view of Lime and his activities, he is not yet ready to accept all the implications of what Calloway has shown him. Schmidt's unquestioned loyalty to her ex-lover still attracts Martins—he remains in love with her even at the film's conclusion, as she impassively walks by his forlorn figure. Yet he has also shown a strong commitment to the idea that evildoers must get what they deserve, as he showed in his initial criticisms of Calloway as well as in the plots of his own novels.

To complete its virtue tableau, *The Third Man* needs to present someone who shows no loyalty to those whom he considers his friends. Harry Lime would be a good candidate for this role, but how can the film show us his character when he is dead?

To resolve this problem, the film demonstrates that, at the very moment when our skeptical doubts about Lime appear to have been resolved, we still have good reason to be unsure of him, for we are deceived about Lime's death. When Martins leaves Schmidt, he thinks that Calloway is tailing him. To his surprise, and ours, the figure that emerges from the shadows is that of his friend Harry Lime, now seen by us for the first time, some two-thirds of the way through the film. Lime only reveals himself after his face has been illuminated accidentally by the light from a neighboring building, and then only to quiet down Martins lest someone call the police. As soon as Martins is quiet, Lime flees. Although Martins gives chase, Lime seems to disappear into thin air. Only later does Calloway figure out the secret of Lime's vanishing—he has descended into the vast sewer network that runs beneath the streets of Vienna and that gives him access to the entire city without attracting the attention of the police.

At this point, Calloway has Lime's coffin disinterred, revealing the body of Joseph Harbin, the medical orderly who actually procured the penicillin. If Calloway's slide show hadn't already convinced Martins that Lime was an evil person, Lime's strategic and apparently cold-blooded killing of his own associate should give him pause. Here is a man who is willing to murder others he has worked with in order to save his own skin. But for Martins' bumbling exposé, the clever plot might have succeeded.

Rather than shy away from the chase, however, Martins continues blithely on his way, demanding that Lime meet with him. Lime attempts to placate him in a scene that is one of the highlights of the film, for the two talk on the Ferris wheel of the famous Prater Amusement Park in Vienna. They are alone in a compartment that slowly ascends over the city. As they do so, Martins confronts his friend. He begins by telling Lime that the police have arrested Schmidt. Lime's seeming indifference upsets the love-struck Martins, while Lime's response recalls the film's earlier portrayal of Martins as a victim of his own fictions. After misquoting the final line from the end of A Tale of Two Cities—"It's a far better thing that I do . . ."[29]—Lime responds in a manner that emphasizes the limitations of Martins' pulp fictional perspective: "Holly, you and I aren't heroes, the world doesn't make heroes . . . Outside of your stories . . . . I've got to be careful."[30] Lime then lets slip that his safety depends on his usefulness to the Russians, a slip that tips Martins off that Lime has betrayed Schmidt to save his own skin.

With its presentation of Lime, The Third Man completes an interesting array of characters with different conceptions of the relationship between loyalty and friendship. At one pole stands Schmidt.[31] She represents a view of friendship as demanding absolute loyalty to one's friends. Nothing that a friend has done can undermine the commitment a person has to being loyal to her friend. At the opposite pole stands Lime. The only person he is loyal to is himself. His willingness to kill Harbin and give Schmidt up to the Russians is evidence that he does not see the commitments of friendship as overriding his instinct for self-preservation. As a result, loyalty plays no role in his conception of the ethical commitments he has to his friends. Because of this, Aristotle would claim, he is not a true friend, but only one whose friendship depends upon convenience.

Occupying a position between these two is Martins. Neither an unwaveringly loyal friend nor merely a participant in friendships of convenience, Martins recognizes that friends need to deserve one's loyalty. What, however, counts as *deserving* a friend's loyalty? This is precisely where the notion of moral intelligence comes in. A morally intelligent person has to be able to assess whether and when a friend deserves one's loyalty, whether actions he has done that one does not approve of result in the defeasance of one's commitment to being loyal to them.

Martins' realization that Lime is not a loyal friend allows him to exercise his moral intelligence by reassessing his own friendship with Lime with the sort of insight that is characteristic of psychotherapy: Once he is able to see that Lime is not the loyal friend Martins believed him to be, a repressed memory floods Martins' consciousness and confirms that view. Remembering an incident from their youth, he tells Lime, "I remember when they raided the gambling joint—you knew a safe way out. . . . . Yes, safe for you . . . . not safe for me."[32] The film here depicts an important step in Martins' exercise of moral intelligence to assess the world around him. With overwhelming evidence of Lime's callousness to those closest to him literally staring him in the face—he notices Lime drawing on the fogged window of their compartment a heart with "Anna" inside—Martins is able to reject the idealized image he has had of Lime and to entertain the thought that he is an evil man. As a result, Martins can rethink the nature of their "friendship". What he discovers is that his own perspective on the past—and "Best friend I ever had"—is radically mistaken, for his "best friend" was always willing to sacrifice Martins to save his own skin.

Armed with this more realistic and morally intelligent view of Lime, Martins asks him if he has ever seen one of the victims of his crimes. Lime responds with a speech that reveals the moral perspective that allows him to commit evil. Moving to the compartment door, Lime opens it, looks down, and asks Martins to look at the people far below. They are so small that they appear to be nothing but *dots*.[33] "Would you feel any pity," Lime asks Martins, "if one of those dots stopped moving forever?"[34] This rhetorical question conveys Lime's ethical perspective to Martins. When viewed from such a distance, Lime implies, people appear so insignificant that it is difficult to be sympathetic to their fate, so that any moral concern for them loses its purchase. If one benefits from harming them—and Lime now admits that he has—there is no reason not to go ahead and do so, for one's own welfare is all that ultimately counts.

This equation of an evil moral perspective with a physically distant one reinforces the metaphoric structure the film uses to present its understanding of how a morally intelligent perspective on one's situation is achieved. In this framework, physically seeing something up close and in detail results in the mobilization of one's moral intelligence. On the other hand, when one maintains a great physical distance between oneself and others, it becomes easy to resort to stock ideas that enable one to harm others without second thoughts, for they lose their humanity when looked at from afar. According to this model, physical distance breeds psychic distance. Even as it presents Lime's view, however, the film criticizes it, for it comes on the heels of Martins' realization that Lime has kept his distance, and hence his detachment, from those who care for him: Martins himself as well as Schmidt.

The conversation between the two "friends" now takes a more sinister turn. Upset that Martins has informed the police that he is alive, Lime threatens to kill Martins, since he appears to be the only witness against him. Martins informs him, however, that his grave has been dug up by the police and Harbin's body found. As he digests this information, Lime's tone changes from threatening to solicitous— Welles' performance here is stunning, as his face registers his reassessment of his situation—as he tells Martins that he still wants to give him a cut of the action. In a fateful admission that will prove to be his undoing, Lime tells Martins that he will meet with him "any place, any time" only not with the police present.[35]

VII. COMPLETING THE TRANSFORMATION

Even though the evidence of Lime's treachery is now overwhelming, Martins still retains traces of his romantic, pulp-fiction-inspired perspective. Earlier in the film, Martins had upbraided Calloway for his failure to pursue Lime's killers and had even taken it upon himself to bring them to justice. Doesn't this commitment now require him to help apprehend a murderer, even if it happens that the murderer is his friend? How could he justify not doing so?

The answer is that he still thinks that his friendship with Lime requires him to be loyal. When Calloway asks him to help set a trap to capture Lime, Martins initially demurs: "Calloway, you expect too much. I know he deserves to hang, you proved your stuff. But twenty years is a long time—don't ask me to tie the rope."[36] Martins here reveals an inability to act on moral ideas that he has himself accepted, for he uses his loyalty to his "friend" to excuse himself from assisting in his capture. He does so even though he believes that Lime deserves to die for the crimes he has committed, thus exhibiting a failure of moral intelligence, an inability to assess the proper way of reconciling his competing allegiances. His seemingly pragmatic solution is inadequate because it arbitrarily exempts him from the responsibility of bringing a murderer to justice, a responsibility that Martins has himself endorsed. His misplaced sense of loyalty, the film suggests, will allow an evildoer to escape unpunished. Martins will have to endure further stimulus to his moral intelligence at Calloway's hands before he is ready to completely embrace an adequate moral perspective.

After his first attempt to use Martins to trap Lime is derailed by the loyal Schmidt's contempt, Calloway provides Martins with the experience he still needs before he can embrace a fully morally intelligent understanding of both Lime and the limits of loyalty. On the way to the airport, while bringing the dispirited Martins to the plane he never does manage to catch, Calloway disingenuously suggests that he has an errand to run in the biggest children's hospital in Vienna, and he asks

Martins to accompany him because he is sure that, as a writer, he will be inter-ested. Recall that earlier Calloway had told Martins that the unlucky children who went insane because the diluted penicillin had not cured their meningitis were hospitalized in a mental ward. Now, he wants Martins to see the actual fruits of Lime's labors—in close-up and in detail. The camera follows Calloway and Mar-tins as they walk around the ward, once again using tilted shots, this time to record Martins' doubts and dismay. As Martins looks at the children in their beds, the camera tracks his movements, showing him looking down into one cot in partic-ular. A nurse shakes a thermometer. Another gives a child oxygen. Finally, one drops into the trash a teddy bear that had been hanging on one child's hospital bed—another victim of Lime's crime has succumbed, this time before Martins' eyes. It takes only a moment longer for Martins to surrender: "I said you win," he tells Calloway, "I'll be your dumb decoy."[37]

Martins had previously refused to cooperate with Calloway because he felt that his friendship with Lime required him to be loyal to Lime. He now sees Lime's punish-ment as morally more compelling than his own loyalty to his former friend. Indeed, as Schmidt's example makes clear, unquestioned loyalty to an evil person can be a moral failing, just as Lime's example has made clear the moral shortcomings of an absence of any loyalty to one's friends. What changes Martins' mind is seeing up close and in detail the devastating effects of Lime's operation on the lives of innocent children, for he cannot maintain any psychic distance when confronted with their actual suffering.

Figure 15.2

By using the harm done to children as the proof that Martins requires, the film brings to mind Ivan's argument in the "Rebellion" chapter of Dostoyevsky's *The Brothers Karamazov*. Ivan argues that his moral perspective as a human being cannot accept a moral outlook that justifies the suffering of innocent children. His target is the optimistic response to the problem of evil—that we should accept the existence of evil as a necessary aspect of God's creation of a world with even greater good. Ivan rejects that moral outlook as inhuman, because it asks us to accept the suffering of children as a necessary price for the existence of the world. For him, the suffering of such innocents is so awful that he refuses to accept it, even when compelled by a moral calculus.

Martins manifests a similar vulnerability to the suffering of innocent children. Unlike Ivan, however, Martins must actually see the harm done to them before he is able to overcome his romanticized view of his friendship with Lime. If Vienna is a city in which there are no absolutes, in which everyone has to compromise to stay alive—a view that Popescu expressed earlier to explain his own presence as a nightclub musician—the film asserts that this need not be a defect. Rather, it asserts that moral intelligence requires flexibility, a refusal to treat any commitment as so absolute that it cannot be overridden by other commitments in the appropriate circumstances. Indeed, this is precisely why moral intelligence is such an important moral virtue, for without it we would not be able to judge when circumstances warrant overriding a commitment we accept.

Martins does not shed his loyalty to Lime easily. Nor should he. As I have said, loyalty to a friend is a virtue that we do, and should, value highly. This does not mean, however, that such loyalty cannot be misplaced, that there are circumstances in which it must give way to more important moral considerations. *The Third Man* presents us with an example of one set of circumstances in which this is true. In so doing, however, it does not provide a counterexample to a moral principle—as Carroll alleges in his discussion of the film[38]—but rather an account of moral intelligence and how it enables one to see the limits of one's specific moral commitments.

It is important to realize that what brings about Martins' willingness to serve Calloway is actually *seeing* the effects of Lime's crime. This is the third in the series of different means the film portrays as capable of settling one's moral perspective on a situation. It began with a critical assessment of pulp fiction as distorting one's view of one's situation. Pulp fiction, it claimed, employed stereotyped moral characters that stunted the use of moral intelligence. It then moved to a positive assessment of the role that a "magic lantern show" could have in achieving a more morally intelligent view. This was because photography can provide the evidence to legitimates a moral reassessment of a situation. It is, finally, seeing the effects of Lime's treachery close up and in detail that results in a perception of a situation made with complete moral intelligence. One has to have eyes that can *see* the significance of that with which one is confronted, however, and, once again, it takes Calloway's directorial skills to allow Martins to do this and, therefore, reach the proper conclusion.

An adequate moral perception of one's situation, then, requires correctly assessing—that is, with moral intelligence—that which appears before one's eyes. Achieving such a perspective can be difficult, because we all employ moral categories that may not fit the situations in which we find ourselves. *The Third Man* suggests that a skilled teacher or director can help us find a more adequate and morally intelligent perspective on our situation.

Once again, the film here suggests that an act of visual perception is central to achieving the appropriate moral perspective on one's situation. What it has now added to its earlier view is that this act of perception requires that we inspect the suffering of others from a vantage point close to them, so that we can see what their lives really are like. Unlike the view from on high that Lime uses to allegorize his own moral perspective, in which others are mere dots compared to his own self, seeing others' situation in close-up mobilizes our moral sympathies in a way that, according to the film, allows us to perceive our own situation and its requirements more clearly.

Somewhat surprisingly, the film does not actually show us the children who are Lime's victims and the objects of Martins' empathy. Rather, its focus is on Martins as he looks at them, as well as on the nurses and their routines. In so doing, the film steers clear of the dangers of including exploitative images of suffering children while still providing its audience with the images it needs to understand the film's point. In particular, its use of the teddy bear to symbolize the child's death is highly effective. So, we audience members do not get a direct view of the sufferings that cause Martins to change his mind; instead, we see Martins and the toy bear. Still, we are looking at things close up and with attention to details. It is this— rather than an unmediated look at reality—that affects us.

I want to suggest that the film has here presented an allegory of film as capable of stimulating moral intelligence because it can show things in close up—quite literally—and also in great detail. Martha Nussbaum has argued that "certain sorts of novels" are the place to "look for instruction" about what I am calling "moral intelligence" because they provide "exemplary, experienced models" of characters who exhibit this virtue.[39] What we can see from our look at *The Third Man* is that films, no less than novels, can be a source for understanding the nature of moral intelligence. Indeed, *The Third Man*'s account of the relationship between loyalty and friendship, a relationship not adequately discussed in the standard philosophical literature, makes a contribution to our understanding of moral intelligence.

In this allegorization of film, Calloway is the stand-in for the filmmakers. Despite Martins' initial hostility—he even, while drunk, attempts to hit Calloway—Calloway maintains a sympathetic attitude toward Martins throughout, always seeking to keep him from harm. At the same time, he selects the visual experiences that bring about Martins' enlightenment, his seeing who Lime is and how he, Martins, therefore must act. So, as it provides a philosophical account of the importance of moral intelligence, *The Third Man* also develops an equally philosophic account of film as the means for achieving it.

The moral position that the film ultimately endorses requires Martins to cooperate with Calloway in Lime's capture, for the morally reprehensible actions of
this man nullify any loyalty that Martins may have had toward him. The penultimate sequence of the film, stunning from a visual point of view and quite sus-
penseful, involves Lime being chased by Martins, Calloway, and the police through
the sewer network beneath the streets of Vienna. In the end, Martins actually kills
Lime, thereby completing his rejection of his commitment to his former friend as
he acts in the role he had once only imagined himself occupying.

VIII. CONCLUSION

I began this chapter by casting doubt upon the possibility that films can have a role
in the development of philosophical ethics. The bulk of the chapter has then used
Carol Reed's *The Third Man* to resolve these skeptical doubts in favor of the idea that
some films—and this one in particular—have a great deal to teach us about ethics.
The central ideas developed by the film are: (1) the significance of moral intelligence
in ethics, (2) there are limits of loyalty as a commitment one has to one's friends, and
(3) works of fiction can both hurt and aid the development of moral intelligence.

Each of these is an issue that has received attention from philosophers. Nonetheless, the film provides us with instruction about their significance that can both sup-
plement and stimulate discussion about them in more traditional philosophical
venues. As a result, the detailed study of this film—dare I say "in close-up"?—provides
support for the idea of fiction films as a source of ethical ideas, if not knowledge.

NOTES

1. Aristotle, *Nichomachean Ethics* (trans. Terence Irwin), 1141a 25–28.

2. Ibid., 1141b 15–23.

3. Iris Murdoch, *The Sovereignty of Good*; Martha Nussbaum, *Love's Knowledge*; and
Lawrence A. Blum, *Friendship, Altruism, and Morality*.

4. *Third Man*, 3–4. All quotations are taken from the film script to *The Third Man*
by Graham Greene.

5. Ibid., 5–6.

6. In *The World Viewed*, Stanley Cavell argues that films embody philosophical
skepticism. Rather than making such universal claims, I think it is more useful to pin-
point specific techniques that films use to present skepticism, as I do here in regard to
The Third Man.

7. Murray Smith uses the term "alignment" to signify this role that a character can
have of being the one through whom we get access to the events in a narrative. He distinguishes it from "allegiance", by which he means our having a positive attitude toward a
character. At this point, although we are aligned with Martins, we don't have a clear allegiance to him. See Murray Smith, *Engaging Characters: Fiction, Emotion, and the Cinema*.

8. *The Third Man*, 17.

9. Ibid.

10. Ibid., 18.

11. Ibid., 19.

12. Ibid., 22.

13. Ibid., 20.

14. Ibid., 21.

15. I discuss the moral implications of Martins' loyalty to Lime, as well as provide a more detailed examination of the film as an illustration of Aristotle's claims about friendship, in *Thinking on Screen: Film as Philosophy*, Chapter 6.

16. *Third Man*, 31.

17. This is the main theme of "The Wheel of Virtue." Carroll's notion of a virtue tableau will be useful later in my argument.

18. See, for example, Anne-Marie Scholz, *"Eine Revolution des Films,"* and Peter Wollen, "The Vienna Project."

19. *Third Man*, 132.

20. Ibid., 133.

21. Ibid., 137.

22. Because Martins has lost Lime—whom he has admired and viewed as his best friend—he puts himself in Lime's place by falling in love with the object of Lime's desire, Schmidt. This odd substitution is later employed by Neil Jordan in *The Crying Game*. I discuss its significance in my *Unlikely Couples*.

23. *Third Man*, 145.

24. Ibid.

25. Ibid., 146.

26. Ibid.

27. Lawrence A. Blum, *Friendship, Altruism, and Morality*. Blum's discussion of friendship as requiring a friend to pay attention to his friend's welfare does involve questions of loyalty to a friend, though Blum does not discuss the issue in those terms.

28. The film's representation of Schmidt could be seen as sexist, for her emotionality keeps her from rationally assessing Lime's character.

29. The final line of Dickens' novel is: "It is a far, far better thing that I do, than I have ever done; it is a far, far better rest that I go to than I have ever known."

30. *Third Man*, 171.

31. I treat love as a form of friendship here, following Aristotle and, I think, the film.

32. *Third Man*, 172–73.

33. Lime's association of people with dots recalls Walt Whitman's characterization of the poet in "As I Sat Alone by Blue Ontario's Shore." The poet, he says, "bestows on every object or quality its fit proportion, neither more or less /. . . . . He sees eternity in men and women—he docs not sec men and women as dreams or *dots*." (lines 144 and 147, emphasis added).

34. *Third Man*, 173.

35. Ibid., 178.

36. Ibid., 179.

37. Ibid., 195.

38. "The Wheel of Virtue," 9ff.

39. See her "The Discernment of Perception," in *Love's Knowledge*, 84–85.

CONTRIBUTORS

Lawrence Blum is Distinguished Professor of Liberal Arts and Education, and Professor of Philosophy, at the University of Massachusetts, Boston. He is the author of four books: *Friendship, Altruism, and Morality* (Routledge, 1980), *A Truer Liberty: Simone Weil and Marxism* (Routledge, 1989, with V.J. Seidler), *Moral Perception and Particularity* (Cambridge University Press, 1994), and *"I'm Not a Racist, But . . . .": the Moral Quandary of Race* (Cornell University Press, 2002). He has written many articles on moral philosophy, moral psychology, moral education, race studies, and multiculturalism, including three on ethics and cinema.

Julia Driver is Professor of Philosophy at Washington University at St. Louis. Her primary areas of research are ethical theory and moral psychology, although she also has an interest in normativity in general, including aesthetic norms. She is the author of *Uneasy Virtue* (Cambridge University Press, 2001) and *Ethics: the Fundamentals* (Blackwell, 2006), as well as numerous journal articles.

Andrew Gleeson teaches philosophy at the University of Adelaide, Australia. He is a graduate of the University of Adelaide and the Australian National University. He has published articles in the philosophy of mind and edited collections in ethics and the philosophy of language.

Peter Goldie is Samuel Hall Chair at The University of Manchester, U.K. His central interests are in ethics, aesthetics, and the philosophy of mind. He is the author of *The Emotions: A Philosophical Exploration* (Clarendon Press, 2000) and of *On Personality* (Routledge, 2004), co-author of *Who's Afraid of Conceptual Art?* (Routledge, 2009), editor of *Understanding Emotions: Mind and Morals* (Ashgate, 2002) and *The Oxford Handbook of Philosophy of Emotion* (Oxford University Press, 2010), and co-editor of *Philosophy and Conceptual Art* (Oxford University Press, 2007).

Karen Hanson is Rudy Professor of Philosophy, and Provost and Executive Vice-President, of Indiana University at Bloomington. She is the author of *The Self Imagined* and co-editor of *Romantic Revolutions*; she has published articles on topics in aesthetics, ethics, philosophy of mind, and the history of American philosophy.

Ward E. Jones teaches philosophy at Rhodes University, South Africa, and is the editor of the journal *Philosophical Papers*. He works primarily in the areas of epistemology, philosophy of mind, ethics, and metaphilosophy.

Deborah Knight is Associate Professor of Philosophy at Queen's University, Canada. Her main research area is the philosophy of art, with emphases on literature and film. Recent publications include chapters in the *Oxford Handbook of Aesthetics* (ed. Jerrold Levinson, Oxford University Press, 2005), *Dark Thoughts: Philosophical Reflections on Cinematic Horror* (ed. Stephen J. Schneider and Jay Shaw, Scarecrow Press, 2003), and *Literary Philosophers? Borges, Calvino, Eco* (ed. Jorge Gracia et. al., Routledge, 2001).

Joseph Kupfer is University Professor of Philosophy at Iowa State University, where he teaches medical ethics, family ethics, philosophy of law, and aesthetics. He has written on privacy, generosity, humility, the parent-child relationship, lying, and architecture. His most recent work includes two books, *Autonomy and Social Interaction* (SUNY, 1990) and *Visions of Virtue in Popular Film* (Westview, 1999), as well as articles on genetic screening in the workplace, romantic love, and the aesthetics of nature.

Tom Martin is Associate Professor and Head of the Department of Philosophy at Rhodes University, South Africa. He has published articles on gender, race, existentialism, and self-deception, as well as the book *Oppression and the Human Condition* (Rowman & Littlefield, 2002).

Murray Smith is Professor of Film Studies at the University of Kent, U.K. He is the author of *Engaging Characters: Fiction, Emotion, and the Cinema* (Oxford, 1995) and *Trainspotting* (BFI, 2002), and the co-editor of *Film Theory and Philosophy* (Oxford, 1997) and *Thinking through Cinema: Film as Philosophy* (Blackwell, 2006). He has published widely on the relationships among ethics, emotion, and film.

Torbjörn Tännsjö is Kristian Claëson Professor of Practical Philosophy at Stockholm University. He has published extensively in moral philosophy, political philosophy, and bioethics. His most recent books are *Understanding Ethics* (2nd revised edition, Edinburgh University Press, 2008) and *Global Democracy: The Case for a World Government* (Edinburgh University Press, 2008).

Paul C. Taylor is an Associate Professor of Philosophy at The Pennsylvania State University, the founding director of the Program on Philosophy After Apartheid at the Rock Ethics Institute, and a founding member of the Jamestown Project at Harvard Law School. His writings explore questions in aesthetics, race theory, Africana philosophy, and social philosophy, and include the book *Race: A Philosophical Introduction* (Polity, 2004). He is currently working on a book called *Black is Beautiful: A Philosophy of Black Aesthetics*.

Samantha Vice is Senior Lecturer at Rhodes University, South Africa. She is co-editor, with Nafsika Athanassoulis, of *The Moral Life: Essays in Honour of John Cottingham* (Palgrave Macmillan, 2008), and has written papers on impartiality and partiality in ethics, goodness, and the work of Iris Murdoch.

Thomas E. Wartenberg is Chair of the Philosophy Department at Mount Holyoke College, where he also teaches in the Film Studies program. He is the author of *Unlikely Couples: Movie Romance as Social Criticism* (Westview Press, 1999) and *Thinking on Screen* (Routledge, 2007), and he has edited (or co-edited) a number of anthologies including *Philosophy and Film* (with Cynthia A. Freeland, Routledge, 1995), *Thinking Through Cinema: Film as Philosophy* (with Murray Smith, Wiley-Blackwell, 2006), and *The Philosophy of Film: Introductory Text and Readings* (with Angela Curran, Wiley-Blackwell, 2004). His recent publications include *Existentialism: A Beginner's Guide* (Oneworld, 2008) and *Big Ideas for Little Kids: Teaching Philosophy Through Children's Literature* (Rowman and Littlefield, 2009).

Stephen Williams is Fellow and Tutor in Philosophy at Worcester College, Oxford, U.K. He works primarily in metaphysics and the philosophy of language. He is also the editor, with Sabina Lovibond, of *Essays in Honour of David Wiggins: Identity, Truth and Value,* (Oxford: Blackwell, 1996).

REFERENCES

Aldgate, Anthony, "What a Difference a War Makes: *The Life and Death of Colonel Blimp*, in Anthony Aldgate and Jeffrey Richards (eds.), *Best of British Film* (London: I.B.Taurus, 1999).

Allais, Lucy, "Wiping the Slate Clean: The Heart of Forgiveness," *Philosophy and Public Affairs* 36.1 (2008), 33–68.

——, "Dissolving Reactive Attitudes: Forgiving and Understanding," *South African Journal of Philosophy* 27/3 (2008), 179–200.

Anzaldúa, Gloria, *Borderlands/La Frontera: The New Mestiza* (San Francisco: Aunt Lute Books, 1987).

Appiah, Kwame Anthony, "Racisms," in David Theo Goldberg (ed.), *Anatomy of Racism* (Minneapolis: University of Minnesota Press, 1990).

Arendt, Hannah, *Eichmann in Jerusalem: A Report on the Banality of Evil* (New York: Penguin Books, 1977).

Aristotle, *Complete Works*, ii, ed. Jonathan Barnes (Princeton, N.J.: Princeton University Press, 1984).

——, *Nichomachean Ethics*, trans. Martin Ostwald (Englewood Cliffs, N.J.: Prentice Hall, 1957).

——, *Nichomachean Ethics*, trans. Terence Irwin (Indianapolis: Hackett Publishing Company, 1985).

Badhwar, Neera (ed.), *Friendship: a Philosophical Reader* (Ithaca: Cornell University Press, 1993).

Bean, Henry, *The Believer: Confronting Jewish Self-Hatred* (New York: Thunder Mouth Press, 2001).

Blum, Lawrence, "Stereotypes and Stereotyping: A Moral Analysis," *Philosophical Papers*, 33/3 (2004), 251–290.

——, *"I'm Not a Racist, but . . . ": The Moral Quandary of Race* (Ithaca, N.Y.: Cornell University Press, 2002).

——, "What do accounts of "racism" do?," in Michael Levine and Thomas Pataki (eds.), *Racism in Mind* (Ithaca: Cornell UP, 2004).

——, *Moral Perception and Particularity* (Cambridge: Cambridge University Press, 1994).

——, *Friendship, Altruism, and Morality* (London: Routledge and Kegan Paul, 1980).

Blumstein, Alfred, "Race and Criminal Justice," in Neil Smelser, William Julius Wilson, and Faith Mitchell (eds.), *America Becoming: Racial Trends and Their Consequences*, ii (Washington, DC: National Academy Press, 2001).

Bok, Sissela, *Lying* (London: Quartet, 1980).

Bolotin, Susan, "Voices From the Post-Feminist Generation," *The New York Times*, October 17, 1982.

Booth, Wayne C., "Of the Standard of Moral Taste," in *The Essential Wayne Booth* (Chicago: University of Chicago Press, 2006).

——, *The Company We Keep: An Ethics of Fiction* (Berkeley: University of California Press, 1988).

Bordwell, David, and Staiger, Janet, and Thompson, Kristin, *The Classical Hollywood Cinema: Film Style and Mode of Production to 1960* (London: Routledge, 1988).

Brandom, Robert, *Making It Explicit* (Cambridge MA: Harvard University Press, 1994).

Capra, Frank, *The Name Above the Title: An Autobiography* (London: W.H. Allen and Co., 1972).

Carr, David, "Los Angeles Retains Custody of Oscar," *The New York Times*, March 7, 2006.

Carroll, Noël, "Sympathy for the Devil," in Richard Greene and Peter Verneze (eds.), *The Sopranos and Philosophy* (Chicago: Open Court, 2004).

———, "The Wheel of Virtue: Art, Literature, and Moral Knowledge," *The Journal of Aesthetics and Art Criticism*, 60/1 (2002), 3–26.

———, "Horror and Humor," *The Journal of Aesthetics and Art Criticism* 57/2 (1999), 145–60.

———, "Film, Emotion, and Genre," in Carl Plantinga and Greg M. Smith (eds.), *Passionate Views* (Baltimore: Johns Hopkins University Press, 1999).

———, *A Philosophy of Mass Art* (Oxford: Oxford University Press, 1998).

———, "Art, Narrative, and Moral Understanding," in Jerrold Levinson (ed.), *Aesthetics and Ethics: Essays at the Intersection* (Cambridge: Cambridge University Press, 1998).

———, *Theorizing the Moving Image* (Cambridge: Cambridge University Press, 1996).

———, *The Philosophy of Horror* (London: Routledge, 1990).

Cavell, Stanley, "Moral Perfectionism," in Stephen Mulhall, ed., *The Cavell Reader* (Cambridge, MA: Blackwell, 1996).

———, *Conditions Handsome and Unhandsome* (Chicago: University of Chicago Press, 1990).

———, *Pursuits of Happiness* (Cambridge, MA: Harvard University Press, 1981).

———, *The World Viewed* (enlarged edn.), Cambridge, MA: Harvard University Press, 1979).

———, *The World Viewed* (Cambridge, MA: Harvard University Press, 1971).

———, *Must We Mean What We Say?* (Cambridge: Cambridge University Press, 1969/1976).

Chapman, Antony J., "Humor and Laughter in Social Interaction and some Implications for Humor Research," in P.E. McGhee and J.H. Goldstein (eds.), *Handbook of Humor Research* (New York: Springer-Verlag, 1983).

Chesterton, G. K., "Killing the Nerve," in *The Well and the Shallows* (London: Sheed and Ward, 1935), 108–109.

Christie, Ian, "Introduction" to Michael Powell and Emeric Pressburger, *The Life and Death of Colonel Blimp*, ed. by Ian Christie (London: Faber and Faber, 1994).

———, and Moor, Andrew (eds.), *The Cinema of Michael Powell* (London: BFI Publishing, 2005).

Cohen, Hubert I, "Review of *Orson Welles*, and *Frank Capra: The Man and his Films*," *Cinema Journal*, 15/1 (1975), 60–5.

Cohen, Ted., *Jokes: Philosophical Thoughts on Joking Matters* (Chicago: The University of Chicago Press, 1999).

Conrad, Joseph, *The Nigger of the "Narcissus,"* edited with an Introduction by C. Watts (London: Penguin, 1987).

Currie, Gregory, "The Paradox of Caring: Fiction and the Philosophy of Mind," in Mette Hjort and Sue Lavers (eds.), *Emotion and the Arts* (Oxford University Press, 1997).

Darwin Awards, <http://www.darwinawards.com>, last accessed: 6 July 2010

de Albuquerque, Klaus, "In Search of the Big Bamboo: Among the Sex Tourists of the Caribbean," *Transition* 77 (1998), 48–57.

De Ruyter, Doret J., "The Importance of Ideals in Education," *Journal of Philosophy of Education*, 37/3 (2003), 467–82.

de Sousa, Ronald, *The Rationality of the Emotions* (Cambridge MA: MIT Press, 1987).

Deutsch, Phyllis, "Sophie's Choice," *Jump Cut*, 29 (February 1984), <http://www.ejumpcut. org/archive/onlinessays/JC29folder/SophiesChoice.html>, last accessed 20 Oct 2006.

Devereaux, Mary, "Beauty and Evil: The Case of Leni Riefenstahl's *Triumph of the Will*," in Jerrold Levinson (ed.), *Art and Ethics* (Cambridge: Cambridge University Press, 1997).

Dewey, John, "The Moral Self," in Larry Iickman and Thomas Alexander (eds.), *The Essential Dewey*, ii (Bloomington: University of Indiana Press, 1998) (first pub. 1932).

Diamond, Cora, "Anything but Argument?," in *The Realistic Spirit* (Cambridge: The MIT Press, 1995).

Dickens, Charles, *A Tale of Two Cities* (New York: Penguin Classics, 2003).

DiMassa, Cara Mia, "'Crash' resonates in LA on race relations," *The Boston Globe*, March 5, 2006.

Dirks, Tim, "Review of *Meet John Doe*," <www.filmsite.org/meet.html>, last accessed 9 November 2007.

Donald, James, and Michael Renov (ed.) *The Sage Handbook of Film Studies* (London: Sage, 2008).

Douglas, Susan J., "Manufacturing Postfeminism," *In These Times* 26/13 (April 26, 2002). Available at <http://www.inthesetimes.com/article/1466/manufacturing_postfeminism/>, last accessed 24 July 2007.

Drazin, Charles, *In Search of the Third Man* (New York: Proscenium Publishers, Inc., 2000).

Du Bois, W.E.B., *The Souls of Black Folk*, in *Writings* (New York: Penguin– Library of America, 1996 [1903]).

Dummett, Michael, *Truth and Other Enigmas* (London: Duckworth, and Cambridge MA: Harvard University Press, 1978).

Dupréel, E., "Le problème sociologique du rire," *Revue Philosophique* 106 (1928), 213–260.

Dyer, Richard, *Stars* (London: British Film Institute, 1979).

Ebert, Roger, "Commentary on *The Third Man*" (8 December, 1996), at "Roger Ebert.com," <http://rogerebert.suntimes>, last accessed 20 March 2007.

Edel, Abraham, "The Evaluation of Ideals," *The Journal of Philosophy*, 42/1 (1945), 561–77.

Ellison, Ralph, "The Little Man at Chehaw Station," in Jon Callahan (ed.), *The Collected Essays of Ralph Ellison* (New York: Modern Library-Random House, 1995).

Emerson, Ralph Waldo, "Fate" (New York: Penguin, 1982 [1860]).

Feinberg, Joel, "The Absurd and the Comic: Why Does Some Incongruity Please?," in *Freedom and Fulfillment: Philosophical Essays* (Princeton, NJ: University Press, 1992), 331–45.

Fine, Gary Alan, "Sociological Approaches to the Study of Humor," in P.E. McGhee and J.H. Goldstein (eds.), *Handbook of Humor Research*, 159–181.

Forster, E.M., "What I Believe," in *Two Cheers for Democracy* (New York: Harcourt, Brace & World, 1951).

Frankfurt, Harry G, "On the Necessity of Ideals," in *Necessity, Volition, and Love* (Cambridge: Cambridge University Press, 1999).

Freeland, Cynthia A., "Realist Horror," in *Philosophy and Film*, eds. Cynthia A. Freeland and Thomas Wartenberg (London: Routledge, 1995).

Freud, Sigmund, *Civilisation and its Discontents* (London: Penguin, 1985).

Frye, Northrop, *Anatomy of Criticism: Four Essays* (Princeton: Princeton University Press, 1957).

Gaita, Raimond, *A Common Humanity: Thinking About Love and Truth and Justice* (Melbourne: Text, 1999).

Gaut, Berys, "Art and Ethics," in Berys Gaut and Dominic McIver Lopes (eds.), *The Routledge Companion to Aesthetics*, 2nd edn. (Abingdon: Routledge, 2005).

——, "The Ethical Criticism of Art," in Jerrold Levinson (ed.), *Art and Ethics* (Cambridge: Cambridge University Press, 1997).

Gendler, Tamar Szabo, "The Puzzle of Imaginative Resistance," *Journal of Philosophy* 97/2 (2000), 55–81.

Glover, Jonathan, *Humanity* (New Haven: Yale University Press, 1999).

Goldie, Peter, "Conceptual Art and Knowledge," in P. Goldie and E. Schellekens (eds.), *Philosophy and Conceptual Art* (Oxford: Oxford University Press, 2007).

——, "Towards a virtue theory of art," *British Journal of Aesthetics*, 47/4 (2007), 1–16.

Goldman, Alvin, *Simulating Minds: The Philosophy, Psychology and Neuroscience of Mindreading* (New York: Oxford University Press, 2006).

Gordon, Robert, *The Structure of Emotions* (Cambridge: Cambridge University Press, 1987).

Greene, Graham, *The Third Man* (London: Faber and Faber, 1998).

Grice, Paul, "Meaning," *Philosophical Review* 66 (1957), 377–88, reprinted in Paul Grice, *Studies in the Ways of Words* (Cambridge, Mass: Harvard University Press, 1989).

Gruner, Charles R., *The Game of Humor* (New Brunswick, NJ: Transaction Publishers, 1997).

Haggis, Paul, "Paul Haggis was carjacked in real life", at www.network54.com/Forum/message?forumid=408205&messageid=1115659830, last accessed 21/06/10.

Hakemulder, Jèmeljan, *The Moral Laboratory: Experiments Examining the Effects of Reading Literature on Social Perception and Moral Self-Concept* (Amsterdam: John Benjamins, 2000)

Hall, Judith A., and Shelley E. Taylor, "When Love is Blind: Maintaining Idealized Images of One's Spouse," *Human Relations* 29/8 (1976), 751–61.

Hanson, Karen, "Minerva in the Movies: Relations Between Philosophy and Film," in Noël Carroll and Jinhee Choi (eds.), *Philosophy of Film and Motion Pictures* (Malden, MA.: Blackwell, 2006).

Hardin, Russell, *One for All: The Logic of Group Conflicts* (Princeton, New Jersey: Princeton University Press, 1995).

Harrison, Jennifer, "Melting Pot," in Stanley I. Kutler (ed.), *Dictionary of American History*, v, 3rd edn. (New York: Charles Scribner's Sons, 2003).

Gale Virtual Reference Library. Thomson Gale. Temple University Libraries. <http://shelob.ocis.temple.edu>, last accessed 27 July 2007.

Hine, Darlene Clark, "Rape and the Inner Lives of Black Women in the Middle West: Preliminary Thoughts on the Culture of Dissemblance," in Beverly Guy-Sheftall (ed.), *Words of Fire: An Anthology of African-American Feminist Thought* (New York: New Press, 1995).

Hirota, Janice M., "Making Products Heroes: Work in Advertising Agencies," in Robert Jackall (ed.), *Propaganda* (London: Macmillan, 1995).

Hobbes, Thomas, *Leviathan*, ed. Michael Oakeshott (New York: Collier Books, 1962).

Holbrook, David, *Sex and Dehumanisation in Art, Thought and Life in Our Time* (London: Pitman 1972).

Holland, R.F., *Against Empiricism* (Totowa N. J.: Barnes and Noble, 1980).

hooks, bell, *Black Looks* (Boston: South End Press,1992).

Hopkins, James, "Conscience and Conflict: Darwin, Freud, and the origins of human aggression," in P. Cruse and D. Evans (eds.), *Emotion, Evolution and Rationality* (Oxford: Oxford University Press, 2004).

Hoess, Rudolf, quoted in "Hoess: Death Dealer at Auschwitz," at http://www.auschwitz.dk/hoess.htm, last accessed October 15, 2006.

Hume, David, *Enquiries Concerning Human Understanding and Concerning the Principles of Morals*, 3rd edn., ed. L. A. Selby-Bigge and P. H. Nidditch (Oxford: Oxford University Press, 1996).

——, "Of greatness of mind," in *A Treatise of Human Nature* (London: Fontana, 1982).

——, "Of the Standard of Taste," in *Essays Moral, Political and Literary*, ed. T.H. Green and T.H. Grose (London: Longmans, 1907).

Hunt, Lester, "Motion Pictures as a Philosophical Resource," in Noël Carroll and Jinhee Choi (eds.), *Philosophy of Film and Motion Pictures: An Anthology* (Oxford: Blackwell, 2006).

Hutcheson, Francis, *Reflections Upon Laughter*, reprinted as the Appendix to *An Inquiry Concerning Beauty, Order, Harmony, Design*, ed. Peter Kivy (The Hague: Martinus Nijhoff, 1973 [1750]).

Jackall, Robert, "The Magic Lantern: The World of Public Relations," in Robert Jackall (ed.), *Propaganda* (London: Macmillan, 1995).

—— (ed.), *Propaganda* (London: Macmillan, 1995).

Jacobson, Matthew, *Whiteness of a Different Color* (Cambridge, MA: Harvard University Press, 1998).

Jensen, Robert and Wosnitzer, Robert, "Crash" and the Self-indulgence of White America, <www.blackcommentator.com/176/176_think_crash_jensen_wosnitzer.htm>, last accessed 6 July 2010.

Johanson, MaryAnn, "Unleashed and Crash (review)," *the flick filosopher*, <http://www.flickfilosopher.com/blog/2005/05/unleashed_and_crash_review.html>, last accessed 20 March 2008.

Kempley, Rita, "'Fools Rush In': Ay Caramba!," *The Washington Post*, February 14, 1997, B07.

Kennett, Jeannette and Cocking, Dean, "Friendship and Moral Danger," *The Journal of Philosophy*, 97/5 (2000), 278–96.

——, "Friendship and the Self," *Ethics*, 108/3 (1998), 502–527.

Kerans, James, "Classics Revisited: *La Grande Illusion*," *Film Quarterly*, 14 (1960), 10–17.

Krazy Kat (comic strip), created by George Herriman (various newspapers, daily 1913–1944).

Kupfer, Joseph, *Visions of Virtue in Popular Film* (Boulder, CO.: Westview, 1999).

Lamarque, Peter, "Reflections on Current Trends in Aesthetics," *Postgraduate Journal of Aesthetics* 1 (2004), 1–9, available at <http://www.british-aethetics.org/uploads/Peter%20LAMARQUE.pdf.>

——, *Fictional Points of View* (Ithaca: Cornell University Press, 1996).

——, "How Can We Fear and Pity Fictions?," *British Journal of Aesthetics* 21 (1981), 291–304.

——, and Olsen, Stein Haughom, *Truth, Fiction, and Literature: A Philosophical Perspective* (Oxford: Oxford University Press, 1994).

Lasswell, Harold D., "Propaganda," in Robert Jackall (ed.), *Propaganda*, (London: Macmillan, 1995), 13–25, originally publ. in Edwin R. Seligman (ed. in chief), *Encyclopaedia of the Social Sciences*, 1st edn., xii (London: Macmillan, 1934).

Laurier, Joanne, "the essential things go unexplained," *World Socialist Web Site*, May 28, 2005, <www.wsws.org/articles/2005/may2005/crsh-m28.shtml>, last accessed 6 July 2010.

Lawrence, D.H., *Lady Chatterley's Lover*, 2nd edn. (Harmondsworth: Penguin, 1961).

Leibniz, G. W., *Theodicy*, ed. with an introduction by Austin Farrer, trans. E. M. Huggard (Teddington, Middlesex: Eco Library, 2008).

Leigh, Mike, *Secrets and Lies* (Faber and Faber, London, 1997).

Lenin, V. I., *What Is To Be Done?*, trans. Joe Fineberg and George Hanna, with revisions to trans. by Robert Service (Harmondsworth: Penguin, 1988).

Lessing, G. E., *Hamburg Dramaturgy*, trans. Helen Zimmern (New York: Dover Publications, 1962).

Levinson, Jerrold (ed.), *Aesthetics and Ethics* (Cambridge: Cambridge University Press, 1998).

Lewis, C.S. *The Four Loves* (New York: Harcourt, Brace, Jovanovich, 1960).

Livingston, Paisley, "Theses on Cinema as Philosophy," *Journal of Aesthetics and Art Criticism* 64/1 (2006), 11–18.

Livingston, Paisley, "Cinematic Authorship," in Noël Carroll and Jinhee Choi (eds.), *Philosophy of Film and Motion Pictures* (Malden, MA.: Blackwell, 2006).

L'Amour, Louis, *The Quick and the Dead* (New York: Bantam, 1999).

Locke, John, *Second Treatise of Government*, ed. Richard Cox (Alington Heights, IL: Harlan Davidson, Inc., 1982).

Loury, Glenn C., *An Anatomy of Racial Inequality* (Cambridge: Harvard University Press, 2002).

Lugones, María, "Playfulness, 'World'-Travelling, and Loving Perception," *Hypatia* 2/2 (1987), 3–19.

Martí, Jose, "Our America," in *Selected Writings* (New York: Penguin, 2002 [1892]).

Martineau, W.H., "A Model of the Social Functions of Humor," in *The Psychology of Humor*, ed. J.H. Goldstein and P.E. McGhee (New York: Academic Press, 1972).

McGhee, P.E. and J.H. Goldstein (eds.), *Handbook of Humor Research* (New York: Springer-Verlag, 1983).

Monro, D.H., *Argument of Laughter* (Notre Dame IN: University of Notre Dame Press, 1963).

Moor, Andrew, *Powell and Pressburger: A Cinema of Magic Spaces* (London: I. B. Taurus, 2005).

Moore, Willis, "On the Nature and Justification of Ideals," *Ethics* 58/2 (1948), 112–7.

Moran, Richard, "The Expression of Feeling in Imagination," *Philosophical Review* 103/1 (1994), 75–106.

Morreall, John, "Enjoying Incongruity," *Humor* 2/1 (1989), 1–18.

———, *Taking Laughter Seriously* (Albany, New York: SUNY Press, 1983).

Mulkay, Michael, *On Humour* (Cambridge: Polity 1988).

Murdoch, Iris, *The Sovereignty of Good* (London and New York: Routledge, 2000).

Mulhall, Stephen, *On Film* (London: Routledge, 2002).

Murray Smith, 'Empathy, Expansionism, and the Extended Mind,' in Amy Coplan and Peter Goldie (eds.), *Empathy: Philosophical and Psychological Perspectives* (Oxford: Oxford University Press, forthcoming 2011).

Nagel, Thomas, *What Does It All Mean?: A Very Short Introduction to Philosophy* (New York: Oxford University Press, 1987).

———, "Moral Luck," in Thomas Nagel, *Mortal Questions* (Cambridge: CUP, 1979).

———, "The Absurd," *The Journal of Philosophy* 68/20 (1971), 716–727.

Nietzsche, Friedrich, *Untimely Meditations*, trans. R. J. Hollingdale (New York: Cambridge University Press, 1983).

———, *The Birth of Tragedy* and *The Genealogy of Morals*, trans. Francis Golffing, (New York: Anchor Books, 1956).

Norton, David L, "Moral Minimalism and the Development of Moral Character," in Peter A. French, Theodore E. Uehling, Jr and Howard K. Wettstein (eds.), *Ethical Theory: Character and Virtue* (*Midwest Studies in Philosophy*, vol. XIII) (Notre Dame: University of Notre Dame Press, 1988).

Nozick, Robert, *Philosophical Explanations* (Oxford: Oxford University Press, 1981).

Nussbaum, Martha, *Poetic Justice: The Literary Imagination and Public Life* (Boston: Beacon Press, 1995).

———, *Love's Knowledge: Essays on Philosophy and Literature* (New York: Oxford University Press, 1990).

Oakeshott, Michael, "The Tower of Babel," in *Rationalism in Politics* (London: Methuen, 1962).

Orwell, George, "Reflections on Gandhi," in *The Collected Essays, Journalism and Letters of George Orwell, iv: 1945–1950, In Front of Your Nose*, ed. Sonia Orwell and Ian Angus (Harmondsworth: Penguin 1968).

———, "Looking back on the Spanish War," in *England Your England and Other Essays* (London: Secker and Warburg, 1953).

Pappas, Gregory, "Dewey's Ethics," in Larry A. Hickman (ed.), *Reading Dewey* (Bloomington: Indiana University Press, 1998), 100–23.

Plantinga, Carl, "Spectator Emotion and Film Criticism" in Richard Allen and Murray Smith (eds.), *Film Theory and Philosophy* (Clarendon: Oxford, 1997).

Plato, *Republic*, trans. G.M.A. Grube (Indianapolis: Hackett, 1974).

Powell, Michael, *A Life in Movies: An Autobiography* (London: Faber and Faber, 2000).

———, and Pressburger, Emeric, *The Life and Death of Colonel Blimp*, ed. Ian Christie (London: Faber and Faber, 1994).

Provine, Robert R., *Laughter: A Scientific Investigation* (New York: Penguin, 2000).

Rawls, John, *A Theory of Justice* (Oxford: Oxford University Press, 1973).

Richards, Jeffrey, "Why We Fight: *A Canterbury Tale*," in Anthony Aldgate and Jeffrey Richards (eds.), *Best of British Films* (London: I. B.Taurus, 1999).

Roberts, Dorothy, *Killing the Black Body: Race, Reproduction, and the Meaning of Liberty* (New York: Vintage, 1997).

Robinson, Jenefer, *Deeper than Reason: Emotion and its Role in Music, Literature and Art* (Oxford: Oxford University Press, 2005).

Rousseau, Jean-Jacques, *The Social Contract*, trans. Donald Cress (Indianapolis: Hackett Publishing, 1983).

Sartre, Jean-Paul, *Anti-Semite and Jew*, trans. George J. Becker (New York: Schocken Books, 1948).

Scholz, Anne-Marie, "*Eine Revolution des Films: The Third Man* (1949), The Cold War, and Alternatives to Nationalism & Coca-colonization in Europe," *Film and History* 31/1 (2001) 44–53.

Schopenhauer, Arthur, *The world as will and representation*, trans. E.F.J. Payne (New York: Dover Publications, 1969 [1818]).

Scruton, Roger, "Laughter," *Proceedings of the Aristotelian Society*, Supplementary Volume 56 (1982), 197–212.

———, *Sexual Desire: A Philosophical Investigation* (London: Weidenfeld and Nicolson, 1986).

Sherman, Nancy. "Aristotle on the Shared Life," in Neera Badhwar (ed.), *Friendship: a Philosophical Reader* (Ithaca: Cornell University Press, 1993).

Shirer, William, *Berlin Diary: The Journal of a Foreign Correspondent, 1934–41* (London, Hamish Hamilton, 1941).

Singer, Irving, *Reality Transformed: Film as Meaning and Technique* (Cambridge, Mass.: MIT Press, 1998).

Smith, Bruce L., "Propaganda," in D. L. Sills (ed.), *International Encyclopaedia of the Social Sciences*, xii (New York: Macmillan, 1968).

Smith, Murray, "Film Art, Argument, and Ambiguity," *Journal of Aesthetics and Art Criticism*, 64/1 (2006), 33–42.

——, "Gangsters, Cannibals, Aesthetes; or, Apparently Perverse Allegiances," in Carl Plantinga and Greg M. Smith (eds.), *Passionate Views: Film, Cognition, and Emotion* (Baltimore: Johns Hopkins University Press, 1999).

——, "Imagining from the Inside," in Richard Allen and Murray Smith (eds.), *Film Theory and Philosophy* (Clarendon: Oxford, 1997).

——, *Engaging Characters* (Oxford: Clarendon Press, 1995).

Solomon, Robert, *About Love* (New York: Simon and Schuster, 1988).

Sontag, Susan, "Jack Smith's *Flaming Creatures*," in *Against Interpretation* (New York: Dell, 1969).

Stephan, Walter, *Reducing Prejudice and Stereotyping in Schools* (New York: Teachers College Press, 1999).

Stout, Jeffrey, *Democracy and Tradition* (Princeton University Press, 2006).

Tabensky, Pedro Alexis (ed.) *Judging and Understanding* (Aldershot: Ashgate, 2006).

Takaki, Ronald, *Iron Cages* (New York: Oxford University Press, 2000).

Tanner, Michael, "Morals in Fiction and Fictional Morality—A Response," *Proceedings of the Aristotelian Society*, Supplementary Volume 68 (1994), 51–66.

Tännsjö, Torbjörn (ed.), *Terminal Sedation: Euthanasia in Disguise?* (Dordrecht: Kluwer, 2004).

——, *Hedonistic Utilitarianism* (Edinburgh: Edinburgh University Press, and Columbia University Press, 1998).

——, "The Morality of Collective Actions," *Philosophical Quarterly* 39 (1989), 221–228.

——, "Moral Conflict and Moral Realism," *The Journal of Philosophy* 82 (1985), 113–117.

Thomson, Judith Jarvis, *Goodness and Advice* (Princeton, NJ: Princeton University Press, 2000).

Truffaut, Francois, *Jules and Jim*, trans. Nicholas Fry (New York: Simon and Schuster, 1968).

Triggs, Jeffrey, "The Legacy of Babel: Language in Jean Renoir's *Grand Illusion*," *New Orleans Review*, 15/2 (1988), 70–74.

Ullmann-Margalit, E. and Morgenbesser, S. (1977), "Picking and Choosing," *Social Research* 44 (1977), 757–85.

Urmson, J.O, "Saints and Heroes," in A.I. Melden (ed.), *Essays in Moral Philosophy* (Seattle: University of Washington Press, 1958).

Van Fraassen, Bas, "Précis of *The Empirical Stance*," *Philosophical Studies*, 121 (2004), 127–34.

——, *The Empirical Stance* (New Haven: Yale University Press, 2002).

Varadarajan, Tunku, "Generation Hex," *Wall Street Journal*, July 28, 2007.

Walton, Kendall, "On Pictures and Photographs: Objections Answered" in Richard Allen and Murray Smith (eds.), *Film Theory and Philosophy* (Oxford: Clarendon Press, 1997).

——, "Morals in Fiction and Fictional Morality," *Proceedings of the Aristotelian Society*, Supplementary Volume 68 (1994), 27–50.

——, "Fearing Fictions," *Journal of Philosophy* 75/1 (1978), 5–27.

Warshow, Robert, "The Gangster as Tragic Hero," in *The Immediate Experience: Movies, Comics, Theatre, and Other Aspects of Popular Culture*, enlarged edn. (Cambridge: Harvard University Press, 2001).

Wartenberg, Thomas E., "Teaching Philosophy Through Film: Aristotle's Theory of Friendship and *The Third Man*", *Film and Philosophy* 13 (2008), 19–34.

——, *Thinking on Screen: Film as Philosophy* (London: Routledge, 2007).

——, "Beyond *Mere* Illustration: How Films Can Be Philosophy," in *The Journal of Aesthetics and Art Criticism* 64/1 (2006), 19–32.

——, *Unlikely Couples: Movie Romance as Social Criticism* (Boulder, CO: Westview, 1999).

Wasserman, David and Robert Wachbroit (eds.), *Genetics and Criminal Behavior* (Cambridge: Cambridge University Press, 2001).

Weatherson, Brian, "Morality, Fiction, and Possibility," *Philosopher's Imprint* 4/3 (2004), 1–27.

Weber, Max, *The Protestant Ethic and the Spirit of Capitalism*, trans. Talcott Parson (New York: Routledge, 1992).

West, Cornel, *The American Evasion of Philosophy* (Madison: University of Wisconsin Press, 1989).

Whitman, Walt, "As I Sat Alone by Blue Ontario's Shore," in *Leaves of Grass* (New York: New York University Press, 1965).

Williams, Bernard, "Practical Necessity," in *Moral Luck* (Cambridge: Cambridge University Press, 1981).

Williams, Linda, "Sex and Sensation," in Geoffrey Nowell-Smith (ed.) *The Oxford History of World Cinema* (Oxford: Oxford University Press, 1996).

Wilson, George, "Rapport, Rupture, and Rape: Reflections on *Talk to Her*," in Anne Wescott Eaton (ed.), *Talk to Her* (London: Routledge, 2008).

Winder, Robert, *Bloody Foreigners* (London: Abacus, 2005).

Wittgenstein, Ludwig, *Philosophical Investigations*, trans. G.E.M. Anscombe (New York: Macmillan, 1953).

Wolf, Susan. "Moral Saints." *The Journal of Philosophy* 79, 1982, 419–39.

Wollen, Peter, "The Vienna Project," *Sight and Sound* 9/7, 1999.

Wood, Michael, "At the Movies" (review of *The Departed* (Martin Scorcese, 2006)), *London Review of Books* 28/22 (16 November 2006).

Young, James, *Art and Knowledge*, (London: Routledge, 2001).

Zillmann, Dolf, "Disparagement Humor," in P.E. McGhee and J.H. Goldstein, *Handbook of Humour Research*. (New York: Springer-Verlag, 1983).

FILMS

Adam's Rib, directed by George Cukor, screenplay by Ruth Gordon and Garson Kanin (MGM, 1949).

The Awful Truth, directed by Leo McCarey, screenplay by Vina Delmar, based on the play by Arthur Richman (Columbia, 1937).

A Bout de Souffle (or, *Breathless*), directed by Jean-Luc Godard, screenplay by Jean-Luc Godard, based on an idea by Francois Truffaut (Imperia, 1959).

Addicted to Love, directed by Griffin Dunne, screenplay by Robert Gordon (Warner Bros., 1997).

American History X, directed by Tony Kaye, screenplay by David McKenna (New Line Productions, 1998).

Arsenic and Old Lace, directed by Frank Capra, screenplay by Julius J. Epstein and Philip G. Epstein, based on the play by Joseph Kesselring (Warner Bros., 1944).

Babe, directed by Chris Noonan, screenplay by George Miller and Chris Noonan, based on the novel *The Sheep-Pig*, by Dick King-Smith (Kennedy Miller Productions, 1995).

Bamboozled, directed by Spike Lee, screenplay by Spike Lee (40 Acres and a Mule Filmworks, October 20, 2000).

The Believer, directed by Henry Bean, screenplay by Henry Bean, based on a story by Henry Bean and Mark Jacobson (The Believer LLC, 2001).

The Best of Eddie Murphy: Saturday Night Live (NBC, 1989).

The Big Lebowski, directed by Joel Coen, screenplay by Ethan and Joel Coen (Working Title/
 PolyGram, 1998).

The Blue Planet: Seas of Life, produced by Alistair Fothergill (BBC, 2001).

Bulworth, directed by Warren Beatty, screenplay by Warren Beatty (Twentieth Century-Fox
 Film Corporation, 1998).

A Canterbury Tale, directed and screenplay by Michael Powell and Emeric Pressburger (The
 Archers, 1944).

Casablanca, directed by Michael Curtiz, written by Julius J. Epstein, Philip G. Epstein, and
 Howard Koch, based on a play by Murray Burnett and Joan Alison (Warner, 1942)

Clockers, directed by Spike Lee, screenplay by Richard Price, based on the novel by Richard
 Price (40 Acres and a Mule Filmworks, September 13, 1995).

Crash, directed by Paul Haggis, screenplay by Paul Haggis and Bobby Moresco (Bulls Eye
 Entertainment, May 6, 2005).

The Crying Game, directed by Neil Jordan, screenplay by Neil Jordan (British Screen Productions, 1992).

Dangerous Liaisons, directed by Stephen Frears, screenplay by Christopher Hampton, based on
 the novel by Choderlos de Laclos (Lorimar Film Entertainment, 21 December 1988).

Dangerous Moonlight, directed by Brian Desmond Hurst, screenplay by Terence Young, Brian
 Desmond Hurst and Rodney Ackland (RKO, 1941).

Dead Man Walking, directed by Tim Robbins, screenplay by Tim Robbins, based on the book
 by Sister Helen Prejean (Working Title/PolyGram, 1995).

Death in Brunswick, directed by John Ruane, written by John Ruane with Boyd Oxlade (Me-
 ridian Films, 1990).

A Diary for Timothy, directed and screenplay by Humphrey Jennings (Crown Film Unit, 1946).

Do the Right Thing, directed by Spike Lee, screenplay by Spike Lee (40 Acres and a Mule Filmworks, June 30, 1989).

Downfall (*Der Untergang*), directed by Oliver Hirschbiegel, screenplay by Bernd Eichinger,
 based on books by Joachim Fest, Trudi Junge, Albert Speer, Gerhardt Boldt, Ernst-Günther
 Schenk, and Siegfried Knappe (Constantin, 2004).

Driving Miss Daisy, directed by Bruce Beresford, screenplay by Alfred Uhry, based on a play by
 Alfred Uhry (Majestic Films International, December 13, 1989).

Eating Raoul, directed by Paul Bartel, screenplay by Paul Bartel (Bartel, 1982).

Fargo, directed by Joel Coen, screenplay by Ethan and Joel Coen (Working Title/ PolyGram, 1996).

Flaming Creatures, directed and conceived by Jack Smith (privately released, 1963).

Fools Rush In, directed by Andy Tennant, screenplay by Katherine Reback, based on a story by
 Joan Taylor (Columbia Pictures Corporation, 1997).

49th Parallel, directed and screenplay by Michael Powell and Emeric Pressburger (The Archers, 1941).

French Kiss, directed by Lawrence Kasdan, screenplay by Adam Brooks (Polygram, 1995).

Gandhi, directed by Richard Attenborough, screenplay by John Briley (Columbia TriStar,
 1982).

The Godfather, directed by Francis Ford Coppola, screenplay by Mario Puzo and Francis Ford
 Coppola, based on the novel by Mario Puzo (Alfran Productions, 1972).

The Godfather, Part II, directed by Francis Ford Coppola, screenplay by Mario Puzo and Francis
 Ford Coppola (Paramount Pictures, 1974).

The Gold Rush, directed by Charles Chaplin, screenplay by Charles Chaplin (Warner Bros, 1925).

The Good Shepherd, directed by Robert de Niro, screenplay by Eric Roth (Universal Pictures, 2006).

The Green Mile, directed by Frank Darabont, screenplay by Frank Darabont, based on the novel by Stephen King (Castle Rock Entertainment, December 10, 1999).

Guess Who's Coming to Dinner, directed by Stanley Kramer, screenplay by William Rose (Columbia Pictures Corporation, December 12, 1967).

It Happened One Night, directed by Frank Capra, screenplay by Robert Riskin, based on a story by Samuel Hopkins Adams (Columbia, 1934).

Harold and Maude, directed by Hal Ashby, screenplay by Colin Higgins (Paramount, 1971).

Harry Potter film series, various directors and screenwriters, based on the novels by J.K. Rowling (Heyday/Warner, 2001-2011).

Heathers, directed by Michael Lehmann, screenplay by Daniel Waters (Cinemarque, 1989).

His Girl Friday, directed by Howard Hawks, screenplay by Charles Lederer, based on a play by Ben Hecht and Charles MacArthur (Columbia Pictures, 1940).

History of the World Part 1, directed by Mel Brooks, screenplay by Mel Brooks (Brooksfilims, 1981).

Holy Smoke, directed by Jane Campion, screenplay by Anna Campion and Jane Campion (India Take One Productions, 1999).

How to Get Ahead in Advertising, directed by Bruce Robinson, screenplay by Bruce Robinson (Handmade, 1989).

In the Heat of the Night, directed by Normal Jewison, screenplay by Stirling Silliphant, based on the novel by John Ball (Mirisch Corporation, August 2, 1967).

Intolerable Cruelty, directed by Joel Cohen, screenplay by Robert Ramsey, Matthew Stone, Ethan Cohen and Joel Cohen (Universal Pictures, 2003).

The Jerk, directed by Carl Reiner, screenplay by Carl Gottlieb and Steve Martin (Aspen Film Society, 1979).

Jerry Maguire, directed by Cameron Crowe, screenplay by Cameron Crowe (Gracie Films, 1996).

Joe Versus the Volcano, directed by Gregory Fitzsimmons, screenplay by Tom McAlister (Frankly Films, 2004).

Jules et Jim, directed by Francois Truffaut, screenplay by Francois Truffaut and Jean Gruault, based on a novel by Henri-Pierre Roche (Carrosse Films and SEDIF, 1962).

Jungle Fever, directed by Spike Lee, screenplay by Spike Lee (40 Acres and a Mule Filmworks, June 7, 1991).

Kind Hearts and Coronets, directed by Robert Hamer, screenplay by Robert Hamer and John Dighton, based on the novel, *Israel Rank*, by Roy Horniman (Ealing, 1949).

King Kong, directed by Merian C. Cooper and Ernest B. Schoedsack, screenplay by James Ashmore Creelman and Ruth Rose (RKO Radio Pictures Inc., 1933).

The King of Comedy, directed by Martin Scorsese, screenplay by Paul Zimmerman (20th Century Fox, 1983).

The Lady Eve, directed and screenplay by Preston Sturges, based on a story by Monckton Hoffe (Paramount, 1941).

The Ladykillers, directed by Alexander Mackendrick, screenplay by William Rose, based on a story by William Rose (Ealing, 1955).

The Life and Death of Colonel Blimp, directed and screenplay by Michael Powell and Emeric Pressburger (The Archers/Independent Producers, 1943).

Lost, created by Damon Lindelhof, J.J. Abrams, and Jeffrey Leiber, various directors and screenplay writers (ABC Studios, 2004–2010).

M*A*S*H, directed by Robert Altman, screenplay by Ring Lardner Jr., based on the novel by Richard Hooker (Aspen, 1970).

A Matter of Life and Death, directed and screenplay by Michael Powell and Emeric Pressburger (The Archers, 1946).

Magnolia, directed and screenplay by Paul Thomas Anderson (New Line, 1999).

Meet John Doe, directed by Frank Capra, screenplay by Robert Riskin, based on a story by Richard Connell and Robert Presnell (Frank Capra Productions, 1941).

Million Dollar Baby, directed by Clint Eastwood, screenplay by Paul Haggis (Warner Bros. Pictures, 2004).

Modern Times, directed and screenplay by Charles Chaplin (Chaplin, 1936).

Monsieur Verdoux, directed by Charles Chaplin, screenplay by Charles Chaplin, based on an idea by Orson Welles (Chaplin, 1947).

Monster's Ball, directed by Marc Forster, screenplay by Milo Addica and Will Rokos (Lee Daniels Entertainment, February 8, 2002).

Monty Python and the Holy Grail, directed by Terry Gilliam and Terry Jones, screenplay by Graham Chapman, John Cleese, Terry Gilliam, Eric Idle, Terry Jones, and Michael Palin (Python, 1975).

Mrs Miniver, directed by William Wyler, screenplay by James Hilton, George Froeschel, Claudine West and Arthur Wimperis, based on a story by Jan Struthers (MGM, 1942).

My Best Friend's Wedding, directed by P.J. Hogan, screenplay by Ronald Bass (Predawn Productions, 1997).

Nashville, directed by Robert Altman, screenplay by Joan Tewkesbury (Paramount, 1975).

One of Our Aircraft is Missing, directed and screenplay by Michael Powell and Emeric Pressburger, (The Archers, 1942).

Parents, directed by Bob Balaban, screenplay by Christopher Hawthorne (Great American Films, 1989).

Philadelphia Story, directed by George Cukor, screenplay by Donald Ogden Steward and Waldo Salt, based on the play by Philip Barry (MGM, 1940).

The Prince and the Pauper, directed by William Keighley, screenplay by Laird Doyle, based on the novel by Mark Twain and the play by Catherine Chishold Cushing (Warner, 1937).

Prison Break, created by Paul Scheuring, various directors and screenplay writers (Rat Entertainment, 2005-).

Pulp Fiction, directed by Quentin Tarantino, screenplay by Quentin Tarantino and Roger Avary (Jersey Films, 1994).

Richard Pryor: Live in Concert, directed by Jeff Margolis (Elkins Entertainment, 1979).

Runaway Bride, directed by Garry Marshall, screenplay by Josann McGibbon and Sara Parriott (Paramount Pictures, 1999).

Secrets and Lies, directed by Mike Leigh, screenplay by Mike Leigh (CiBy2000/Thin Man production in association with Channel Four Films 1996).

Shadow of a Doubt, directed by Alfred Iitchcock, screenplay by Thornton Wilder and Sally Benson (Skirball Productions, 1943).

Short Cuts, directed by Robert Altman, screenplay by Robert Altman and Frank Barhydt, based on short stories by Raymond Carver (Fine Line, 1993).

Sophie's Choice, directed by Alan J. Pakula, screenplay by Alan J. Pakula, based on the novel by William Styron (ITC, 1982).

The Sopranos, created by David Chase, various directors and screenplay writers (HBO Original Programming, Brad Grey Television and Chase Films, 1999–2007).

SpongeBob SquarePants, created by Stephen Hillenburg, various writers and directors (Nickelodeon, 1999-present).

The Stranger, directed by Orson Welles, screenplay by Anthony Veiller (International Pictures, 1946).

The Third Man, directed by Carol Reed, screenplay by Graham Greene (London Film Productions, 1949).

Tom and Jerry, created, directed and written by William Hanna and Joseph Barbera (MGM, 1940–58).

Vertigo, directed by Alfred Hitchcock, screenplay by Alec Coppel and Samuel Taylor, based on a novel by Pierre Boileau and Thomas Narcejac (Paramount, 1958).

White Like Me, directed and screenplay by John Patrick Stanley (Warner, 1990).

Who Framed Roger Rabbit?, directed by Robert Zemeckis, screenplay by Jeffrey Price and Peter Seaman, based on a book by Gary K. Wolf (Touchstone/Amblin/Silver Screen Partners, 1988).

The Wire, created by David Simon, various directors and screenplay writers (HBO, 2002–2008).

INDEX